THE
BATTLE
100

THE
BATTLE
100

THE STORIES BEHIND HISTORY'S
MOST INFLUENTIAL BATTLES

BY MICHAEL LEE LANNING
MAPS BY BOB ROSENBURGH

SOURCEBOOKS, INC.®
NAPERVILLE, ILLINOIS

Published by Sourcebooks, Inc.
P.O. Box 4410, Naperville, Illinois 60567-4410
(630) 961-3900
FAX: (630) 961-2168
www.sourcebooks.com

Library of Congress Cataloging-in-Publication Data

Lanning, Michael Lee.
The battle 100 : the stories behind history's most influential battles
/ by Michael Lee Lanning ; maps by Bob Rosenburgh.
     p. cm.
Includes bibliographical references and index.
ISBN 1-57071-799-0 (hardcover : alk. paper)
1. Battles. 2. Military history. 3. Naval history. 4. Strategy. 5. Military art and science—History. I. Title: Battle one hundred. II. Title.
D25.L36 2003
355.4'09—dc21

2003153539

Printed and bound in the United States of America
ED   10   9   8   7   6   5   4   3

DEDICATION

Dedicated to James Garland Moore
and Glenna Gene Knox Moore

TABLE OF CONTENTS

FOREWORD

"Between a battle lost and a battle won, the distance
is immense and there stand empires."
—Napoleon Bonaparte

Battles win wars, topple thrones, and redraw borders. Every age of human history has experienced battles that have been instrumental in molding the future. Battles, and their outcomes, have been the single greatest factor in choices available to any given people. Religion, politics, academia, and philosophy have certainly contributed to the twists and turns of history, but they have been able to have impact only when a tribe, nation, or kingdom has maintained a strong military that could win battles and ensure the endurance of their way of life.

The significance of pivotal battles must not be underestimated, for those countries that win battles ultimately win wars. Winners can prosper, control their own territory, and dominate their neighbors. Losers, on the other hand, find themselves subjugated or annihilated and their communities destroyed. Battles influence the spread of culture, civilization, and religious dogma. They introduce weapons, tactics, and leaders who dominate future conflicts. Some battles have even been influential not for their direct results, but for the impact of their propaganda on public opinion.

Great military leaders have always understood the significance of single battles. Prussian General Frederick the Great, who militarily kept his country a world power for most of the eighteenth century, said it best: "War is decided by battles and it is not decided except by them."

In 1812 another Prussian, General Karl Von Clausewitz, declared in his masterful *On War,* "Battles decide everything."

The following list is not a ranking of decisive engagements, but rather a ranking of battles according to their influence on history. Each of the one hundred narratives details location, participants, and leaders of the battle, and also provides commentary on who won, who lost, and why. Narratives also evaluate each battle's influence on the outcome of its war and the impact on the victors and losers. A rationale for the battle's inclusion and its rank on the list concludes each of the entries.

Land battles dominate the list, with only a dozen naval engagements and a mere two air campaigns included. While many land campaigns on this list have depended on naval and/or air support, the axiom that "no battle is won until the infantryman occupies the objective" has remained true throughout history. Some naval battles nevertheless have been influential because control of the sea-lanes directly affects what occurs on the land. Naval battles have also allowed or prevented land invasions from the sea.

Air power has existed only over the past century—a small portion of the more than three thousand years this list considers. Except for the two air battles included—the atomic bombings of Japan and the defense of Britain—air warfare has merely supported ground fighting. The impotent Allied bombing of Iraq during Operation Desert Storm in 1991 again confirmed this truth. Although the 1990s air strikes in Bosnia, combined with economic embargoes and political pressure, helped topple the oppressive government, the war and its ethnic cleansing did not cease until ground combat troops acting as peacekeepers arrived. In the War on Terror, air power has played a key role in ending the power of the Taliban in Afghanistan. Despite the destruction caused by the bombs, however, no area of the country was free until the arrival of ground forces from either one of the Afghani opposition groups or the United States. Without a doubt, air attacks can harass populations and even influence campaigns, but battles and wars continue to be decided by ground forces.

It is difficult at best, of course, to compare military battles on land, sea, and air, separated by as many as thirty-five centuries. The key to understanding these rankings is to keep in mind that the list assesses long-term influence of the battles rather than any one battle's decisiveness or direct outcome.

It is even more difficult to find sources that agree on the numbers of participants and casualties. For the earlier battles, there is even disagreement on the specific dates and locations. Various spellings of commanders' names and inconsistent official battle designations for ancient fights riddle historical documents. The dates, locations, numbers, and names included in this ranking are either the most common or the results of comparison and analysis.

[Note: For ease of comparison, when one battle narrative references another battle included on the list, the ranking of the referenced battle will follow its name, e.g. Waterloo (9), Marathon (28), and Midway (44).]

1

YORKTOWN

American Revolution, 1781

The Battle of Yorktown was the climax of the American Revolution and directly led to the independence of the United States of America. While others may have been larger and more dramatic, no battle in history has been more influential. From the days following their victory at Yorktown, Americans have steadily gained power and influence up to their present role as the world's most prosperous nation and the only military superpower.

The idea that a group of poorly armed, loosely organized colonists would have the audacity to challenge the massive, experienced army and navy of their rulers seemed impossible when the revolution's first shots rang out at Lexington and Concord in 1775 (74). The rebels' chances of success seemed even more remote when the American colonies formally declared their independence from Great Britain on July 4, 1776.

Despite the huge imbalance of power, the Americans understood that time was on their side. As long as George Washington and his army remained in the field, the newly declared republic survived. Washington did not have to defeat the British; he simply had to avoid having the British defeat him. The longer the war lasted, the greater the odds that the British would become involved in wars that threatened their own islands and that the British public would tire of the war and its costs.

During the first year of the war, Washington had lost a series of battles around New York but had withdrawn the bulk of his army to fight another day. Many British commanders had unintentionally aided the American effort with their military ineptness and their belief that the rebels would diplomatically end their revolt.

Participants on both sides, as well as observers around the world, had begun to take the possibility of American independence seriously only with their victory at Saratoga in October 1777 (15). The poorly executed plan by the British to divide New England from the southern colonies by occupying New York's Hudson River Valley had resulted not only in the surrender of nearly six thousand British soldiers but also in the recognition of the United States as an independent nation by France. The American victory at Saratoga and the entrance of the French into the war also drew Spain and the Netherlands into the fight against England.

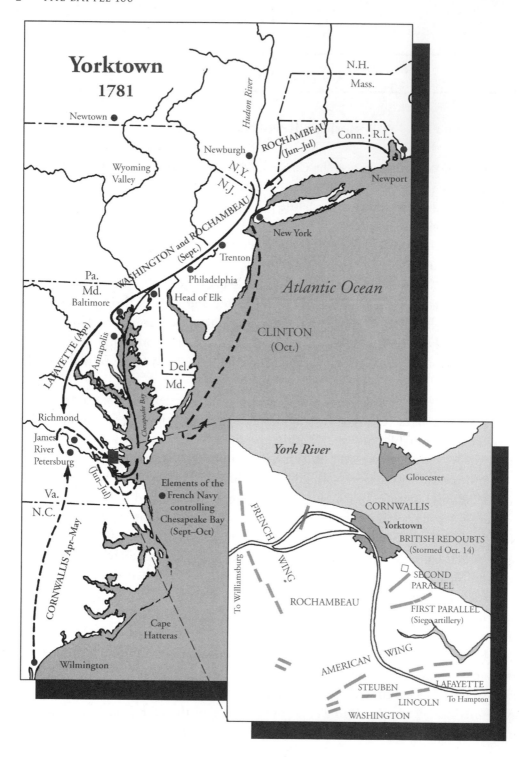

Yorktown
1781

By 1778, neither the British nor the Americans could gain the upper hand, as the war in the northern colonies had come to a stalemate. The British continued to occupy New York and Boston, but they were too weak to crush the rebel army. Washington similarly lacked the strength to attack the British fortresses.

In late 1778, British commander General Henry Clinton used his superior sea mobility to transfer much of his army under Lord Charles Cornwallis to the southern colonies, where they occupied Savannah and then Charleston the following year. Clinton's plan was for Cornwallis to neutralize the southern colonies, which would cut off supplies to Washington and isolate his army.

Washington countered by dispatching Nathanael Greene, one of his ablest generals, to command the American troops in the South. From 1779 to 1781, Greene and other American commanders fought a guerrilla-like campaign of hit-and-run maneuvers that depleted and exhausted the British. In the spring of 1781, Cornwallis marched into North Carolina and then into Yorktown on the Virginia peninsula flanked by the York and James Rivers. Although his army outnumbered the Americans two to one, Cornwallis fortified the small town and waited for additional men and supplies to arrive by ship.

Meanwhile, more than seven thousand French infantrymen, commanded by Jean Baptiste de Rochambeau, joined Washington's army outside New York, and a French fleet led by Admiral Paul de Grasse waited in the Caribbean, prepared to sail northward. Washington wanted de Grasse to blockade New York while the combined American-French armies attacked Clinton's New York force.

Rochambeau and de Grasse proposed instead that they attack Cornwallis. On August 21, 1781, Washington left a few units around New York and joined Rochambeau to march the two hundred miles to Yorktown in only fifteen days. Clinton, convinced that New York was still the rebels' primary target, did nothing.

While the infantry was on its march, the French navy drove away the British ships in the area at the Battle of Chesapeake Capes on September 5. De Grasse then blockaded the entrance to Chesapeake Bay and landed three thousand men to join the growing army around Yorktown.

By the end of September, Washington had united his army from the north with the rebel southerners. He now had more than 8,000 Americans along with the 7,000 French soldiers to encircle the 6,000 British defenders. On October 9, the Americans and French began pounding the British with fifty-two cannons while they dug trenches toward the primary enemy defensive redoubts.

The American-Franco infantry captured the redoubts on October 14 and moved their artillery forward so they could fire directly into Yorktown. Two days later, a

British counterattack failed. On October 17, Cornwallis asked for a cease-fire, and on the 19th he agreed to unconditional surrender. Only about one hundred and fifty of his soldiers had been killed and another three hundred wounded, but he knew that future action was futile. American and French losses numbered seventy-two killed and fewer than two hundred wounded.

Cornwallis, claiming illness, sent his deputy Charles O'Hara to surrender in his place. While the British band played "The World Turned Upside Down," O'Hara approached the allies and attempted to surrender his sword to his European peer rather than the rebel colonist. Rochambeau recognized the gesture and deferred to Washington. The American commander turned to his own deputy, Benjamin Lincoln, who accepted O'Hara's sword and the British surrender.

Several small skirmishes occurred after Yorktown, but for all practical purposes, the revolution was over. The upheaval and embarrassment over the defeat at Yorktown brought down the British government, and the new officials authorized a treaty on September 3, 1783, that acknowledged the independence of the United States.

Yorktown directly influenced not only the United States but also France. The French support of the United States and their own war against Britain wrecked France's economy. More importantly, the idea of liberty from a tyrant demonstrated by the Americans motivated the French to begin their own revolution in 1789 that eventually led to the age of Napoleon and far greater wars.

The fledgling United States had to fight the British again in 1812 to guarantee its independence, but the vast area and resources of North America soon enlarged and enriched the new nation. By the end of the nineteenth century, the United States had become a world power; by the end of the twentieth, it was the strongest and most influential nation in the world.

Before Yorktown, the United States was a collection of rebels struggling for independence. After Yorktown, it began a process of growth and evolution that would eventually lead to its present status as the longest-surviving democracy and most powerful country in history. The American Revolution, beginning at Lexington and Concord and drawing strength from Saratoga, culminated at Yorktown in the most influential battle in history.

HASTINGS

Norman Conquest of England, 1066

The Norman victory at the Battle of Hastings in 1066 was the last successful invasion of England—and the first and only since the Roman conquest a thousand years earlier. Its aftermath established a new feudal order that ensured that England would adopt the political and social traditions of continental Europe, rather than those of Scandinavia. The single battle also gained the country's crown for the Norman leader William.

Prior to the Battle of Hastings, the Vikings ruled Scandinavia, Northern Europe, and much of the British Isles. Areas they did not directly control were still vulnerable to their constant raids. Earlier Viking victories in France had led to intermarriage and the creation of a people who called themselves the Normans. Other Vikings conquered the British Isles and established their own kingdoms. Royal bloodlines ran through the leaders of all of the monarchies, but this did not prevent them from fighting each other.

Claims of crowns and territories reached a state of crisis with the death of Edward the Confessor, the King of England in 1066, who had left no heir. Three men claimed the throne: Harold Godwin, brother-in-law of Edward; William, the Duke of Normandy and a distant relative of Edward's; and King Harald Hardrada of Norway, the brother of Harold Godwin.

Both Harald and William assembled armies to sail to England to secure their claims. Godwin decided that William presented more of a threat and moved his English army to the southern coast across from Normandy. Weather, however, delayed William, and King Harald's ten thousand Vikings arrived first. On September 20, the Vikings soundly defeated the local forces around the city of York and seriously weakened the English army in the region.

Hearing of the battle, Godwin turned his army north and covered the two hundred miles to York in only six days. At Stamford Bridge, he surprised the Vikings and soundly defeated them. The retreating Viking survivors filled only twenty-four of the three hundred ships that had brought them to England.

Godwin had inflicted the most decisive defeat on the Vikings in more than two centuries, but there was no time to celebrate. A few days later, he learned that the

Normans had landed at Pevensey Bay in Sussex and were marching inland. Godwin hurried back south with his army and on October 1 he arrived in London, where he recruited additional soldiers. On October 13, Godwin moved to Sussex to take defensive positions along the Norman line of march on Senlac Ridge, eight miles northwest of the village of Hastings. He did not have long to prepare because William approached the next day.

Godwin possessed both advantages and disadvantages. He had the advantage of the defense, and his army of 7,000 was about the same size as that of the Normans. Only about 2,000 of his men, however, were professionals. These housecarls, as they were known, wore conical helmets and chain-mail vests and carried five-foot axes in addition to metal shields. The remaining Saxons were poorly trained militiamen known as fyrds, who were basically draftees levied from the shires. Many of the fyrds, and most of the housecarls, were exhausted from their march as well as from the fierce battle with the Vikings.

William's army contained about 2,000 cavalrymen and 5,000 infantrymen, equally armed with swords or bows or crossbows. Despite the lack of numerical superiority and an enemy defense that would only allow for a frontal assault, William attacked.

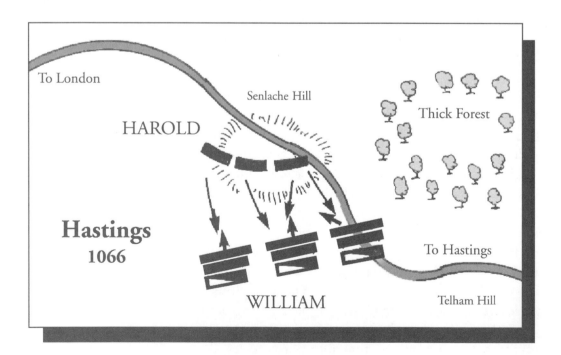

The Normans advanced behind a rain of arrows from their archers, but the Saxon shields turned aside most of the missiles. Several direct attacks by infantry fared no better. William then personally led a cavalry charge but was turned back by marshy ground and the Saxon defenses. Defeat, or at best stalemate, appeared to be the outcome of the battle for the invaders. The Normans were further demoralized when a story swept the ranks that William had been killed.

When the Norman leader heard the rumor, he removed his visor and rode to the head of his army. His soldiers, seeing that he was alive, rallied and renewed the assault. William also ordered his archers to fire at a high angle rather than in a direct line in order to reach behind the Saxon shields. The battle remained in doubt until William's cavalry turned and wildly fled from the battlefield. Whether the cavalry was retreating from fright or as a ruse, it had the same results. The Saxons left their defenses to pursue, only to be struck by the Norman infantry. At about the same time, an arrow hit Godwin in the eye, and he was killed by the advancing infantry. The leaderless Saxons began to flee.

William, soon to be known as the Conqueror, pursued the retreating Saxons and seized Dover. With little resistance, he entered London on December 25, 1066, and received the crown of England as King William I. Over the next five years, William brutally put down several rebellions and replaced the Anglo-Saxon aristocracy with his own Norman followers. Norman nobles built castles from which to rule and defend the countryside. Norman law, customs, traditions, and citizens intermingled with the Saxons to form the future of England as a nation.

Later the adage would declare, "There'll always be an England." The fact remains that the England that eventually came to exist began on the Hastings battlefield, and 1066 became a schoolbook standard marking the expansion of English culture, colonization, and influence around the world.

STALINGRAD

World War II, 1942–43

Stalingrad was the last great offensive by the German Nazis on the Eastern Front. Their defeat in the city on the Volga River marked the beginning of a long series of battles that would lead the Russians to Berlin and Hitler's Third Reich to defeat. The Battle of Stalingrad resulted in the death or capture of more than a quarter million German soldiers, and denied the rich Caucasus oil fields to the Nazis.

Despite the lack of success by the German army to capture the cities of Moscow and Leningrad in their blitzkrieg offensive in the fall and winter of 1941 (22), Hitler remained determined to conquer Russia in order to destroy Communism and gain access to natural resources for the Third Reich. With his army stalled outside the cities to the north, Hitler directed an offensive against Stalingrad to capture the city's industrial assets and to cut communications between the Volga and Don Rivers. Along with the attack against Stalingrad, German columns were to sweep into the Caucasus to capture the oil fields that would fuel future Nazi conquests.

In the spring of 1942, German Army Group A headed into the Caucasus while Group B marched toward Stalingrad. Initially both were successful, but the German army, depleted by the battles of the previous year, was too weak to sustain two simultaneous offensives. The Germans might have easily captured Stalingrad had Hitler not continued to redirect units to the Caucasus. By the time he concentrated the offensive against Stalingrad, the Soviets had reinforced the area. Stalin directed the defenders of the city that bore his name, "Not a step backward." Hitler accepted the challenge and directed additional forces against the city.

On August 23, 1942, more than a thousand German airplanes began dropping incendiary and explosive bombs. More than 40,000 of the 600,000 Stalingrad civilians died in the fiery attack. The survivors picked up arms and joined the soldiers in defense of their city. The next day, the Sixth German Army, commanded by General Friedrich Paulus, pressed into the edge of the town and assumed victory when they found it mostly in ruins. They were wrong. Soldiers and civilians rose from the rubble to fight back with small arms and even hand-to-hand combat as they contested every foot of the destroyed town.

Elements of the Soviet Sixty-second Army joined the fight. Clashes over the city's Mamaev Mound resulted in the hill changing hands eight times as the battle line advanced and retreated. Near the center of the city, the Stalingrad Central Railway station changed hands fifteen times in bitter, close infantry combat. German artillery and air power continued to pound the city, but the Russians maintained such close contact with their opponents that much of the ordinance exploded harmlessly to their rear.

By September 22, the Germans occupied the center of Stalingrad, but the beleaguered Russian soldiers and civilians refused to surrender. The time they provided Soviet General Georgi Zhukov to reinforce the city's flanks with additional soldiers, tanks, and artillery pieces. On November 19, the Russians launched a counter-offensive against the north and south flanks of the Germans.

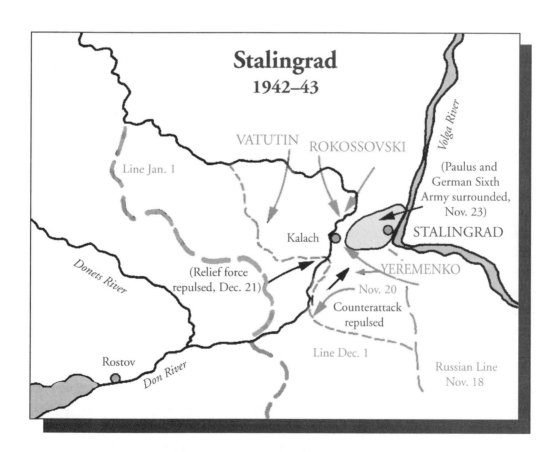

The two attacks focused on lines held by Romanian, Italian, and Hungarian forces who were allied with the Germans, rather than the better trained and disciplined Nazi troops. On November 23, the two pinchers linked up west of Stalingrad, trapping more than 300,000 German soldiers in a pocket thirty-five miles wide and twenty miles long.

General Paulus requested permission from Hitler to withdraw prior to the encirclement, but he was told to fight on. Marshal Hermann Goering promised Hitler that he could supply the surrounded Paulus with 500 tons of food and ammunition per day. Goering and his Luftwaffe failed to deliver even 150 tons a day while the Russians destroyed more than 500 transport aircraft during the supply effort. A relief column led by General Erich von Manstein, one of Hitler's finest officers, attempted to reach the surrounded army but failed.

The Russians continued to reduce the German perimeter. By Christmas, the Germans were low on ammunition, nearly out of food, and freezing in the winter cold. On January 8, the Russians captured the last airfield inside the German lines and demanded the surrender of the entire army. Hitler radioed Paulus, "Surrender is forbidden. Sixth Army will hold their position to the last man and last round...." He also promoted Paulus to field marshal and reminded him that no German of that rank had ever surrendered on the battlefield.

The Germans did not hold out to the last round or the last man. By January 31, their numbers had plummeted to 90,000, many of whom were wounded. All were hungry and cold. Units began to give up, and within two days all resistance ceased. Field Marshal Paulus surrendered himself, 23 generals, 90,000 men, 60,000 vehicles, 1,500 tanks, and 6,000 artillery pieces.

Of the 90,000 Germans captured at Stalingrad, only about 5,000 survived the harsh conditions of the Soviet prisoner-of-war camps. Those who were not worked to death died of starvation and disease. Paulus, however, was not harshly treated by his captors but remained under house arrest in Moscow for eleven years. He was allowed in 1953 to return to Dresden in East Germany, where he died in 1957.

The siege of Stalingrad provided sufficient time for the German Army Group A to withdraw from the Caucasus. The loss of Army Group B in the rubble of Stalingrad and the toll experienced by Army Group A before its withdrawal, however, weakened the German army on the Eastern Front to the point where it could never again mount a major offensive. More than two years would pass before the Red Army occupied Berlin, but Stalingrad opened the way to the future victories that led to Hitler's Bunker and the defeat of Nazi Germany.

Victory at Stalingrad did not come easily or cheaply for the Russians. Nearly half a million soldiers and civilians died in defense of the city. Almost all of its homes, factories, and other buildings were destroyed. But the Russians had won, and that victory united the Russian people, giving them the confidence and strength that drove them on to Berlin.

Stalingrad proved to the Russians and their allies that they could both stop and defeat the great German army. The battle was the turning point of World War II. Victory at Stalingrad for the Germans would have led to victory in the Caucasus Mountains. With the oil and other resources from that area, the German army would have been able to turn more of their power to the Western Front. If the German armies in the east had survived to face the British, the Americans, and their Allies in the west, the war definitely would not have concluded as quickly. Perhaps even the eventual allied victory might have been in doubt.

While Stalingrad was the turning point of World War II, and the valor of its defenders will never be in doubt, the Soviet brand of Communism in whose name the battle was fought has not survived. Stalingrad did not even survive to see the demise of the Soviet Union. In the purge of all references to Stalin after his death, the city was renamed Volgograd. Yet, the brave defenders of Stalingrad, who fought for themselves and their city, deserve recognition as fighting one of history's most decisive and influential battles.

4

LEIPZIG

Napoleonic Wars, 1813

The allied victory over Napoleon at Leipzig in 1813 marked the first significant cooperation among European nations against a common foe. As the largest armed clash in history up to that time, Leipzig led to the fall of Paris and the abdication of Napoleon.

After the Russian army and winter had handed Napoleon a nasty defeat in 1812, Europeans felt confident that peace would prevail after more than a decade of warfare. They were wrong. As soon as Napoleon returned to France from icy Russia, he set about rebuilding his army, conscripting teens and young men. He strengthened these ranks of inexperienced youths with veterans brought back from the Spanish front.

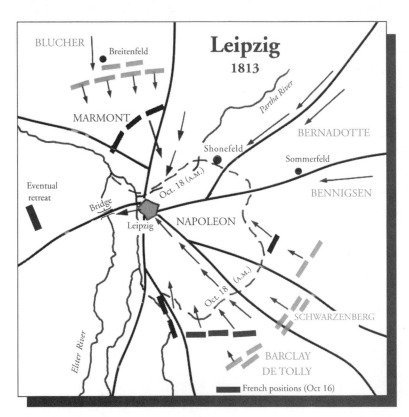

While Napoleon had been weakened by Russia, he believed that the other European countries were too distrustful of each other to ally against him. In early 1813, he decided to advance into the German provinces to resume his offensive. Just as he had done before, he planned to defeat each army he encountered and assimilate the survivors into his own force.

European leaders were correct to fear that Napoleon could accomplish his objectives, but they remained reluctant to enter into alliances with neighbors who were former, and possibly future, enemies. Karl von Metternich, the foreign minister of Austria, saw that neither his nor any other European country could stand alone against the French. Even though he had previously negotiated an alliance with Napoleon, he now began to assemble a coalition of nations against the French emperor.

Metternich's diplomacy, combined with the massing of the French army on the German border, finally convinced Prussia, Russia, Sweden, Great Britain, and several smaller countries to ally with Austria in March 1813. Napoleon disregarded the alliance and crossed into Germany with the intention of defeating each opposing army before the "allies" could actually unite against him.

Napoleon won several of the initial fights, even defeating the Prussians at Lutzen on May 2. He soon realized, however, that his new army was not the experienced one he had lost in Russia. More importantly, he had not been able to replace much of his cavalry lost in the Russian winter, limiting his reconnaissance and intelligence-gathering capabilities

When Napoleon learned that armies were marching toward Dresden from the north, south, and east against him, he negotiated a truce that began on June 4. Metternich met with Napoleon in an attempt to reach a peace settlement but, despite generous terms that allowed France to retain its pre-war borders and for him to remain in power, Napoleon refused to accept the agreement.

During the negotiations, both sides continued to add reinforcements. On August 16, the truce ended and combat resumed. For two months, the Allies harassed the French but avoided a pitched battle while they solidified their plans for a major attack. Napoleon's army, forced to live off the land and to rapidly march and countermarch against the multiple armies around them, steadily became more exhausted.

In September, the Allies began a general offensive in which the French won several small battles. Yet the Allies forced them back to Leipzig in October. Napoleon had 175,000 men to defend the town, but the Allies massed 350,000 soldiers and 1,500 artillery pieces outside his lines.

On the morning of October 16, Napoleon left part of his army in the north to resist an attack by the Prussians while he attempted to break through the Russian and

Austrian lines in the south. The battle raged all day as the front swept back and forth, but by nightfall both sides occupied the same positions as when the battle began.

Little action took place on October 17 because both sides rested. The battle on October 18 closely resembled that of two days earlier. Nine hours of furious combat accomplished little except to convince Napoleon that he could not continue a battle of attrition against the larger Allied force. The odds against him increased when the Swedish army arrived to join the Allies and a unit of Saxons deserted the French to join the other side.

Napoleon attempted to establish another truce, but the Allies refused. During the night, the French began to withdraw westward by crossing the Elster River. A single stone bridge, which provided the only crossing, soon created a bottleneck. Napoleon deployed 30,000 soldiers to act as a rear guard to protect the crossing, but they were stranded when the bridge was destroyed. A few swam to safety, but most, including three senior officers, were killed or captured.

Once again, Napoleon limped back toward Paris. Behind him he left 60,000 dead, wounded, or captured French soldiers. The Allies had lost a similar number, but they could find replacements far more quickly and easily than Napoleon. Other countries, including the Netherlands and Bavaria—which Napoleon had added to his confederation by conquest—now abandoned him and joined the Allies. On December 21, the Allies invaded France and, following their victory at Paris on March 30, 1814, forced Napoleon into exile on Elba.

Napoleon soon returned, but after only one hundred days he suffered his final defeat by the Allies at Waterloo on June 18, 1815 (9). Metternich continued his unification efforts and signed most of the Allies to the Concert of Europe, which provided a balance of power and a peace that lasted until the Crimean War in 1854. Most of the alliance survived another three decades until the ambitions of Germany brought an end to European peace.

The Battle of Leipzig was important because it brought Napoleon a defeat from which he could not recover. More important, however, was the cooperation of armies against him. This alliance is so significant that Leipzig is frequently called the Battle of the Nations. For these reasons, Leipzig ranks as one of history's most influential battles.

Leipzig also eclipses Waterloo in its influence. While the latter was certainly more decisive, a victory by Napoleon at Leipzig would likely have broken the alliance and placed the French in a position to once again defeat each of the other nation's armies. A French victory at Leipzig would have meant no defeat of Napoleon at Paris, no abdication to Elba, and no return to Waterloo.

5

ANTIETAM

American Civil War, 1862

The Battle of Antietam, the bloodiest day in American history, stopped the first Confederate invasion of the North. It also ensured that European countries would not recognize the Confederacy or provide them with much-needed war supplies. While the later battles at Gettysburg (17) and Vicksburg (49) would seal the fate of the rebel states, the defeat of the rebellion began along Antietam Creek near Sharpsburg, Maryland, on September 17, 1862.

From the day the American colonies gained their independence at the Battle of Yorktown in 1781 (1), a conflict between the United States' North and South seemed inevitable. Divided by geographical and political differences, and split over slavery and states' rights issues, the North and South had experienced mounting tensions during the first half of the nineteenth century. Finally, the election of Republican Abraham Lincoln in 1860 provided the spark that formally divided the country. Although Lincoln had made no campaign promises to outlaw slavery, many in the South viewed him as an abolitionist who would end the institution on which much of the region's agriculture and industry depended. In December 1860, South Carolina, acting on what they thought was a "state's right" under the U.S. Constitution, seceded from the Union. Three months later, seven other southern states joined South Carolina to form the Confederate States of America.

Few believed that the action would lead to war. Southerners claimed it was their right to form their own country while Northerners thought that a blockade of the Confederacy, supported by diplomacy, would peacefully return the rebel states to the fold. However, chances for a peaceful settlement ended with the Confederate bombardment of Fort Sumter, South Carolina, on April 12–14, 1861. Four more states joined the Confederacy a few days later.

Both sides quickly mobilized and aggressive Confederate commanders achieved success against more reluctant and cautious Union leaders. While warfare on land favored the Confederates, they lacked a navy, which allowed the U.S. Navy to blockade its shores. This prevented the South from exporting their primary cash crop of cotton, as well as importing much-needed arms, ammunition, and other military supplies that the meager Southern industrial complex could not provide.

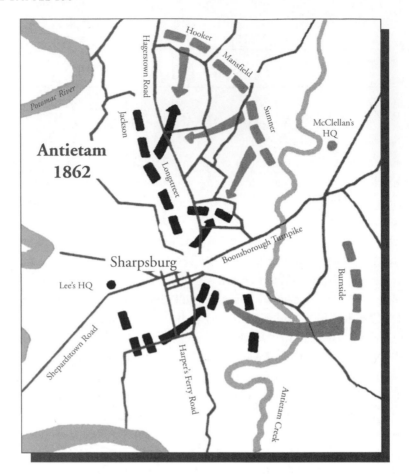

In May 1862, General Robert E. Lee took command of what he renamed the Army of Northern Virginia. Lee soon became one the most beloved commanders in history. Yet, while his men adored him, his critics noted his inability to control his subordinate leaders.

Despite his shortcomings, Lee outmaneuvered and out-generaled his opponents in his initial battles. He turned back the Union march on Richmond and then moved north to win the Second Battle of Bull Run near Manassas, Virginia, on August 30, 1862. Both Lee and Confederate President Jefferson Davis realized, however, that the South could not win a prolonged war against the more populous and industrialized North. To endure and succeed, the South would need war supplies and naval support from Britain, France, and possibly even Russia. While these countries were sympathetic with the Southern cause, they were not going to risk bad relations or even war with the United States unless they were convinced the rebellion would succeed.

Following their victory at the Second Battle of Bull Run, Lee and Davis devised a plan that would meet their immediate needs for supplies as well as their long-range goal of European recognition. They would take the war into the North. On September 6, the Army of Northern Virginia crossed into Maryland with the intention of raiding and gathering supplies in southern Pennsylvania.

Union General George B. McClellan paralleled Lee, keeping his army between the invading rebels and Washington, D.C., where Lincoln feared they would attack. On September 9, 1862, Lee issued Order Number 191, calling for half of his force to move to Harrisburg, Pennsylvania, to control the region's rail center, while the other half marched to Harpers Ferry to capture the town's gun factory and to secure lines back to the South. Four days later, a Union soldier discovered a copy of the order in a field, wrapped around three cigars. He kept the cigars, but Lee's order was shortly in McClellan's hands.

Even though McClellan now possessed the complete Confederate battle plan and his forces outnumbered the rebels 76,000 to 40,000, he remained cautious because his own intelligence officers incorrectly warned that the Confederates' force was far larger. On September 14, McClellan began to close on Lee's army only to be slowed by small forces in passes in South Mountain. The brief delay allowed Lee to form his army along a low ridge near Antietam Creek just east of Sharpsburg, Maryland.

McClellan finally attacked on the morning of September 17, but his characteristic hesitation and poor communications caused the battle to be composed of three separate fights rather than one united effort. The battle began with a murderous artillery barrage, followed by an infantry assault on the Confederate left. Attacks and counterattacks marked the next two hours, with neither side able to maintain an advantage. Meanwhile, at mid-morning, Union troops assaulted the rebel center that stood protected in a sunken road. By the time the rebels withdrew four hours later, the depleted, exhausted Union force was unable to pursue past what was now known as the "Bloody Lane."

In the afternoon, still another Union force attacked the rebel right flank to secure a crossing of Antietam Creek. Even though the waterway was fordable along much of its banks, most of the fight was concentrated over a narrow bridge. After much bloodshed, the Union troops pushed the Confederates back and were about to cut off Lee's route back south when rebel reinforcements arrived from Harpers Ferry. Even so, the third battlefront, like the other two, lapsed into a stalemate.

On the morning of September 18, Lee and his army withdrew back to Virginia. Since he was not forced to retreat, Lee claimed victory. McClellan, overly cautious as usual, chose not to pursue, although it is possible that if he had done so he could have defeated Lee and brought the war to a quick conclusion.

Between the two armies lay more than 23,000 dead or wounded Americans wearing either blue or gray. A single day of combat produced more casualties than any other in American history—more dead and wounded than the U.S. incurred in its Revolution, the War of 1812, the Mexican War, and the Spanish-American War combined. Casualties at Antietam even outnumbered those of the Longest Day, the first day of the Normandy Invasion (13), by nine to one.

The influence of Antietam reached far beyond the death and wounds. For the first time, Lee and the rebel army failed to accomplish their objective, and this provided a much-needed morale boost for the Union. More importantly, when France and England learned of the battle's outcome, they decided that recognition of the Confederate States would not be advantageous.

The battle also changed the objectives of the United States. Prior to Antietam, Lincoln and the North had fought primarily to preserve the Union. Lincoln had waited for the opportunity to bring slavery to the forefront. Five days after Antietam, he signed the Emancipation Proclamation. Although the Proclamation did not free slaves in Union states and, of course, had no power to do so in areas controlled by the rebels, it did advance the freeing of slaves as an objective of the war.

Prior to the battle and the proclamation, European nations, although opposed to slavery, still had sympathies for the Southern cause. Now with slavery an open issue and the Confederate's ability to win in question, the South would have to stand totally alone.

While it took two and a half more years of fighting and the battles of Gettysburg and Vicksburg to finally end the war, the Confederate States were doomed from the time they withdrew southward from Antietam Creek. An improving Union army, combined with a solid refusal of outside support for the Confederacy, spelled the beginning of the end.

Antietam ranks as one of history's most influential battles because if the South had been victorious outside Sharpsburg, it is very possible that France, England, and possibly even Russia would have recognized the new country. Their navies would have broken the Union blockade to reach the cotton needed for their mills and to deliver highly profitable war materials. France, who already had troops in Mexico, might have even provided ground forces to support the South. Lincoln most likely would not have issued his Emancipation Proclamation and might have been forced to make peace with the rebels, leaving the country divided. Although future events, such as the two world wars, would likely have made the former enemies into allies, it is doubtful that, in their state of division, either the United States or Confederate States would have been able to attain the level of world influence or to develop into the political, trade, and military power that the unified United States would become.

6

CAJAMARCA

Spanish Conquest of Peru, 1532

Francisco Pizarro conquered the largest amount of territory ever taken in a single battle when he defeated the Incan Empire at Cajamarca in 1532. Pizarro's victory opened the way for Spain to claim most of South America and its tremendous riches, as well as imprint the continent with its language, culture, and religion.

Christopher Columbus's voyages to the New World offered a preview of the vast wealth and resources to be found in the Americas, and Hernán Cortés's victory over the Aztecs had proven that great riches were there for the taking. It is not surprising that other Spanish explorers flocked to the area—some to advance the cause of their country, most to gain their own personal fortunes.

Francisco Pizarro was one of the latter. The illegitimate son of a professional soldier, Pizarro joined the Spanish army as a teenager and then sailed for Hispaniola, from where he participated in Vasco de Balboa's expedition that crossed Panama and "discovered" the Pacific Ocean in 1513. Along the way, he heard stories of the great wealth belonging to native tribes to the south.

After learning of Cortés's success in Mexico, Pizarro received permission to lead expeditions down the Pacific Coast of what is now Colombia, first in 1524–25 and then again in 1526–28. The second expedition experienced such hardships that his men wanted to return home. According to legend, Pizarro drew a line in the sand with his sword and invited anyone who desired "wealth and glory" to step across and continue with him in his quest.

Thirteen men crossed the line and endured a difficult journey into what is now Peru, where they made contact with the Incas. After peaceful negotiations with the Incan leaders, the Spaniards returned to Panama and sailed to Spain with a small amount of gold and even a few llamas. Emperor Charles V was so impressed that he promoted Pizarro to captain general, appointed him the governor of all lands six hundred miles south of Panama, and financed an expedition to return to the land of the Incas.

Pizarro set sail for South America in January 1531 with 265 soldiers and 65 horses. Most of the soldiers carried spears or swords. At least three had primitive muskets called arquebuses, and twenty more carried crossbows. Among the members of the expedition were four of Pizarro's brothers and all of the original thirteen adventurers who had crossed their commander's sword line to pursue "wealth and glory."

Between wealth and glory stood an army of 30,000 Incas representing a century-old empire that extended 2,700 miles from modern Ecuador to Santiago, Chile. The Incas had assembled their Empire by expanding outward from their home territory in the Cuzco Valley. They had forced defeated tribes to assimilate Incan traditions, speak their language, and provide soldiers for their army. By the time the Spaniards arrived, the Incas had built more than 10,000 miles of roads, complete with suspension bridges, to develop trade throughout the empire. They also had become master stonemasons with finely crafted temples and homes.

About the time Pizarro landed on the Pacific Coast, the Incan leader, considered a deity, died, leaving his sons to fight over leadership. One of these sons, Atahualpa, killed most of his siblings and assumed the throne shortly before he learned that the white men had returned to his Incan lands.

Pizarro and his "army" reached the southern edge of the Andes in present-day Peru in June 1532. Undaunted by the report that the Incan army numbered 30,000, Pizarro pushed inland and crossed the mountains, no small feat itself. Upon arrival at the village of Cajamarca on a plateau on the eastern slope of the Andes, the Spanish officer invited the Incan king to a meeting. Atahualpa, believing himself a deity and unimpressed with the small Spanish force, arrived with a defensive force of only three or four thousand.

Despite the odds, Pizarro decided to act rather than talk. With his arquebuses and cavalry in the lead, he attacked on November 16, 1532. Surprised by the assault and awed by the firearms and horses, the Incan army disintegrated, leaving Atahualpa a prisoner. The only Spanish casualty was Pizarro, who sustained a slight wound while personally capturing the Incan leader.

Pizarro demanded a ransom of gold from the Incas for their king, the amount of which legend says would fill a room to as high as a man could reach—more than 2,500 cubic feet. Another two rooms were to be filled with silver. Pizarro and his men had their wealth assured but not their safety, as they remained an extremely small group of men surrounded by a huge army. To enhance his odds, the Spanish leader pitted Inca against Inca until most of the viable leaders had killed each other. Pizarro then marched into the former Incan capital at Cuzco and placed his handpicked king on the throne. Atahualpa, no longer needed, was sentenced to be burned at the stake as a heathen, but was strangled instead after he professed to accept Spanish Christianity.

Pizarro returned to the coast and established the port city of Lima, where additional Spanish soldiers and civilian leaders arrived to govern and exploit the region's riches. Some minor Incan uprisings occurred in 1536, but native warriors were no match for the Spaniards. Pizarro lived in splendor until he was assassinated in 1541 by a follower who believed he was not receiving his fair share of the booty.

In a single battle, with only himself wounded, Pizarro conquered more than half of South America and its population of more than six million people. The jungle reclaimed the Inca palaces and roads as their wealth departed in Spanish ships. The Inca culture and religion ceased to exist. For the next three centuries, Spain ruled most of the north and Pacific coast of South America. Its language, culture, and religion still dominate there today.

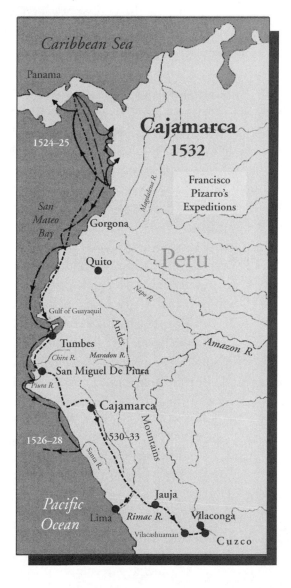

7

ATOMIC BOMBING OF JAPAN

World War II, 1945

The United States dropped atomic bombs on the Japanese cities of Hiroshima and Nagasaki in August 1945 to hasten the end of World War II in the Pacific. Although it would be the first, and to date the only, actual use of such weapons of "mass destruction," the mushroom clouds have hung over every military and political policy since.

Less than five months after the sneak attack by the Japanese against Pearl Harbor (62), the Americans launched a small carrier-based bomber raid against Tokyo. While the attack was good for the American morale, it accomplished little other than to demonstrate to the Japanese that their shores were not invulnerable. Later in the war, U.S. bombers were able to attack the Japanese home islands from bases in China, but it was not until late 1944 that the United States could mount a sustained bombing campaign.

Because of the distance to Japan, American bombers could not reach targets and safely return to friendly bases in the Pacific until the island-hopping campaign had captured the Northern Mariana Islands. From bases on the Mariana Islands, long-range B-29 Superfortresses conducted high altitude bombing runs on November 24, 1944. On March 9, 1945, an armada of 234 B-29s descended to less than 7,000 feet and dropped 1,667 tons of incendiaries on Tokyo. By the time the fire storm finally abated, a sixteen-square-mile corridor that had contained a quarter million homes was in ashes, and more than 80,000 Japanese, mostly civilians, lay dead. Only the Allied fire bombing of Dresden, Germany, the previous month, which killed 135,000, exceed the destruction of the Tokyo raid.

Both Tokyo and Dresden were primarily civilian rather than military targets. Prior to World War II, international law regarded the bombing of civilians as illegal and barbaric. After several years of warfare, however, neither the Allies nor the Axis distinguished between military and civilian air targets. Interestingly, while a pilot could drop tons of explosives and firebombs on civilian cities, an infantryman often faced a court-martial for even minor mistreatment of noncombatants.

Despite the air raids and their shrinking territory outside their home islands, the Japanese fought on. Their warrior code did not allow for surrender, and soldiers and civilians alike often chose suicide rather than giving up. By July 1945, the Americans were launching more than 1,200 bombing sorties a week against Japan. The bombing had killed more than a quarter million and left more than nine million homeless. Still, the Japanese gave no indication of surrender as the Americans prepared to invade the home islands.

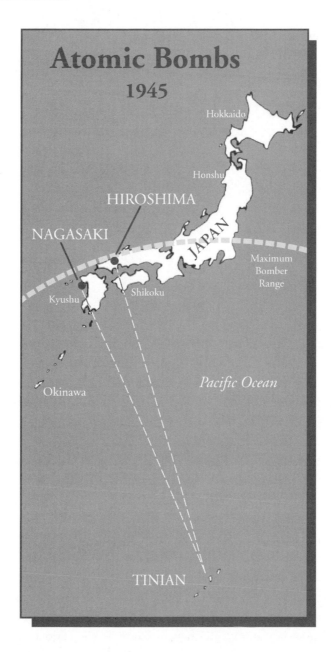

While the air attacks and plans for a land invasion continued in the Pacific, a top-secret project back in the United States was coming to fruition. On July 16, 1945, the Manhattan Engineer District successfully carried out history's first atomic explosion. When President Harry Truman learned of the successful experiment, he remarked in his diary, "It seems to be the most terrible thing ever discovered, but it can be made the most useful."

Truman realized that the "most terrible thing" could shorten the war and prevent as many as a million Allied casualties, as well as untold Japanese deaths, by preventing a ground invasion of Japan. On July 27, the United States issued an ultimatum: surrender or the U.S. would drop a "super weapon." Japan refused.

In the early morning hours of August 6, a B-29 named the *Enola Gay* piloted by Lieutenant Colonel Paul Tibbets lifted off from Tinian Island in the Marianas. Aboard was a single atomic bomb weighing 8,000 pounds and containing the destructive power of 12.5 kilotons of TNT. Tibbets headed his plane toward Hiroshima, selected as the primary target because of its military bases and industrial areas. It also had not yet been bombed to any extent, so it would provide an excellent evaluation of the bomb's destructive power.

At 8:15 A.M., the *Enola Gay* dropped the device called "Little Boy." A short time later, Tibbets noted, "A bright light filled the plane. We turned back to look at Hiroshima. The city was hidden by that awful cloud…boiling up, mushrooming." The immediate impact of Little Boy killed at least 70,000 Hiroshima residents. Some estimates claim three times that number but exact figures are impossible to calculate because the blast destroyed all the city's records.

Truman again demanded Japan surrender. After three days and no response, a B-29 took off from Tinian with an even larger atomic bomb aboard. When the crew found their primary target of Kokura obscured by clouds, they turned toward their secondary, Nagasaki. At 11:02 A.M. on August 9, they dropped the atomic device known as "Fat Man" that destroyed most of the city and killed more than 60,000 of inhabitants.

Conventional bombing raids were also conducted against other Japanese cities on August 9, and five days later, 800 B-29s raided across the country. On August 15 (Tokyo time), the Japanese finally accepted unconditional surrender. World War II was over.

Much debate has occurred since the atomic bombings. While some evidence indicates that the Japanese were considering surrender, far more information indicates otherwise. Apparently the Japanese were planning to train civilians to use rifles and spears to join the military in resisting a land invasion. Protesters of the bombs ignore the conventional incendiaries dropped on Tokyo and Dresden that claimed more casualties. Some historians even note that the losses at Hiroshima and Nagasaki were far fewer than the anticipated Japanese casualties from an invasion and continued conventional bombing.

Whatever the debate, there can be no doubt that the dropping of the atomic bombs on Japan shortened the war. The strikes against Hiroshima and Nagasaki are the only air battles that directly affected the outcome of a conflict. Air warfare, both before and since, has merely supplemented ground fighting. As confirmed by the recent impotent Allied bombing of Iraq in Desert Storm (86) and in Bosnia, air attacks can harass and make life miserable for civilian populations, but battles and wars continue to be decided by ground forces.

In addition to hastening the end of the war with Japan, the development and use of the atomic bomb provided the United States with unmatched military superiority—at least for a brief time, until the Soviet Union exploded their own atomic device. The two superpowers then began competitive advancements in nuclear weaponry that brought the world to the edge of destruction. Only tentative treaties and the threat of mutual total destruction kept nuclear arms harnessed, producing the Cold War period where the U.S. and the USSR worked out their differences through conventional means.

8

HUAI-HAI

Chinese Civil War, 1948

The Battle of Huai-Hai was the final major fight between the armies of the Chinese Communist Party (CCP) and the Nationalist Party of Kuomintang (KMT) in their long struggle over control of the world's most populous country. At the end of the battle, more than half a million KMT soldiers were dead, captured, or converted to the other side, placing China in the hands of the Communists who continue to govern today.

Struggles for the control of China and its provinces date back to the beginnings of recorded history. While some dynasties endured for many years and others for only short periods of time, the Chinese had fought among themselves and against foreign invaders throughout history only to find themselves divided once again at the start of the twentieth century. Political ideologies centered in Peking and Canton. Divisions in the country widened when the Japanese invaded in 1914. During World War I, the Chinese faced threats from within, from the Japanese, and from the newly formed Soviet Union.

When World War I finally ended, the Chinese continued their internal struggles with local dictators fighting to control small regions. In 1923, the country's two major parties, the CCP under Mao Zedong and the KMT controlled by Chiang Kai-shek, joined in an alliance to govern the country. The two sides had little in common, and in less than five years, the shaky alliance had come apart when their leaders' views on support from the Soviet Union clashed. Mao encouraged Soviet support while Chiang opposed it.

By 1927, the two parties were directly competing for control of China and its people. Mao focused on the rural areas while Chiang looked to the urban and industrial areas for his power. From 1927 to 1937, the two sides engaged in a civil war in which Chiang gained the upper hand through a series of successful offensives. Chiang almost destroyed the CCP army in 1934, but Mao and 100,000 men escaped before he could do so. For the next year, the Communists retreated from the Nationalists across 6,000 miles of China to Yenan (80), a retreat that became known as the Long March. Only 20,000 survived.

In 1937, Chiang and Mao once again put their differences aside to unite against another invasion by Japan. Mao and his army fought in the rural northern provinces, primarily employing guerrilla warfare. Mao also used this opportunity to solidify his support from the local peasants while stockpiling weapons provided by the Allies and captured from the Japanese. His army actually gained strength during the fighting. Meanwhile Chiang faced stronger Japanese opposition in the south, which weakened his army.

Despite efforts by the United States to mediate an agreement, the Communists and Nationalists resumed their armed conflict soon after the conclusion of World War II. In contrast to their weaker position prior to the war, the Communists now were stronger than the Nationalists. On October 10, 1947, Mao called for the overthrow of the Nationalist administration.

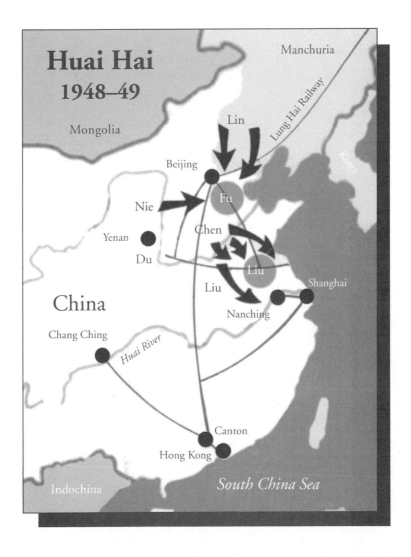

Mao, a student of Washington, Napoleon, and Sun Tzu, began to push his army south into the Nationalist zone. Where the Nationalists often looted the cities they occupied and punished their residents, the Communists took little retribution, especially against towns that did not resist. Now the Communists steadily achieved victories over the Nationalists. During the summer of 1948, the Communists experienced a series of victories that pushed the major portion of the Nationalist army into a cross-shaped area extending from Nanking north to Tsinan and from Kaifeng east through Soochow to the sea.

Mao decided that it was time to achieve a total victory. On October 11, he issued orders for a methodical campaign to surround, separate, and destroy the half-million-man Nationalist army between the Huai River and the Lung Hai Railway—the locations that gave the resulting battle its name. Mao divided his battle plan into three phases, all of which his army accomplished more smoothly and efficiently than anticipated.

The Communists divided the Nationalist-held territory into three areas. Then beginning in November, they attacked each in turn. Early in the campaign, many Nationalists, seeing no hope for their own survival, much less a Nationalist victory, defected to the Communists. Chiang, who also was encountering internal divisions within his party, attempted to reinforce each battle area, but poor leadership by the Nationalist generals, combined with Communist guerrilla activities, made his efforts ineffective. Chiang even had air superiority during the entire battle but was unable to coordinate ground and air actions to secure any advantage.

Over a period of two months, the Communists destroyed each of the three Nationalist forces. Support for Chiang from inside and outside China dwindled with each successive Communist victory. The United States, which had been a primary supporter, providing arms and supplies to the Nationalists, suspended all aid on December 20. U.S. Secretary of State George C. Marshall stated, "The present regime has lost the confidence of the people, reflected in the refusal of soldiers to fight and the refusal of the people to cooperate in economic reforms."

Within weeks of the U.S. announcement, the Communists overran the last Nationalist position and ended the Battle of Huai-Hai. Of the six highest-ranking Nationalist generals in the battle, two were killed in the fighting and two captured. The remaining two were among the few who escaped. By January 10, 1949, the half-million members of the Nationalist army had disappeared.

Within weeks, Tientsin and Peking fell to the Communists. On January 20, Chiang resigned his leadership of the Nationalists. The remaining Nationalist army and government continued to retreat until they finally withdrew to the island of Formosa. On Formosa, renamed Taiwan, Chiang regained power and developed the island into an Asian economic power. Mainland China, however, remained under the control of Mao and his Communists, who are still in power today.

The Communist takeover of China achieved by the Battle of Huai-Hai greatly influenced not only that country but the entire world. Over the next two decades, Mao focused almost exclusively on wielding complete control over his country. He ruthlessly put down any opposition and either executed or starved to death more than 20 million of his countrymen in order to bring to China the "joys" and "advantages" of Communism. Fortunately for the rest of the world, Mao remained focused on his own country. He disagreed with the Soviets on political and philosophical aspects of Communism, and the two nations viewed each other as possible opponents rather than allies.

China's internal struggles and its conflicts with its neighbors have restricted its active world influence. Even though it remains today the largest and strongest Communist nation and the only potential major Communist threat to the West, China remains a passive player, more interested in internal and neighboring disputes than in international matters.

Had the Nationalists been victorious at Huai-Hai, China would have played a different role in subsequent world events. There would have been no Communist China to support North Korea's invasion of the South, or North Vietnam's efforts to take over South Vietnam. Had Chiang, with his outward views and Western ties, been the victor, China might have taken a much more assertive role in world events. Instead, the Battle of Huai-Hai would keep China locked in its internal world rather than opening it to the external.

9

WATERLOO

Napoleonic Wars, 1815

The Allied victory over Napoleon Bonaparte at the Battle of Waterloo in 1815 brought an end to French domination of Europe and began a period of peace on the continent that lasted for nearly half a century. Waterloo forced Napoleon into exile, ended France's legacy of greatness, which it has never regained, etched its name on the list of history's best known battles, and added a phrase to the vernacular: "Waterloo" has come to mean decisive and complete defeat.

When the French Revolution erupted in 1789, twenty-year-old Napoleon left his junior officer position in the King's artillery to support the rebellion. He remained in the military after the revolution and rapidly advanced in rank to become a brigadier general six years later. Napoleon was instrumental in suppressing a Royalist uprising in 1795, for which his reward was command of the French army in Italy.

Over the next four years, Napoleon achieved victory after victory as his and France's influence spread across Europe and into North Africa. In late 1799, he returned to Paris, where he joined an uprising against the ruling Directory. After a successful coup, Napoleon became the first consul and the country's de facto leader on November 8. Napoleon backed up these aggrandizing moves with military might and political savvy. He established the Napoleonic Code, which assured individual rights of citizens and instituted a rigid conscription system to build an even larger army. In 1800, Napoleon's army invaded Austria and negotiated a peace that expanded France's border to the Rhine River. The agreement brought a brief period of peace, but Napoleon's aggressive foreign policy and his army's offensive posturing led to war between France and Britain in 1803.

Napoleon declared himself Emperor of France in 1804 and for the next eight years achieved a succession of victories, each of which created an enemy. Downplaying the loss of much of his navy at the Battle of Trafalgar in 1805 (36), Napoleon claimed that control of Europe lay on the land, not the sea. In 1812, he invaded Russia and defeated its army only to lose the campaign to the harsh winter. He lost more of his army in the extended campaign on the Spanish peninsula.

In the spring of 1813, Britain, Russia, Prussia, and Sweden allied against France while Napoleon rallied the survivors of his veteran army and added new recruits to meet the enemy coalition. Although he continued to lead his army brilliantly, the stronger coalition defeated him at Leipzig in October 1813 (4), forcing Napoleon to withdraw to southern France. Finally, at the urging of his subordinates, Napoleon abdicated on April 1, 1814, and accepted banishment to the island of Elba near Corsica.

Napoleon did not remain in exile for long. Less than a year later, he escaped Elba and sailed to France, where for the next one hundred days he struck a trail of terror across Europe and threatened once again to dominate the continent. King Louis XVIII, whom the coalition had returned to his throne, dispatched the French army to arrest the former emperor, but they instead rallied to his side. Louis fled the country, and Napoleon again claimed the French crown on March 20. Veterans as well as new recruits swelled Napoleon's army to more than 250,000.

News of Napoleon's return reached the coalition leaders while they were meeting in Vienna. On March 17, Britain, Prussia, Austria, and Russia agreed to each provide 150,000 soldiers to assemble in Belgium for an invasion of France to begin on July 1. Other nations promised smaller support units.

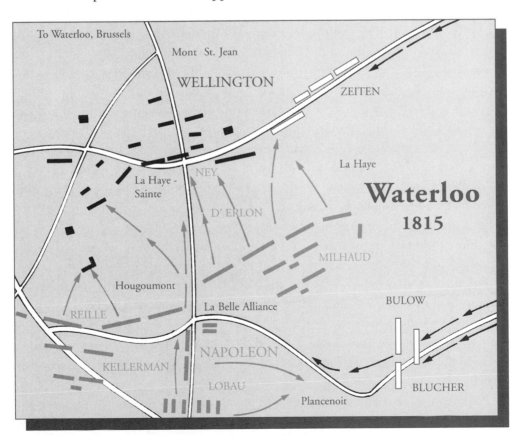

Napoleon learned of the coalition plan and marched north to destroy their army before it could organize. He sent part of his army, commanded by Emmanuel de Grouchy, to attack the Prussians under Gebhard von Blücher in order to prevent their joining the Anglo-Dutch force near Brussels. Napoleon led the rest of the army against the British and Dutch.

The French army won several minor battles as they advanced into Belgium. Although the coalition commander, the Duke of Wellington, had little time to prepare, he began assembling his army twelve miles south of Brussels, just outside the village of Waterloo. There he arrayed his defenses on high ground at Mount St. Jean to meet the northward-marching French.

By the morning of June 18, Napoleon had arrived at Mount St. Jean and deployed his army on high ground only 1,300 yards from the enemy defenses. Napoleon's army of 70,000, including 15,000 cavalrymen and 246 artillery pieces, faced Wellington's allied force of about 65,000, including 12,000 cavalry and 156 guns, in a three-mile line. Both commanders sent word to their other armies to rejoin the main force.

A hard rain drenched the battlefield, causing Napoleon to delay his attack as late as possible on June 18 so that the boggy ground could dry and not impair his cavalry and artillery. After ordering a sustained artillery bombardment, Napoleon ordered a diversionary attack against the allied right flank in the west in hopes of getting Wellington to commit his reserve. The British defenders on the west flank, including the Scots and Coldstream Guards, remained on the reverse slope of the ridge during the artillery bombardment and then came forward when the French advanced.

The attack against the Allied right flank failed to force Wellington to commit his reserve, but Napoleon pressed on with his main assault against the enemy center. As the attack progressed, Napoleon spotted the rising dust of Blucher's approaching army, which had eluded Grouchy's, closing on the battlefield. Napoleon, disdainful of British fighting ability and overly confident of his own leadership and the abilities of his men, continued the attack in the belief that he could defeat Wellington before the Prussians joined the fight or that Grouchy would arrive in time to support the assault.

For three hours, the French and the British fought, often with bayonets. The French finally secured a commanding position at the center at La Haye Sainte, but the Allied lines held. Late in the afternoon, Blücher arrived and seized the village of Plançenoit in Napoleon's rear, which forced the French to fall back. After a brutal battle decided by bayonets, the French forced the Prussians to withdraw. Napoleon then turned back against Wellington.

Napoleon ordered his most experienced battalions forward from their reserve position for another assault against the Allied center. The attack almost breached the

Allied defenses before Wellington committed his own reserves. When the survivors of Napoleon's best began to withdraw from the fight, other units joined the retreat. The Prussians, who had regrouped, attacked the French flank, sending the remainder running in disorder to the south. Napoleon's last few reserve battalions led him to the rear where he attempted, without success, to regroup his scattered army. Although defeated, the French refused to give up. When the Allies asked a French Old Guard officer to surrender, he replied, "The Guard dies, it never surrenders."

More than 26,000 French were killed or wounded and another 9,000 captured at Waterloo. Allied casualties totaled 22,000. At the end of the one-day fight, more than 45,000 men lay dead or wounded within the three-square-mile battlefield. Thousands more on both sides were killed or wounded in the campaign that led to Waterloo.

Napoleon agreed once again to abdicate on June 22, and two weeks later, the Allies returned Louis to power. Napoleon and his hundred days were over. This time, the British took no chances; they imprisoned Napoleon on remote St. Helena Island in the south Atlantic, where he died in 1821.

Even if Napoleon had somehow won the battle, he had too few friends and too many enemies to continue. He and his country were doomed before his return from Elba.

France never recovered its greatness after Waterloo. It returned territory and resumed its pre-Napoleon borders. With Napoleon banished, Britain, Russia, Prussia, and Austria maintained a balance of power that brought European peace for more than four decades—an unusually long period in a region where war was much more common than peace.

While a period of peace in itself is enough to distinguish Waterloo as an influential battle, it and Napoleon had a much more important effect on world events. While the Allies fought to replace the king of France on his throne, their leaders and individual soldiers saw and appreciated the accomplishments of a country that respected individual rights and liberties. After Waterloo, as the common people demanded a say in their way of life and government, constitutional monarchies took the place of absolute rule. Although there was post-war economic depression in some areas, the general plight of the common French citizen improved in the post-war years.

Through the passage of time, the name Waterloo has become synonymous with total defeat. Napoleon and France did indeed meet their Waterloo in southern Belgium in 1815, but while the battle brought an end to one age, it introduced another. Although the French lost, the spirit of their revolution and individual rights spread across Europe. No kingdom or country would again be the same.

10

VIENNA

Austria-Ottoman Wars, 1529

The Ottoman Turks' unsuccessful siege of Vienna in 1529 marked the beginning of the long decline of their empire. It also stopped the advance of Islam into central and western Europe, and ensured that the Christian rather than the Muslim religion and culture would dominate the region.

In 1520, Suleiman II had become the tenth sultan of the Ottoman Empire, which reached from the Persian frontier to West Africa and included much of the Balkans. Suleiman had inherited the largest, best-trained army in the world, containing superior elements of infantry, cavalry, engineering, and artillery. At the heart of his army were elite legions of janissaries, mercenary slaves taken captive as children from Christians and raised as Muslim soldiers. From his capital of Constantinople, the Turkish sultan immediately began making plans to expand his empire even farther.

Suleiman had also inherited a strong navy, which he used with his army to besiege the island fortress of Rhodes, his first conquest. Granting safe passage to the defenders in exchange for their surrender, the Sultan took control of Rhodes and much of the Mediterranean in 1522. This victory demonstrated that Suleiman would honor peace agreements. In following battles where enemies did not surrender peacefully, however, he displayed his displeasure by razing cities, massacring the adult males, and selling the women and children into slavery.

By 1528, Suleiman had neutralized Hungary and placed his own puppet on their throne. All that now stood between the Turks and Western Europe was Austria and its Spanish and French allies. Taking advantage of discord between his enemies, Suleiman made a secret alliance with King Francis I of France. Pope Clement VII in Rome, while not allying directly with the Muslim sultan, withdrew religious and political support from the Austrians.

As a result, by the spring of 1529, King Charles and his Austrians stood alone to repel the Ottoman invaders. On April 10, Suleiman and his army of more than 120,000, accompanied by as many as 200,000 support personnel and camp followers, departed Constantinople for the Austrian capital of Vienna. Along the way, the huge army captured towns and raided the countryside for supplies and slaves.

All the while Vienna, under the able military leadership of Count Niklas von Salm-Reifferscheidt and Wilhelm von Rogendorf, prepared for the pending battle. Their task appeared impossible. The city's walls, only five to six feet thick, were designed to repel medieval attackers rather than the advanced cast-cannon artillery of the Turks. The entire Austrian garrison numbered only about 20,000 soldiers supported by 72 cannons. The only reinforcements who arrived in the city were a detachment of 700 musket-armed infantrymen from Spain.

Despite its disadvantages, Vienna had several natural factors supporting its defense. The Danube blocked any approach from the north, and the smaller Wiener Back waterway ran along its eastern side, leaving only the south and west to be defended. The Vienna generals took full advantage of the weeks before the arrival of the Turks. They razed dwellings and other buildings outside the south and west walls to open fields of fire for their cannons and muskets. They dug trenches and placed other obstacles on avenues of approach. They brought in supplies for a long siege within the walls and evacuated many of the city's women and children, not only to reduce the need for food and supplies but also to prevent the consequences if the Turks were victorious.

One other factor greatly aided Vienna: the summer of 1529 was one of the wettest in history. The constant rains delayed the Ottoman advance and made conditions difficult for the marching army. By the time they finally reached Vienna in September, winter was approaching, and the defenders were as prepared as possible.

Upon his arrival, Suleiman asked for the city's surrender. When the Austrians refused, he began an artillery barrage against the walls with his 300 cannons and ordered his miners to dig under the walls and lay explosives to breach the defenses. The Austrians came out from behind their walls to attack the engineers and artillery-men and dig counter-trenches. Several times over the next three weeks, the invaders' artillery and mines achieved small breaches in the wall, but the Viennese soldiers quickly filled the gaps and repelled any entry into the city.

By October 12, the cold winds of winter were sweeping the city. Suleiman ordered another attack with his janissaries in the lead. Two underground mines near the city's southern gate opened the way briefly for the mercenaries, but the staunch Viennese defenders filled the opening and killed more than 1,200. Two days later, Suleiman ordered one last attack, but the Viennese held firm once again.

For the first time, Suleiman had failed. Scores of his never-before-defeated janissaries lay dead outside the walls. The Turkish army had no choice but to burn their huge camp and withdraw back toward Constantinople, but before they departed they massacred the thousands of captives they had taken on the way to Vienna. Along their long route home, many more Turks died at the hands of raiding parties that struck their flanks.

The loss at Vienna did not greatly decrease the power of the Ottoman Empire. It did, however, stop the Muslim advance into Europe. Suleiman and his army experi-enced many successes after Vienna, but these victories were in the east against the Persians rather than in the west against the Europeans. The Ottoman Empire survived for centuries, but its high-water mark lay somewhere along the Vienna city wall.

Following the battle for Vienna, the countries of the west no longer viewed the Turks and the janissaries as invincible. Now that the Austrians had kept the great menace from the east and assured the continuation of the region's culture and Christianity, the European countries could return to fighting among themselves along Catholic and Protestant lines.

If Vienna had fallen to Suleiman, his army would have continued their offensive the following spring into the German provinces. There is a strong possibility that Suleiman's Empire might have eventually reached all the way to the North Sea, the alliance with France notwithstanding. Instead, after Vienna, the Ottomans did not venture again into Europe; the Empire's power and influence began its slow but steady decline.

11

ZAMA

Second Punic War, 202 B.C.

The Battle of Zama featured the two strongest nations of the time and two of the most influential military commanders of all time. The Romans, led by Publius Scipio, faced the Carthaginians, commanded by Hannibal Barca. At the close of the battle, Rome dominated the western Mediterranean and established what would become the greatest empire of the age.

By the third century B.C., Rome and Carthage were emerging as the two strongest military powers in the western Mediterranean. For twenty-three years, the two rivals had fought over control of Sicily. Then in 241 B.C., the Roman navy defeated the Carthaginians at the Battle of Aegates Islands, ending what became known as the First Punic War.

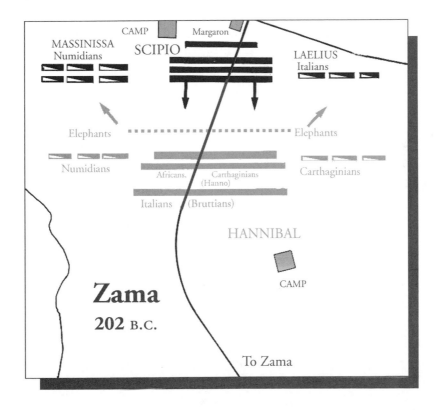

The victory over the Carthaginian navy had given Rome control of the sea, but it had done little to diminish Carthage's land force. Twenty years later, Hannibal Barca led the Carthaginian army into Spain and within two years subjugated the entire country. In 218 B.C., Rome declared war against Carthage, initiating the Second Punic War. Hannibal responded by marching toward Italy with 50,000 men and 40 elephants. Despite the loss of many men and some of his animals, Hannibal successfully crossed the Alps while battling hostile mountain tribesmen as well as the elements.

For the next sixteen years, Hannibal fought the Romans as he advanced south toward Rome. Only his lack of siege equipment and reinforcements prevented his capture of the Roman capital. In 207 B.C., Hannibal ordered his brother Hasdrubal, who commanded the Carthaginian army in Spain, to join him for a final campaign. The Romans, however, discovered Hasdrubal's route of march and ambushed him at the Battle of Metaurus River (59). Rome announced this victory to Hannibal by delivering his brother's severed head to his camp. Despite the loss of his brother and his reinforcements, Hannibal continued operations in Northern Italy.

In 205 B.C., Scipio assumed command of the Roman legions and decided the best way to remove Hannibal from Roman soil was to take the war closer to Carthage. He quickly defeated the remaining Carthaginian army in Spain and then sailed to North Africa, where he won several victories near Carthage itself. Upon hearing the news of Scipio's victories, Hannibal sailed to Carthage to defend his homeland.

Hannibal brought about 12,000 soldiers with him and quickly recruited 25,000 more infantry and cavalry soldiers. He secured 80 elephants as well. Scipio, boosted by reinforcements from home and his own recruiting among local tribes opposed to Carthage, amassed an army of 30,000 infantrymen and 9,000 cavalry. In October 202 B.C., the two most powerful armies in the western Mediterranean led by the two most influential leaders of their generation met at Zama, about five miles southwest of Carthage.

Scipio arranged the core of his army of infantrymen in three parallel lines, with the most inexperienced in the front and the veterans in the rear. Cavalry stood on both flanks. The Roman commander made one modification to this standard formation. Between each company of about 120 men, Scipio left a gap of ten to twenty meters. Hannibal arranged his army in a similar fashion but without the gaps and with an additional rank of elephants in front of his infantry.

When Hannibal's elephants began their advance, the Romans blew horns, stuck their swords on their shields, and made as much noise as possible. The startled elephants broke into a panic, some charging forward through the gaps deliberately left in the Roman lines, and others running for the rear or to the flanks. The Roman cavalry counterattacked against the Carthaginian horsemen and drove them back. Yet, despite the elephant fiasco and the retreat of his cavalry, Hannibal's army advanced. The Carthaginians broke through the first line of defense before the Roman cavalry attacked their rear. This maneuver allowed Scipio's second and third ranks to envelop Hannibal's infantry.

By the end of the day, nearly one-half of the Carthaginian army lay dead on the fields of Zama. Almost that many more were captive, but Hannibal and a few others escaped. Rome's losses totaled only about 1,500 men.

Scipio next moved against the city of Carthage and, despite his lack of siege equipment, he probably could have destroyed the city. Instead, he granted a generous peace, which spared Carthage and even allowed Hannibal to assume its leadership. Hannibal, however, continued to plot against Rome and eventually was exiled to Syria. There he joined still another group in opposition to Rome and ultimately chose to commit suicide in 183 B.C. rather than be captured.

The peace between Rome and Carthage lasted nearly fifty years before the Carthaginians again took up their swords. The Third Punic War did not last long; there would be no fourth. After a four-year siege, Carthage fell to Rome in 146 B.C. (95). The Roman army killed the male adults, sold the women and children into slavery, and razed the city. Thus Carthage ceased to exist.

The victory at Zama made Rome the most powerful force in the western Mediterranean. Its control extended over all of the Italian peninsula, Sicily, Corsica, Sardinia, and Spain. With the defeat of Carthage, Rome could now turn its military might toward the east and the conquest of the Greeks. Although it would be another century and a half before the Roman Empire emerged, the seeds for it were planted on the Zama plain. Scipio, with the newly bestowed title of "Africanus," retired as the dominant military leader of his time.

Although it is doubtful that Carthage, because of their lack of resources and will, could have ever defeated and occupied Rome, with a victory at Zama they could have remained a sufficient threat to prevent Rome's future conquests and development of an empire. Instead, defeat ended the North African power; nothing remains of Carthage. In fact, since Hannibal's time, not a single group or nation in North Africa has been able to assemble a military force capable of effective military operations beyond its own borders.

12

TENOCHTITLÁN

Spanish Conquest of the Aztecs, 1521

With a force of less than seven hundred men supported by fewer than a hundred horses and twenty cannons, Hernán Cortés invaded and conquered the Aztec Empire of more than five million people. Never before had such a small force captured such a large region and secured such massive wealth.

From the time of the "discovery" of the New World during the voyages of Christopher Columbus in the last decade of the fifteenth century, adventurers, soldiers, and explorers crossed the Atlantic to pursue the great wealth of the native peoples. The greatest of these treasures was reported to be held by the Aztec Empire, which controlled most of Central Mexico and the Yucatán Peninsula.

The Aztecs, originally a nomadic tribe from the north, had ruled the region since their arrival in about 1200. Over a period of three hundred years, they had neutralized or assimilated most of the local tribes and had amassed great stores of gold, silver, and precious stones. Although advanced in many ways—including construction, astronomy, and trade—their leaders included human sacrifice as an integral part of their worship of the sun and other gods.

Hernán Cortés ventured to the New World in 1511 and for several years lived the life of a gentleman farmer on the Caribbean island of Hispaniola. Cortés, intrigued by the stories of gold and riches in Mexico, received permission in 1518 to conduct an exploration of the Mexican coastline. Cortés intended to become a conqueror and allowed no obstacle to block his way.

In February 1519, Cortés sailed along the Yucatán coast before landing at what is today Tabasco. Once his seven hundred men were ashore, he burned his fleet in order to leave no means of escape for his small army. Cortés made allies of local tribes who opposed Aztec rule and learned from them about the rich city of Tenochtitlán in the central part of the country. Along the way inland, he recruited additional native tribes as allies. He also made plans to exploit the Aztec myth of a light-skinned, bearded god-king named Quetzalcoatl who, according to legend, had taught them about agriculture and government.

The Aztecs put up a token resistance when Cortés's army neared Tenochtitlán, but the fear of the Spaniards' horses and firearms, combined with the legend of the "white god" Quetzalcoatl, quickly brought their surrender. Cortés entered the city on November 8, 1519, seized the Aztec leader Montezuma, and demanded restitution in gold and other treasure. No sooner had Cortés began to assemble the Aztec wealth than word reached him that an expedition under command of Pánfilo de Narváez had landed at Veracruz with orders to arrest Cortés for overextending his orders and to return him to Hispaniola.

Cortés divided his army, leaving half in Tenochtitlán and marching the remainder back to the coast. Upon arrival at Veracruz, he aggressively attacked at night, captured Narváez, and convinced the survivors to join him in taking the riches of Mexico. Shortly after his return to Tenochtitlán, however, the Aztecs revolted and forced Cortés to withdraw from the city on June 30, 1520.

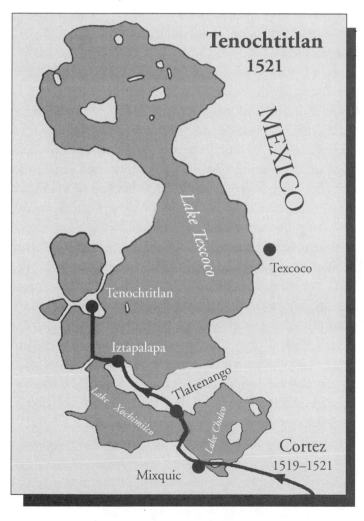

During the next year, Cortés reorganized his small Spanish army and recruited additional local tribesmen. In the spring of 1521, he again marched against Tenochtitlán, this time with an army of 700 Spaniards and more than 60,000 Tlaxcalan tribesmen. Tenochtitlán was a difficult city to attack because it was built on fill in the middle of a large lake, approachable only by a series of causeways. Cortés constructed towers so his firearms and crossbows could fire into the city, and prepared boats to cross the open waters.

For three months, Cortés laid siege to the city while the Aztec defenses weakened from a lack of supplies and the spread of European diseases, including smallpox and measles, to which they had little resistance. After nearly ten weeks of assaults and counterassaults, the Spaniards gained a foothold and then fought street by street until they neutralized the defenders on August 13, 1521. Outside the city, tribes traditionally opposed to Aztec occupation attacked village after village, destroying them and scattering the survivors.

Cortés, forgiven by the Spanish government once they realized the wealth he had captured, immediately began the export of gold and other treasures. During the next forty years, more than one hundred tons of gold, double the amount held in all of Europe, were delivered to the coffers of Spain. Nearly 7,000 tons of silver, as well as other treasures, crossed the Atlantic from Mexico. In addition to wealth, the Spanish brought New World crops to Europe, including potatoes, beans, and maize.

A grateful Spanish government named Cortés the Captain General of New Spain. Several years later, he led other expeditions in the New World before retiring to Spain, where he lived in splendor until his death in 1547.

The battle of Tenochtitlán established Spain as the leader of Central America for the next three hundred years. Even today, the language and religion of Spain dominate the region. The wealth exploited from its lands funded Spanish conquest in South America and throughout the world. As a direct result of the battle, Spain remained the world's most powerful country until the debacle of the Spanish Armada a half-century later (16).

Cortés's victory at Tenochtitlán changed the course of history and the future of a continent and its peoples. The only comparable battle is the even more influential victory of Francisco Pizarro at Cajamarca a decade later (6), which gave Spain control of most of South America.

13

NORMANDY

World War II, 1944

The Battle of Normandy established an Allied foothold on the beaches of Western Europe during World War II that provided a base for the eventual thrust into the German heartland. To counter the Normandy invasion, the Germans transferred many of their troops from the Eastern Front, a move that allowed the Soviets to advance more rapidly toward Berlin.

For two years after the beginning of World War II, the German war machine had marched unchecked to the English Channel in the west and to Central Russia in the east. The Battle of Britain (40) and the entry of the United States into the war stopped Hitler's plan to invade England, and the hard-fought battles of Moscow (22) and Stalingrad (3) finally slowed his war against the Russians.

The three most powerful Allies—the United States, Britain, and the Soviet Union—differed on the best plan to defeat the Axis—Germany, Italy, and Japan. Russia's Josef Stalin wanted an immediate U.S.-British invasion of Western Europe to take pressure off his forces in the east. The U.S. preferred to strike at Germany as quickly as possible and therefore agreed with the Soviets. The British were not in such a hurry, remembering their disastrous losses in France in the previous World War. "Memories of the Somme and Passchendaele were not to be blotted out by time or reflection," Winston Churchill later wrote. One British officer, Lieutenant General Frederick Morgan, stated more bluntly in his memoirs, "Certain British authorities instinctively recoiled from the whole affair, as well they might, for fear of the butcher bill."

The British and Americans finally agreed to first neutralize the German forces in North Africa, which would then allow them to invade Italy, take the Italians out of the war, and protect sea-lanes to the much-needed Middle Eastern oil fields. In November 1943, after securing North Africa and Italy, Churchill and Roosevelt met face-to-face with Stalin at the Teheran Conference, where the Soviet leader persuaded them to conduct a cross-channel attack against the French coast. Plans began immediately for what was named Operation Overlord, better known as D-Day.

The Allies selected General Dwight D. Eisenhower to command the Supreme Headquarters and Allied Expeditionary Forces, and British General Bernard Montgomery to command the ground units. Initially, the Allied planners considered

Calais in northern France, across the narrowest point of the English Channel from Dover. Aware that this would also appear obvious to German planners, the Allies instead selected a fifty-mile stretch of the Normandy coast between Caen and the Cotentin Peninsula as the invasion point.

Plans included initial bombings of rail and roadways to prevent transport of enemy reinforcements to the beachhead, to disrupt their rear areas, and to establish air superiority. Ships would then bombard the beaches before the ground attack went ashore.

The planners divided the Normandy beaches into five areas. The British Third Division would be responsible for Sword on the far east. Farther west would be the Canadian Third at Juno, then the British Fiftieth at Gold in the center, the U.S. First and part of the Twenty-ninth at Omaha, and farthest west, the U.S. Fourth at Utah. British Commandos and American Rangers would accompany the divisions to neutralize particularly difficult targets. Prior to the landings, paratroopers and glider infantry would land behind the beaches to secure bridges and disrupt communications. The British Sixth Airborne was responsible for the territory behind Sword Beach, while the U.S. Eighty-second and 101st Airborne divisions would land behind Utah Beach.

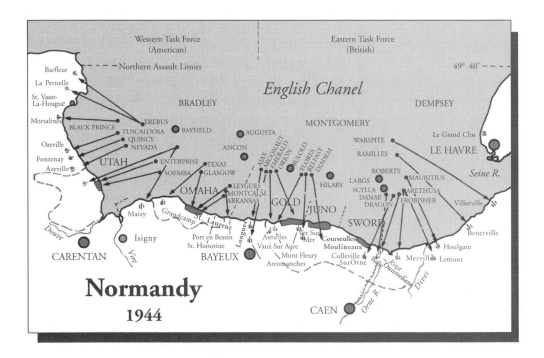

During the spring and early summer of 1944, the Allies assembled and trained their ground, air, and naval forces at bases throughout Britain under the utmost secrecy. Gradually 800,000 men, 5,000 ships, and 10,000 aircraft assembled to execute the invasion.

The 175,000 Allied ground forces landing on the Normandy beaches would face about 80,000 German defenders under command of Field Marshals Erwin Rommel and Gerd von Rundstedt. Although the Germans anticipated that the invasion would come at Calais, they had nonetheless lined the Normandy beaches with concrete bunkers, beach obstacles, anti-personnel and tank mines, and barbed wire entanglements. They had also flooded low areas with water from nearby rivers. Additional tank divisions were stationed in the French interior as reinforcements.

The dates picked by the Allies coincided with tide and weather. The days that appeared most advantageous were June 5–7. Such conditions would not again occur until June 18–20. The invasion force was loaded and ready on June 4 to cross the channel the next day, but adverse weather delayed the invasion. Eisenhower's staff informed him the weather might break briefly on the 6th but they could not guarantee good conditions.

Eisenhower knew his troops were ready and growing restless. He was also aware that every day he waited offered the Germans more opportunities to learn of his plan and to strengthen their defenses. Early on June 5, Eisenhower gave the order for the invasion to proceed the next day. He told his staff, "I don't like it, but…I don't see how we can possibly do anything else." A short time later he simply ordered, "O.K., let's go."

Along the Normandy coast, the Germans had not been maintaining a high state of alert because they thought any invasion would be to their east and that the weather was too bad for a channel crossing. Rommel even took the opportunity to return home to Germany for his wife's birthday.

The weather did have its effects, bad and good, for the invaders. Clouds obscured many of their air targets and the drop zones for the paratroopers and glider infantry. High winds further spread the airborne forces over vast areas instead of the planned concentrated drop zones. While this disrupted the assembly of the units, it thoroughly confused the Germans, who were suddenly faced with Allied paratroopers all over their rear areas. The dispersal of the paratrooper divisions into small groups also confused the Germans into thinking the airborne attack was just a diversion for a full invasion elsewhere.

The front-line German defenders quickly learned differently as day broke and the fog lifted. Thousands of Allied troops under cover of air and sea bombardment rushed ashore. The Allies had complete air superiority, with only two German fighters breaking through to strafe the landing boats. Despite the Allied armada of ships and multiple divisions coming ashore, some German leaders, especially Hitler, still believed the attack was merely a diversion. Hitler declared the main attack would still come at Calais and held back the reserve tank divisions.

On the beaches, the Allies met widely varying degrees of resistance. Fighting was particularly heavy at Omaha, where Allied intelligence had failed to note the recent arrival of the German 352nd Division. Most of the Allied tanks had sunk in the high surf on their way to the beach, and the naval and air bombardment was concentrated too far inland to neutralize the coastal bunkers. Finally, however, the U.S. engineers breached the German defenses and the Rangers led the way off the beach. For every yard of beach secured, one American soldier fell dead or wounded.

During the next six days, the five beach invasion forces linked together and pushed inland to unite with the airborne forces. Eight more divisions came ashore as engineers put in mobile harbors for resupply and reinforcements at the beachhead. Allied casualties totaled more than 11,000, including 2,500 dead, less than a quarter of the number some planners had feared.

From the beachhead, the Allies pressed forward to liberate France and to prepare for the invasion of Germany itself. Many hard battles lay ahead, but Normandy had opened the door to fortress Europe. Any thought of Germany's winning the war lay in ruins on the Normandy beachhead.

In addition to hastening the end of Hitler's Germany, the invasion on the Western Front did as planned in siphoning German troops from the Eastern Front. Soviet units moved faster and, with the consent of the other Allies, captured Berlin to end the war in Europe.

For their part, the Russians garnered a buffer zone between the west and their homeland in which they could spread Communism. This space caused an early split among the Allies, which quickly broke open into a Cold War. The Cold War legacy of World War II was, however, inevitable because of the ideological differences between the Allies.

There is some conjecture that if the invasion had failed, the U.S. and Britain would have sued for peace with Germany. This is highly unlikely. Britain could not and would not have allowed German occupation of France only a few miles across the Channel. Hitler had to be stopped, even if it required many more years and additional invasions to accomplish the objective.

14

SALAMIS

Persian-Greek Wars, 480 B.C.

The Greek naval victory in the waters around the island of Salamis in 480 B.C. and the subsequent land battles that followed completed the defeat of the Persians that had begun at Marathon a decade earlier (28). This victory established independence for the Greek city-states, which provided both the environment and the military might for Alexander the Great to establish his great empire a century later. That empire ensured the dominance of Greek philosophy throughout Western civilization for centuries to come.

Despite their defeat by the Greeks at Marathon in 490 B.C., the Persians had still maintained a formidable army as well as a navy that controlled the seaways. Darius I, who had lost at Marathon, intended to mount another offensive against Greece, but he first had to put down a rebellion in Egypt. Before he could do so, he died in 486 B.C. His son Xerxes replaced him and quickly proved his military skills by defeating the Egyptian rebels. Xerxes then turned toward Greece to avenge his father's defeat and to expand the borders of the Persian Empire westward.

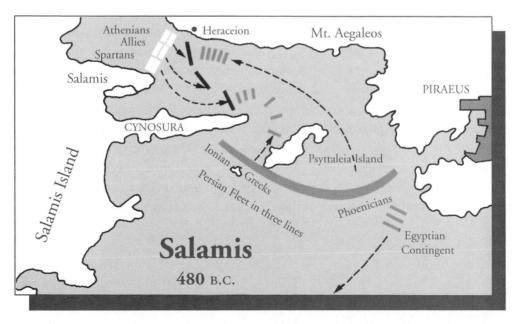

Athenians Allies Spartans — Heraceion — Mt. Aegaleos — PIRAEUS — Salamis — CYNOSURA — Salamis Island — Ionian Greeks — Persian Fleet in three lines — Psyttaleia Island — Phoenicians — Egyptian Contingent

Salamis

480 B.C.

During the decade following their victory at Marathon, the Greeks had drifted back to fighting internally. However, when word reached them that Xerxes was headed in their direction with an army of possibly more than a million men and as many as 1,200 ships, the southern Greek city-states of Athens, Sparta, and Cyclades united to combat the invaders. The northern provinces, which were the most difficult to defend and first in the path of the advancing Persian force, were reluctant to join the alliance. In an attempt to garner support from the northern city-states, the southern alliance dispatched a small army of Spartans to defend the pass at Thermopylae. Before the battle began, most of the Spartans retreated, leaving only 300 of their men and 1,100 Borotian allies to defend the pass. They did so valiantly until all were killed. While they left a lasting legacy of fighting ability and valor, the fight had little or no direct influence on the succeeding battle.

From Thermopylae the Persians continued south toward Athens with their army marching near the shoreline. The Persian navy sailed along the shore carrying the provisions for the huge land force. Some accounts, particularly those from Greece that attempted to enhance their subsequent victory, estimated the size of the Persian army at upwards of two million; one report went as high as five million. Even counting support personnel and camp followers, these numbers are vastly exaggerated, as neither the Persian population nor any supply system of the period could have supported such a vast army. In reality the Persian land force likely numbered about 200,000.

Whatever its exact size, the Greeks realized that they could not stand against such a large force. Their leader, Themistocles of Athens, determined that their only hope for victory was at sea. If they could defeat the Persian navy, their army would have to withdraw for lack of supplies. Despite misgivings from several of his subordinates, Themistocles convinced his allies to abandon the Greek mainland and withdraw to the nearby island of Salamis. From there they would deploy their joint navy against the Persian fleet.

Xerxes entered Athens and quickly defeated the small Greek stay-behind force defending the Acropolis. While the Persians looted and burned the city, Themistocles sent messengers claiming to be Greek deserters to report that the Greeks were divided from internal strife and were preparing to retreat on their ships. The Persian leader responded by planning to attack and destroy the Greek vessels before they could sail away.

Xerxes established an elaborate camp, complete with a golden throne on the side of Mount Aeguleas, overlooking the waters around Salamis from which to observe the anticipated victory. On the morning of September 23, 480 B.C., Xerxes mounted his throne and signaled his ships to attack. The Persian navy, reduced to about a thousand vessels by a recent storm, still outnumbered the Greeks' by three to one. However, the 370 Greek triremes, with their triple banks of oars, were faster and larger than their opponents' ships. The Greeks also had the advantage of knowing the waters on which the battle was fought. More importantly, each Greek sailor and soldier realized that he and his mates were all that stood between their families and the Persian army. The very existence of Greece was in their hands.

The Persians approached in the crescent formation typical of the period. The Greek ships rammed them head-on and grappled ships together so their infantry could board and destroy the enemy crews. A small Greek force of about thirty galleys remained in reserve and then struck the Persian flank just as the rest of the Greek force began to gain an advantage.

Over a period of nearly eight hours, Xerxes watched from his hillside throne as nearly half his navy sank to the bottom of the sea. Greek losses totaled only forty ships. For the first time in history, a naval battle had determined the outcome of a war. With much of his navy destroyed and the supply vessels for his army now threatened, Xerxes had no choice but to turn back to Asia Minor. He left behind an army of about 100,000 to hold the Greek mainland, but by the following August they had surrendered to the Greeks.

The Persian navy remained strong despite their defeat at Salamis. However, the Greeks replaced them as the dominant navy in the Mediterranean. It took another century and many more internal wars for Alexander the Great to unite all of Greece and defeat the Persian Empire, but the cornerstone of the eventual victory was in place. The Battle of Salamis guaranteed the lasting independence of Greece and the advancement of a culture and philosophy that would influence all of Europe and eventually spread to North America.

If Xerxes had been victorious at Salamis, it is doubtful that the divided Greeks would have even been able to unite to expel the Persians from their territory. If Salamis had gone the other way, it is quite possible that Persia, rather than Greece, would have exerted the dominant influence on Europe and the West.

15

SARATOGA

American Revolution, 1777

The Battle of Saratoga was the turning point of the American Revolutionary War. The rebel victory prevented the British from dividing the colonies along the Hudson River Valley and greatly boosted the morale and confidence of the Americans. More importantly, the battle proved that the Americans could defeat the British in a conventional battle, and it brought support from France and other European countries that recognized the Americans might very well be successful in their revolution.

From the first days of the American Revolution, the rebel colonists had suffered from a lack of arms and supplies, the absence of a navy, and the weak and wavering commitment of the colonists themselves. Only about a third of the American population actively supported the rebellion, while an equal number remained loyal to the Crown. The remaining third were neutral.

Out-manned and out-gunned, the Continental Army under General George Washington had fought a series of losing battles in the war's first two years, culminating with the loss of New York City in the autumn of 1776. Washington reacted by adopting a simple strategy. Short of manpower, arms, ammunition, rations, and equipment while opposing one of the world's strongest and best-equipped forces, he decided to follow a protracted defensive war rather than seek immediate victory on the battlefield. As long as his army existed, so did the United States. What the rebels could not achieve by fighting, they could by waiting, and Washington determined that he could afford to lose longer than the British could afford to win.

Washington did, however, need the occasional victory to maintain the morale of his troops and to encourage enlistments. He achieved this with surprise attacks at Trenton on December 26, 1776, and against Princeton on January 3, 1777.

Meanwhile, British generals, tired of the lack of decisive action, developed plans to crush the rebellion. General William Howe, in command of the British army in New York, lobbied London for permission to move on the rebel capitol of Philadelphia with an offensive in the summer of 1777. With their capitol destroyed, the rebels, Howe believed, would surrender. In Canada, General John Burgoyne proposed a move down the Hudson River Valley in two columns while Howe moved north from New York.

The two armies meeting in Albany would separate the New England states, where the rebellion had the most support, from the southern colonies, which provided many of the supplies for the army. Of the two plans, Burgoyne's made the most sense. However, officials in London approved both plans, which called for more offensive operations than the British army in North America could properly conduct.

Howe further complicated the British plans when he took a circuitous route by sea through Maryland instead of marching directly over land from New York to Philadelphia. Although Washington attempted to defend the American capital, he refused to risk his army in a sustained battle. By October, the British had scored a hollow victory by occupying Philadelphia, while Washington left the city to the invaders and withdrew to winter quarters.

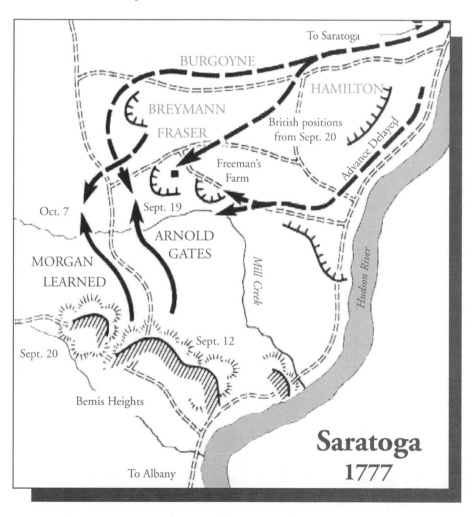

Burgoyne had his setbacks as well. Howe's slow advance against Philadelphia prevented his moving north to support Burgoyne's offensive. Then the British column in the east, commanded by Colonel Barry St. Leger, had the opposite effect than intended. It consisted of about 800 regulars and irregulars and about a thousand Native American allies, and was designed to elicit support from Americans wavering between Revolutionists and Loyalists. But the colonists, veterans of more than a century of warfare with Native Americans, were outraged to see the British teamed with their traditional enemies. St. Leger moved down Lake Ontario to Fort Stanwix about forty-five miles east of Oswego before the Americans could gather a force large enough to stop him. When many of his Indians deserted, St. Leger decided to retreat back to Canada without a significant fight.

Burgoyne's column initially appeared more successful when on July 1, the British captured Fort Ticonderoga with little resistance. The route to Albany, however, was heavily wooded, infested with summer insects, and filled with challenges provided by the American commander, General Horatio Gates, who destroyed bridges, felled trees across roads, and even rerouted streams to create a series of obstacles to delay the British march.

Gates used what time he gained to add militia units to his own army. By the time Burgoyne reached Saratoga, 10,000 Americans, who were dug in on Bemis Heights about ten miles south of the town, outnumbered his 6,500 British soldiers. On September 19, Burgoyne attempted to flank the American positions by sending General Simon Fraser and 2,000 men to seize high ground near Freeman's Farm.

Gates countered with a force led by General Benedict Arnold and a unit of expert riflemen commanded by General Daniel Morgan. Although Morgan's men killed many of the British officers with their expert marksmanship, Burgoyne's artillery finally broke the American ranks and forced the rebels to withdraw back to Bemis Heights. Gates's losses totaled about 300, about half the number of British casualties.

Over the next two weeks, more than a thousand additional militiamen joined Gates's defenses. Burgoyne, confronted with supply shortages and demoralized troops, determined that he had to attack. On October 7, he once again ordered Fraser and 1,600 men against the American left flank. Gates sent Morgan and others to meet the advance in the vicinity of Freeman's Farm. In a brief fight, the Americans repelled the British, inflicting 600 casualties, including Fraser, on the enemy, as opposed to 150 friendly losses.

The British withdrew to Saratoga where more and more Americans arrived to surround them. On October 17, Burgoyne surrendered his surviving but exhausted army of nearly 7,000 to Gates.

Burgoyne's surrender had an immediate impact on the Revolution as well as a long-lasting effect on the future of the United States. Burgoyne's failure to cut the colonies in half further united the rebels' efforts, especially when his multitude of small arms and artillery pieces fell into their hands.

The effect of the battle's outcome extended far beyond the Hudson River Valley. The French, sympathetic with the rebellion, now saw that joining the rebels could help them gain a new ally against their long-time English enemies. Three months after the Battle of Saratoga, France and the United States signed a treaty of alliance. A month later, the French declared war against Great Britain. Encouraged by the French action, Spain and the Netherlands joined the war against England over the next two years.

The support of the French brought much-needed weapons and supplies to support the rebel army. More importantly, the powerful French navy protected rebel ports while also slowing the movement of men and supplies from England to the United States. Instead of a rebellion confined to North America, the British now faced a multifaceted war of international proportions.

While the first shots of the Rebellion echoed at Lexington and Concord (74), the Battle of Saratoga was the turning point that led directly to the final victory at Yorktown (1), and ultimately to the rise of the United States as the single world power. Its ranking would be even higher except for the simple fact that Washington and his fellow rebels were already committed to a long war. Victory was the only option. A British victory at Saratoga might have further prolonged the conflict, but had Saratoga not led to victory, there is little doubt that some other battle eventually would have. Nevertheless, Saratoga deserves its ranking because it was one of the most influential battles in history's most influential revolution.

16

THE SPANISH ARMADA

Spanish-English Wars, 1588

The defeat of the Spanish Armada marked the decline of Spain and the rise of England as a world power. In addition, the battle showed that the future of naval warfare lay in long-range cannons rather than the traditional tactic of ramming and boarding.

As part of their exploration and exploitation of the riches of the Western Hemisphere, the Spanish had maintained the world's most powerful military for nearly a century. The Spanish navy ruled the seas while their army marched across Europe, imposing their culture and Catholic religion on the masses. By the latter part of the sixteenth century, Spain dominated the continent and only England provided a viable threat to their hegemony.

For many years, the English and Spanish had remained allies against common enemies, and friends through various marriages between their royal families. However, when Elizabeth I became queen of England in 1558, she declared the Protestant Church of England as the country's religion; she permitted English privateers, many of whom closely resembled pirates, to capture Spanish treasure ships from the New World; she allowed attacks on Spanish seaside villages; and she increased England's support of Protestant rebels against Spanish occupation of the Netherlands.

King Philip II, ruler of Spain and an avid Catholic, endured these transgressions until Elizabeth ordered the execution of her Catholic rival Mary, Queen of Scots, in February 1587. At that point he decided to act; however, like Caesar before him and Napoleon and Hitler later, he faced the problem of crossing the English Channel. For a successful operation, Philip knew that he must destroy, or at least dominate, the English navy so that his ships could transport his army across the Channel from the Continent.

Philip thought that with God on his side, as well as a strong navy that had defeated the Turks at Lepanto the previous decade (53), he could easily achieve his objectives. The English too had placed their faith in God, but they also had taken measures to strengthen their fleet. Whereas the Spanish lighter ships were designed to close in on and ram enemy ships so boarding parties could clear the decks, the English had been building larger vessels armed with heavier, long-range cannons. While the Spanish ships carried more soldiers than sailors for hand-to-hand fighting, the English vessels contained mostly sailors and cannon gunners.

To invade England, Philip faced not only the English Channel but also other obstacles. First, the English privateer Sir Francis Drake landed at Cape St. Vincent while he was raiding the Spanish coast and destroyed Spain's primary source of barrels used to hold its navy's shipboard provisions. Then the Spanish fleet commander died, leaving Philip no choice but to appoint the inexperienced Duke of Medina Sidonia to replace him.

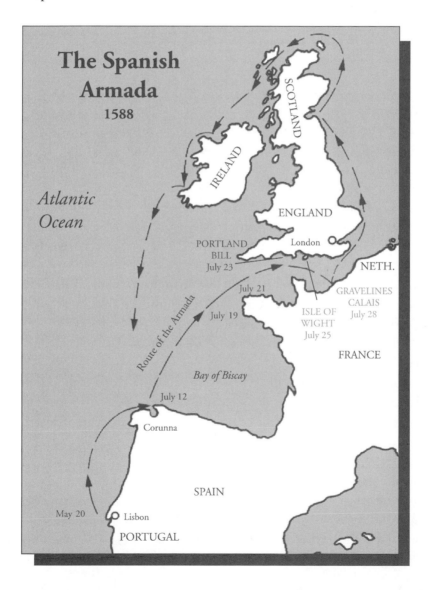

On May 20, 1588, the Spanish Armada set sail for England with 130 ships, 2,500 guns, and 30,000 men, two-thirds of whom were soldiers. A heavy storm and rotting provisions (caused by uncured barrels that had replaced the ones Drake had destroyed) forced the fleet to put into Corunna for repairs and supplies. Finally, on July 12, the Spanish Armada sailed north to bring Catholicism and escort the Spanish army, led by the Duke of Parma in the Netherlands, to England.

Elizabeth had expected the invasion and had put her own fleet of 34 warships and 6,000 men to sea under command of Lord Howard of Effingham. Another 163 privateer vessels, led by such able captains as Drake, reinforced the English fleet. Unlike the Spanish Armada, the English vessels had the advantage of nearby friendly ports to resupply or to refit.

The Spanish neared the English coast on July 19 in a seven-mile-wide crescent, the formation that had proven successful in previous battles for closing with enemy vessels and boarding them. The English, however, did not close to boarding range but rather sailed only near enough to rake the Spanish formation with their long-range guns while remaining out of range of the enemy cannons. On July 21, 23, and 25, the English attacked as the Spanish sailed north into the Channel, futilely expending their own ammunition at targets beyond their range.

The superior English cannons damaged the Spanish ships and killed many of their crewmembers. An internal explosion destroyed the Spanish *San Salvador*. Another Spanish ship, the *Rosario,* was captured and claimed as a prize by Drake. English losses were negligible.

By July 27, the Armada was running low on ammunition and put into Calais on the French coast. Knowing that a direct attack against the anchored Spanish fleet was extremely risky, the English unloaded eight small ships, set them afire, and let them drift into the Spanish formation. Many of the Armada cut their anchor cables and fled in confusion.

Although the floating fires did not sink or damage a single ship, the Armada had no choice but to continue their flight. Medina Sidonia decided to sail north around Scotland and then south down the coast of Ireland back to Spain. Along the way his crews suffered from hunger, thirst, and disease while severe storms sank or beached many of his ships. Most of the crews that went aground in Scotland and Ireland were executed or imprisoned. By the time the Armada returned to Spanish waters in September, only half their original number remained.

Despite the Armada's disastrous losses, Spain had sufficient resources to launch additional ships. King Philip reinforced his army and navy to maintain his kingdom, but the defeat of his Armada ended hopes of additional conquests. From 1588 onward, Spain's power declined. In contrast, the English gained unity and confidence from the battle and soon started to expand their empire into North America and India as the Protestant Reformation gained strength in Europe.

In addition to its influence on the future of Spain and England, the battle of the Spanish Armada strongly influenced future naval warfare. The traditional crescent formation used to ram and board opponents went to the bottom of the English Channel along with much of the Spanish fleet. Future naval warfare would utilize line astern formations with man-of-wars firing broadsides with powerful, long-range cannons. Gun crews, not cutlass-armed boarders, would decide future naval battles.

While Spain remained sufficiently strong after the loss of the Armada to maintain its colonies in Central and South America, the strength gained by the English enabled them to dominate the settlement of North America. Had the battle gone differently, the Spanish and Catholicism might have dominated Europe, as well as what would later become the United States and Canada.

17

GETTYSBURG

American Civil War, 1863

The successful stand by the United States Army at Gettysburg, Pennsylvania, in July 1863 marked the "high tide" of the rebellious Confederate States of America. By turning back the second and final invasion of the North by General Robert E. Lee and his Army of Northern Virginia, the Union army preserved the country.

Following the battle of Antietam (5), which had stopped Lee's first invasion of the North the previous September, the Confederate army fought a series of successful battles in Virginia at Fredericksburg and Chancellorsville. However, despite the victories, the war was exhausting the few resources available within the Southern states, and the Union blockade of Confederate ports continued to severely limit supplies arriving by ship from Europe. Lee and Confederate President Jefferson Davis once again decided that it was time to invade the North. They hoped that the invasion would allow the Army of Northern Virginia to forage the countryside and factories of Maryland and Pennsylvania for supplies to stockpile for future operations. Lee believed that he could defeat any Union army sent to intercept him and that a victory in Federal territory would strengthen the Northern peace movement that was demanding an end to the war. The Southern leaders also still hoped a great victory might win recognition and support from European nations, despite the slavery issue.

In June 1863, Lee crossed the Potomac River and marched north into southern Pennsylvania. As with his invasion the previous year, he aimed his army toward the rail center of Harrisburg. Meanwhile, in Washington, President Abraham Lincoln remained concerned about the recent Confederate victories in Virginia and the inability of his generals to defeat the rebel army. When he learned of Lee's move northward, Lincoln promoted General George Meade, who then became the fifth commander of the Army of the Potomac in only ten months.

Meade began moving his army to intercept the advancing Confederates. Their ultimate clash came by chance and began when Confederate General A.P. Hill learned that much-needed shoes for his infantrymen were available for the taking at a Gettysburg factory. On July 1, just west of the town, a Union cavalry patrol met the advancing rebels. Although badly outnumbered, the Northern cavalrymen held the line until additional rebel troops under General Richard Ewell arrived and pushed the

Union force back through Gettysburg and onto Cemetery Ridge and Culp's Hill. Ewell, who had replaced the famous Stonewall Jackson when he was killed at Chancellorsville, was not as aggressive as his predecessor and failed to act on an opportunity to roll up the exposed Union flank. Lee arrived in time to order Ewell to attack "if practicable," but the reluctant general felt that it was not and conceded his attack against the Union right flank.

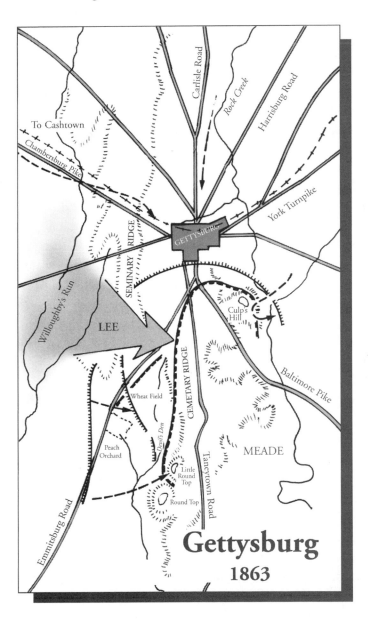

Gettysburg
1863

During the late afternoon and evening of July 1, the remaining Confederate and Union armies converged on Gettysburg. Unfortunately for Lee, his cavalry commander J.E.B. Stuart rode off on a raid of his own, leaving Lee without reconnaissance or intelligence capability.

By the morning of July 2, Meade had the Union army of 90,000 arrayed in a fishhook pattern running from the hook on Culp's Hill in the north for three miles southward along Cemetery Ridge to Little Round Top. Across an open field three-quarters of a mile to the west stood Lee's 76,000-man army along the high ground of Seminary Ridge.

Previous Civil War battles had proven what commanders had learned throughout the ages: the advantage lay with the defense, especially when the defenders outnumbered the attackers. In recognition of this adage and his observations of the Union defenses to his front, Lee's commander on his right flank, General James Longstreet, advised against an attack. Lee nevertheless ordered Longstreet to advance toward Little Round Top, believing that if Longstreet could secure this hill, the Confederate artillery could place enfilade fire on the Union lines and easily turn their flank. The initial Union line in front of Little Round Top was out of position and gave way early in the battle; however, other regiments quickly filled the gap and occupied the high ground. After a bloody, close battle, they forced back Longstreet's advance from the Union's left flank.

Having failed in the attacks on the left and right flanks, Lee now decided to assault the Union center. When Longstreet again recommended not attacking, Lee responded, "The enemy is there, and I am going to attack him there."

On the morning of July 3, Lee ordered a division commanded by George Pickett from Longstreet's command and two divisions from A.P. Hill's corps to attack the Union center. Although all three divisions advanced, the attack would forever be known as Pickett's Charge.

After a mostly ineffective artillery barrage, the 15,000 rebel soldiers began their long march across the open field to the Union lines at 3:00 P.M. For three-quarters of a mile, the 200 guns of the Union artillery shredded the long gray line. At 200 meters, the Union infantrymen began to pour musket shots into the advancing rebels. Despite the carnage, the disciplined Confederates made it to the Union defenses and even broke through briefly before reinforcements threw them back from what became known as "the high tide of the Confederacy."

Less than half of the assault force staggered back to Seminary Ridge. Lee met the survivors saying, "It's all my fault...I'm sorry." The three-day fight left more than 23,000 of Lee's best troops dead, wounded, captured, or missing. Meade's casualties also numbered about 23,000.

Lee anticipated a counterattack on the morning of July 4, but the cautious Meade was satisfied with a partial victory. Nor did he pursue Lee's army as it retreated back to Virginia, even though the flooded Potomac would have aided an attack.

Some accounts blame the loss at Gettysburg on Stuart for being absent and not providing Lee with sufficient information. Others point at Longstreet for his reluctance. The real blame, however, belongs to none other than Robert E. Lee for piecemealing his attack and for assaulting across open ground into the heart of the Union defenses. Even accounts that claim Lee was ill or suffering heart problems cannot excuse his faulty tactics and deplorable decisions.

After Gettysburg, the South was never again able to resume an effective offensive. Although fighting continued for nearly two more years, after their defeat at Gettysburg the Confederacy was on its way to becoming a lost cause. Gettysburg directly led to the eventual surrender of Lee and other rebel generals that resulted in the reunification of the United States. From that point, the United States has continued to gain riches and strength to become the world's only superpower.

Had Lee won at Gettysburg, or listened to Longstreet to fight another day, the war would have lasted longer. It is doubtful, however, that the Confederacy could ever have prevailed even if victorious at Gettysburg. Its stance on slavery kept European allies at a distance, and the South simply could not match the North in resources and industry. The more populated North could field more soldiers, and after the Emancipation Proclamation, free and runaway slaves readily volunteered to add even more regiments to the Union army.

All of these factors combined make Gettysburg one of history's most influential battles. Yet it remains less pivotal than the Battle of Antietam fought the previous year. Antietam established that the Confederacy would have to stand alone. Gettysburg proved that it could not.

18

ARBELA-GAUGAMELA

Macedonian Conquests, 331 B.C.

Alexander the Great's victory at Arbela-Gaugamela in 331 B.C. led to the end of the Persian Empire and opened the way for the Greeks to extend their influence eastward all the way to India. The victory ensured the dominance of Greek civilization and culture for centuries to come.

In the mid-fourth century B.C., Philip of Macedon had organized and trained a powerful army that first defeated and then united the Greek states into the new Greek Empire, which became the most powerful military and economic force in the West. Only the Persian Empire in the East rivaled its world power. Philip had begun plans to conquer Persia, but an assassin killed him before he could attack his rival. Philip's son Alexander assumed the Greek throne at twenty years of age, but he brought to the crown years of battlefield experience gained at his father's side, as well as a classical education provided by Aristotle.

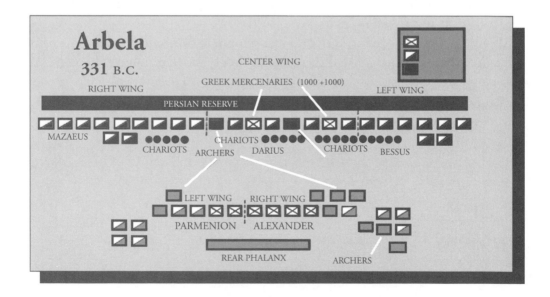

At the time Alexander assumed command, battle-planning and strategy had not yet been developed. Tactics were crude at best; opponents met head-on, and the victor was usually the larger, better-armed force. Alexander introduced tactical maneuvers for enveloping the enemy and for coordinating his infantry and cavalry attacks. Before Alexander, warfare resembled a street fight; after him, it resembled a massive, albeit unrehearsed, stage production.

In 334 B.C., the Greek army defeated the Persians at the Granicus River and then marched to Issus, where again they were victorious. Although Persia remained strong, Alexander decided to add more territory to his Empire before completing his defeat of the Persians. He drove down the eastern Mediterranean coast, capturing all of what is now Israel and then occupying Egypt. Legend has it that after a visit to the great temples of Egypt, the Greek leader professed his belief that he was the son of the Greek god Zeus, rather than King Philip. His soldiers, who already worshiped him for his leadership and tremendous bravery in the midst of the fiercest fighting, had little difficulty accepting him as a deity.

Alexander halted his offensive only long enough to establish the city of Alexandria at the mouth of the Nile River. In addition to providing a port for his navy and a resupply point for his army, Alexandria quickly became the commercial, scientific, and literary center of the Greek world.

In 331 B.C., Alexander took his veteran army of 40,000 infantry and 7,000 cavalry and retraced his steps along the Mediterranean back toward Persia, where he crossed the Tigris and Euphrates Rivers with little resistance. Darius III, the Persian King, monitored Alexander's advance as he assembled soldiers from throughout his kingdom. By late September, Darius III had gathered an army of 200,000 infantry and cavalry supported by 200 war chariots and 15 elephants. Some estimates swell the army to a half-million, but it is doubtful that so many soldiers would have been available or sustainable by the supply system of the period.

Darius positioned his army on a large open area about seventy miles west of the town of Arbela. He then leveled the plain so that his chariots could move more easily.

Alexander arrived at the village of Gaugamela, opposite Darius's defenses, in late September. Some accounts state that the Greeks rested for several days, while others report that they waited only hours before attacking. On the morning of October 1 (the exact date confirmed by accounts of a lunar eclipse), Alexander advanced. Because he was outnumbered at least five to one, Alexander could only attack the Persian center. To prevent being easily surrounded, Alexander placed his infantry in the middle, his cavalry on the flanks, and his strong reserve in the rear.

Darius countered with his own attack against the Greek center. His chariots and elephants, followed by the cavalry, broke through the front ranks only to fall to the Greek infantry. The Persian cavalry made their way through the Greek front, but instead of turning to assault the unprotected flanks of the Greek army, they continued to the rear to loot supplies and kill camp followers.

Alexander ignored his own rear and personally led a force through the gap left by the Persian horsemen while committing his reserve against the exposed Persian flanks. His tactics were superior, but the large numbers of Persians prevented a quick Greek victory. The Persians held until they saw Alexander break through the center and approach Darius and his command group. When Darius retreated, his army, although still numerically superior, broke ranks and fled. The Greek cavalry pursued and killed many of the fleeing Persians. Darius escaped, but much of his army lay dead. Casualty estimates for the Persians vary from 40,000 to 100,000. Greek losses were less than 500.

Alexander and his army quickly captured the major Persian cities, while Darius fell to an assassin in his own government. Alexander did not stop at defeating the Persian Empire but continued his offensive toward the Caspian Sea and occupied the territory all the way to northwest India. No army ever stopped Alexander except his own. After eight years of constant warfare, Alexander's subordinates finally convinced him to return home. Along the way, despite his claims of divinity, Alexander died at the early age of thirty-three, his death likely the result of malaria compounded by alcoholism.

Given the preparation time and his overwhelmingly superior numbers, Darius should have defeated the Greeks at Arbela-Gaugamela. The deciding factor was not, however, numbers or time but rather leadership. Alexander was simply the better general. Perhaps a Persian victory or, more importantly, the death of Alexander in the battle, would have changed the future world. Instead, Alexander used the victory as a pivotal point for joining the East and West. The battle provided Alexander the opportunity to spread Greek civilization throughout vast territories while establishing more than twenty new cities that became regional trade and cultural centers.

Arbela-Gaugamela also influenced other military leaders who adopted the Greek tactics that had defeated far more numerous foes. These methods of military operation strongly influenced the leaders of the future Roman Empire and also provided inspiration and knowledge for the Napoleonic conquests more than two centuries later.

19

MEXICO CITY

U.S.-Mexican War, 1847

The Battle of Mexico City brought an end to the war between the United States and Mexico, solidified the States' claim to Texas and much of the West, and established the U.S. as the dominant country in the Western Hemisphere. Mexico City and the battles that led up to it also significantly influenced the development of artillery and served as training grounds for many of the officers on both sides of the American Civil War.

Following the defeat of the Mexicans by the Texans at the Battle of San Jacinto (23) in 1836, the border between the two countries was in constant dispute. Texas claimed the Rio Grande as the boundary, while Mexico claimed the boundary to be about two hundred miles farther north along the Nueces River. Few American or Mexican settlers occupied the territory, but both sides coveted the large expanse of land. The border dispute became even more heated when the United States annexed Texas in 1845.

Difficulties between the two countries might have been resolved by diplomacy except that the expansion-minded United States government was focused on its "Manifest Destiny" to stretch the nation from the Atlantic to the Pacific Oceans. President James K. Polk dispatched John Slidell as an envoy to Mexico City with an offer to purchase the disputed area, but the Mexican government refused to meet with him.

During the winter of 1845–46, President Polk sent an army of 4,000 men commanded by Major General Zachary Taylor to the northern bank of the Rio Grande. Mexico likewise sent an army to the south side of the river. For several months the two sides peacefully observed each other from across the river. This peace was disturbed, however, when on April 22, a Mexican cavalry patrol crossed the Rio Grande and killed or captured sixty-four American soldiers. When word reached Polk of the incident, he sent a message to Congress saying, "Mexico has…shed American blood on American soil," and demanding a declaration of war. Congress officially declared war on Mexico on May 13.

General Taylor spent the summer reinforcing and training his army. In September, he defeated the Mexicans in several small battles north of the Rio Grande and then crossed the river and captured Monterrey on the 25th. Taylor pushed deeper into

Mexico the following spring and defeated a Mexican army led by General Antonio López de Santa Anna, who, despite his defeat at San Jacinto, had recently returned to head Mexico's army.

While Taylor was winning battles in northern Mexico, political moves in Washington were changing the way the war would progress. Polk knew that Taylor, who was becoming a national hero through his battlefield leadership, had ambitions for the presidency. The U.S. Army's senior officer, General Winfield Scott, had been lobbying Polk for permission to take command in Mexico, so Polk agreed to Scott's proposal of a "second front" consisting of a landing at Veracruz and an offensive against Mexico City. The president also readily agreed to transfer most of Taylor's soldiers to Scott's command.

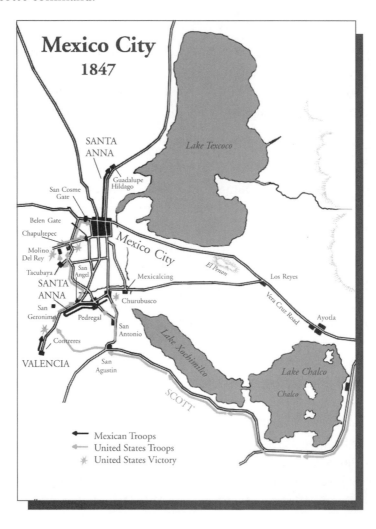

Scott landed near Veracruz on March 9, 1847, with an army of 10,000. He quickly moved inland to get away from the malaria- and yellow fever-infested coastal plain. Santa Anna, however, had learned of the American advance and established a blocking position at the village of Cerro Gordo, but Scott conducted a flanking attack along a route discovered by Captain Robert E. Lee to secure a victory on April 18.

A month later, Scott, using the same route as Hernán Cortés had three centuries earlier, marched to Puebla and occupied the city. Scott, thoroughly confident in his predominately West Point-trained officers and his artillery, decided to push on to Mexico City. Although outnumbered three to one, he attacked and defeated the Mexicans six miles south of Mexico City at Contreras and Churubusco on August 20, 1847.

Scott exploited his advantage with unrelenting attacks. The tactic was at times costly. At Molino del Rey, he assaulted a church bell factory falsely rumored by the Mexicans to be casting cannons. The attack on the well-defended factory on September 8 was successful, but cost 800 casualties to secure an unimportant objective.

The losses at Molino de Rey did not stop Scott's advance on Mexico City. By September 13, when the Americans attacked Chapultepec, a fortified hill guarding the entrance to Mexico City, the Mexican army was so depleted that it resorted to employing military cadets as young as thirteen. The young cadets fought and died, earning the title of "heroic children" in Mexican lore.

The fall of Chapultepec cleared the way for the Americans to enter Mexico City along the causeways over the water that surrounded the city. Mexican officials, fearful that the enemy's artillery would level the historic capital, pleaded with Santa Anna to surrender. Although his army still outnumbered the Americans by two to one, Santa Anna withdrew. On the morning of September 14, the Americans defeated the few remaining defenders and occupied the city. The conquerors, including a detachment of Marines, raised the U.S. flag over the Mexican National Palace—the "Halls of Montezuma" that would later be hailed in the Corps official hymn.

Santa Anna made a halfhearted attack on Scott's rear at Puebla, but the war was effectively over except for political negotiations. By the time Scott occupied Mexico City, however, the war was out of favor back at home. While some Americans, including Polk, thought the U.S. should annex all of Mexico southward to the Yucatán Peninsula, many thought the U.S. should have not have gone to war at all.

Finally, on February 2, 1848, the United States and Mexico agreed to the Treaty of Guadalupe Hidalgo. It recognized the Rio Grande as the Texas border and gave the U.S. lands stretching to the Pacific Ocean. The U.S., in an unusual gesture for a victorious force, also agreed to pay Mexico more than fifteen million dollars.

The treaty formed the borders of the continental United States that, with minor adjustments, survive to this day. It also established the United States as the most powerful military force in the hemisphere and earned the respect of European officials. It finalized what had begun at San Jacinto and ranks therefore as one of the most influential battles in American history.

Mexico City and the battles that led up to it were also important for the training and experience they provided the future leaders of both sides in the American Civil War. Along with the skills of leadership they gained, these officers learned how to maximize artillery and to employ long supply lines.

The battle also adversely impacted long-term Mexican-American relations. Mexico saw the war as an aggressive effort to seize their land. During World War I, Germany attempted to exploit these feelings by promising the return of their lands if Mexico would join them in fighting against the Americans. Beliefs that the western U.S. should be a part of Mexico still linger today south of the border.

The Battle of Mexico City also affected politics in the U.S. Although Taylor did not lead the attack on the Mexican capitol, he won the presidency in 1848. Scott, who ran unsuccessfully for president that same year, remained in the army and later designed the plan that helped defeat the rebel Confederacy.

Finally, it is interesting to consider the impact if the U.S. had claimed all of Mexico. What would have been the influence of the country's resources on America's future? Where would the Mexican state have stood in the Civil War? If it had gone with the South, would it have tipped the scales of that war to a victory for the rebels with its manpower and other resources?

20

ACTIUM

Wars of the Second Triumvirate, 31 B.C.

Octavian's naval victory over the joint fleets of Antony and Cleopatra off the shore of Actium in 31 B.C. ended the Roman Republic and established the Empire, which would endure for the next five hundred years. It also ensured that Rome's cultural influence would concentrate in the West rather than the East.

With the advance of Rome as a cultural and military power, Roman citizens had formed a republic led by a triumvirate, a group of three leaders. The First Triumvirate ended with the assassination of Julius Caesar in 44 B.C. to be replaced by the Second Triumvirate composed of Mark Antony, Marcus Lepidus, and Caesar Octavianus or Octavian. Shortly after the Second Triumvirate defeated Caesar's assassins at Philippi in 42 B.C., Lepidus faded from power, leaving Antony and Octavian in charge of the Republic.

Even though Antony married Octavian's sister, he continued to compete with Octavian for Rome's leadership. By 33 B.C., Octavian ruled Rome and the west provinces, while Antony controlled Egypt and the east. Much of Antony's power, and many of his future problems, came from his alliance and romance with the Egyptian queen, Cleopatra. The relationship between Antony and Cleopatra—forever glorified in a play by William Shakespeare—benefited both in that Egypt remained free of Roman dominance, and the Republic gained a valuable trade and military ally.

Octavian, however, did not like sharing power with Antony, let alone the Egyptian queen. The rivalry came to a head when Antony married Cleopatra without first divorcing Octavian's sister, prompting Octavian to begin a rumor campaign that Antony intended to move the center of the Republic to Egypt and include Cleopatra in the government. Octavian secured a copy of Antony's will and read it to the Senate, revealing his rival's intentions of declaring his and Cleopatra's children as heirs to his Roman leadership. The Roman Senate, angered over Antony's personal life and insulted that he intended for an Egyptian to be their queen and the mother of their future leader, agreed with Octavian that military action had to be taken.

Early in 31 B.C., Octavian sailed with a fleet of 400 galleys and his army of 40,000 to the narrow Greek peninsula that separated the Ionian Sea from the Ambracian Gulf. About this same time, the joint armies and navies of Antony and Cleopatra, totaling 460 galleys, occupied Actium to the south and across the narrow waterway from Octavian.

For several months, the two forces engaged in indecisive skirmishes. The only significant action occurred when Octavian's navy blocked Antony's resupply route. By the end of the summer, Antony's supplies were dwindling dangerously, and his army was becoming demoralized. His only two options were either to march inland into Greece, where there were few supplies, or to take to the sea and fight his way back to Egypt. He chose the latter.

At dawn on September 2, Antony sailed into the Ionian Sea with his fleet of 400 galleys arrayed into three lines while Cleopatra's navy of 60 ships, including her personal treasure vessel with purple sails, brought up the rear. Antony's soldiers, including several senior leaders, protested against having the battle with Octavian fought at sea rather than on land. When they could not dissuade Antony, many deserted or went over to the other side. As a result, Octavian and his primary admiral, Marcus Agrippa, knew their opponent's plan and deployed their ships in line across his route of escape.

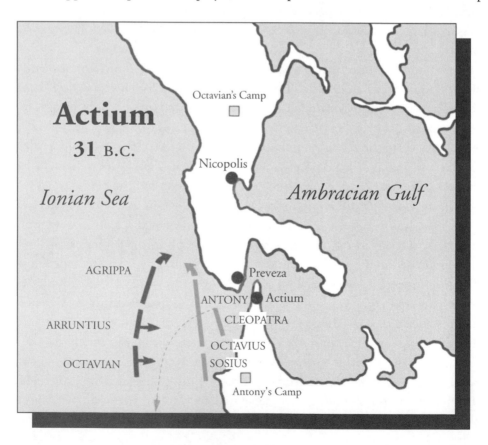

For most of the day, both sides attempted to turn the other's northern flank. Neither was successful and neither appeared to gain an advantage, but in the afternoon, a gap opened in Antony's northern lines. Instead of filling the space with her ships, Cleopatra exploited the opportunity by sailing through the opening and into the open sea toward Egypt. When he became aware of her departure, Antony assembled forty of his swiftest boats and broke away to join her. Antony's remaining navy, abandoned and leaderless, surrendered. Antony's soldiers, stranded ashore, also surrendered or melted into the countryside. By September 9, Octavian was in control of Actium as well as its surrounding land and waters.

The following year, Octavian launched an offensive against Egypt to complete his defeat of Antony and Cleopatra. Antony's legions, aware of how he had abandoned his army at Actium, deserted without a fight. Antony committed suicide rather than be taken prisoner; a few days later, Cleopatra took her life as well.

Octavian returned to Rome as a hero in possession of the treasures of Egypt and as the single Roman leader. Three years later, the Senate declared him "Augustus," giving birth to the Roman Empire that survived for the next five hundred years.

As far as sea battles go, Actium was not very large. Although the two forces were fairly equal in size, Octavian's navy was united, while his opponents' was deeply divided. Ultimately, the brief battle hinged on the internal political struggle within the armed forces of Antony and Cleopatra. The romantic struggle between the two also played a major role. Cleopatra saved herself and her treasure ship by abandoning Antony. Antony saved himself by following her and abandoning his own army and navy. Whatever their rationale, the chance for the Republic or the new Empire to be ruled from Egypt rather than Rome ended when the two lovers' ships broke through the line, abandoned the remainder of their force, and sailed to Egypt.

21

MECCA

Muhammad's Conquest of Arabia, 630

Muhammad's victory at Mecca in 630 gave him control of western Arabia and the opportunity to spread his religious beliefs. Following the battle, Mecca became the holy center of Islam from where Muhammad and his followers would build one of the world's leading religions.

By the latter part of the sixth century, Mecca had become a major center on the overland trade route that paralleled the west coast of Arabia. Merchants in the town included Christians and Jews, but the population was mostly pagan. A sanctuary within Mecca housed stone idols that drew nomadic Arab tribesmen on annual pilgrimages. During the sacred months of these visits, individuals and tribes set aside their feuds, giving Mecca the reputation of a peaceful place that catered to all sorts of travelers. This image was, of course, good for trade and the enrichment of the town's leaders.

In about 570, a boy named Muhammed was born in Mecca to a family of merchants. By the time this boy reached the age of six, both his parents had died and he had been left in the care of his grandfather. A short time later, he began the life of a trader with caravans that took him all over the Middle East. During his travels, Muhammad encountered the religious practices and holy sites of Jews and Christians. The more he studied these believers in one God, the more he became dissatisfied with the idolatry of his own people.

When he was twenty-five, Muhammad returned to Mecca and married a rich widow fifteen years his senior. His wife's wealth allowed him to quit the caravans and spend his time praying, meditating, and studying religious ideas. Muhammad believed he had been hearing God's voice for years, but not until he was forty years old did these heavenly revelations manifest themselves as what would become the religion of Islam.

In 610, Muhammad spent six months meditating in a cave on Mount Hira, where he claimed the angel Gabriel appeared in a vision telling him that he would be entrusted with the word of Allah (God). Muhammad came down from the mountain preaching the tenets of Islam in Mecca. He explained that Islam meant "Submit or surrender to God," and that one who submits or surrenders is a "Muslim." All Muslims were to believe that Allah was the one and only God and that Muhammad was his messenger.

The merchants and other residents of Mecca mostly ignored the new prophet as they focused on trade and profits. For several years, Muhammad gathered few followers in Mecca outside his own family. He was, however, able to convert a group of about 200 in Medina, another trade center 210 miles to the north. By 622, the leaders of Mecca had tired of Muhammad's preaching and began to feel threatened by his message. Their increased persecution forced him and his family to flee the city and join his followers in Medina.

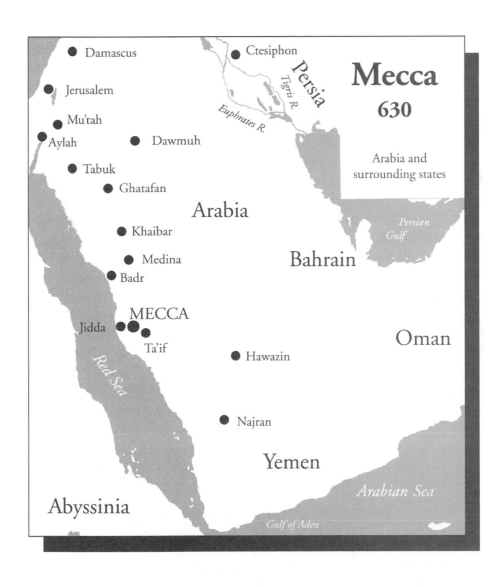

Muhammad and his Medinian followers raided Meccan caravans. Muhammad's preaching, combined with his policy of equal shares for all participants in the caravan raids, brought new followers. By 624, Muhammad's band totaled more than 300 as they again left Medina to raid Meccan caravans. When Abu Sufyan, leader of the Meccan merchants, learned that Muhammad was attacking along the trade routes, he gathered an army of 1,300 to defend his next caravan. The Muslims and Abu Sufyan's army met in March 624 at the oasis of Badr, located seventy-five miles southwest of Medina. Muhammad showed that he had military as well as prophetic abilities by deploying his men on the high ground surrounding the area's only water source. Muhammad later claimed divine assistance in the battle that followed, but whatever the reason, he proved victorious against a much larger force.

Abu Sufyan escaped Badr and formed an even larger army. Three years later, he led 10,000 men to Medina, where he discovered that Muhammad's followers had also increased. The 3,000 Muslims had dug a trench all the way around Medina from which they repulsed several attacks over the next three weeks. Abu Sufyan, unable to penetrate the defenses and not prepared to conduct a siege, withdrew.

During the next year, Muhammad continued to spread the word of Islam. In 628, he and other leaders in the region agreed to the Treaty of Hudaybiya that granted Muslims peaceful entry into Mecca for worship.

A year later, the Meccan officials ceased honoring the treaty, and once again Muhammad prepared to ensure religious freedom through military might. This time, the Muslims had the larger force with more than 10,000 warriors who firmly believed in one God and one Prophet. In January 630, Muhammad led his army out of Medina toward Mecca. When he reached the city, its inhabitants put up only a token defense before laying down their arms and welcoming Muhammad as their savior.

Muhammad enshrined his birthplace of Mecca as the Holy City of Islam and continued to send out messengers to bring the words of Allah to the region. Two years later, Muhammad died at age sixty-two. He left behind records of his revelations from Gabriel, as well as other tenets of Islam. Fifteen years after his death, his followers completed the Holy Book of Islam, the Koran.

After the Battle of Mecca, religious and military followers of Islam grew exponentially. Islam and the Muslim army expanded from Mecca to Jerusalem and on into Syria, Iran, Egypt, and Iraq in less than a decade. The Islamic armies then continued into Europe, where they again succeeded until their westward expansion was stopped at the Battle of Tours in 732 (24).

Jews, Christians, and pagans continued to live in the Middle East after the Battle of Mecca, but from the day of Muhammad's victorious entrance into the city, the future of Islam was assured. From the Middle East, it has spread until today it is one of the most practiced religions in the world, as well as the dominant influence on the governments of many nations.

This advancement of Islam to the status of a major religion and political force would not have taken place without Muhammad, the founder of the religion itself. From the time he came down from Mount Hira in 610 with his message from Allah until he captured Mecca twenty years later, he and Islam were one and the same— equally vulnerable to destruction. Every battle he fought was significant; while some may have been larger, such as Badr, and others brought more converts to his cause, such as Medina, the future of the Prophet and Islam were not assured until his victory at Mecca.

22

MOSCOW

World War II, 1941

Poor military decisions by Adolf Hitler, severe winter weather, and a desperate defense stopped the German invasion of the Soviet Union on the outskirts of Moscow in 1941. This first major defeat of the Nazi army was the turning point on the Eastern Front that significantly influenced the outcome of World War II.

By late 1940, the Royal Air Force and the daunting English Channel had finally slowed the Nazi advance westward. While the German leader Adolf Hitler disdained the English as "shopkeepers," his real hatred focused on Communism and the Soviet Union. He therefore postponed his invasion of Great Britain to attack the Communists.

Hitler's generals favored a blitzkrieg move against Moscow. By capturing the Soviet capital, they believed they could destroy the primary Communist industrial center and gain control of the railways throughout the vast country. Hitler's control of this rail hub would help prevent Soviet or Allied reinforcements from joining the war. Furthermore, the generals argued that Nazi occupation of the Soviet capital would destroy the Communists' morale and hasten their surrender.

Despite the success and experience of his generals, Hitler, a veteran World War I corporal, commanded that the primary offensive be aimed at Leningrad and Stalingrad, because he believed that the capture of the two cities bearing their leaders' names would doom the country and dishearten the people. Moscow would be only a secondary target. On June 22, 1941, Germany began its invasion with a three-pronged attack. Army Group North marched toward Leningrad while Army Group South attacked toward Kiev, the Ukraine, and ultimately Stalingrad. Army Group Center was to penetrate the Soviet heartland between the two columns and then swing north in a pincer movement to link up with Group North, cut off much of the Communist army, and capture Leningrad.

Although delayed by a month due to a late spring, the German invasion initially repeated the same success it had when the Germans had slashed across France. The Nazis killed hundreds of thousands of Soviets and destroyed or captured their artillery and support vehicles in less than a month of fighting.

By July 19, Army Groups North and Center were both nearing their objective of Leningrad when Army Group Center briefly halted at Smolensk. Group Center was in position either to drive two hundred miles toward Moscow or turn to meet Group North and join the attack against Leningrad. Hitler chose instead to order much of Group Center to reinforce Group South, whose attack was slowing.

The maneuver was successful, and within two months, the reinforced Group South surrounded Kiev and forced the surrender of more than a half-million Russians and nearly a thousand tanks on September 26. Even though Leningrad continued to hold out against Group North during the battle in the south, Hitler ordered the forces of Group Center to return to Smolensk after their victory at Kiev to attack Moscow.

While the road from Smolensk to the Kremlin had been virtually undefended when Group Center departed to the south two months earlier, the route was now densely covered with tank obstacles, mines, and reinforcements brought in from the east. Still, despite the Soviet preparations, the German two-pronged attack from Smolensk on September 30 quickly gained the advantage. In a little more than a week, the Germans killed or captured another half-million Soviets and secured more than a thousand enemy tanks and five thousand artillery pieces as they advanced to within sixty miles of Moscow.

By October 8, it appeared the Nazi swastika would soon be flying over the ruins of the Kremlin; it very well might have been except for the Russian "resource" that had stopped many armies in the past, including that of Napoleon. Autumn rains fell in torrents and turned the crude Russian roads into quagmires, causing the German offensive along with their vehicles to get bogged down in the deep mud. Again the Soviets used the delay to reinforce their defenses along the Mozhaisk Line, fifty miles outside the city.

When the rains turned to snow and ice, the Germans used the frozen ground to resume their attack and finally penetrated the Mozhaisk Line on November 15. But on November 20, a severe blizzard swept across the lines, beginning one of the harshest winters in Russian history. Because Hitler and his generals had expected to defeat the Soviets in the fall, they had made no preparations for clothing or supplying their army during the winter cold. Guerrillas and partisans harassed the long supply routes back to Germany, further slowing the arrival of warm clothing and other supplies. Frostbite and other cold-related problems soon added to the long list of German casualties.

On December 2, the Army Group Center made one last desperate assault on the Soviet lines. A few units reached the edge of the city and were even able to see the spires of the Kremlin in the distance before Soviet soldiers and armed factory workers beat back their advance. On December 5, Hitler finally allowed his exhausted, nearly frozen army to withdraw to more defendable positions.

Soviet Marshal Semyon Timoshenko led most of the defense of Moscow before Marshal Georgi Zhukov replaced him prior to the final battle. Zhukov, who had impressed Stalin with his defense of Kiev, soon exhibited the aggressiveness that marked his leadership for the remainder of the war. Using recently arrived reinforcements, Zhukov counterattacked on December 6 and, over the next month, pushed the Germans back more than a hundred miles as his soldiers and the weather continued to inflict heavy casualties on the Nazis.

While the Army Group Center began their retreat, the Group North's attack against Leningrad slowed and eventually stopped. The Germans were able to besiege the city for the next thirty months, but they never managed to penetrate its defenses. An angry Hitler fired and replaced many of his generals and then focused again on Stalingrad, where within a year his army suffered the critical defeat that broke its back. Even though the battle for Stalingrad (3) was even more influential than that for Moscow, the winter the Germans spent outside the gates of the Kremlin foreshadowed the final Soviet and Allied victory over the Nazis.

23

SAN JACINTO

Texas War of Independence, 1836

Although it was an extremely small battle by any standard, the defeat of the Mexicans by the Texans at San Jacinto in 1836 easily ranks as one of history's most decisive and influential battles. The victory enabled Texas to establish its independence and provided lands that would eventually compose much of the western United States. Conflicts between the U.S. and Mexico over the borders of that region produced a major war between the two countries a decade later.

Shortly after Mexico gained its independence from Spain early in the nineteenth century, the Mexican government encouraged immigrants to move into its northern territories. Settlers from the United States were welcomed if they agreed to become Mexican citizens and convert to Catholicism. Beginning in 1821, Americans moved to Texas to establish farms and villages. By 1836, they numbered more than 30,000, compared to only about 4,000 native Mexicans in the vast territory.

Political unrest and corruption in the Mexican government spawned revolutionary movements throughout the country, but none were as successful as those in Texas. In 1835, Texans resisted Mexican control and took over the towns of Gonzales and San Antonio. On March 2, 1836, Texas formally declared its independence.

General Antonio López de Santa Anna immediately formed an army and moved north to put down the rebellion. Santa Anna had declared himself dictator shortly after his election as president in 1833. In addition to his political title, he also was proud of his perceived military abilities and often referred to himself as the "Napoleon of the West."

General Sam Houston, a former Tennessee congressman and a veteran of the War of 1812, took command of the few men who made up the army of Texas. Houston had already established several small garrisons along Santa Anna's route to slow the Mexican army while he sought reinforcements and trained his army. One of these garrisons, led by William Travis, Jim Bowie, and David Crockett, held out for thirteen days at the Alamo in San Antonio before being overrun on March 6. Santa Anna granted no quarter to the 180 Texans who had refused to surrender.

Three weeks later, Santa Anna surrounded the Texan defenses commanded by James Fannin near Goliad. Again the Mexicans slaughtered the defenders, including those who attempted to surrender. The Alamo and Goliad provided Houston the time to assemble and train an army of 800, which he kept on the move ahead of Santa Anna.

Santa Anna had lost about 1,500 men at the Alamo, yet his army still numbered about 4,000. In mid-April, Houston learned that Santa Anna had detached about a thousand men to range ahead of his army in an attempt to catch up with the Texans. Although outnumbered, Houston decided that the odds would get no better. On April 19, he established a camp north of Galveston near the convergence of the San Jacinto River and the Vince and Buffalo Bayous. Santa Anna, thinking he had trapped the Texans, stopped about 2,000 yards away and hastily established defenses of brush, packs, and saddles. He sent for the rest of his army while he planned his attack to destroy the rebel Texans.

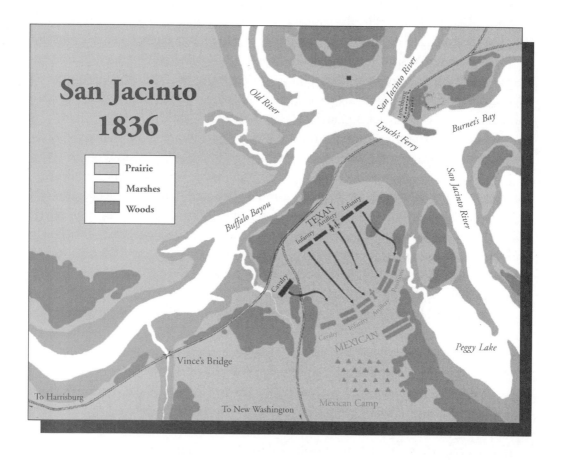

Houston realized that he had to react quickly before the Mexican armies converged. On April 20, he sent a small cavalry force to skirmish with the Mexican pickets in order to determine the exact outline of Santa Anna's defenses.

About 500 reinforcements joined Santa Anna on the morning of April 21, bringing his total to 1,500 soldiers. He decided to rest his men for one more day and then attack.

Actions were occurring more quickly on the Texas side of the lines. Houston dispatched Erastus "Deaf" Smith to destroy Vince's Bridge, which cut off the avenue for additional Mexican reinforcements, and also eliminated the Texans' only avenue of retreat. Houston's army now would have to achieve their slogan of "victory or death."

At about 4:00 P.M., the Texans formed an infantry line nine hundred yards long and two men deep. The Mexican camp lay quiet, confident that the Texans were neither strong enough nor sufficiently motivated for an assault. They were wrong. The Texans made it to within two hundred yards before the Mexicans realized they were under attack. Santa Anna's few artillery pieces answered the fire from the Texans' two cannons, but neither side's artillery was particularly effective. Infantrymen would decide the outcome of the battle of San Jacinto.

Just as the Texans reached the Mexican lines, Smith rode down the line shouting that the bridge was down. The Texans fired a volley into the Mexican ranks and then charged forward, using their muskets as clubs and drawing their long knives for hand-to-hand fighting. The Mexicans never got their defenses organized. One of Santa Anna's staff officers, Colonel Pedro Delgado, later wrote in his account of the battle, "I saw our men flying in small groups, terrified, and sheltering themselves behind large trees. I endeavored to force some of them to fight, but all efforts were in vain." Santa Anna later wrote of the battle, "So sudden and fierce was the enemy's charge that the earth seemed to move and tremble."

In only eighteen minutes, the battle was over. Many Mexicans who tried to surrender fell to Texans who shouted, "Remember the Alamo!" and "Remember Goliad!" Others drowned trying to swim the San Jacinto to safety. Houston's casualties totaled ten men killed and thirty wounded, including himself, with a musket shot to his ankle. More than 600 Mexicans lay dead on the battlefield. Nearly all of the remainder of Santa Anna's army, including the general, were captured.

Santa Anna agreed to a treaty that granted Texas its independence and the withdrawal of the remainder of his army to Mexico. Both the Mexican Congress and Santa Anna soon disavowed the treaty, but they never re-entered Texas with an army capable of reclaiming their former territory. Texas soon applied to the U.S. for statehood, but slavery issues kept it independent for the next nine years. Its admission into the U.S. led to the Mexican War in 1846, and ultimately influenced the American Civil War.

The San Jacinto battlefield has changed little since Texas gained its independence from Mexico. Except for a tall spire commemorating the battle, which Texans typically brag is taller than the Washington Monument, the field is as it was in 1836. A plaque on the monument provides a sufficient summary of the influence of the battle on today's single superpower and wealthiest nation in the world. It states, "Measured by its results, San Jacinto was one of the decisive battles of the world. The freedom of Texas from Mexico won here led to annexation and to the Mexican War, resulting in the acquisition by the United States of the states of Texas, New Mexico, Arizona, Nevada, California, Utah, and parts of Colorado, Wyoming, Kansas, and Oklahoma. Almost one-third of the present area of the American nation, nearly a million miles of territory, changed sovereignty."

TOURS

Muslim Invasion of France, 732

The victory of the Franks at the Battle of Tours in 732 stopped the Muslim advance into Europe and ensured that Christianity would remain the dominant religion of the region. It also united the previously divided Franks and established a line of rulers that included Charlemagne, the great conquerer, two generations later.

During the later part of the seventh century and the early years of the eighth, the Muslims expanded their borders to garner riches and to spread their religious beliefs. Their conquests of Syria, Egypt, and North Africa produced great numbers of converts to Islam, and they became dedicated and efficient soldiers in the expanding Muslim armies. In 710, the Muslim Moors and Berbers from North Africa, under the leadership of Musa ibn Nusair, invaded Spain and within two years controlled the entire peninsula.

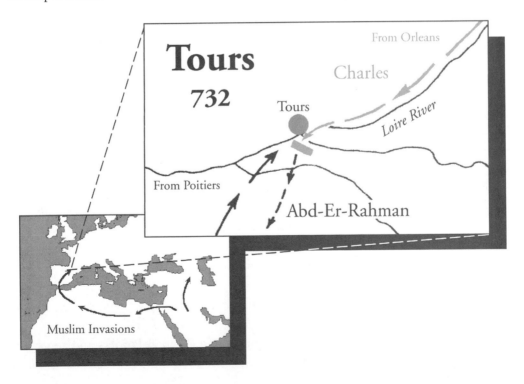

The first major setback for the Muslims occurred in 718, when the Byzantine Empire defeated them at the Battle of Constantinople (41). The Muslims then decided to expand from Spain across the Pyrenees into Gaul (modern France). The great wealth of the region was certainly attractive to the Muslims, as was the opportunity for more converts to their religion. The Franks, who suffered many internal divisions, appeared capable of little resistance.

In the summer of 732, the Muslim emir of Spain, Abd-er-Rahman, led an army of more than 60,000 cavalrymen northward. At the Garonne River, a Frankish army under command of Duke Eudes of Aquitaine attempted to block the invasion, but the Muslims quickly overwhelmed them. Eudes and the survivors of his army fled to Paris, where they agreed to put aside previous differences with other Frankish factions and unite under King Charles to stand against the invaders. Other groups of Franks previously opposed to Charles also joined his army to fight their common enemy.

Charles's army of approximately 30,000, mostly infantry, marched south as Abd-er-Rahman advanced northward, burning churches and looting along the way. Both sides moved slowly, as their large forces had to live off the land. In October, somewhere near Tours, the two armies met. The Franks, mostly infantrymen armed with swords and axes, formed closely packed defensive squares. Across the field, the Muslim horsemen, carrying long swords and spears, prepared to attack using their tactic of a mass charge.

Before the fight began, however, the Muslims delayed long enough to secure the loot they had gathered on their march at a point far behind the battlefield. For several days, the two sides observed and probed each other's lines. Finally on a morning in mid-October, Abd-er-Rahman's army charged the Frankish squares. Charles's infantrymen held steady as they hacked and stabbed the cavalrymen and their mounts. Again and again, the horsemen charged, only to be killed or beaten back.

The battle ceased only with the arrival of darkness. At daybreak the next morning the battle renewed and continued for several days until Abd-er-Rahman died in the fight. His depleted, exhausted army decided it was better to secure the loot they had already taken and return to Spain than to risk more charges against the Frankish defenses. Charles, fearing the Muslims might turn and charge once again, did not pursue the withdrawing army. Without a cavalry force, the Frankish infantry would also have had little success in catching up with the retreating horsemen. No reliable casualty figures exist.

The survivors of Abd-er-Rahman's army retreated through Poitiers and across the Pyrenees into Spain. Small Muslim raids into southern Gaul continued for the next several years, but no subsequent large-scale invasions took place. The high tide of Islam rested in Spain. Western Europe remained Christian.

Charles's victory at Tours had immediate as well as long-term impact. For his stout defenses against the charging Muslims, he gained the title of Martel or "the Hammer," and the Franks remained united under his leadership. Charles rewarded the veterans of his army with land grants, much of which he confiscated from the Catholic Church. This briefly earned him the Pope's displeasure, but the church leaders, aware of the good that Charles had done for Christianity, quickly forgave him.

Upon Charles's death in 741, his sons claimed what became the Frankish throne. His grandson Charles, by further uniting the kingdom and increasing its military and political power into what became France, earned the title of "the Great" or "Charlemagne," and eventually became the emperor of the restored Holy Roman Empire.

The victory at Tours not only led to the success of Charles, his heirs, and the Frankish Kingdom, but also it stopped the spread of Islam into Western Europe and occupation by the Muslims. This last point is somewhat debatable, however, as several internal Islam factions already had been weakening Abd-er-Rahman's army and the overall Muslim influence. Whether or not the Muslims would have remained in Gaul if victorious, or merely looted it and gone back to Spain, is unknown. It is also possible that if the Muslims had been successful at Tours and remained to spread their religion in the region, the remainder of Europe, previously in opposition to the Gauls, might have united against the invaders.

Whatever might have occurred, it is certain that the Gauls under Charles defeated a much larger army of Muslims led by Abd-el Rahman near Tours in 732. At the end of the battle, the defeated Muslims retreated to Spain without their leader and never again mounted a substantial invasion. That certainly earns the Battle of Tours a ranking as one of the most influential battles in history.

25

INDUS RIVER

Mongol Conquest of Central Asia, 1221

Genghis Khan completed his conquest of Asia and amassed the largest land empire in history at the Battle of Indus River in 1221. After the victory, the Mongol Empire reached from the Arctic Ocean to the Persian Gulf, and Khan joined the ranks of the most influential military leaders of all time.

Until the mid-twelfth century, the vast region north of China had been ruled by a multitude of clans and tribes who were in a near-constant state of warfare for control of territory and power. The Mongols were among the strongest tribes for a long period, but a neighboring clan and their Chinese allies defeated them in 1161. The Mongol leader had a son whom a rival clan kidnapped at age nine when they killed his father. In his teens, the boy escaped, rejoined his Mongol tribe, and quickly earned the reputation of a fierce warrior.

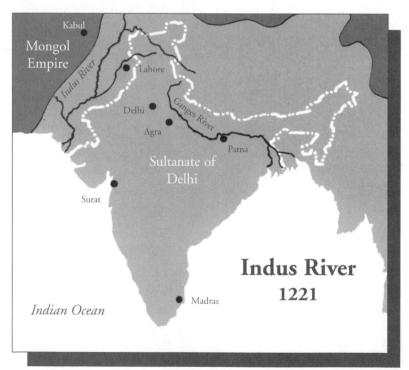

By the time he reached his twenties, the young warrior had earned the position of leadership of his clan. He attacked and defeated neighboring tribes and assimilated them into his own group. By the age of twenty-five, the young leader had systematically defeated all of the tribes in Mongolia and united them into a single federation. At about this time, he also assumed the title Genghis Khan—variously translated as "universal lord," "rightful lord," or "precious lord."

Khan required that each of the subordinate tribes in his federation maintain a standing force prepared to defend their territory or to mass with other armies to assume the offensive. Although often described as a "horde of barbarians," the Mongol army achieved its victories through Khan's brilliant organization, superior tactics, and superb discipline. Khan organized his army using a system of ten—ten men to a squad, ten squads to a company, ten companies to a regiment, and so on, up to "tuméns" of ten thousand warriors. Khan's sons and other trusted family members assumed the senior leadership positions and enforced rigid training and disciplinary standards.

All members of the Mongol army were mounted on horseback, half of them heavy cavalry warriors armed with lances and swords and protected by leather helmets and breastplates, the other half light cavalry archers armed with bows and arrows. Each soldier led several horses that carried additional arrows as well as sufficient supplies for sustained operations.

Khan employed scouts and spies to penetrate enemy lines and glean up-to-date intelligence. When the reconnaissance detected a weakness, Khan massed his force of as many as a hundred thousand warriors and attacked with his heavy cavalry leading.

Khan had stabilized Mongolia, so he turned his army to external conquests in 1211. By the end of that year, he had overrun Northern China, and four years later he completed his occupation of the country with the capture of Beijing. In 1218, he added the Korean Peninsula to his Empire and then turned westward to capture the Central Asian region that today includes Iran, Iraq, and Turkestan. Other parts of his army attacked north out of Mongolia into Russia to expand the Empire's northern border all the way to the Arctic Ocean.

Only one army now stood between the Mongols and control of all Central Asia, but that force was a formidable one. Much of Central Asia had fallen to the Mongols with their victory over Shah Muhammad in a series of battles in 1220, but the Muslim leader's son Jalal al-Din escaped and formed an army of 30,000 in present-day Afghanistan. In the autumn of 1221, Khan personally led 40,000 Mongol warriors through the Bamian Pass in the Hindu Kush Range in pursuit of the Muslim army.

Jalal al-Din withdrew toward India but decided to make his stand when he reached the Indus River. The Muslims formed their defense with the river to their backs and with their right flank protected by a bend in the waterway. A mountain ridge anchored their left flank. Jalal al-Din did not wait for the Mongols to approach his defenses; he attacked with his cavalry on the right wing against Khan's left flank. When the surprised Mongols dropped back, Jalal al-Din assaulted the Mongol center with his own center, which he reinforced from his left flank.

The Muslim leader assumed that the mountain range would protect his exposed flank, but he was wrong. Prior to the opening of the battle, Khan dispatched 10,000 men under one of his best generals to scale the high ground. Just as the Muslims gained the advantage, the Mongols came down from the ridgeline and attacked the exposed flank. Khan personally led a counterattack against the opposite flank at the same time.

The double envelopment separated the Muslim army into parts that the Mongols then methodically butchered. Many Muslims attempted to swim the Indus to safety. A few, including Jalal al-Din, made it to the far bank, but most drowned in the treacherous waters. By the end of the day, the last opposition to Mongol occupation of Central Asia were dead on the battlefield or in the waters of the Indus River.

Khan returned home to govern his Empire and conduct a few additional offensives to further expand his borders. By 1226, the Mongols ruled from Poland in the west to Korea in the east and from Vietnam in the south to Russia's Arctic coast in the north—the largest empire in history. Khan died a year later, but his sons and their sons ruled the Empire for the next 150 years before it began to fall to outside forces. China and Russia eventually took over much of the Empire, but the remainder of Mongolia still exists today because of Genghis Khan and his "horde of barbarians."

The Battle of the Indus River is the most important Mongol victory because it assured their control of Central Asia. While it alone did not establish the Mongol Empire, the Battle of Indus River represents all the fights that earned Khan a place among history's most influential military leaders and established his Empire as the largest ever.

26

ALESIA

Gallic Wars, 52 B.C.

Julius Caesar's victory over the Gauls at Alesia in 52 B.C. established Roman dominance over Europe that would continue for the next five hundred years. It also established Caesar as the most influential Roman leader and led to the end of the Republic and the formation of the Empire.

Julius Caesar spent the first half of his life in Rome as a successful politician. In his early forties, he sensed the decline of the Roman Senate's power and sought alliances to increase his personal influence. In 60 B.C., Caesar joined Gnaeus Pompey and Marcis Crassus in the First Triumvirate, with each taking charge of individual parts of the government and portions of the empire.

Within Caesar's area were Cisalpine Gaul (now northern Italy) and Narbonese Gaul (now the southern French coast). Along with his governing responsibilities, Caesar inherited four Roman legions composed of about 20,000 well-armed, well-trained soldiers. Caesar immediately began to use his legions to increase his territory and power by expanding his borders into northern France, or Gaul as it was known at the time.

The Celtic tribesmen who inhabited Gaul vastly outnumbered the Roman legions, but Caesar was aware that the Celts spent about as much time fighting each other as opposing external enemies. Caesar, with no prior military experience, kept his tactics simple. Instead of innovations, he relied on the fighting proficiency of his legions and his personal leadership to motivate them.

Caesar's initial forays into Gaul were successful. He also invaded and pacified the British Isles and modern Belgium during his first five years of command. In 53 B.C., the first major threat to Caesar's expansion arose when the Celts in Gaul rebelled against Roman occupation. The previously fragmented Celtic tribes had been united under the leadership of Vercingetorix, who had attacked and massacred the Roman garrison at Cenebum.

When he learned of the defeat, Caesar, who feared the loss of all Roman territory northwest of the Alps, went to Provence and personally assumed command of his legions that now numbered more than 50,000 men. He met and defeated a Gaul force at Cenabum on the Loire River and then pursued Vercingetorix and his army northward.

Caesar gained several victories in the early months of 52 B.C., but the harsh winter and the Gauls' scorched-earth policy left little food or resources for the advancing Romans. By late spring, both sides were tiring of the mobile warfare, so Vercingetorix occupied the fortress town of Alesia, north of Dijon, evacuated the city's civilian population, and moved provisions, including livestock, inside the walls. To gain additional time to build his supplies and fortifications, Vercingetorix sent his cavalry to attack the Romans. The Roman legions formed their traditional fighting hollow square and easily fought off the Gauls, but the delay allowed Vercingetorix to reinforce his defenses.

Alesia provided an excellent defensive position for the Gauls. It stood on a flat hilltop that dropped off in steep cliffs on all sides. City walls were an extension of the mountainside. The Oze and Ozerain Rivers, which ran east to west at the base of the hill, provided further protection. Vercingetorix added trenches along the approaches to the city, which now protected his army of 90,000.

Caesar approached the fortification, but he did not attack; rather he lay siege and began digging a ten-mile-long trench around the town. When Caesar realized that Vercingetorix had dispatched messengers throughout Gaul to assemble a relief force, he ordered his army to dig a second, fifteen-mile trench around the first. Caesar and his legions now stood between two trench lines, one oriented to besiege Alesia, the other to defend against a relief force.

In early October, an army of more than 100,000 Gauls approached Caesar's outer trenches from the west. The veteran Roman legions beat back the mostly inexperienced farmers and peasants. Vercingetorix tried to break out of Alesia but the Romans turned back that assault as well. A third attack then resumed from outside the Roman trenches. The Gauls concentrated at a weak spot in the defenses and almost broke through. Just when it seemed they would be successful, Caesar, wearing a bright red cloak so all would recognize him, hurried to the front, rallied his troops, and beat back the attackers.

The Gauls could not mount another assault, and their supplies were nearly depleted within the walls of Alesia. Vercingetorix surrendered. No record of the casualties from the fight exist, but Caesar recorded later in his *Commentaries of the Gallic Wars* that each of his soldiers was awarded a captured Gaul as a slave.

Caesar also noted in his third-person account in *Commentaries* the style of leadership that secured his victory at Alesia and other battlefields. According to Caesar, "The situation was critical and as no reserves were available, Caesar seized a shield from a soldier in the rear and made his way to the front line. He addressed each centurion by name and shouted encouragement to the rest of the troops, ordering them to push forward and open their ranks so they could use their swords more easily. His coming gave them fresh heart and hope. Each man wanted to do his best under the eyes of his commander despite the peril."

Following the battle, the Romans placed Vercingetorix in chains and brought him to Rome where, after displaying him at victory parades and imprisoning him for years, they executed him. All of Gaul now belonged to Rome and would for the next five hundred years, and the Roman occupation influenced the language as well as the Gaul's culture and civilization.

Not everyone was happy with Caesar's victories and assumed power. The Roman Senate ordered him home to become a private citizen in 49 B.C. Caesar returned to Rome at the head of his Legions and defeated all opposition to his leadership, making way for the end of the Republic and the establishment of the Empire. In 45 B.C., Rome declared Caesar dictator for life and consul for the next decade. A year later, he fell to the knives of assassins.

The influence of Caesar, which began with his victory at Alesia, did not end with his death on the Ides of March, 44 B.C. The Roman Empire became the largest of its age and was the most influential power for more than five centuries. Roman culture and civilization continue to exert influence even today.

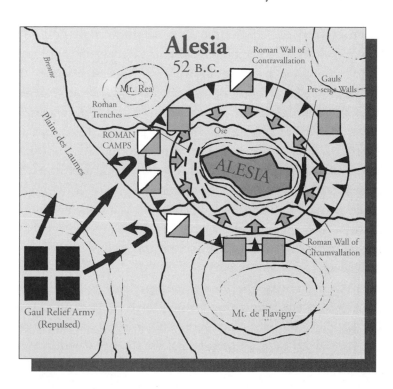

27

SEDAN

Franco-Prussian War, 1870

The Prussian victory over the French at Sedan in 1870 led to the unification of the German states into one country and set the stage for two world wars in the following century. The resulting imbalance of power changed previous European alliances and inspired French colonization throughout the world. Sedan also refined aspects of modern warfare, such as the General Staff concept, the use of railways to move men and supplies, and the telegraph for communications.

From the time of their defeat by the French in the first decade of the nineteenth century, the Prussians had dedicated their resources to rebuilding their army to the glory days of Frederick the Great. By mid-century, Chancellor Otto von Bismarck and General Helmuth von Moltke had developed an army strong enough to easily defeat former ally Austria in a dispute over neighboring provinces. While the victory verified the military strength of Prussia, it also further divided the German states.

Bismarck and Moltke realized that the most expeditious method of unifying the country was to find a common enemy. The Prussian leaders did not have to look far. Just across the border were their traditional French enemies, ruled by Emperor Napoleon III, nephew of the great Bonaparte. Like his uncle, Napoleon III also needed a war, in his case to stabilize his position as his country's leader.

The French declared war on the Prussians on July 19, 1870, ostensibly due to disagreements regarding succession to the Spanish throne. Unfortunately for the French, their military was totally unprepared for conflict, while the Prussians had been honing their battle techniques and securing equipment for decades. The French mobilization was marked by inefficiency and chaos. Many reserve soldiers reported with no uniforms or weapons, and leaders were often separated from their units. Across the lines, the Prussians, using the telegraph and railroads, assembled their army quickly and efficiently.

Despite their shortcomings, the French launched the war's first offensive from their assembly area at Metz against the Prussian town of Saarbrücken on August 2. Napoleon III, at the front and in command, inspired his men by declaring, "Whatever road we take beyond our frontiers, we shall find glorious traces of our fathers. We will prove ourselves worthy of them."

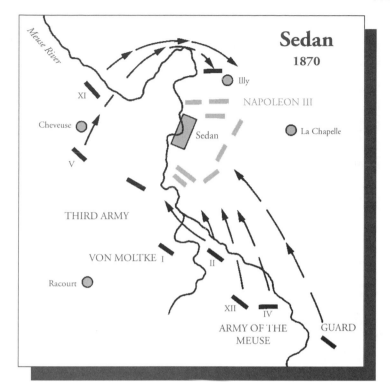

Motivated by the words of their emperor, and more importantly because Saarbrücken was lightly defended, the French won the war's first battle. However, the Prussians immediately counterattacked, sending the French reeling back across the border. After a few ineffective efforts to stop the advancing Prussians, Napoleon withdrew his 170,000-man army to Metz. The Emperor placed Marshal François Bazaine in command and moved west about a hundred miles to Châlons. From there he ordered an army of 130,000 men commanded by General Maurice McMahon to reinforce Metz.

Meanwhile, Moltke was not sitting idly by. He dispatched one army to besiege Metz and directed two other forces toward Châlons. Half the forces initially sent to Metz soon joined the advance toward Napoleon's troops. When the three columns neared Châlons, the French faced the options of proceeding toward Metz and hitting the advancing Prussians head on or withdrawing westward to protect the approach to Paris. Napoleon chose to do neither. Instead, he swung his army northward and occupied the small border fortress of Sedan.

Moltke's three columns followed, quickly surrounding the city and pounding the French with their superior artillery. On September 1, the French attempted a breakout, but the Prussians, despite suffering 9,000 killed and wounded, turned back the attack. With 17,000 casualties of his own, Napoleon raised a white flag late in the afternoon and surrendered more than 100,000 men and 400 cannons.

France had suffered its worst defeat since Waterloo. Although the Battle of Sedan did not conclude the war, it ended the French desire to fight. Metz surrendered on October 27, and Paris fell on January 19. After spending a few months under arrest in Prussia, Napoleon went into exile in England. France yielded the border provinces of Alsace and Lorraine and paid an indemnity of five billion francs—equivalent to about three billion dollars at the time.

In addition to gaining land and money, the Prussians achieved their objective of a unified Germany. Moltke continued to lead the army, while Bismarck turned his attention to building Germany's industrial base. Soon Germany stood as the most powerful country on the continent.

The impact of the Battle of Sedan reached far beyond the unification of Germany. France, hostile to their conquerors, began making allegiances with previous enemies, such as England and Russia. Then, unable to expand its borders in Europe, France sought worldwide colonization. In 1883, the French army expanded its holding in Southeast Asia to include all of today's Vietnam. Additional French colonies flourished in Africa and the Pacific.

Also, other countries appreciated the Prussian use of railroads and the telegraph and began integrating them into their war planning. Armies around the world also copied the Prussian General Staff model.

While Sedan produced more than three decades of peace for the now strong and united Germany, the other European countries both resented and feared their power. Inevitably, the two sides would again clash on the battlefield—the effects of which would escalate into World War I. Germany, still led by many Prussian officers, had excellent equipment and organization, but its forces could not stand against the French, English, Russian, and American allies. Alongside the French also stood legions from their colonies established after the defeat at Sedan. Among these were more than 100,000 Vietnamese soldiers fighting Germany under the French tri-color.

It is interesting to consider the consequences of a French rather than a German victory at Sedan. Had France won the Franco-Prussian War, perhaps the German states would have not united, or at least not as soon. Two world wars might never have happened. Vietnam might have remained free of the French, and the long American-Vietnamese war might have never taken place.

Of course, the Prussians, a name that has become synonymous with the military mind itself, were not denied at Sedan. Although it did not last long, the Prussians and, later, the Germans, believed they deserved the glory that began with their victory at Sedan.

28

MARATHON

Persian-Greek Wars, 490 B.C.

The battle on the plains of Marathon in 490 B.C. ended a major Persian invasion of Europe and established the Greeks as a dominant military force. It also provided the unification that would eventually lead to the emergence of Greece as the propagator of Western civilization.

In 556 B.C., Cyrus succeeded his father as the ruler of the Persian district of Anshan, which was under the control of the Medians. Shortly thereafter, Cyrus, soon to be known as "the Great," led a three-year revolt in which he defeated the Medians and incorporated them into his army so he could take even more territory. By the time of his death in battle twenty-five years later, Cyrus had expanded his Persian Empire from the eastern Indus River border with India to the Aral, Caspian, Black, and Mediterranean Seas.

Included in the Empire was the west coast of Asia Minor, known as Ionia, which was inhibited by Greek colonists. Some of these colonists rebelled briefly in 512 B.C. and then more substantially in 499 B.C. In the latter rebellion, the Ionian Greeks requested assistance from the city-states in Greece. Athens responded with a fleet of twenty warships, and the city of Eritrea—on the island of Euboea—provided five more. Despite the assistance from the Greek city-states, the Ionian rebellion was quickly defeated, and Darius, the Persian leader, swore vengeance against the Greek cities for their assistance in the rebellion.

In 492 B.C., Darius conquered the kingdoms of Thrace and Macedonia on the northern Greek border. Before he could attack south, however, a storm damaged his fleet. Two years later (some accounts say only one year), the Persians returned and quickly captured and burned Eritrea. The Persian force of about 20,000 infantry and 1,000 cavalry then landed on the Greek mainland at the Plain of Marathon, about twenty-six miles northeast of Athens. The Persians hoped to intercept the Greeks reinforcing Eritrea while also waiting for the remainder of their army and navy to join them.

Athens responded with an army of 10,000 supported by 1,000 thousand soldiers from the city of Plataea. The Athenian commander dispatched a runner to Sparta requesting reinforcements. The young soldier, Pheilippides (or Pheidippides), reportedly ran the 150 miles in two days, only to be told that the Spartans could not join the fight, in accordance with their religious beliefs, until after the next full moon. Pheilippides took only two more days to return to Marathon with the message.

For nine days, the Greeks and Persians stood in long lines across the two-mile-wide plain, neither side willing to attack and lose the advantage of the defense. The Greeks were waiting for the Spartans while the Persians were waiting for the remainder of their army from Eritrea.

On a morning in mid-September, the Greek commander noticed that the Persian cavalry was no longer on the plain. Some accounts speculate that the horsemen were on reconnaissance toward Athens, while others suggest that they may have gone for fresh water. Whatever the reason, the Persian cavalry was absent, and the Greek infantry took advantage.

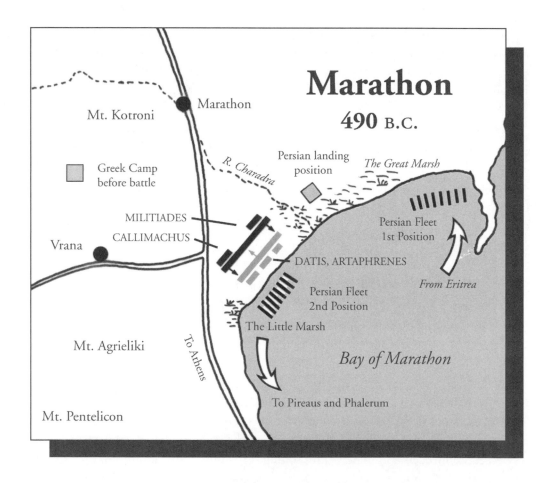

Greek commander Miltiades ordered his men forward, first at a walk and then at a trot when they came within range of the Persian archers. The Greeks, armed with swords, spears, and shields, first struck the Persian flanks, moving them backward until the attackers began to envelop the center. Miltiades ordered more men against the Persian flanks, which forced the center into a hasty withdrawal toward the beach. The Greeks killed many of the retreating Persians and even captured seven of the Persian ships as they attempted to rescue their retreating army.

By the end of the day, more than 6,000 Persian bodies littered the Marathon plain. Greek losses totaled only 192 men. Two small Greek cities had defeated the great Persian Empire. When the Spartans finally arrived, shortly after the battle concluded, they could only admire the work of their fellow Greeks.

However, there was little time for celebration. Miltiades knew the surviving Persians and their reinforcements would set sail for undefended Athens. The Athenians immediately began a forced march for their home city. They arrived only hours before the Persians, who, when they found the same army waiting that had soundly defeated them at Marathon, turned their ships toward Persia.

Marathon, through the writings of Greek historian Herodotus and others, quickly became celebrated as history's first great decisive battle. Stories about the fight survive as fact and influence even today's classical scholars and events. For example, the story of the soldier's run of more than twenty-six miles to Athens to report the victory lives on in the Olympic race known as the marathon.

Marathon became a symbol for great feats. It was decisive at the time; however, it was not as influential as the battle at Salamis ten years later (14) that ended Persian influence in Greece for good. Still, Marathon did provide a significant turning point in stopping the invasion of the west from the east. It was the first great victory by Europe over Asia, and from the seeds sown on the plain of Marathon grew the future of Greek and Western civilizations.

29

QUEBEC

French and Indian War, 1759

The Battle of Quebec gave Britain claim to most of North America and reduced French holdings to a few islands in the Caribbean. It also influenced the independence movement in the American colonies, which would eventually lead to the Revolutionary War and the establishment of the United States.

During the first several hundred years of European settlement in North America, the English, French, and Spanish had established themselves as the primary colonizers. Initially, the colonies had grown slowly and there had been more than enough land for all. By the middle of the eighteenth century, however, certain claims for territories, particularly in the Ohio River Valley, were overlapping. On May 28, 1754, the dispute resulted in a brief skirmish between French and English colonists at Great Meadows, where the Ohio and Allegheny Rivers converge. Some accounts credit a twenty-one-year-old Virginian with firing the first shot. Whether this claim is true or not, the skirmish is where young George Washington gained his first combat experience.

Minor disputes grew into full military operations the following year when English General Edward Braddock failed in a general offensive against the French and their Native American allies. By 1756, hostilities between England and France spilled over into Europe in what became known as the Seven Years' War. In North America, the conflict expanded into the French and Indian War.

Combat between the French and English in North America remained fairly low-key until William Pitt assumed power in London. In 1759, Pitt dispatched additional troops to North America and sent British ships to guard the coastline and prevent French reinforcements. Pitt planned a four-pronged attack into Canada via Lake Erie, Lake Ontario, Lake Chaplain, and the St. Lawrence River. The ultimate goal of the offensive was the capture of Quebec—the only walled city in North America—which lay at the northeast end of a long, narrow point bordered on three sides by cliffs as high as 350 feet. At the southwest approach were the Plains of Abraham, named for a former owner of the property.

General James Wolfe, a thirty-two-year-old veteran of the army of the Duke of Marlborough, led the attack three hundred miles up the St. Lawrence to Quebec. Wolfe's army numbered about 9,000, while the French garrison of Quebec, commanded by

General Marquis Louis de Montcalm, totaled about 14,000. Many of the French troops, however, were local militiamen and lacked the training and discipline of Wolfe's regulars. Wolfe also had the advantage of superior seamen manning the boats that transported him up the river. Among the captains was James Cook, who would later earn the reputation as one of the great world explorers.

Wolfe arrived near Quebec on June 27, 1759, and initially landed a force commanded by General George Townshend on the river's north bank below the city. Montcalm had anticipated that this was the most likely avenue of assault and had reinforced the area's defenses. After several unsuccessful attacks and the loss of about 500 men, Townshend withdrew on September 3.

For the next several days, Wolfe continued probing attacks as he shelled the city with his ships. During one of his reconnaissance tours around the city, he noticed a narrow trail leading from the river to the Plains of Abraham. During the night of September 12–13, Wolfe landed 4,500 troops at the base of the cliff below the Plains. They quietly made their way up the trail, fooling the few sentries at the top by responding to their challenges in French.

By daybreak, Wolfe had his army assembled on the Plains facing Quebec. Montcalm, not waiting for additional troops to arrive, foolishly marched out of the city with about 4,500 soldiers. The two equal-sized forces met on the Plains in the formal military style typical of European warfare of the time.

The French line advanced to within forty yards of the British, who fired a withering volley of musket balls, which stopped and then broke the attacking formation. In less than fifteen minutes, 1,400 French soldiers fell, including the fatally wounded Montcalm. British casualties totaled about half that of the French, but their commander had also fallen. Wolfe lived only long enough to be informed of the victory by his subordinates.

The remaining French retreated to within the walls of Quebec, but the militias soon deserted. On September 18, the city surrendered. The French and Indian War did not officially end until the Treaty of Paris in 1763, but only two minor fights followed the Battle of Quebec. Wolfe wrote in his final orders before the assault on the city, "A vigorous blow struck at this juncture may determine the fate of Canada." He was absolutely correct.

Provisions of the Treaty of Paris gave England all of the land east of the Mississippi River and north of the Great Lakes claimed by the French. France ceded their territory west of the Mississippi to Spain. The Union Jack now flew over all of Canada, primarily as the result of a single battle fought by a total of fewer than ten thousand men. French holdings and influence in North America dwindled to a few island colonies in the Caribbean.

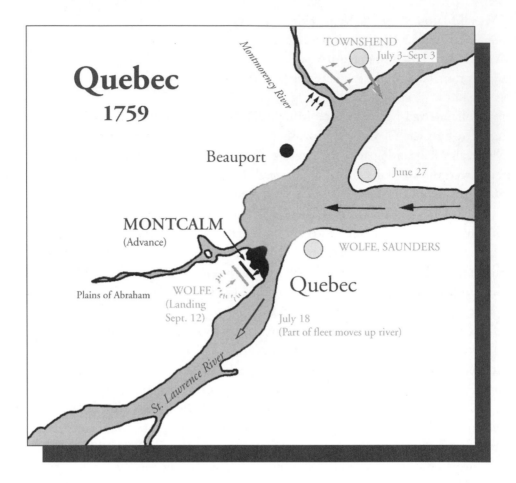

The victory at Quebec influenced more than just the fate of Canada. Many American colonists—including George Washington, who helped win the war for the British—began to think that not only did they want the French out of America, but the British as well. These seeds of independence grew when England began levying heavy taxes on the colonists to pay for the expenses incurred during the war.

Another long-term effect of the battle was the death of General Wolfe. During the American Revolution, the British never were able to field a commander capable of ending the rebellion. Many have speculated that had Wolfe lived to lead the British, the thirteen colonies might have remained as such. Of course this is mere conjecture. Although Wolfe was a young man at Quebec, he was already in the advanced stages of tuberculosis, and it is doubtful he would have survived the disease to fight the rebellious Americans.

30

MILVIAN BRIDGE

Roman Empire Civil Wars, 312

The victory by Constantine at the Battle of Milvian Bridge unified the strife-torn Roman Empire and reorganized its western region into a power that would last a thousand years. Constantine's religious revelations prior to the battle also opened the way for the acceptance of Christianity as the principal religion of the Empire and led to its dominance in Europe and eventually throughout the Western Hemisphere.

By the third century, the Roman Empire reached from Britain to Persia and from the North Sea to the Nile River. While vast territory and resources made the Empire powerful, they also made it vulnerable. Control of the Empire changed regularly, one military leader or another constantly seizing the government. Between the years 235 and 284, a total of twenty-six men claimed the position of Emperor.

Finally in 284, Diocletian, a soldier from the eastern Adriatic coast, gained control and made reforms that stabilized the government. Diocletian divided the Empire into West and East to better manage its size. A co-emperor with the title of "augustus" ruled each region. A second, or deputy, leader called "caesar" assisted the augustus and assumed the highest position upon the co-emperor's death or retirement.

Diocletian's organization and leadership brought a peace that lasted until he and his co-emperor retired in 305. His system of succession should have maintained the peace, but conflicts arose over who would become the new ceasars when their predecessors assumed the positions of augustus. Civil war broke out across the Empire when several leaders claimed power. In 308, Diocletian re-entered public life and called a conference of the competing factions that briefly stabilized the government. Two years later, civil war began again and lasted until 311. This time the conflict concluded with the Empire divided into four regions, each ruled by an augustus—Constantine in Gaul, Maxentius in Italy, Licinius in the Balkans, and Maximinus in the East.

Soon after the division, Maxentius feared that Constantine would attempt to take over all of the Western Empire and dispose him of his position. Maxentius planned to invade Gaul, but before he could strike, Constantine learned of his plans and mounted his own offensive.

In the early spring of 312, Constantine led his army of about 45,000 into north-ern Italy. Maxentius sent a series of armies to stop the invaders, but Constantine defeated each as he advanced closer to Rome. Maxentius took command of his last 75,000 troops and marched north, crossed the Milvian Bridge over the Tiber River, and took up defensive positions near the village of Saxa Rubra.

When Constantine's army approached Maxentius's position in October 312, both sides arranged their armies in the standard formation, with infantry in the center and cavalry on the flanks. Constantine's army contained men of several different nationalities, some pagans, and others, including Constantine, sun worshipers. A few Christians also filled the ranks.

Accounts vary, but all agree that Constantine experienced something the night before the battle—a sign or a dream or a voice—that told him to place his faith in Christ. The most accepted version is that he saw a flaming cross in the sky on which was written *in hoc signo vinces* ("by this sign thou shall conquer"). Constantine had his soldiers mark their shields with a cross and vowed to covert to Christianity if victorious in the pending battle.

The morning of October 28 (some accounts say a day earlier), Constantine advanced his cavalry against the enemy's horsemen. Maxentius's cavalry quickly gave way and retreated, leaving his infantry vulnerable. They, too, joined the retreat southward to Rome. The narrow Milvian Bridge over the Tiber became so congested that many of the retreating soldiers, including Maxentius, tried to swim the river. Maxentius, weighted down by his armor, sank and drowned.

Constantine now ruled all of the Western Roman Empire. Prior to his invasion of Italy, Constantine had made a non-aggression pact with Licinius in the Balkans, and after his victory he fulfilled his promise of offering his sister in marriage to his ally. In February 313, Constantine and Licinius met in Milan and issued an edict that provided the first formal policy of religious toleration in the empire. According to the Edict of Milan, "The Christians and all other men should be allowed full freedom to subscribe to whatever form of worship they desire."

Constantine and Licinius remained allied over the next decade. Constantine campaigned against hostile Germanic tribes, while Licinius defeated Maximinus for control of the Eastern Empire. Licinius, however, did not join Constantine in his conversion and, in fact, continued to persecute Christians after the Edict of Milan. The two leaders finally clashed in 323, with Constantine emerging victorious and in command of the entire Empire.

Less that a decade later, Constantine recognized that he could not alone control the vast Empire and once again divided it. He maintained leadership of the Western Roman Empire and relocated his capitol to the ancient Greek town of Byzantium, which he renamed Constantinople. Rome remained the center of the Eastern Roman

Empire as well as that of the Christian religion. While Rome maintained its religious influence, the political and military power of the Eastern Roman Empire quickly began to erode, until it totally collapsed less than a century and a half later. Meanwhile the Western Roman Empire, later renamed the Byzantine Empire, flourished for more than a thousand years until it fell to the Muslims in the Battle of Constantinople in 1453 (41).

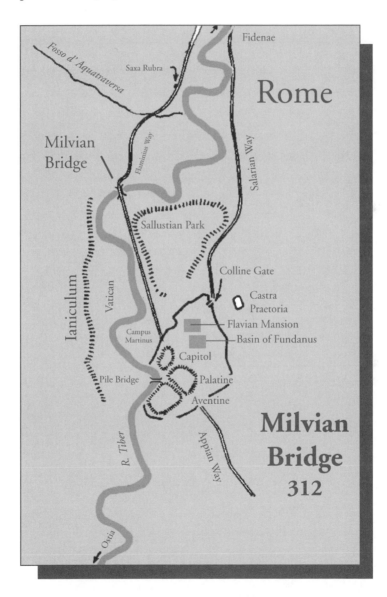

The Battle of Milvian Bridge set the stage for the stabilization and dominance of the Western Roman Empire while opening the way for the downfall of the Eastern Roman Empire. More importantly, it assured the acceptance and advancement of Christianity. Once persecuted, Christians could now worship freely and bring their message of forgiveness and afterlife to the pagan majority. Over the years, Christianity became the predominate religion of Europe and eventually spread through the Western Hemisphere with the explorations and colonization.

While few Christian churches today celebrate or even acknowledge the Battle of Milvian Bridge, it was more influential in the spread of their beliefs than any other military event. Without the vision and victory of Constantine, the Christian religion might not have reached its level of current influence.

31

MANZIKERT

Byzantine-Turkish Wars, 1071

The victory of the Seljuq Turks over the Byzantines at Manzikert brought most of Asia Minor under Muslim control. It marked the decline of the Byzantine Empire and opened the way for a century of religious crusades in which huge armies fought not for empires or riches but for control of holy sites.

From their capital in Constantinople, the Byzantines had long provided a Christian buffer between the Muslims and Europe. The Muslim failure to capture Constantinople in 718 and their loss to the Franks at Tours in 732 (24) had left Europe to Christianity, while Byzantine rule of Asia Minor and much of the Mediterranean coastline had ensured Christian access to sites in the Holy Land.

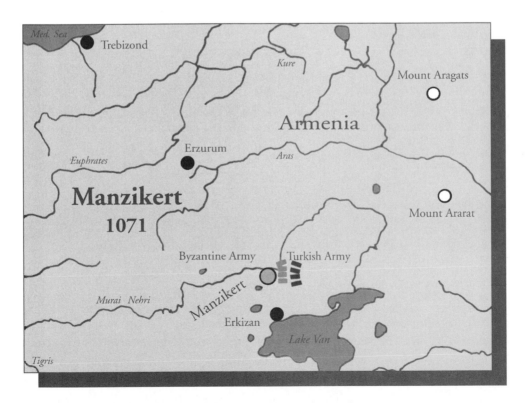

The Byzantines maintained this control until the mid-eleventh century when they had begun to weaken as the Muslims united and became stronger. Byzantium, like many empires both before and after it, had become comfortable in its power and acquired more and more outsiders and mercenaries to man its army. Even the emperor's personal bodyguard was a collection of hired English and Viking soldiers. Meanwhile, one of the many nomadic armies to come out of Central Asia was the Seljuq Turks, hordes of horsemen who raided Persia. These Seljuq Turks differed from other nomadic horsemen, however, in that when they conquered Persia, they adopted the Muslim religion and began to unite all the people into a single force from headquarters in Baghdad.

In 1065, Alp Arslan assumed the leadership of the Seljuq Turks and their Muslim allies. He increased his territory and added captured forces to his army under the common banner of Islam. As Alp Arslan's power grew, he looked west to take from Byzantium the rich area that makes up much of current Turkey.

Meanwhile, the Byzantine leader died in 1068, and the leadership passed to Romanus IV Diogenes. Romanus, although young, was an experienced general. Unfortunately for him and his empire, he inherited an army marked with internal strife and flagging morale. One of its strongest units was composed of men recruited from the same region that would soon be contested.

Both Romanus and Alp Arslan conducted operations in Asia Minor for several years with varying degrees of success. In 1071, Alp Arslan captured the city of Manzikert in eastern Asia Minor, left a small occupation force behind, and returned to Syria. When Romanus found out about the fall of Manzikert, he marched to recapture the city. After retaking Manzikert, Romanus remained nearby with about half of his army while dispatching the other half to raid farther eastward in the vicinity of Lake Van.

Unbeknownst to the Byzantine leader, Alp Arslan had learned of the recapture of Manzikert and had quickly moved from Syria to meet the Byzantines. Surprised by the approach of the Muslim army, Romanus abandoned Manzikert and attempted to join the other half of his army. In a narrow valley just west of the town, the Byzantines and Turks met with about 40,000 men each.

Alp Arslan attempted to negotiate a peace agreement, but Romanus demanded an immediate surrender of the Muslim army. When Alp Arslan refused, Romanus attacked using the traditional Byzantine tactic that called for a forward advance with infantry and cavalry to break the enemy line and then push the remaining opponents against a terrain feature, such as a river or mountain, to finish them off. Initially, the tactic worked for Romanus. The Byzantines forced the Turks backward, but the open plain did nothing to hinder their retreat, and in the midst of the battle, Byzantine soldiers recruited from the Manzikert region deserted Romanus to join the Turks.

At the approach of darkness, Romanus halted his advance and withdrew toward his initial defenses. When he saw this, Alp Arslan turned his army to attack. More Byzantines fled, leaving behind only Romanus and his most loyal followers, who survived to become prisoners. Eventually ransomed, Romanus returned home only to be murdered by members of his own court.

The Byzantine Empire did not end with Manzikert, but the battle greatly eroded its power and influence, reducing it eventually to only the area around Constantinople and the region to its west. If this had been the battle's only impact, it would not rank as high or perhaps even make this list at all. Byzantium was well past its prime, and if it had not been defeated at Manzikert, it would have soon fallen elsewhere. But now, the Turks, not the Byzantines, ruled Asia Minor and much of the Middle East, including the Holy Land. Alp Arslan's son killed him a short time later, but the Turks continued their dominance of the region.

The real impact of the battle is what came afterward. With the remainder of the Byzantine Empire so weakened it could barely defend its own reduced borders, it could no longer guarantee Christians access to the holy sites in Jerusalem and surrounding towns. Knights in England, France, and other European countries soon formed armies to conduct Crusades against the "infidels" who controlled the Holy Land. During the next century, thousands would die to gain access to holy relics and sites. The real legacy of Manzikert was not glory, but rather bloodshed for the sake of religious beliefs.

32

SAN JUAN HILL

Spanish-American War, 1898

The Battle of San Juan Hill brought an end to Spain's influence in the Western Hemisphere and vaulted the United States to the status of a world and colonial power. More importantly, the battle and the war further narrowed the chasm between the American North and South as it helped put the bitterness of the Civil War behind them.

From the time the United States gained its independence, it had begun pushing its borders westward through settlements, purchases from foreign powers, and the spoils of war. By 1844, many Americans believed that their "Almighty God" had "manifestly destined" the United States to dominate all of North America. By the latter part of the nineteenth century, most Americans thought that this Manifest Destiny extended throughout the hemisphere.

Following its bloody civil war, the United States had put its energy into Reconstruction in the Southern states and Native American uprisings in the West. When the Indians were on reservations, the U.S. began enhancing its navy and looking beyond its borders for colonies and world influence. Businessmen and journalists in particular saw the financial benefits of Manifest Destiny and lobbied for intervention in Cuba.

Cuban rebels had been fighting their Spanish colonizers for more than twenty years before U.S. businessmen became concerned over the security of their property and investments on the island. American journalists, aware that conflict sells papers, joined the businessmen in encouraging U.S. intervention in the rebellion. President William McKinley attempted diplomatic solutions to the problem, but he was forced to ask for a declaration of war on Spain when the USS *Maine* mysteriously blew up and sank in Havana harbor on February 15, 1898.

The American Asiatic Squadron, already in the Far East, quickly moved against the Spanish fleet in the Philippines and won the Battle of Manila Bay (46) on May 1, 1898. Invasion of Cuba by the U.S. Army took longer and faced many more obstacles.

While the navy had career professionals aboard modern ships, the army had fewer than 30,000 men, most of whom were spread across a string of western forts and equipped and trained to fight Indians. However, within days of the declaration of war, more than a million men volunteered for service. For the first time since before the Civil War, Americans from the North and South united against a common foe.

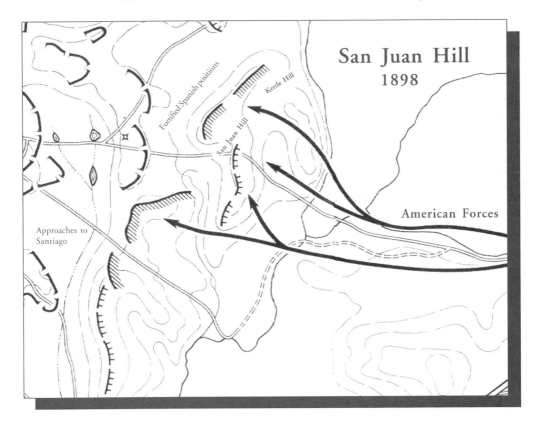

San Juan Hill
1898

Fortified Spanish positions

Kettle Hill

San Juan Hill

American Forces

Approaches to
Santiago

On June 14, the U.S. V Corps, composed of 17,000 soldiers, departed Tampa, Florida, for Cuba with Major General William R. Shafter in command. Shafter, weighing more than three hundred pounds, had more problems than just his weight. His army contained many poorly trained volunteer units, including the much-publicized First Volunteer Cavalry, the self-proclaimed "Rough Riders." Led by the able Colonel Leonard Wood, the Rough Riders had as their second-in-command Lieutenant Colonel Theodore Roosevelt, an officer with no military experience but with ambitions for adventure, glory, and future political campaigns. Among the most experienced and disciplined soldiers in Shafter's V Corps were the all-black Twenty-fourth and Twenty-fifth Infantry and the Ninth and Tenth Cavalry regiments.

This odd assortment of units was made even more unusual when McKinley recalled the gray-bearded former Confederate Joseph (Fighting Joe) Wheeler to active duty as a subordinate to Shafter. The old rebel's presence and stories about him in the newspapers—for example, Wheeler had the tendency in the heat of battle to call the Spaniards "Yankees"—helped heal former divisions among the whites. No one recorded what the four black regiments thought of serving under a major general who was a former Confederate officer.

The invasion force began landing at Daiquirí and Siboney on June 22 and moved toward the port city of Santiago. Spanish General Arsenio Linares deployed his army of 10,000 in Santiago and along the crests of San Juan and Kettle Hills outside the city. He had also sent 500 soldiers to defend the nearby village of El Caney to the northeast.

Hilly terrain, thick vegetation, and few roads limited the American attack to a frontal assault. Outdated rifles that still used black powder charges exposed shooters' positions and hindered the advance. On the other side, the Spanish had modern, bolt-action rifles, smokeless powder, and several new German-manufactured machine guns. Yet, although well-armed, the Spanish soldiers were poorly motivated and had little interest in risking their lives to defend one of the last vestiges of Spanish colonial power. Spain and its military were well past their prime.

The American attack began on the morning of July 1, with an assault against El Caney. Shafter thought this portion of the battle would be over quickly and that the victors could secure his right flank. In fact, the badly outnumbered but well-fortified Spanish held out through the entire day, still fighting even when the main attack went forward.

Behind a barrage of artillery, the Americans began a frontal assault up San Juan and Kettle Hills. Well-aimed Spanish rifle fire cut into the ranks, sending several of the volunteer units into wild retreat. The Rough Riders and the black cavalry regiments filled the void and carried the heights. More than 1,500 Americans were dead or wounded. Spanish casualties were about the same, but most had avoided capture by fleeing to Santiago.

The Americans dug in on the captured high ground and began planning an assault on Santiago, but no further ground attack was necessary. On the morning of July 3, the Spanish fleet, blockaded in Santiago harbor, attempted to break out into the open sea. Unlike its army, the American navy had modern weapons and ships with well-trained crews. In less than four hours, the entire Spanish fleet was sunk or captured. More than 500 Spanish sailors were dead or wounded, and another 1,800 were taken prisoner. American naval casualties totaled one dead and one wounded.

On July 17, the remaining Spanish army surrendered. Americans, already losing more soldiers to tropical diseases than they had to battle, redeployed home. A few months later, the United States further realized its Manifest Destiny when the Treaty of Paris awarded it Cuba, Puerto Rico, the Philippines, and other territories in the Caribbean and Pacific.

The Battle of San Juan Hill, along with Manila Bay, made the United States a significant power. While the battle had international impact, its most influential effect was within American borders. National pride and unity, absent since the Civil War, resurfaced as patriotism blossomed and isolationism became less prevalent.

The victories at San Juan Hill and Manila Bay also provided the experience needed to advance the might of the American military. The sea battles proved the capabilities of modern warships, while the land war demonstrated the need to modernize the army's weapons and training. The casualties to tropical diseases spurred research that defeated yellow fever and allowed the building of the Panama Canal, a facility that influenced all future commercial and military shipping. Junior leaders who "won their spurs" in Cuba, later modernized, trained, and led the American forces in World War I.

33

CRÉCY

Hundred Years' War, 1346

At the Battle of Crécy on August 26, 1346, the English established the longbow as the weapon that would dominate battlefields of the next century. Their victory over the French also established them as the most efficient professional army of the period and led to their occupation of the port of Calais, which provided them with military and trade access to France for the next hundred years.

In 1337, England and France began a series of battles that would continue for more than a century. The two competed for the wool trade in Flanders, and the English were extremely angry over the open support the French provided the Scottish rebellion. The disputes came to a head when King Charles IV died in 1328, leaving behind no direct heir to the French throne. King Edward III of England initially recognized Philip of Valois's ascension to the throne, but a decade later decided that his own claim, based on his mother's lineage, gave him the right to rule France.

On the surface, Edward's quest seemed ambitious. The French population of twenty million was five times that of England. France also had powerful feudal nobility who were both trained in and appreciative of warfare, and who manned their armies with a draft system that required all adult males to serve in the military. The English, on the other hand, had fewer men, but they recruited volunteer professionals who understood arms and military tactics.

For several years, small English forces raided France. In 1340, the English navy defeated the French at the Battle of Sluys, giving Edward control of the English Channel and the power to launch a full-scale invasion. On July 12, 1346, Edward landed at Normandy with an army of about 12,000 professional soldiers who were veterans of the Scottish wars. About 7,000 of these were archers armed with longbows with a range of 250–300 yards. Edward faced little resistance at Normandy, and his army pushed inland, pillaging the countryside. Looting, torture, rape, and murder not only kept his army happy but also demoralized the French in his path.

King Philip VI quickly massed his army and marched to intercept Edward. About 12,000 heavily armored knights and cavalrymen and 6,000 mercenary Genoese crossbow men composed the heart of the French army. Another 20,000 to 30,000 French draftee peasants, neither trained nor motivated, accompanied the force.

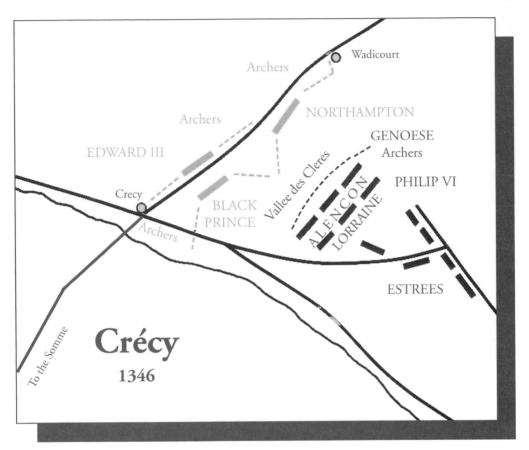

Wadicourt

Archers

Archers

NORTHAMPTON

GENOESE
Archers

EDWARD III

PHILIP VI

Crecy

Vallée des Cleres

BLACK
PRINCE

ALENCON
LORRAINE

Archers

ESTREES

To the Somme

Crécy
1346

The French attempted to pin the English against the flooded Somme River, but Edward forded the waterway and made his way to a hillside near the village of Crécy where he prepared his defenses. Edward deployed his army into three groups of infantry with archers on their flanks along a line about 2,000 yards long. He added obstacles of sharpened stakes and trenches to the front. In his rear Edward held back 700 men-at-arms and 2,000 archers as a reserve. Even in the midst of these lengthy preparations, the English still had time to gather supplies from the countryside and get some rest before the battle.

Philip approached the English defenses on the afternoon of August 26, 1346, but he decided to rest his force before attacking, though many of his knights, who commanded their own armies, did not want to delay the fight. Unwilling to wait, some of the French advanced. The crossbowmen from Genoa led the way, but they fired their first volley of arrows at too great of a distance to reach the English defenders.

Edward's longbowmen responded with volley after volley that struck many of the Genoese and several knights to their rear. More French knights, ignoring the range of the longbows, charged forward, only to be struck down by a hail of arrows. Succeeding charges of the French horsemen were slowed by the bodies of their comrades as well as the arrows that continued to rain from the sky. The best-trained English bowmen could fire up to a dozen arrows a minute while even the inexperienced bowmen could get off half that many in the same time.

The French made at least a dozen—and perhaps as many as fifteen—charges against the English line. A few broke through to engage the men-at-arms in direct combat, but they were quickly killed. The most successful French attack came against the English right flank commanded by Edward's sixteen-year-old son known as the Black Prince. When pressed by his subordinates to commit the reserve to support his son, Edward is reported to have said, "Let the boy win his spurs."

By late evening, the Black Prince and the English army had indeed won their spurs. More than 1,500 French knights were killed or captured, and the kings of Majorca and Bohemia lay dead on the field. Several thousand more soldiers of Philip's army, including most of his crossbow men, were also slain. Several high-ranking French nobles were taken prisoner. Philip, although he had been in the midst of the fighting, managed to escape. The English, who had sustained only about a hundred deaths, maintained their disciplined lines and did not pursue.

Edward then moved against the port of Calais. Although the siege continued for a year, the English eventually took the city with few casualties. The heavily fortified port provided the English with protected access to France for their armies and trade for the remainder of the war.

Other than the eventual capture of Calais, the Battle of Crécy had little effect on the remainder of the Hundred Years' War. Its greatest influence should have been changes in warfare tactics brought about by longbowmen. Unfortunately for the French, the fact that the innovative weapon could defeat mounted knights was a lesson they would have relearn again and again, including their disastrous attack at Agincourt (79) nearly three-quarters of a century later.

The Battle of Crécy certainly deserves its reputation as the birthplace of the English army as an international force, thanks to its discipline and the introduction of the longbow. While the longbow had already strongly influenced previous battlefields, at Crécy it proved that it was the weapon of the future and that warfare would have to adjust to technology.

34

TSUSHIMA STRAIT

Russo-Japanese War, 1905

The Japanese defeat of the Russian Baltic Fleet in the Tsushima Strait in 1905 brought an end to Russia's naval prowess and catapulted Japan into a role of military dominance in the Pacific and the world. The outcome of the battle exacerbated the discord in Russia that would eventually lead to the Communist Revolution. It also encouraged Japan in its expansionist policy that would nearly destroy the country during World War II.

Until the nineteenth century, Japan remained isolated. The Japanese rarely ventured from their home islands, and they turned away visitors to their shores. However, the advancement in sailing ships increased the demand for trade opportunities. Japan finally opened its borders in 1854 but recognized that it had to maintain a strong navy to defend itself. In the 1870s, Japan began sending its brightest naval cadets to England, the reigning sea power of the time, to study shipbuilding and sea warfare. At home, the Japanese also concentrated on developing their land forces.

In 1894, the Japanese went to war with China over Korea and the Liaodong Peninsula, with its strategic harbor at Port Arthur. The Japanese won easily, but diplomatic pressure from European nations forced the return of most of the captured territory to China. Japan did not appreciate external pressures on decisions made on "their territory" and became even more dismayed when Russia made arrangements shortly after the war to build a railway down the Liaodong Peninsula to occupy Port Arthur.

Japan tried to negotiate with Russia for access to much-needed coal and iron ore resources in Manchuria, but the Russians refused any kind of trade agreement. On February 8, 1904, the Japanese navy, under command of Admiral Heihachiro Togo, conducted a sneak attack against the Russian fleet anchored at Port Arthur (78). Because the attack was not decisive, Togo withdrew to the Yellow Sea, where he sank most of the remaining Russian Far Eastern Fleet. The few remaining Russian ships attempted to break out of Port Arthur on August 10 but were destroyed by Togo's gunners. Japanese ground forces meanwhile had landed at Inchon, Korea, with the objective of marching into and occupying Manchuria.

With the ships of its Pacific fleet at the bottom of the ocean or captive of the Japanese, Russia had few options. The best move to make at this point would have been to sue for peace and salvage what they could. Instead, Czar Nicholas III took the worst possible course of action by instructing his Baltic Fleet to sail to Port Arthur to avenge the loss of the Pacific Fleet. The problems with this order were numerous, particularly regarding the fact that Japan was more than 18,000 miles from the Baltic Sea, halfway around the world. Furthermore, the Russian ships were old and their crews poorly trained.

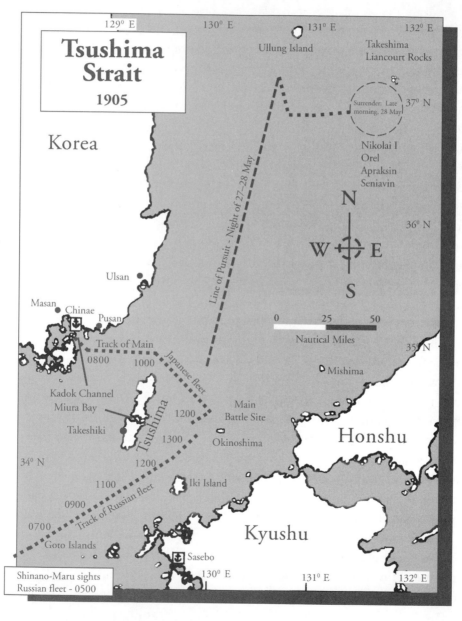

The Baltic Fleet commander Admiral Zinovy Rozhestvensky did his best to repair his ships and train his crews before setting sail for Japan on October 15. Days later, the Russian fleet confused English trawlers in the North Sea for Japanese gunboats and fired on them, bringing Russia to the brink of war with Britain. While an apology and a promise of full compensation for the losses averted further combat, the very idea that the Russians thought the Japanese would be on the other side of the world from their home waters is a good measure of their lack of intelligence gathering and training.

After more than seven months at sea, broken only by a short stay at Cam Ranh Bay, Vietnam, the Russian Baltic Fleet steamed into the sixty-three-mile-wide Tsushima Strait, which separates Japan and Korea. Awaiting them were four Japanese battleships, eight cruisers, twenty-one destroyers, and a mixture of torpedo boats and support ships—a fleet approximately equivalent to Russia's fleet of eight battleships, eight cruisers, nine destroyers, and support and hospital ships. However, the Russian sailors were tired and poorly trained, while the Japanese were rested and confident. The Japanese ships were also capable of a superior speed of sixteen knots compared to the Russians' top speed of ten knots.

At 5:05 A.M. on May 27, 1905, Togo's scouts spotted the Russian vessels approaching the Tsushima Strait. His message to Tokyo exhibited his confidence: "I have just received the news that the enemy's fleet has been sighted. Our fleet will forthwith proceed to sea to attack the enemy and destroy him."

Togo did just that. In a message that he must have adapted from studying British Admiral Nelson at Trafalgar (36), he signaled his fleet: "The rise or fall of the Empire depends upon today's battle. Let every man do his utmost."

In the early afternoon, the Japanese ships approached the Russians and used their greater speed and training to close within 6,000 meters before turning and "crossing the T" of the enemy ships. The advancing Russians could only fire their forward guns as the Japanese fleet traversed their front firing full broadsides. Within a half-hour the battle was decided. Most of the Russian battleships were at the bottom of the strait or sinking. Although the remainder of the fleet attempted to escape to Vladivostok, the pursuing Japanese sank them one by one. Only a single Russian cruiser, two destroyers, and a support craft managed to limp into the friendly port while three additional destroyers escaped to the Philippines.

With the loss of only three torpedo boats and one hundred men killed, the Japanese sank or captured two-thirds of the Russian Fleet, killing more than 4,300 sailors and capturing nearly 6,000—including their commander, Admiral Rozhestvensky. Not since Nelson at Trafalgar and Dewey at Manila (46) had a naval force achieved such a one-sided victory.

The United States, now itself a world power through its acquisitions after the Spanish-American War, stepped forward with an offer by President Theodore Roosevelt to mediate a peace agreement. Delegates from Russia and Japan met in New Hampshire in August 1905, where they ended the conflict by signing the Treaty of Portsmouth. Although the Japanese had won the war, Roosevelt pressured them to return two captured Russian battleships. The Japanese reluctantly agreed, but this forceful persuasion from the U.S. established a grudge they would not forget.

The Russians were glad to have peace, but the people's dissatisfaction with the Czar and royal leadership drew them ever closer to the revolution that would eventually topple the Czar and replace his government with Communism.

For the Japanese, the effects were immediate and far-reaching. While Japan honored Togo as a hero and enshrined his flagship *Mikasa* as a national memorial, the real monument to the war was the end of Japanese isolationism. Japan now had uncontested access to the resources of Korea, resources that expanded the island nation into a world power with the strongest navy in the East. Many Japanese began to visualize their country as the leader of all Asiatic peoples, free of European colonization and control.

Unfortunately for the Japanese and much of the rest of the world, the victory at Tsushima had been too easy. The battle proved only that Japan could win a short war against an under-motivated, poorly prepared enemy. Forty years later, they learned the rest of the lesson—a sneak attack against the poorly armed Americans at Pearl Harbor (62) might earn an early battle victory, but in the end the cost would be the unconditional surrender of the very country that had been protected from the world for so many centuries.

35

GRANADA

Spanish-Muslim Wars, 1491–1492

The victory of King Ferdinand over the Moors at Granada ended seven centuries of Muslim control of the Iberian Peninsula. It also provided an environment where a united Spain could begin the exploration that led to their discovery, settlement, and exploitation of the New World.

Various factions had fought for the control of the Iberian Peninsula long before the Battle of Granada. Rome had controlled the region from the time it defeated Carthage in the third century B.C., until the Vandals (who later fell to the Visigoths) replaced them in the fourth century A.D. During this period, the Muslims spread their empire from Arabia to Syria and Morocco, and in 711, crossed the Straits of Gibraltar from Morocco to conquer the Spanish.

From their new bases in Spain, the Muslims, or Moors, attempted to expand farther into Europe. However, after their defeat at Tours in 732 (24), they concentrated in expanding and improving their settlements in Andalusia, which occupied the southern two-thirds of the peninsula. While the Pyrenees Mountains in northern Spain officially separated Christians from Muslims, many Spanish Catholics continued to live south of the mountains in the provinces of Castile and Aragon.

Moorish immigrants in Andalusia primarily settled into areas according to their lineage. Arabs settled in the east, Berbers in the central hill country, and Syrians in the south. Each brought elements of their own language, culture, and architecture that would have a long-lasting influence on the peninsula. Despite varied backgrounds, the Moors coexisted fairly well with the Christians and Jews who remained within their territory.

For several hundred years, the Moors lived reasonably peacefully despite several changes of leadership in the Muslim world. There were sufficient internal struggles, however, to prevent any significant united effort to expel the Christian settlements in the north, and through the years, the Moorish leadership steadily weakened while the Christians grew stronger and more united.

In the eleventh century, the Christian Spaniards began expanding south into Moorish territory, and in 1085 they captured the city of Toledo. Farther advances were steady but extremely slow. The Christian Spanish front, under a succession of able leaders who included El Cid and Alfonso VII, were satisfied with undertaking minor, low-risk campaigns that captured the occasional Moorish city. These campaigns were so infrequent that it took nearly four centuries before the Spanish had reduced the Moorish holding to the southern province of Granada.

Spanish King Ferdinand II conducted several offensives against Granada in the 1470s, and for some time he forced the Moors to pay a tribute to maintain the peace. However, war with Portugal distracted Ferdinand, and the Moors promptly ceased payment of the annual tribute and brought in additional soldiers from Morocco. In 1481, Ferdinand returned his focus to the Moors and through a series of battles continued to reduce their territory.

In 1491, Ferdinand and his wife Isabella, whose marriage had united the provinces of Castile, Aragon, and Leon, decided to undertake a final offensive to push the Moors off the peninsula. During the summer, the Spanish army constricted the Moorish defenses to the walled city of Granada. Moorish leader Muhammad XI, fearful that if he asked for help from Muslim North Africa he would lose his power to his allies, decided to stand alone against the Spanish.

No accurate estimate exists of the number of soldiers inside or outside the walls of Granada. Some accounts state that the Spanish army numbered 80,000, but this is probably at least double their actual strength. Whatever their total, it is apparent from what occurred that the Spanish did not have enough troops to assault the walls, while the Moors were not strong enough to attempt a breakout. Ultimately, the Spanish were satisfied to besiege the city and wait for hunger to take its toll.

For months, little occurred. The two sides taunted each other, usually over their differing prayers and religious beliefs, and brief skirmishes took place. Generally, however, the siege was so peaceful that even Queen Isabella was able to visit the front lines.

By November, supplies and morale in Granada had dwindled. On the 25th, Muhammad XI agreed to surrender on the condition that he be granted safe passage to Morocco and that his people be treated fairly. Not everyone was pleased with giving up without a fight, including members of the Moorish leader's own family. When Muhammad departed the city, he looked back and broke into tears. His mother, standing at his side, is said to have exclaimed, "You may weep like a woman for what you could not defend like a man."

The Moors left behind in Granada held out until January 2, 1492, before formally surrendering. The Spanish entry into the city ended nearly eight hundred years of Muslim dominance on the peninsula.

Ferdinand kept his promise and allowed the Moorish leaders to safely flee to North Africa and did not harm those who remained behind. Within a decade, however, Catholic zeal increased to the point that the Christians forced the remaining Moors either to leave the country or convert.

While the immediate result of the fairly bloodless victory at Granada ended Muslim occupation and paved the way for the formation of Catholic Spain, there were extensive results as well. To further their Eastern trade routes, Ferdinand and Isabella funded the explorations of Christopher Columbus within months of the victory. His "discovery" of the New World soon brought more explorers, many of whom were military veterans of the wars against the Moors, who subdued the native populations and claimed most of Central and South America as Spanish territory. Thus, within a year of Granada, the Spanish expanded their holding from the peninsula to a New World that would provide the riches and resources to elevate the country to a great world power.

While Moorish influence in Spain was on the decline for centuries before Granada, it is still interesting to speculate about what could have occurred had the Moors won the battle and Muslim explorers rather than Christians had been the first to travel to the New World. Muslim religion and culture would have undoubtedly taken hold and altered the entire future of the Americas and the world. Although this scenario is difficult to envision, it does lend credence to the influence of Granada. What might have happened if the Moors had won is unknown; the fact is that the Spanish raced from Granada to firmly establish their religion, language, and culture in the New World.

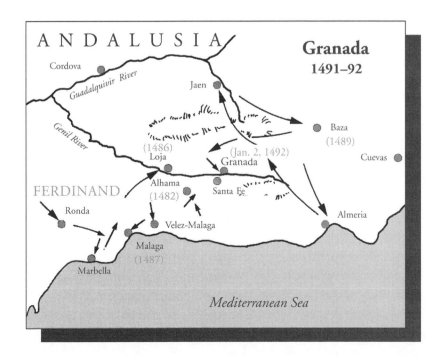

36

TRAFALGAR

Napoleonic Empire Wars, 1805

The British became masters of the world's seas for a century following their victory over the French and Spanish fleets off the coast of the Cape of Trafalgar in 1805. This naval battle was also a contributor to Napoleon's downfall and Horatio Nelson's rise to heroic status.

In less than a decade, Napoleon of France had advanced from a junior artillery officer to emperor. His mastery of land warfare had gained victory after victory as he either allied with, or conquered, most of Western Europe. England remained the only viable threat to Napoleon's world empire, a situation he was determined to correct by invading and conquering Britain. However, the twenty-mile wide English Channel separated the French army from their objective. To conquer the English army, the French first would have to win at sea.

In the spring and summer of 1805, Napoleon repeatedly ordered his naval commander Admiral Pierre de Villeneuve to attack and destroy the English fleet. Villeneuve, who understood the might of the English navy, remained reluctant to engage in a pitched battle until Napoleon threatened to relieve him of his command.

On October 19, Admiral Villeneuve joined his eighteen warships with fifteen vessels from the Spanish navy at Cádiz in southern Spain and sailed for the Strait of Gibraltar. Two days later, they met the British fleet commanded by Admiral Horatio Nelson about ten miles off the Cape of Trafalgar. Although outnumbered (thirty-three French ships to twenty-seven British), Nelson's fleet was better-trained and prepared. Nelson also had a newly developed flag signal system to communicate among his ships, as well as a detailed plan.

When the two opposing fleets sighted each other at dawn on October 21, they began their maneuvers. Although they were only nine miles apart, the extremely light winds caused a delay of six hours before the ships came within gunnery range. During that time, Nelson continued to signal his ships with additional attack instructions. He also sent a signal that became one of naval warfare's most famous messages, when he instructed his signal officer to flag: "England confides that every man will do his duty." The signal officer suggested that "expects" instead of "confides" would make the hoisting of the flag message much faster. Nelson agreed. Many British sailors did not welcome the message, for they felt that they had never failed do so. Regardless, every man soon did do his duty, and the message joined the most famous phrases ever issued in battle.

As the two fleets approached each other, Villeneuve turned north in a single line. Nelson, as planned, divided his ships into two columns and attacked at right angles from the west. Initially, this gave the Franco-Spanish fleet the advantage, but once the British breached the line, they had the upper hand. Nelson then proceeded to plummet the French and Spanish ships.

By late afternoon, eighteen of the Franco-Spanish vessels had surrendered. Of the ships that escaped, only three remained battle-ready. More than 14,000 French and Spanish sailors were killed or captured. The British did not lose a single ship, and their casualties totaled fewer than 1,500.

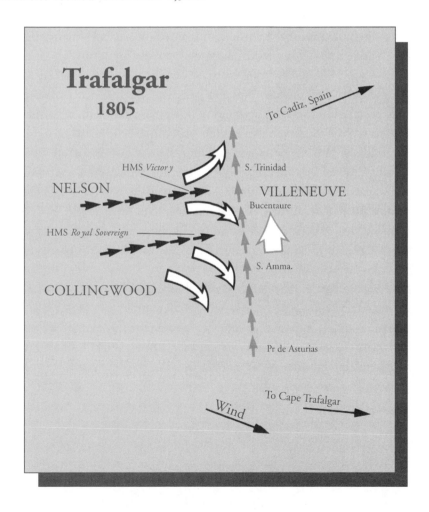

Among those casualties, however, was Nelson. Early in the afternoon, a French sniper high in the riggings of a nearby vessel shot the admiral on the deck of his flagship *Victory*. Nelson lived long enough to learn of his decisive victory; his dying words were, "Thank God, I have done my duty." Nelson's men embalmed his body in a cask of brandy for return to a hero's funeral at St. Paul's Cathedral in London. Stories later circulated that sailors drank from the cask on its way back to England. Whether true or not, to this day the British navy refers to grog as "Nelson's Blood."

Nelson's victory at Trafalgar made the English navy the strongest in the world. Their dominance of the seas remained unchallenged for more than a century until the Battle of Jutland during World War I. This control of the sea lanes enhanced England's ability to colonize around the world so that it became true that the sun never set on the British Empire. It was a sun that rose on that October day in 1805 off Cape Trafalgar.

The defeat of the Franco-Spanish fleet did not, however, mean the defeat of the French army. Napoleon's ground forces remained the strongest on the continent, and it would be another decade before the emperor finally faced total defeat.

If the French had prevailed at Trafalgar, they would have controlled the seas, invading and probably conquering England. Under these circumstances, all of Europe as well as the New World colonies would have been under French rule.

Other immediate and far-reaching influences also came out of the Battle of Trafalgar. Control of the seas increased England's world trade and the need for additional ships and seamen. They could build ships, but men to crew them were in short supply. England turned to impressing sailors, particularly from the United States, despite the successful American Revolution. The impressment of American sailors into the British navy, combined with restrictive trade practices, eventually led the two countries to fight the War of 1812.

Longer range, the Battle of Trafalgar also influenced the largest war of its time. As the British influence dominated Europe and expanded around the world, the Germans began to resent British land and sea power. In the latter part of the nineteenth century, the Germans began to expand their armed forces and eventually challenged the British, thus leading to World War I.

37

ADRIANOPLE

Gothic Invasion of the Roman Empire, 378

The Gothic victory at Adrianople in 378 killed more than 20,000 Roman soldiers, proved that "barbarians" could defeat the civilized Romans in their own territory, and marked the beginning of the end of the Roman Empire. More importantly, it delineated the point in history when the infantry no longer dominated the battlefield, as the battle introduced the power of horse-mounted armies.

As the Roman Empire conquered its neighbors and expanded its borders, it increased the number of its enemies along with its territory. The Roman army won most of its battles and always managed, even after major defeats, to regroup and achieve later victories. However, by the latter part of the fourth century, Franks, Jutes, Saxons, Vandals, Persians, and Goths were all threatening the empire. Some of these groups united together against Rome, while others fought among themselves for territory and natural resources. Rome encouraged the fighting among its enemies and even recruited some of the best warriors into its own army.

In 376, a large group of nomadic people known as Visigoths, or Goths, requested permission from Roman Emperor Valens to settle south of the Danube River near the town of Adrianople, which is now in western Turkey. The Goths, led by Fritigern, originated in Scandinavia but over a period of several generations had migrated into eastern Russia before arriving in the Balkans in the third century. Like most of the migrant people of the period, the Goths survived by raiding and pillaging.

Valens, already involved in combat against the Persians on his east border, welcomed the Goths, thinking that they might provide recruits for his legions. Several hundred thousand Goths soon settled about eight miles outside of Adrianople but found the local officials reluctant to sell them food or other supplies. The local authorities demanded that the Goths turn their weapons over and that they leave their children as hostages to insure good behavior.

As a result, the Goths revolted and destroyed the local Roman army. Fritigern then began his preparations to defend his newly won territory against the Roman reinforcements he knew would soon arrive. Upon hearing about the Gothic revolt, Valens ceased his campaign against the Persians and turned his army of 40,000 infantry and cavalry toward Adrianople. He requested further assistance from Rome but did not wait for it. He approached the Goth camp, which was composed of a huge circle of wagons on an open plain.

Valens deployed his 30,000 infantrymen against the camp and divided his 10,000 cavalrymen into two flanking units. Both Valens and Fritigern were more than willing to negotiate rather than jump into an immediate battle. Valens wanted to rest his tired troops after their long march, while Fritigern had an even better reason: although he outnumbered the Romans with his 50,000 infantrymen, his more than 20,000 cavalrymen were foraging outside the camp. He immediately dispatched runners to order the return of his horsemen.

Negotiations quickly broke down. Although outnumbered, Valens had neither respect for the fighting abilities of the "barbarians" nor a desire to share the glory of victory with leaders of the other Roman armies coming to his support. On August 9, 378, Valens ordered his men forward against the Goth defenses.

The Goths flung spears and other missiles at their attackers, but the enemies soon came face-to-face, as the Romans battled with swords, clubs, and shields. Valens's men began to best the Goths, but on a hillside on the right flank Goth cavalrymen assembled. In a short time, their number grew to 20,000, and they swept down the hill against the Roman flank. Roman infantrymen and cavalry were quickly and literally pinned between the Goth camp and the attacking horsemen. The space was so limited that some Romans could not even raise their swords until their mortally wounded comrades fell to the ground and made room.

Much of Valens's army died between the attacking Goth infantry and cavalry. Most of those who escaped the encirclement were caught by pursuing Goths and shown no mercy. By the end of the battle, Valens and more than 20,000 of his men lay dead. More Romans died at the hands of the Goths at Adrianople than in any battle since Teutoburger Wald more than three hundred years earlier (42). Goth causalities were described as "relatively light."

Shortly after the battle, Roman historian Ammianus Marcellinus wrote, "The plain was covered with corpses, showing the mutual ruin of combatants. The groans of the dying, or of men horribly wounded, were intense and caused much dismay on all sides. Amidst all this great tumult and confusion, our infantry were exhausted by toil and danger, until at last they had neither the strength left to fight nor the spirit to plan anything."

Following the battle, the Goths moved against the Roman garrison in Adrianople, but lacking siege weapons, their infantry and cavalry could not penetrate the city's walls. Over the next five years, Valens's successor, Theodosius, was able to force the Goths back across the Danube, but after Fritigern's victory, Rome's enemies knew the Empire was not invincible. Rome did not give up easily, adapting what it learned at Adrianople and continuing to recruit soldiers from conquered territories. But eventually their enemies outnumbered their allies. After almost constant warfare, Alaric, another Goth, besieged Rome in 410, and for the first time in a thousand years, the city fell to an attacker. Although the Goths eventually adopted much of the Roman culture, the end of the Western Roman Empire, which had begun at Adrianople, was complete.

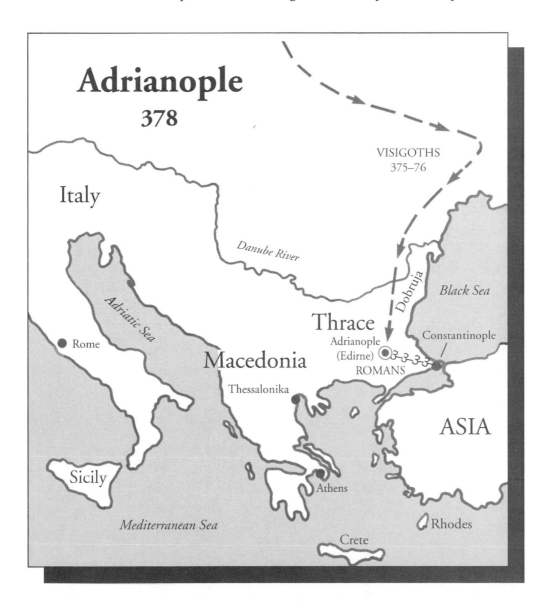

While Adrianople was important because of the Romans' defeat, the battle's real impact was on future warfare. From the beginning of time until Adrianople, the foot soldier armed with sword, club, and/or pike ruled the battlefield. Horsemen had been used to screen the flanks and conduct reconnaissance, but heretofore they had not been employed directly against enemy forces, as evidenced by the fact that horses and their riders wore no metal mail or other types of protection.

This changed after Adrianople. The Gothic cavalrymen became the predecessors of the knights of the Middle Ages and for cavalry units that would dominate the battlefield for the next thousand years. Not until the English longbow archers' defeat of the French cavalry at Crécy in 1346 (33) would the legacy of Adrianople begin to fade into the historical icons of military tactics that were no longer successful.

38

MARNE

World War I, 1914

The French and British resistance and counterattack along the Marne River in September 1914 stopped the German invasion of France and prevented the fall of Paris and the country. In its aftermath lay hundreds of miles of mostly static trench lines where the two sides battled for the next four years with little result other than carnage and death.

For centuries, European tribes and then nations had vied for control over portions of the continent. War, rather than peace, prevailed as various countries united against common enemies to add to their kingdoms or to resist foreign invasions. The Prussian victory in the Franco-Prussian War in 1871 finally brought an uneasy peace that lasted for more than thirty years, but the resultant unification of the German states provided an imbalance in European power that could only lead to future conflict.

By the turn of the century, France and Russia were allied against Germany and Austria, with each side planning to dominate the other if and when war broke out again. The French had begun preparing Plan 17 for an offensive against Germany since its humiliating financial and territorial losses to Prussia in 1871. Plan 17 included a massive attack through the rugged hills and forest of Alsace into Germany.

Meanwhile, the newly united Germany also began planning for the next war and by 1894 had adopted a plan developed by General Alfred von Schlieffen for the invasion of France. The Schlieffen Plan, wary of a two-front war, called for defeating France before Russia could mobilize and join the fight. Only minimal forces would remain on the Eastern Front, but once France fell, the German army would turn toward Moscow.

Both sides readied for war while waiting for the spark that would set their armies marching against each other. That spark came on June 28, 1914, when a terrorist from Serbia, an ally of Russia, assassinated Francis Ferdinand, the archduke of Austria, an ally of Germany. Various halfhearted negotiations took place for a month before war broke out on July 28.

The Germans immediately began executing their Schlieffen Plan, which had remained constant with few modifications since its adoption more than a decade earlier. Helmuth Johannes von Moltke, the nephew of the great Helmuth Karl von Moltke, served as the chief of the general staff and overall commander of German forces. As planned, Moltke left a small force along the border with Russia while he massed his army of nearly a million men for an assault against France.

Moltke planned to take Paris in six weeks, with a rapid advance west through Belgium and then south to Paris. His "hook" would encircle the French army, capture the capital, and ensure surrender. The Belgian army, however, put up more resistance than the Germans anticipated, though not enough to completely stop the offensive. In response to the violation of Belgian neutrality, Britain entered the war and immediately began deploying four divisions to meet the German advance into France.

Despite the British reinforcements, the Germans continued their offensive. General Joseph Joffre, the French commander, realized that Paris would soon be threatened and began to recall units that had attempted but failed to execute their Plan 17 attack along the German border. He also called upon Parisian military commander General Joseph Gallieni to gather all available soldiers and willing civilians into the Sixth Army and hurry to the front. Gallieni gathered his army and drafted the entire Paris civilian taxi fleet to ferry the men to the front lines. Most of the cabs made two round-trips as they quickly delivered more than 6,000 men to the front.

The German advance began to slow. Supply lines, still mostly serviced by horse- or mule-drawn wagons, had difficulty keeping up with the infantry, causing shortages of ammunition and food. Moltke learned that the Russians were fighting harder than anticipated and even believed a rumor that Russia was sending reinforcements to France via Scotland. Instead of continuing the Schlieffen Plan to take Paris, he decided to withdraw several divisions and dispatch them to the Russian front. He ordered that the "hook" be shortened to encircle the city of Verdun rather than the French capital.

Meanwhile, the German army advanced across the Marne River near Paris on September 3, before Moltke's order to turn toward Verdun reached them. Shortly after the Germans moved away from Paris, a reconnaissance airplane spotted the change of direction and reported the exposed flank to the French high command.

Gallieni recognized the German vulnerability and convinced Joffre that it was an opportune time for a counterattack. The British were reluctant to join the counterattack, but Joffre met with their commander Sir John French and stated, "I cannot believe that the British army will refuse to do its share in this supreme crisis….history will severely judge your absence." He concluded, "The honor of England is at stake." Convinced that indeed their honor was in question, the British joined the action.

The French and British armies launched their counterattack against the exposed German flank along the Marne River on September 6. A thirty-mile gap quickly opened, allowing the Allies to penetrate between two German armies. Fighting raged along the three hundred-mile front for two days before the Germans began to withdraw on the 9th.

The German leaders relieved Moltke of his command on September 14 for his failure to take Paris and his decision to send reinforcements to the Russian front. The Germans had already defeated the Russians at the Battle of Tannenberg (63) before the extra troops arrived from France. On the Western Front, the opposing sides settled into trench warfare that would kill the better part of a generation of young men on both sides over the next four years.

The Battle of the Marne was certainly a French victory, as it saved their capital and prevented a loss similar to that of the Franco-Prussian War in 1871. It did not, however, defeat the Germans. Instead it led only to years of subsequent warfare and millions of deaths. Even the armistice in 1918 only postponed the still larger battles of World War II that would finally decide the victors.

The French victory at the Marne was pivotal to Europe and, therefore, the world. Had the French lost, the Germans, with their Tannenberg win as well, would have dominated Europe unchallenged. Defeated countries, including France, Belgium, and Russia, would have been unable to rally resources and manpower for a second world war. Hitler would have remained just one more nameless misfit, and the great Soviet revolution certainly would have been delayed, if not completely suppressed. The war would have also been over before the United States could join the fight, thus slowing, or limiting, the American advance to the status of a world power.

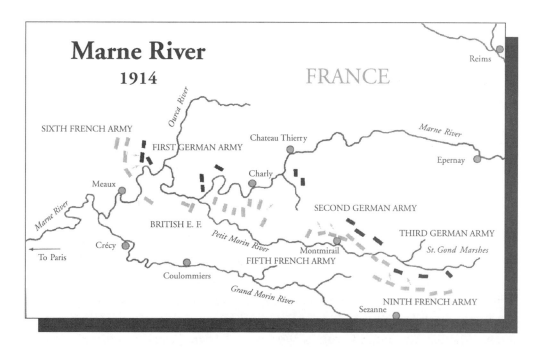

39

CHÂLONS

Roman Empire-Huns Wars, 451

The Roman victory over Attila and his Huns at Châlons in 451 blocked a major Asian advance into Western Europe. The defeat so weakened the Hun army that Attila failed in his invasion of Italy the following year, a failure that would lead to the breakup of his empire a year later.

Late in the fourth century, bands of nomadic tribesmen known as Huns had swept out of the great steppes of Asia to raid the settlements of the Germanic peoples and the Eastern Roman Empire. By the early fifth century, Huns had united into a single army under the leadership of King Ruga to become so threatening that the emperor of the eastern Roman Empire paid them an annual tribute in gold.

In the mid-fifth century, Attila assumed the leadership of the Huns, leading raids throughout a wide area that today encompasses Hungary, Greece, Spain, and Italy. From these attacks, he amassed great wealth and an enormous army, as captured prisoners had the option of allegiance to him or death. Attila organized his army on a base of ten, and he expected each subordinate tribe to field an army of ten thousand, called a tumén, structured with ten horsemen forming a basic unit, ten units forming a company of one hundred, ten companies forming a squadron of one thousand, and ten squadrons forming a tumén.

The Hun tuméns went into combat on horseback clothed in crude leather armor and armed with bows and multiple arrow quivers. They also carried swords and clubs for close combat and led one or more pack horses that carried additional arrows, food, and water. Each Hun soldier was self-sustainable. The only wagons that accompanied the tuméns were war chariots carrying multiple archers.

By the middle of the fifth century, the Hun army had grown to at least 100,000, some accounts estimating that number at a half-million. Horsemen dominated the Hun army, but Attila had added some infantry, particularly from captured tribes.

In 450, Attila decided to turn his conquest westward, where he expected little resistance. He was well aware that the two strongest forces in the region, the Western Roman and Visigoth armies, opposed each other over their own territorial claims. In a short time, Attila sacked and burned many of Europe's great cities, including Metz, Reims, Mainz, Strasbourg, Cologne, Worms, and Trier.

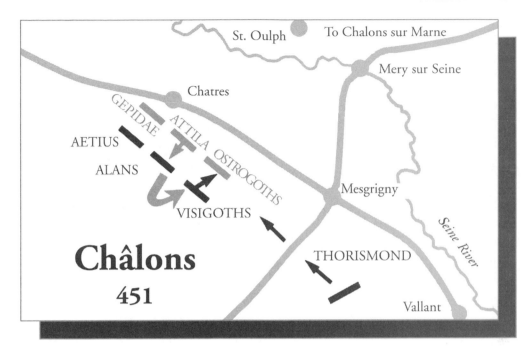

Attila bypassed Paris (some claim because of the prayers of a young girl, but more likely because of the city's significant defenses) and continued southward to besiege Orleans. Emperor Valentinian III of the Western Roman Empire saw that he was in danger of losing all his territory and ordered his military commander, Flavius Aetius, to assemble his army and march to relieve Orleans. Aetius faced a difficult task. His regular army was small, and many of the mercenaries that he traditionally hired for operations were already allied with Attila.

Aetius finally convinced one of his adversaries, Visigoth King Theodoric I, to join with the Romans against a common enemy. The size of their combined armies was probably about half the size of the Huns' when they approached Orleans in early June 451. Attila, not wanting to be pinned between the approaching army and the city walls, withdrew toward the Marne River plain. He left behind a rear guard of about 15,000, but Aetius destroyed this force in a daring night attack that gave the rest of his army confidence that they could defeat the great Huns.

Like many of the facts about the following battle, its exact location remains unclear. Most agree that the two armies finally met in the Champagne region of France near the town of Châlons-sur-Marne. Most accounts agree that the Huns were on the north and the allies on the south, each arrayed in a line of three groups. Attila positioned his strongest force, the Hun army, in the center, with other tribal groups on his flanks. Aetius did just the opposite, placing his weakest force in the center and the stronger on the wings.

The fight began early on a summer morning. A skirmish over a hill on the Hun left flank started the battle and diverted some of the Huns from the center to reinforce the wing, thus weakening Attila's attack a short time later against the Roman-Visigoth center. Attila pushed back the enemy center, but this maneuver exposed his right, forcing the Huns to turn and defend rather than continue into the enemy rear. Meanwhile, on the other wing, the Romans and Huns fought to a stalemate, preventing either side from enveloping the other.

After hours of close combat, the battlefield was covered with what all sources agree were "countless bodies." Unable to gain an advantage, Attila ordered a withdrawal to more defendable terrain, from which his archers quickly turned back the pursuing Romans and Visigoths. Attila, however, did not renew his attack. Instead, a short time later, the Huns began their march toward the east. The allies did not pursue the retreating Huns because Aetius feared the Visigoths might turn against the Romans now that the Huns were no longer a threat. The Roman leader convinced the Visigoths to return home to protect their own territory, which allowed Attila to safely reach his bases in modern Hungary to rebuild for an invasion of Italy the following year.

Attila raided deep into Italy before Pope Leo I met with him and convinced him to cease his offensive. Whether because of the Pope's intervention or because of the weakened Hun army, Attila turned his army back homeward. A year later, the great Hun leader died of a severe nosebleed, and within twenty years infighting brought an end to his empire and its army.

Historians still debate the impact of the Battle of Châlons. While it was not greatly decisive in that Attila avoided defeat and kept his army intact, the battle's significance was major. Châlons marked the zenith of the Huns. Their failure to advance throughout Europe left the Christian religion and culture uncontested. When the weakened Hun army could not take Rome the following year, the power of the papacy and the Empire greatly increased. For the next thousand years, the Catholic religion and culture dominated Western Europe.

40

BRITAIN

World War II, 1940–41

History's first battle fought totally in the air saw the British defeat the Germans—a victory that stalled the Nazi's efforts to subdue all of Europe. The Battle of Britain also preserved precious assembly and staging areas needed for air attacks against the German heartland and the eventual landings at Normandy (13) that would lead to the final defeat of Germany.

From the time of their invasion of Poland (65) in 1939 and through the fall of France in 1940, the German war machine advanced with little resistance. By the summer of 1940, Adolf Hitler controlled all of Western Europe with the single exception of Great Britain. Although the Germans had defeated the British in France and forced their evacuation across the Channel at Dunkirk, the English still possessed a formidable navy and air force. Aware of the British strength and of his own shortages of watercraft to support a cross-Channel invasion, Hitler was willing to negotiate a peace so he could concentrate his power against the Soviets in the east.

The British and their new prime minister, Winston Churchill, were unwilling to negotiate with the Nazis. Instead they welcomed the opportunity to fight and even bragged that they were now at the advantage since they were no longer encumbered with allies.

Angered by the British reaction, Hitler began plans to invade the islands. On July 16, 1940, he announced, "As England, despite her hopeless military situation, still shows no sign of willingness to come to terms, I have decided to prepare, and if necessary to carry out, a landing operation against her. The aim of this operation is to eliminate the English motherland as a base from which war against Germany can be continued and, if necessary, to occupy it completely."

A successful land invasion of the British Isles had not occurred since that of 1066 at Hastings (2). Hitler and his generals knew that they had to neutralize British naval and air assets before any successful ground invasion could begin.

The British understood the magnitude and importance of the impending battle. In a speech to the House of Commons on June 18, the prime minister declared, "The Battle of Britain is about to begin. Upon this battle depends the survival of Christian civilization. Upon it depends our own British life, and the long continuity of our institutions and our Empire. The whole fury and might of the enemy must very soon be turned on us. Hitler knows that he will have to break us in this island or lose the war. If we can stand up to him, all Europe may be free and the life of the world may move forward into broad, sunlit uplands. But if we fail, then the whole world, including the United States, including all that we have known and cared for, will sink into the abyss of a new Dark Age made more sinister, and perhaps more protracted, by the lights of perverted science. Let us therefore brace ourselves to our duties, and so bear ourselves that, if the British Empire and its Commonwealth last for a thousand years, men will still say, 'This was their finest hour.'"

At the opening of the Battle of Britain, the Germans had about 1,200 bombers and 1,100 fighters commanded by General Hermann Goering. The Royal Air Force (RAF), commanded by Air Marshal Hugh Dowding, had about 1,100 fighter aircraft—only about 700 of which were airworthy at any one time. Ultimately, the primary aircraft that dominated the action were the German Messerschmitt Bf109s and the British Hurricanes and Spitfires.

Britain's greatest limitation was its inferior numbers; its greatest advantage was its crude but functional radar sites that could forewarn of German attacks. This radar allowed British pilots to remain on the ground and take to the air only when necessary, saving fuel and wear on their aircraft. Pilots were also more rested.

The Germans also faced distinct disadvantages. First, the range of their aircraft allowed only about a quarter of an hour over targets once the planes reached England from their Belgian and French fields. Second, because they were operating over enemy territory, German crews who were shot down or forced to crash-land could not be recovered to fly another day.

The Battle of Britain progressed through three phases. On July 10, German bombers, accompanied by fighters, attacked British ships and ports from Dover to Plymouth. Phase One came to a climax with a raid by more than a thousand German planes on August 15. While exact figures are in dispute, approximately 75 German planes went down, compared to only about 35 RAF aircraft.

Before Phase One concluded, the Germans were already engaging in Phase Two by striking the British radar stations, airfields, and aircraft factories. The most intense action took place between August 24 and September 6. German fighters brought down more than 450 Hurricanes and Spitfires, killing more than a hundred British aviators—one fourth of their total number of qualified fighter pilots. German losses were nearly double that in both planes and pilots. German aircraft manufacturers could not keep pace with these losses or with the numbers of planes the British factories were producing.

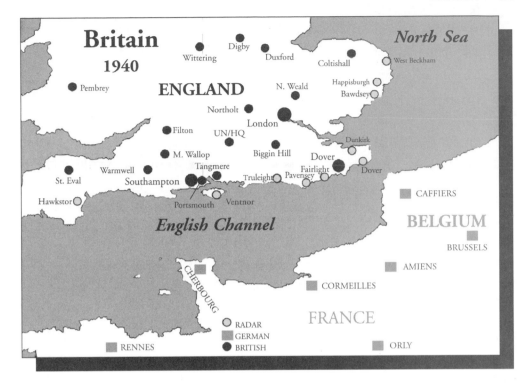

A minor incident at the beginning of Phase Two led to Phase Three and greatly influenced the eventual British victory. On the night of August 24–25, a German bomber missed its oil-storage-yard target near London and dropped its bombs on civilian houses in the city. In response, the British dispatched bombers against Berlin the following night. Physical damage to Berlin was minimal, but Hitler and the German people were infuriated and demanded revenge.

On September 7, Hitler opened Phase Three by shifting operations from radar stations, airfields, and factories to the bombing of London. He could have made no greater mistake. London was farther from German airfields, allowing less time for fighter cover of the bombers. German casualties escalated, while British resolve solidified. The bombing also rallied support for Britain from the United States and other countries.

Germany continued its attacks against London for the next two months before shifting part of its efforts to industrial centers. All the while the RAF continued to reduce the numbers of German planes and pilots. The last major assault on London occurred on May 10, 1941. Sporadic attacks continued, but Hitler was never again able to launch a significant air attack against Britain. Germany had suffered its first major defeat of the war.

During the ten-month battle, the British lost nearly 1,000 planes and 500 crewmembers. German bombs killed more than 43,000 civilians in London and wounded five times that many. In what Churchill called their "finest hour," neither the British military nor people faltered. The Germans, in contrast, lost at least 1,700 planes—although the exuberant British claimed to have downed nearly a thousand more than that number.

It is, of course, difficult to speculate on what might have happened had the British "few" not stopped the German air assault. Even with air superiority, the Germans would still have had to deal with the British army and navy at a time when Germany lacked sufficient assets to mount an amphibious attack across the Channel. Although lightly defended, much of the British coast itself offered a formidable obstacle, with its high cliffs and rocky shores. Also, if Germany had tried to invade across the Channel, the United States would probably have entered the war earlier. If Germany had knocked Britain out of the war, it is possible—albeit unlikely—that the U.S. would have allowed Nazi control of all of Europe. Without having to fight on two fronts, the Germans may have been able to defeat the Soviets, and Hitler could have taken charge of all of Western Europe and perhaps much of the Middle East and North Africa.

However, the Battle of Britain ended any German hopes of invading the British Isles. It left Britain able and determined to rebuild its army and military machine. More importantly, it provided a secure land base near the European continent for Britain and its Allies, especially the United States once it joined the war the following December, to prepare to counter the Nazis. It also proved that conventional bombing could not subdue an enemy. The British and Americans would learn this lesson for themselves as they squandered thousands of planes and airmen in later attacks against the German heartland. Yet, the Battle of Britain is well deserving of the honor as one of only a few air battles that greatly influenced a war's outcome. Only the U.S. atomic bombing of Japan (7) is more significant in the annals of air war influence.

41

CONSTANTINOPLE

Byzantine-Turkish War, 1453

The victory of the Turks at Constantinople in 1453 ended the thousand-year-old Byzantine Empire and opened Eastern Europe to the spread of Islam. Although the battle dissolved the dominance of Christianity in the region, refugees from the defeated Empire greatly influenced education, arts, and trade in Italy and surrounding countries, significantly contributing to the Renaissance.

Prior to the Byzantines' final battle, Constantinople had stood for more than a thousand years as a buffer between the Muslim and Christian worlds. Its natural defenses of water on three sides and a triple wall on its landward approach had withstood more than twenty attacks over the years. The city's defenses had been further bolstered by a single wall that ran along its coastline and a massive chain that blocked the entrance to its harbor on the Golden Horn. Twenty-six galleys had stood behind the barrier to further strengthen the fortress.

While Constantinople's defenses were strong, the Byzantine Empire itself was crumbling. After losing its eastern territories to the Muslims in the Battle of Manzikert in 1071 (31), the Empire eroded. By the mid-fifteenth century, Constantinople was its only major holding. Within its walls, Emperor Constantine XI could muster only about 5,000 soldiers to defend the city and his Empire. Constantine's request to the Christian west for support against an anticipated Muslim attack brought only about 3,000 additional troops, because Rome and Western Europe found the Orthodox Church of the Empire almost as repulsive as the Muslims. However, among those answering the call for help was Giovanni Giustiniani, an Italian soldier of fortune renowned for his defense of walled cities.

The lands to the east of Constantinople were ruled by the Muslims. Following the Battle of Manzikert, the Muslims had fought for nearly four centuries against each other and outside invaders until about 1400, when the Ottoman Turks gained control of the region. After wars with Tamerlane and his Mongols in the early fifteenth century, the Ottoman Turks looked to expand, rather than just defend, their territory.

In 1451, Mohammed II assumed the leadership of the Ottoman Turks and set out to destroy the remnants of the Byzantine Empire. In April 1453, he moved against Constantinople with an army of 80,000 men, more than 300 warships, and

70 cannons captured in the Balkans. Among these was a 27-foot-long gun capable of firing a 600-pound stone projectile.

On April 6, the Muslim artillery began a barrage against the city's walls. After twelve days of pounding, Mohammed ordered his infantry forward. The Byzantine soldiers and their European allies fought back with the willful determination of those whose lives, families, and homes depended upon it. After a fierce battle, the Muslims withdrew. Mohammed's European engineers then attempted to dig under the walls and lay mines to breach the obstacle. Constantine's advisors, however, caught the Muslims in the act and either flooded the passages or collapsed them with explosives. Mohammed ordered subsequent artillery barrages followed by ground attacks on May 1, 12, and 21. Once again, the Byzantines, under the able leadership of Giustiniani, held and even repaired the damage to the city's walls.

Mohammed paused long enough to drag 70 light vessels a mile overland near the town of Pera and relaunch them in the Golden Horn behind the chain barricade. With the city now completely cut off, Mohammad ordered another artillery barrage and infantry attack. In the forward units of the Muslim army was another anomaly of the religious differences in the region. More than 12,000 elite mercenaries known as janissaries, many of whom had been captured from their Christian families as children and then were raised as elite Muslim warriors, led the attack.

The exhausted, outnumbered Byzantines fought valiantly, but the janissaries broke through the wall and into the city on May 29. Thousands of Muslim soldiers followed. Constantine took a sword and charged into the invaders, reportedly shouting, "God forbid that I should live an emperor without an empire! As my city falls, I will fall with it."

Constantine, along with most of his army, did indeed fall. The few military survivors, along with the city's civilian population, were either murdered or sold into slavery. Mohammad allowed his army three days to rape and loot before restoring order and offering prayers to Allah at the city's historic church, Saint Sophia. The Muslim leader spared most of the city's buildings, not out of compassion but rather because he planned to make Constantinople the center of the Ottoman Empire. It would remain so for more than four and a half centuries, until World War I.

The direct influence of the Battle of Constantinople was the end of the Byzantine Empire. It also opened the way for Muslim expansion westward that would spread all the way to Vienna before finally being stopped.

While the fall of Constantinople and the resultant loss of Greece and surrounding territory ended a great period of advancement in the arts and culture in that region, it also encouraged the spread of civilization. Greek philosophers, educators, tradesmen, and artists fled the Muslim advance and took up residence in Italy, France, and other regions where they significantly contributed to the Renaissance. The fall of Constantinople may have destroyed one of the great protectors of world culture, but its defeat spread its most creative and influential citizens throughout Europe.

The battle also directly influenced trade and exploration. With Constantinople and much of the Mediterranean in Muslim hands, the Christian European nations had to look for new trade routes. Within fifty years, European navigators had ventured around the African Horn and across the Atlantic to explore the New World. These explorations would, of course, have eventually taken place regardless, but the Battle of Constantinople certainly expedited them.

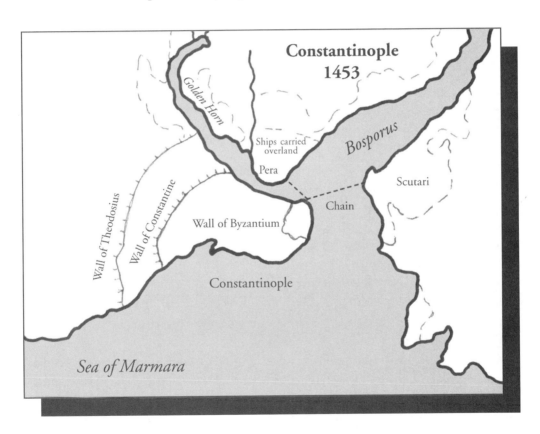

42

TEUTOBURGER WALD

Roman Empire-Germanic Wars, A.D. 9

The northern expansion of the Roman Empire ended in the Teutoburger Wald, when the Germanic tribes defeated Rome's legions in A.D. 9. The Rhine River then became the Empire's northern border and the point where Latin customs, culture, and language stopped, thus precluding their influence on those who would evolve into the German people.

By the latter part of the first century B.C., Rome had expanded its empire into the Middle East, North Africa, Western Europe, and Britain. When Gaul fell to the Romans, the only remaining resistance to their northern expansion came from nomadic Germanic tribes. What these groups lacked in finesse, they made up for in their fierce fighting ability. From their bases in Gaul, the Romans finally pacified most of the tribes and limited their operations to occasional raids. For a time, Rome even hired many of the Germanic tribesmen as mercenaries in their own legions.

In A.D. 6, Publius Quintilius Varus assumed command of occupied Gaul and the regions home to Germanic tribes north of the Rhine River. Varus, a more experienced administrator than soldier, imposed taxes payable in gold, silver, and other rare metals upon the tribesmen. Minor revolts broke out, but the Germanic tribes initially lacked the unity to launch anything more than token resistance. It was not until A.D. 9 that Arminius, a German mercenary in service to the Romans, provided the tribes the leadership and the plan they needed. Arminius convinced the German tribes that, while it was impossible to defeat the Romans in conventional battle, they could defeat them by way of guerrilla warfare—especially if the area of the fight was in their favor.

Arminius continued to serve on Varus's staff as one of the Roman leader's primary military advisors, even as he secretly conspired with the "enemy" Germanic tribes. When Varus prepared to move his army of about 18,000 legionnaires and 10,000 camp followers south of the Rhine to winter quarters, Arminius recommended that the army go through the Teutoburger Wald, or Teutoburg Forest, to put down a small rebellion on their way.

The Roman legions proceeded into the thickly forested, swampy region where they found not a "small rebellion," but rather 20,000 to 30,000 fierce Germanic warriors flanking their path. The Germans had to close only near enough to shoot arrows and throw spears into the Roman columns, as the terrain and elements assisted them in defeating their enemy. Trees, gullies, and swamps hampered the Romans' movement, while a torrential downpour prevented their assuming offensive formations for a counterattack. In addition, several thousand German mercenaries in hire of the Romans deserted early in the fight, choosing to return home or join the attackers. Varus finally maneuvered his men into a clearing where he could form a defense.

Arminius, who had abandoned the Roman column shortly before the battle began, joined his fellow German tribesmen in the attack but stopped the assault once the Romans established their defenses. Although his tribesmen outnumbered the Romans, they were not trained or armed to attack a fixed position. Instead, they waited, knowing Varus would have to eventually continue his march.

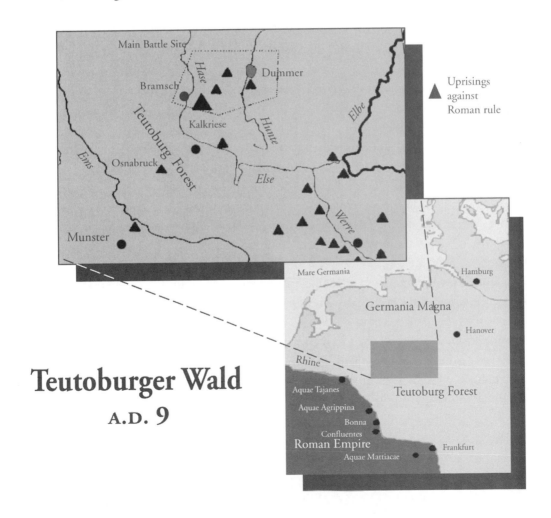

Teutoburger Wald
A.D. 9

While archeologists have found only parts of the line of march, and possibly one of the Roman camps, apparently most of the following battle took place near the present German town of Detmold. Evidence indicates that Varus burned his wagons and tried at least once, and possibly twice, to break out of the forest and outdistance his attackers. The largest fight occurred when the eight hundred Roman cavalrymen abandoned the primary column and attempted a breakout on their own, but the thick woods impeded their horses. Few, if any, escaped. The Germanic tribesmen then picked off the remaining Roman soldiers in ones and twos.

With his cavalry gone, his infantry mostly dead, and capture imminent, Varus committed suicide. The remaining Romans surrendered, only to be tortured and sacrificed to the various Germanic tribal gods. Years later, bones of the Roman dead still littered the forest.

The immediate effect of the defeat of Rome was the widespread fear that the Germans would invade Italy and destroy the Empire. Rome was in no danger from Germanic tribes, however, because Arminius could not hold together the loose confederation whose soldiers were more interested in looting the Roman bodies than in continuing the offensive southward. The army dispersed without conducting any other military operations.

Rarely had so few accomplished so much with so little effort. The tribesmen blocked the advance of Rome into the north central and northeastern regions of Europe; established the Rhine River as the northern boundary of the Empire; and, unlike Gaul and other conquered areas, preserved their own language and civilization, such as it was. The Rhine River stood as the Germanic boundary for more than four centuries before Germanic tribesmen again joined forces to destroy the Roman Empire.

Had Varus defeated the Germanic tribesmen in the Teutoburger Wald, the Latin influence would have eventually prevailed there as in Gaul. There would have been no subsequent Anglo-Saxon raids on Britain and therefore no England. While Arminius failed to sustain the German tribal unity that defeated the Romans, the brutal battle in the Teutoburger Wald laid the foundation for the future German culture, assisted in the establishment of England, and eventually led to the fall of Rome.

43

VALMY

French Revolution, 1792

The French victory in the relatively bloodless Battle of Valmy on September 20, 1792, guaranteed the success of their revolution and the formation of the Republic. Valmy marked the genesis of the French military power and introduced the concept of a national armed force that would dominate Europe for the next two decades. Wolfgang von Goethe, a German observer of the battle, later remarked, "From this place and from this day forth commences a new era in the world's history."

On July 14, 1789, French commoners, angry at excesses by their royal leaders and encouraged by the recent successful rebellion in America, had stormed the Bastille in Paris. The rebellion soon spread and produced a document titled "Declaration of the Rights of Man and the Citizen" that called for an end to the monarchy and the formation of a constitutional government.

King Louis XVI, obviously opposed to the idea, attempted to rally the French nobles, including senior military officers, to combat the rebellion. Many nobles fled, and Louis himself tried to leave the country to secure military assistance from neighboring monarchs, but the rebels captured him and returned him to Paris. By the summer of 1791, the revolutionaries controlled France, and Louis was briefly reinstated as the head of the new constitutional government.

Meanwhile, French nobles who had fled the country sought assistance from other monarchs to return Louis to his throne. Motivated by the threat to their own rule if the French rebels succeeded, the kings of Austria and Prussia agreed to crush the rebellion. By the time the two declared war on France in the spring of 1792, the kingdoms of Spain, Sweden, Savoy, and Russia had also agreed to provide financial support for the operation.

The royal allies assumed that their mission to end the rebellion and restore Louis to his throne would be an easy one. After all, the allies, particularly the Prussians, were battle-tested from the Seven Years' War and had the best armies in the world.

Despite its perceived weaknesses, the French army, which had mostly sided with the rebels, had several advantages. The remaining officers and the sergeants who now composed its leadership were a capable lot. More importantly, they had the most advanced artillery corps in Europe, and their crews had joined the revolution. These two aspects of the "old" French army were also greatly influenced by an additional factor: the French people liked their new freedoms so much that they were willing to fight to maintain them. Instead of a small army made up of professionals and mercenaries who fought for money, the French could now field a huge force made up of "citizen soldiers," who fought for nationalism and personal freedom.

However, regardless of their idealism, the French had much to learn before they could successfully face the experienced Prussians and Austrians. In the initial fights along the border with the Austrian Netherlands (modern Belgium), the French retreated with little resistance. The allied army, commanded by Prussian field marshal Karl Wilhelm Ferdinand, the Duke of Brunswick, followed the rebel army into France and quickly captured Longwy on August 27, and Verdun a week later. Brunswick continued his march through the Argonne Forest until he neared the village of Valmy, about a hundred miles east of Paris, where French General François Kellermann was determined to mount a defense.

By the time the two armies met on September 20, they were about equal in size. Brunswick had 34,000 men and 54 cannons, while Kellermann commanded 36,000 soldiers supported by 40 pieces of artillery. The allies approached within 2,500 yards of the French defenses before they opened up with their cannons. Brunswick anticipated that the inexperienced French would flee in panic at the pounding of the guns. Instead, the French returned fire with their own artillery batteries. Since both sides were firing at near maximum range, neither inflicted serious casualties.

Brunswick attempted to advance his infantry, but the wide-open area separating the two forces proved to be an artillery-killing field, forcing the Prussian marshal to withdraw his infantry before they sustained significant losses. Brunswick and his subordinates faced a difficult situation. The French were no longer running from combat, and they occupied substantial defensive positions supported by accurate cannon fire. Discretion truly being the better part of valor, Brunswick decided that reinstating a foreign king did not justify the possible loss of his army. The Prussians and their allies withdrew from the battlefield and turned toward home.

Losses at the Battle of Valmy totaled only about two hundred Prussians and three hundred Frenchmen. While battle casualties were negligible, the influence of the fight was significant. The French army had proven it would and could defend its revolution. The day after the battle, a newly appointed National Convention officially declared France a republic, and a few months later, the government publicly executed King Louis XVI.

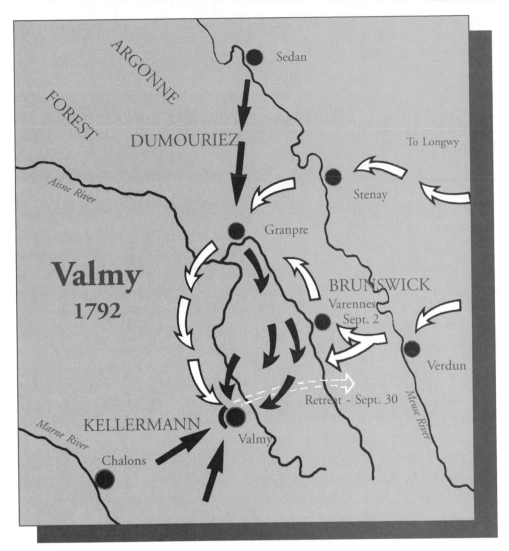

Valmy spawned far more than just the formation of the French Republic. The defense of Valmy began an offensive by the French army that did not cease until Waterloo in 1815 (9). When Corsica declared their independence from the Republic a year later, a young Corsican officer named Napoleon declared his continued loyalty to France. He soon used his artillery and leadership skills to assume the leadership of the military, and ultimately France itself. It eventually took an alliance of most of Europe to stop the general and his national army. While Valmy had been nearly bloodless, its influence would lead to the bloodiest battles and the most costly wars the world had ever seen.

44

MIDWAY

World War II, 1942

The U.S. Navy combined superior intelligence-gathering and aircraft carrier tactics with more than a little luck to defeat a Japanese fleet at the Battle of Midway in 1942. The battle, marking the end of Japanese expansionism in the Pacific, was the first of a long series of defeats that would lead to Japan's eventual surrender to the Allies.

Following their successful surprise attacks on Pearl Harbor (62), the Philippines, and other targets in December 1941, the Japanese had experienced another five months of total success. With little difficulty, they had captured Malaysia, Singapore, the Dutch East Indies, the Philippines, and other islands in the central and western Pacific. Still hungry for further territorial conquests, the Japanese had begun operations early in 1942 to seize bases in Papua New Guinea and the Solomon Islands in order to isolate and neutralize Australia and India.

In April and May, two events took place that caused the Japanese to accelerate their plan to expand eastward. The first factor was the air raid against Tokyo led by Lieutenant Colonel James Doolittle from the U.S. carrier *Hornet* on April 18, 1942. Although the bombers had inflicted little damage, the Japanese high command was extremely embarrassed that they had not prevented an attack on their home islands.

The second event occurred when Japanese and American carrier fleets met in the Coral Sea on May 7–8. Both sides had launched their airplanes to engage each other's fleets in history's first naval battle during which no enemy ships were within gun or visual range. Neither side had been able to claim victory when the two fleets finally parted. Americans had lost the carrier *Lexington*, an oiler, and a destroyer; the carrier *Yorktown* had been seriously damaged. The Japanese had lost a small carrier, a destroyer, and several support vessels; they had sustained damage to another small carrier. However, the most important result of the Battle of the Coral Sea was not total losses, but rather the fact that the U.S. had stopped a Japanese advance for the first time.

To seize more territory in order to better defend their homeland and to expand their Empire, Japanese Admiral Isoroku Yamamoto ordered a diversionary attack against the Alaskan Aleutian Islands while the main attack, composed of four carriers and more than eighty support ships, would capture Midway Island, located about

1,000 miles west of Hawaii. With Midway in their control, the Japanese could defend the sea lanes around their home islands, while also providing a base for more attacks on Hawaii. Ultimately, the Japanese hoped that victory at Midway and destruction of the U.S. fleet would force the Americans to sue for peace and leave all of Asia under the flag of the Rising Sun.

What the Japanese did not know was that American signal operators had broken many of their radio codes, thus revealing their plans. They were also unaware that repair crews at Pearl Harbor, working day and night, had made the *Yorktown* battle-ready once again. The *Yorktown* and supporting vessels, designated Task Force (TF) 17 and commanded by Rear Admiral Frank Jack Fletcher, sailed from Pearl Harbor on May 28. TF 16, led by Rear Admiral Raymond Spruance with the carriers *Enterprise* and *Hornet,* had departed for Midway two days earlier. The two task forces united on June 2, approximately 350 miles northeast of Midway.

On June 3, the Japanese fleet—commanded by the same Admiral Chuichi Nagumo who had led the raid against Pearl Harbor, and composed of the carriers *Akagi, Kaga, Hiryu,* and *Soryu*—came under attack about 600 miles west of Midway by land-based fighters and bombers from the island. Japanese fighters easily shot down the older American planes with no damage to the fleet. On the morning of June 4, Nagumo, still unaware of the proximity of the U.S. carriers, sent half his aircraft to bomb Midway. A U.S. observer plane followed the attackers back to their ships and relayed their exact location to Spruance and Fletcher. Aboard the Japanese carriers, still unaware of the U.S. fleet, the crews began reloading their planes with bombs for a second attack on Midway.

The Americans launched torpedo planes against the enemy vessels, but the Japanese shot them down before they could inflict any damage. A second wave also failed. One U.S. torpedo squadron lost all of its fifteen planes and twenty-nine of its thirty crewmen. Nagumo, finally aware of the presence of U.S. carriers, ordered his airplanes to remove their bombs and reload with torpedoes so he could attack and destroy the American ships.

This change in plans left bombs, torpedoes, and fully fueled airplanes on the decks of the Japanese carriers. Skill, combined with plain luck, allowed American dive-bombers to appear at just the right time. While the few Japanese planes in the air continued to engage low-flying torpedo planes, the dive bombers swept down almost unopposed. The Douglas SBD "Dauntless" dive-bombers delivered their explosives onto the flight decks and down the exposed elevators of the Japanese ships. Three heavy carriers, the *Akagi, Kaga,* and *Soryu,* were on their way to the bottom of the sea in less than five minutes.

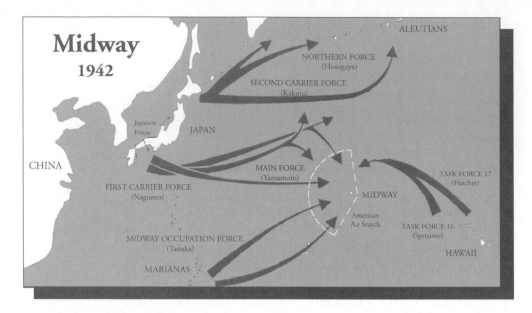

The *Hiryu,* some forty miles away from the main battle, launched its planes and crippled the carrier *Yorktown.* U.S. planes struck the *Hiryu,* which sank on June 5. A Japanese submarine finished off the veteran U.S. carrier on June 6 as its crew still struggled to save their ship.

The Japanese fleet, minus its carriers, turned toward home. Too weakened to pursue, the Americans sank still another heavy cruiser before the Japanese moved out of range.

American losses at the Battle of Midway totaled one carrier, one destroyer, 150 planes, and about 300 men. Japan lost four carriers, leaving only five in their entire navy; 275 airplanes; and more than 4,000 men, including many of their most experienced pilots. More importantly, U.S. shipbuilders were already turning out additional carriers and other vessels, while the Japanese lacked the resources to replace their losses.

Japan never mounted another significant offensive after Midway. Their numbers of men and ships dwindled as the resources of the Allies steadily increased. Soon the Americans were island-hopping across the Pacific, regaining captured territory and securing bases near Japan to begin a massive bombing campaign. The real influence of Midway is that it turned the tide of the war in the Pacific. Before Midway, Japan experienced only victory; after the battle, they met a succession of defeats.

A Japanese victory at Midway definitely would have prolonged the war in the Pacific, but it is unlikely that the U.S. would have sued for peace and left Japan in charge of the Pacific and Asia. The U.S. and its allies had agreed at the beginning of

World War II on a "Europe first" policy, meaning the Americans sent minimum assets to the Pacific while concentrating on first winning the war against Germany. After the Battle of Midway, leaders in the U.S. realized they could defeat the Japanese and still primarily focus their assets against the Germans. Had Midway gone the other way, the U.S. would most likely have diverted assets from the Europe to the Pacific. Midway certainly influenced the eventual unconditional surrender of Japan, but the fact remains that Japan was doomed from the time of their sneak attack on Pearl Harbor.

45

ORLEANS

Hundred Years' War, 1429

The French triumph over the English siege at Orleans in 1429 was the turning point of the Hundred Years' War. It not only united the various French factions into one nation, but it also introduced Joan of Arc as the most influential woman in military history.

From the earliest establishment of their respective kingdoms, France and England clashed. The passage of time elevated their rivalry into hatred, and by the mid-fourteenth century, a series of conflicts had escalated into a war that lasted for more than a century. The intensity of fighting during the Hundred Years' War (1337–1453) ebbed and flowed depending on who was seated on the respective thrones of the two countries. In addition, the spread of the bubonic plague often reduced both armies to a point where they could not continue operations.

The Black Death also increased religious fervor as the plague-racked people sought explanations for the widespread disease. Some Frenchmen blamed God for the plague; many turned to the heavens for salvation while blaming the Jews and the English for their troubles. Regardless, French, Jews, and English suffered equally from the disease.

During the war's early years, the plague kept the invading English army at bay so that the French maintained a slight advantage. That changed when the English and their longbows won decisive victories at Crécy (32) in 1346 and Agincourt (79) in 1415. After his defeat at Agincourt, the French king Charles VI offered his daughter to the English king Henry V in marriage and peace. A short time later, both Henry V and Charles VI died. The English claimed that Henry V's nine-month-old son should inherit both crowns, while France supported Charles's son, Charles VII, as its sovereign.

Charles VII, the dauphin (oldest son), had the birthright but little else, as he was weak both physically and mentally. Nevertheless, the supporters of Charles VII claimed the throne, and the English and French resumed their century-long war. The Duke of Bedford (John of Lancaster), acting as regent for the young English king, dispatched an army of 5,000 commanded by the Earl of Salisbury (Thomas de Montacute) to occupy the French stronghold at Orleans.

On October 23, 1428, Salisbury arrived at Orleans only to discover that his army was too small to encircle the defenses of the entire city. He established a series of strong points along roads and waterways into the town and then futilely pounded the walls with his cannons. Several French relief columns unsuccessfully attempted to reach Orleans while the only setback to the English was the loss of Salisbury to a shell fragment on November 3.

The siege, now under the leadership of the Duke of Suffolk (William de la Pole), continued into the spring of 1429 until Orleans and France itself appeared to be in their last days. Relief came from a most unexpected source.

Joan of Arc, born in 1412 to religious parents in the northeastern French village of Domrémy, began at about age thirteen to hear voices of saints she later identified as Michael, Margaret, and Catherine. Joan apparently did not tell anyone until she was seventeen that she was hearing voices or that they were telling her to free her country. In 1429, she approached Robert de Baudricourt, the captain of a nearby town militia, and convinced him to provide her an escort to see Charles VII.

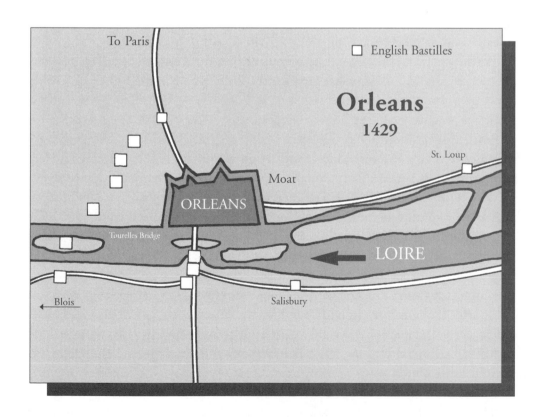

Charles agreed to see the young woman and then had his church leaders interview her. When they supported her claims of voices from the saints, Charles dispatched her to Orleans. Nowhere in the glamorized, and often fictionalized, history of Joan is there any rationale why Baudricourt, Charles, church leaders, or military commanders allowed a peasant girl to take charge of the French army. Yet from the time she entered Orleans through a gap in the English lines on April 29, 1429, French commanders accepted the guidance she passed along from the saints, including a risky offensive to break the siege, the banishment of prostitution, and the cessation of fighting on Sundays.

Joan began her campaign by sending a letter to the English commander requesting they give up the siege. Referring to herself in the third person, Joan wrote, "She is sent by God to reclaim the royal blood, and is fully prepared to make peace, if you will give her satisfaction; that is, you must render justice, and pay back all that you have taken."

The English refused. On May 1, Joan announced that it was time to take forcefully what the English would not yield peacefully. In full armor, she mounted a white horse and led the French against an English strongpoint at Saint Loup. With Joan in the lead, the French destroyed the fort with the loss of only two men.

On May 5, Joan again led her army out of the city's walls to attack the English holding the Tournelles bridge that spanned the Loire River south of Orleans. On the second day of fighting, an arrow struck Joan in the neck, but after ten minutes of prayer, she was back leading her troops. On May 7, the French swept the English from the bridge, killing about 500 men. Two days later, the English evacuated the remainder of their positions around Orleans and withdrew.

Because it was Sunday, Joan waited a day to attack the retreating English. By the time she resumed, word had swept the countryside about Joan herself, bringing thousands of volunteers to her army. On June 18, the French inflicted 4,000 casualties on the English and then won several more small battles over the next weeks. On July 16, Joan escorted Charles to Reims for his official coronation as King of France.

Charles had begun to take credit for Joan's successes even before his coronation. Shortly after the ceremony, he authorized Joan to attack Paris, where she experienced her first defeat. Charles systemically reduced Joan's army to only a few hundred soldiers. She continued to campaign, but without sufficient troops, she could not accomplish the objectives assigned by her voices.

In May, a group of Burgundians, allied with the English, captured the young warrior. The English religious leaders and court system tried her for witchcraft and heresy.

On May 30, 1431, Joan was burned at the stake in Rouen's marketplace. Charles made no effort to rescue her. She was nineteen years old.

The spirit of Joan lived on, drawing the different French factions together into a unified nation that expelled the English and ended the Hundred Years' War. Whether Joan's voices came from Heaven or she suffered a psychological disorder makes little difference with regard to her impact on her country. Before Joan and the Battle of Orleans, France was facing domination by the English. After Joan and Orleans, France became united and inspired to maintain its independence. From the battlements of Orleans sprang a strong nation that eventually led to the age of Napoleon.

Had the French lost at Orleans, it is uncertain if they ever would have emerged as an independent nation. If the English had been victorious, their culture would have prevailed and changed the future of France. With France as a part of England, rather than separate and usually at odds, the French would have also influenced government and culture of Britain and its other possessions.

46

MANILA BAY

Spanish-American War, 1898

The last great naval battle of the nineteenth century was also the first battle between ships crafted entirely from steel. By the end of the fight, the Spanish fleet was at the bottom of Manila Bay, and the Americans were expanding in influence and territory from a regional force to a world and colonial power.

The Battle of Manila Bay actually began half a world away. The United States had long viewed Cuba as a potential state and became increasingly troubled by the Spanish occupation and military presence on the island. At the close of the nineteenth century, several factors merged to thrust the United States into a war on the side of the Cuban rebels who had been fighting against the Spanish for twenty years. American businessmen escalated their demands for protection of their interests and properties in Cuba at the same time that yellow journalism in New York was sensationalizing all news out of Cuba and encouraging military action. President William McKinley attempted diplomatic solutions, but when the mysterious explosion and sinking of the USS *Maine* in Havana harbor cost the lives of 266 men on February 15, 1898, he had to act.

McKinley ordered the U.S. Atlantic Fleet to blockade Cuba; Spain responded by declaring war. The Americans began planning an invasion of the island, but their first combat actions took place at sea rather than on land. The U.S. Army was small, ill-trained, and ill-prepared for battle; however, the U.S. Navy was one of the largest and most powerful in the world. It was prepared and well-positioned for war with Spain.

The U.S. Asiatic Squadron, commanded by Commodore George Dewey, had been stationed in Hong Kong since the previous summer. For more than six months, Dewey had trained the crews of his four cruisers, two gunboats, and one revenue cutter for an attack on the Spanish fleet in the Philippines. Dewey gathered maps of the islands and also interviewed visitors to the Philippines for additional information.

On April 25, the day hostilities were formally declared, Dewey received orders from the Navy Department to "proceed at once to the Philippine Islands. Commence operations…against Spanish fleet. You must capture vessels or destroy."

Dewey, confident that he had sufficient intelligence on the location of the Spanish ships, sailed directly to the islands and into Subic Bay on April 30, only to find the waters empty. He then learned that the fleet under Admiral Patricio Montojo y Pasarón had sailed to Manila.

Assuming the Spanish fleet would be formidable, Dewey planned a dangerous night attack through an entrance to Manila Bay that he could only hope was not mined or otherwise obstructed. The American commander later wrote that word in Hong Kong was that his ships were sailing to certain destruction. He added that wagers were being offered with no one willing to put money on the Americans, even at long odds. Actually, Spanish capabilities were vastly overrated. The Spanish navy, long past its prime, was composed of lightly armed, deteriorating ships with poorly trained, unenthusiastic crews.

Admiral Montojo was well aware of his commands' shortcomings. Some accounts speculate that he moved his ships from Manila Harbor to the nearby Cavite Navy Yard, so the city would not be damaged by an exchange of shellfire. Actually, the Spanish commander anticipated the results of the battle and moved his fleet to the shallow waters of Cavite, where their superstructures would remain above the water line even after sinking. This would allow more of his sailors to survive the anticipated defeat.

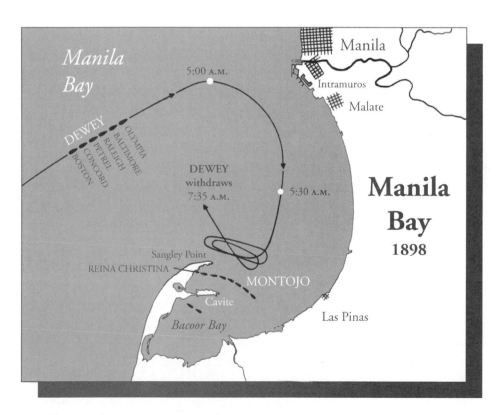

Early on the morning of May 1, Dewey's fleet made its way through the twenty-three-mile approach to Cavite. The Spanish shore batteries either did not detect the ships or feared reprisal if they fired. At 5:40 A.M. Dewey began his attack when he gave his initial order to the captain of his flagship *Olympia*, "You may fire when you are ready, Gridley," a command that became one of the most famous declarations in American naval history.

Dewey made five passes, shelling the Spanish fleet while receiving little return fire. At 7:35 A.M., he withdrew to feed his crews breakfast and to be sure he had sufficient ammunition. At 11:00 A.M., the Americans resumed their attack. The surviving Spanish surrendered at 12:20 P.M.

All of the Spanish ships were destroyed or captured, and 167 men were killed and 214 wounded. Several American ships had been hit by cannon fire, but none were seriously damaged. Six American sailors were slightly wounded. Their only fatality was a victim of heat prostration in an engine room.

A small party of U.S. Marines went ashore to raise the first American flag on Spanish soil, but Dewey had too few men to secure Manila. All he could do was blockade the island until sufficient ground forces arrived more than two months later. A long war would develop between the U.S. Army and the Filipino rebels who desired independence instead of colonialism, but the Americans eventually prevailed.

The U.S. navy and army were equally successful in the Caribbean and in Cuba itself, and by the end of July, the war was over. Spain's formal surrender on December 10 gave the United States control of Cuba and Puerto Rico, which bolstered defenses of its southern borders, along with control of the Philippines, Guam, and the Hawaiian Islands. The U.S. was now a colonial power with naval bases in the Pacific Ocean that allowed them trade access with China and other Asian nations.

The American victory at Manila Bay also showed the world the potential influence of steel ships. Shipyards around the world were soon launching Dreadnought Class battleships that would rule the seas until the advent of power aircraft carriers forty years later.

Dewey's victory at Cavite demonstrated to the world that, through superior ship-building and aggressive commanders, the Americans had joined the ranks of global naval powers. The Battle of Manila Bay simultaneously ended Spanish power in the Caribbean and the Pacific and began the ascension of U.S. prominence as a major participant in world events. The current role of the United States Navy as the most powerful on the seas emerged with Dewey and his victory in the Philippines.

47

KURSK

World War II, 1943

The World War II Battle of Kursk was the largest and most intense clash of armored forces in history, and it directly influenced conventional warfare for the next half-century. It also marked the end of German offensive operations on the Eastern Front and opened the way for operations that eventually would carry the Soviets all the way to Berlin.

After their defeat at Stalingrad in the winter of 1942–43, the Germans were desperate for a victory to regain the advantage against the Soviets, which would allow them to transfer troops from the Eastern Front to counter the anticipated Allied invasion of Italy, and perhaps break the coalition between the East and West. Hitler's generals presented several plans of action, including cessation of major offensives by forces that were already overextended. Hitler disagreed and sided with Field Marshal Wilhelm Keitel who declared, "We must attack on political grounds."

On April 15, 1943, Hitler ordered the plan for an attack against the Kursk salient, a bulge in the lines around the western Russian city that stretched 150 miles from north to south and extended a hundred miles into German-held territory. An attack from both the north and south would cut off the Soviet defenders, who then could be killed or captured. Hitler demanded that the best weapons, ammunition, and commanders be committed to the battle, and in his orders he declared, "Every commander, every private soldier, must be indoctrinated with awareness that the decisive importance of this offensive victory at Kursk will be a beacon for the whole world."

German leaders initially planned to attack in early May, but Hitler waited until sufficient numbers of the latest models of tanks were available. Then the offensive was delayed further by the spring thaw that turned the Russian countryside into a muddy bog, coupled with German losses in North Africa. It was not until July that the Germans were finally prepared to crush the Kursk salient.

The delay may have strengthened the German attack force, but it helped the Russian defenders even more. Marshal Georgi Zhukov had assumed command of the Red Army, and his military sense, combined with intelligence reports, helped him anticipate that Kursk would be the next German target. For three months, he reinforced the defenses with additional tanks and men, and also laid thousands of anti-personnel and anti-tank mines along the most likely approaches. The Russians used civilian labor from nearby villages to bury 2,700 mines per mile of front line before the start of the battle. By July, Zhukov had 1.3 million men, 3,300 tanks, 20,000 artillery pieces, and 2,400 aircraft integrated into his defenses.

Traditionally, an attacking force must outnumber the defenders at least three or four to one to expect victory. At Kursk the Germans had 900,000 men, 2,700 tanks, 10,000 artillery pieces, and 2,000 aircraft—a force significantly smaller than that of the defenders. Because the bulk of their troops were from the elite Waffen SS Divisions, the German commanders believed in the abilities of their own soldiers, and, despite a disastrous German loss at Stalingrad (3), they had little respect for the Russians.

On the night of July 3, German engineers began to clear paths through the minefields. The sappers performed well, but the Russians captured several who revealed the exact attack time. Planes bombed the forward Russian lines on July 4–5, followed by sustained artillery barrages. Ten minutes before the ground attack was to begin, the Russian artillery countered with their own barrages.

The Germans attacked on schedule, though undetected mines and the Russian artillery slowed their progress. The advance in the south made it thirty miles into the salient, but the northern offensive made it only ten miles before it could proceed no farther. On July 12, the Germans regrouped near Prokhorovka for a final attack. Following air and artillery preparation fires, the Germans advanced, only to be surprised by the Russians who came out of their defenses to meet the onslaught. An intense armor battle between 700 German and 850 Russian tanks quickly closed to a few meters, with the main guns on either side firing directly into each other. In several instances, tanks that had exhausted their ammunition supply simply rammed their foes.

By the end of the day, more than half the German tanks were destroyed. About an equal number of Russian tanks were inoperative, but many were salvageable once the Russians could recover them.

The Russians began a general counterattack the following day. By July 17, Hitler realized that his "beacon for the world" had been extinguished and ordered a withdrawal. The Russian counter-offensive quickly secured the nearby town of Orel (now Oryol) and by the end of August had pushed into the Ukraine to Kharkov. German losses at Kursk numbered 100,000 men and ultimately totaled a half-million by the end of the Russian counter-offensive. The Soviets did not announce their losses until after the collapse of the Communist government nearly fifty years later, when they finally admitted that the defense of Kursk and the subsequent offensive cost them 250,000 killed and 600,000 wounded.

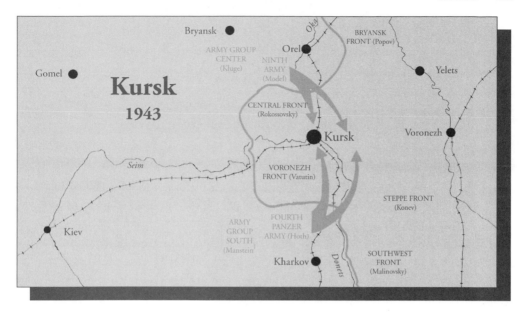

Kursk
1943

Stalingrad had stopped the German advance into the Soviet Union. Kursk put an end to German offensive actions in the Eastern Theater, and the Nazi forces began a long retreat before the advancing Russians that took them all the way into the heartland of Germany and finally to Berlin.

No tank battle of comparable size took place until the Arab-Israeli wars of the 1960s and 1970s, and Operation Desert Storm in the 1990s (86). While these wars rivaled the numbers of participants at Kursk, none came close to matching the intensity and destruction of the Soviet-German battle.

The influence of the Battle of Kursk extended far beyond its impact on World War II, as it became a primary subject of study at armor schools around the world. In the atomic/nuclear age where battlefield mobility meant survival, major post-war armies, including those of the Soviet Union and the United States, focused on armor-heavy forces. Battle plans and weapons development concentrated on future tank battles on the European plains. For fifty years after the Battle of Kursk, the world's most powerful nations prepared to match their tanks in decisive battle. Only after the collapse of the Soviet Union, the increase in terrorism, and the emergence of the United States as the world's only superpower, did the emphasis on tank warfare finally diminish.

48

BLENHEIM

War of the Spanish Succession, 1704

The Battle of Blenheim set the stage for the emergence of the British as the strongest European military force of the period, and began the decline of the French as the world's leading army. Blenheim also eliminated Bavaria as a French ally; retained the Austrian government; influenced the future development of Germany; and established John Churchill, the Duke of Marlborough, as one of history's most influential combat leaders.

During the final decades of the seventeenth century, France, through the military genius of Henri de Turenne and Sébastien de Vauban, had established itself as the most powerful nation in Europe. When King Charles II of Spain died without an heir in 1700, Louis XIV of France claimed the Spanish throne for his grandson. Two years later, Louis refused to recognize the ascension of Anne to the British throne at the time of the death of her father, William II. The English, along with their allies from the Netherlands and Austria, determined that they had to challenge France for the Spanish throne as well as for their own continued independence.

Britain dispatched its most talented commander, John Churchill, the Duke of Marlborough, with an army of 10,000 to the continent, where he joined an allied army of 50,000 in the Netherlands. For the next two years, Churchill struggled to get his Dutch allies to fight when and where he desired. He also found the French army under Marshal François de Neufville, duc de Villeroi, to be more than a worthy opponent in battles along the Rhine River.

In the early summer of 1704, when the combined army of French and Bavarians threatened Vienna and Austria, Churchill left the Dutch to defend the Netherlands and moved his English army south. In five weeks, Churchill marched more than 250 miles to the Danube River, where he united with an Austrian force commanded by Eugene of Savoy.

Churchill deployed his expanded army of 52,000 troops along the small Nebel River that ran south to the Danube. He took command of the center sector and assigned Lord John Cutts responsibility for the left flank that bordered the junction of the two rivers. Eugene took charge of the northern (or right) flank and the army's cavalry. Across the lines was an army of 60,000 French and Bavarian troops under

Count Camille de Tallard, with its right flank anchored at the village of Blenheim near the juncture of the Danube and Nebel rivers.

The French, having larger numbers, superior defensive positions, and a river as an obstacle, felt secure. After a night of meticulously detailed planning, Churchill ordered his men forward on the morning of August 13, 1704. His initial attack plan resembled that of the Greeks at Marathon (28) as he held back his center while his flanks hurried forward against the surprised French and Bavarian flanks.

Churchill, dressed in a red tunic and mounted on a white horse, observed the battle's progress from a hillside while he calmly ate his lunch. He watched both Cutts and Eugene face substantial opposition, but their well-disciplined troops continued the attack. When the French commander committed his reserve forces to bolster the flank defenses, Churchill then led his infantry and cavalry across the Nebel and sliced through the enemy's center. The elite French cavalry charged in an attempt to fill the gap, but the English beat them back. The resolve of the remaining soldiers weakened as they witnessed the retreat of what was considered the best of the French army.

Churchill wheeled his center army toward the Danube, rolling up the flanks of the surviving French force. Many died in place; still others drowned in their attempts to flee across the Danube. Eugene continued his attack on the right flank, scattering or killing the reminder of the army. By the end of the day, Tallard and 14,000 of his soldiers were prisoners. More than 20,000 French and Bavarian soldiers were dead. Allied losses totaled about 12,000.

A few days later, Churchill recorded his own account of the battle. He wrote, "We have cut off great numbers of them, as well in the action as in the retreat, besides upwards of twenty squadrons of the French, which I pushed into the Danube, where we saw the greater part of them perish. Monsieur Tallard, with several of his general officers being taken prisoners at the same time, and in the village of Blenheim, which the enemy had entrenched and fortified, and where they made the greatest opposition, I obliged twenty-six entire battalions, and twelve squadrons of dragoons, to surrender themselves as prisoners at discretion. We took likewise all their tents standing, with their cannon and ammunition, as also a great number of standards, kettle-drums, and colors in the action, so that I reckon the greatest part of Monsieur Tallard's army is taken or destroyed."

Churchill and Eugene emerged from the battle with reputations as the greatest commanders of their generation. Both continued their successes in battles and maintained tremendous popularity and respect among their soldiers and countrymen. Eugene eventually served as a trusted advisor to the Austrian court. Napoleon, Frederick the Great, and others later expressed their admiration for his battle leadership. After several more victories, Churchill returned to England where his countrymen built him a home appropriately named Blenheim Palace.

The effects of the Battle of Blenheim stretched far beyond the lives of its victorious commanders. For the first time in two generations, the French experienced defeat in a significant battle. They were no longer perceived as an invincible force. The allied victory also effectively eliminated Bavaria as a participant in the war and saved Vienna and Austria from French occupation. This meant that the Hapsburgs and Hohenzollerns would rule Bavaria and other territory that ultimately would become parts of Germany rather than France. In England, news of the victory solidified Anne's claim to the throne and stabilized her reign.

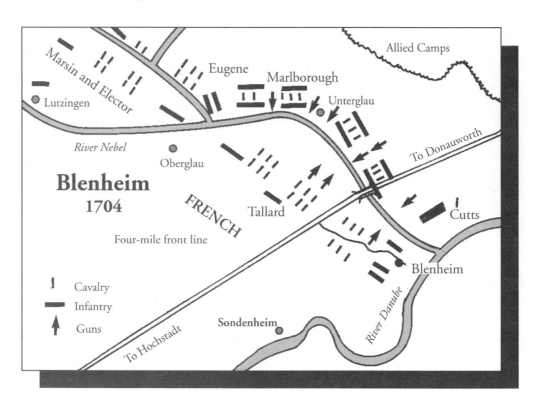

49

VICKSBURG

American Civil War, 1863

The surrender of Vicksburg on July 4, 1863, eliminated the primary obstacle to Union control of the Mississippi River and divided the Confederacy into two sectors. It also established Ulysses S. Grant as a dominating general, a step that led to his eventual command of the Union army that would defeat Robert E. Lee and end the rebellion.

While most of the major battles fought during the first two years of the American Civil War occurred in the East, the Confederate states in the West were vital as sources of manpower and supplies. The Confederates moved these resources along the part of the Mississippi River that they controlled, from northern Tennessee to the Gulf of Mexico. Union commanders recognized the need to sever this rebel transportation line, as well as the advantages of controlling it for their own troop and supply purposes.

To take the river, the Union navy blockaded its Gulf entrance and sent low-draft gunboats northward to open the waterway. At the same time, Union vessels moved southward from Illinois to control the northern part of the vast river. These warships were virtually unopposed on the water, as the South had few boats of their own. However, rebel fortifications armed with heavy cannons dominated high ground along the river, preventing navigation by the Union flotillas. As a result, the Union had to coordinate their naval operations with ground commanders to remove these enemy strongholds.

In February 1862, Union forces under Grant captured Forts Henry and Donelson along the Cumberland River, which carried supplies from the Mississippi to the Tennessee interior. The following April, New Orleans fell to Captain David Farragut. The Union now held both ends of the Mississippi River, but the rebels still controlled its interior by way of various small forts along its banks. However, the strongest river defenses proved to be the guns perched high on the cliffs of Vicksburg, Mississippi. U.S. President Abraham Lincoln declared, "Vicksburg is the key!…The war can never be brought to a close until that key is in our pocket."

Lincoln, always looking for aggressive generals, awarded Grant a promotion to command the Army of Tennessee after his capture of Fort Donelson. Grant moved south but quickly discovered that he faced a formidable foe. Not only did he encounter the powerful guns on the Vicksburg bluff but also Confederate forces equal in size to his own. The Confederate army under General John Pemberton and local rebel units commanded by General Joseph Johnston used Vicksburg as their headquarters.

From January through March 1863, Grant made four unsuccessful attempts to capture, or at least isolate, Vicksburg. These operations even included attempts to dig a canal to bypass the bend in the river below Vicksburg. Grant was further delayed by a Confederate raid that destroyed much of his supply base.

Finally, in April, Grant devised an elaborate plan integrating the land and naval forces that would spread out and weaken the Confederate defenses. On the night of April 16, Admiral David Porter made his way south past the Vicksburg batteries with twelve vessels, losing only one to cannon fire. The following day, a Federal cavalry division under General Benjamin Grierson set out from La Grange, Tennessee, on a sixteen-day raid through central Mississippi toward Baton Rouge, Louisiana. On April 22, a supply flotilla slipped past the Vicksburg guns and joined the Union fleet south of the city. Another diversionary attack took place against Haynes' Bluff northeast of Vicksburg on April 29–30. Confederate units deployed to counter these actions, but in doing so they fragmented their defenses, just as Grant had hoped.

During these operations, Grant moved the bulk of his army by land down the western banks of the Mississippi past Vicksburg to Hard Times, Louisiana. There, under the protection of Porter's gunboats, he transported his army across the river into Mississippi. By May 7, Grant had an army of 41,000 prepared to move against the southern and eastern approaches to Vicksburg. Before advancing to the river city, Grant ensured the security of his rear by first attacking the Confederate forces defending Jackson, Mississippi, fifty miles east of the river, on May 14. He quickly routed the rebels and forced them to retreat.

Grant left a small force in Jackson to destroy captured Confederate supplies while turning the bulk of his army west toward Vicksburg. The rebels briefly held up Grant's advance on May 16 at Champion's Hill, but the Union army reached the outskirts of Vicksburg on the 19th.

Although Pemberton had only had about 30,000 soldiers opposing 70,000, the rebel commander had nine miles of defensive trenches circling the city. On May 17 and again on the 22nd, Grant assaulted the city's defenses only to be beaten back. After the second failed attack, Grant decided to settle into a siege. With Porter's gunboats preventing any resupply by water and his own army blocking land access to the city, Grant planned to starve Vicksburg into submission. To hasten their surrender, he began a sustained artillery bombardment.

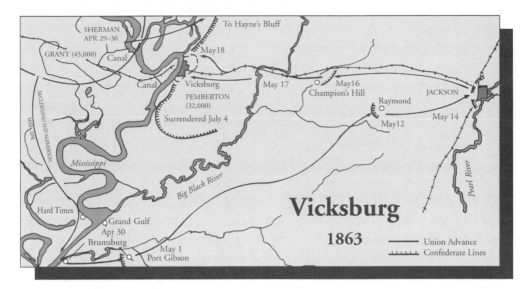

On July 4, the cannon fire, combined with disease and hunger, forced Pemberton to surrender. The other remaining rebels at fortifications on the Mississippi either surrendered or withdrew over the next few days. Grant sent word to Washington that the Mississippi River was now open from the Union states in the North all the way to the Gulf of Mexico. It would remain so for the remainder of the war.

During the final days of Vicksburg, the much more publicized Battle of Gettysburg (17) was concluding with a Union victory. Gettysburg ended Confederate offensive operations in the East while Vicksburg opened the way for the defeat of the rebels in the West and South. While Gettysburg was more influential in that it stopped the rebel threat against the Northern states and Washington, D.C., Vicksburg hastened the end of the war by dividing the Confederacy into Eastern and Western sections and providing the Union a route for men and supplies to push the war into Georgia. While neither Vicksburg nor Gettysburg were as influential as Antietam (5), both were critical in preserving the Union and making it possible for a unified United States to become a world power of unprecedented industrial and military might.

50

PLASSEY

Seven Years' War, 1757

Outnumbered nearly twenty to one, the British used treachery, skill, and luck to defeat the Indian army and their French allies at Plassey in 1757. The victory led to the establishment of India as an English colony, which, in turn, produced much of the wealth that financed the industrial and technological advances that would make Great Britain the most powerful country of its time.

By the middle of the eighteenth century, the Mogul Empire in India, established by Babur in 1526 at the Battle of Panipat (56), had disintegrated into self-appointed nobles controlling various areas and opposing or allying with each other as the circumstances warranted. By allying themselves with French or English trading companies, these local lords became entangled in an even larger dispute when the Seven Years' War broke out in 1756.

Siraj-ud-daula, the ruler of Bengal, took advantage of the British distraction with the war against France, Austria, and Russia to increase his power and financial situation. Believing that the British had a huge amount of money stored at Fort William in Calcutta, Siraj-ud-daula assembled an army of 50,000 and quickly captured the city on June 16, 1756. Most of the British inhabitants escaped aboard ships, but the Indians captured about 150 soldiers, whom they herded into a single fifteen-by-eighteen-foot cell. By morning, only twenty-three had survived what became known as the Black Hole of Calcutta.

The British immediately responded, both to the outrage at Calcutta and to the need to protect their interest in the country, by ordering Robert Clive, who had come to India in 1744 as a clerk for the British East India Company, to assemble an army and move against Siraj-ud-daula. Although he had no military experience prior to his posting to India, Clive had earned a commission when he took charge of several small operations against native insurrections. By 1756, he had advanced in rank to lieutenant colonel.

Clive could assemble a force of only 1,000 British soldiers and 2,000 natives. This was sufficient, however, to retake Calcutta from soldiers Siraj-ud-daula had left to occupy the city, who numbered fewer than 1,000. Negotiations followed between Clive and Siraj-ud-daula, with neither side making any serious attempt to maintain peace. Siraj-ud-daula strengthened his army by adding artillery manned by French gunners, who willingly joined the Indian leaders.

Clive, aware that Siraj-ud-daula's army now numbered 50,000 and was supported by more than fifty French artillery pieces, needed more than just additional military power. He sought allies within Siraj-ud-daula's army and came to terms with Mir Jafar, who commanded the bulk of Siraj-ud-daula's soldiers. Mir Jafar agreed to withhold his command of nearly 45,000 in exchange for the throne of Bengal.

In June 1757, Siraj-ud-daula moved to retake Calcutta and destroy the British army. Preferring offense to defense, Clive advanced from the city to meet his opponent. Near the village of Plassey, ninety miles north of Calcutta, the forces met on June 23.

Clive assembled his 3,000 men and ten cannons in and around a mango grove on a hillside along the rain-swollen Hooghli River. Siraj-ud-daula deployed his army in a semicircle and bombarded the British with his superior French artillery, but the British positions on the back slope of the hill protected them from shot and shell. The British cannons returned fire with better results, but after four hours of bombardment, neither side had gained an advantage.

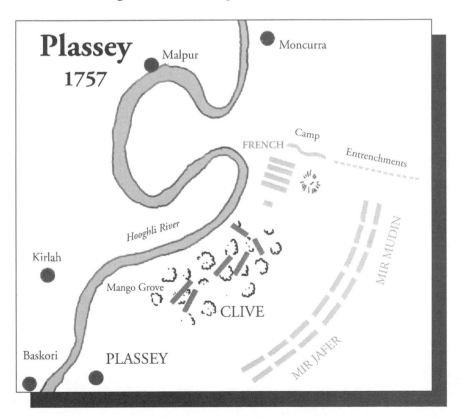

At midday, a monsoon rain swept the battlefield and soaked the powder of both the French artillerymen and the Indian infantry. Clive, however, had kept his power dry by placing it under waterproof tarps. When the rains stopped, Siraj-ud-daula, assuming the British powder was also wet, ordered his infantry to advance. His most loyal general, Mir Mudin Khan, was killed, and many of his followers were mowed down by cannon grape shot and musket fire. Mir Jafar kept his word and withheld his force.

Clive counterattacked to destroy the remainder of Mir Mudin's force and to capture the French artillery. Siraj-ud-daula fled the battlefield, but Mir Jafar's men captured and executed him. Clive, according to a letter he wrote a few weeks later, lost only twenty-two men, and only fifty more were wounded. He estimated that they had killed more than five hundred of Siraj-du-daula's soldiers.

The British allowed Mir Jafar to assume the throne of Bengal, but Clive joined him as the governor of the region. Mir Jafar might have been the royal ruler, but the British controlled the land, the trade, and the people. They collected rents on the land, as well as taxes on everything it produced. As harsh as the British treatment and rule was, it was generally better than that of the previous local nobles. British language, customs, and culture quickly spread across the country.

The defeat of the French artillery at Plassey ended any French territorial and trading claims to India. Britain awarded Clive and his officers riches and titles. The British East India Company did even better. For the next two centuries, India remained Britain's crown jewel as it provided income, natural resources, strategic bases, and personnel to defend and expand the Empire.

The influence of the Battle of Plassey continues in India today, as British customs and language remain prevalent. It is, of course, debatable what might have occurred if Mir Jafar had remained loyal to Siraj-ud-daula and joined the attack on Clive. If he had done so, the British would almost certainly have lost the battle, and maybe the entire country. France, not Britain, might have assumed the role of colonizer, changing many succeeding battles, events, and destinies.

51

CHAERONEA

Macedonian Conquests, 338 B.C.

The Battle of Chaeronea ended the independence of the Greek city-states and united them under the control of Philip II of Macedonia. The battle also paved the way for the League of Corinth and introduced Philip's son, Alexander, who would establish himself as one of history's most powerful and influential military leaders.

During the fifth century B.C., the Greek city-states had advanced the development of the arts, government, and military, but they often fought among themselves over territory and religious sites. During a period of two centuries, Sparta, Athens, and Thebes each had, in turn, become the strongest and most advanced city, but none had gained sufficient control to unite the city-states into a single Greek nation. In 362 B.C., the major and minor city-states agreed to various unions to form two opposing armies that met at the Battle of Mantinea. The fights' only accomplishments were the deaths of several leaders and further division of the city-states. Conflicts of varying magnitude continued over the next several decades.

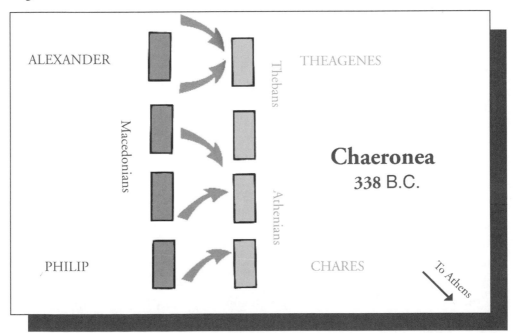

While the Greek city-states fought their internal wars, a leader emerged in the kingdom of Macedonia to the north. Philip II assumed the Macedonian crown in 359 B.C. and immediately began operations to secure the country's borders against barbarian tribes to their north. As a boy, Philip had been held hostage in Thebes, where he had learned to appreciate Greek culture, including their military system. He adopted the Greek phalanx for his army, but modified it to make it even more efficient and lethal. Philip increased the length of the phalanx spears by several feet and doubled the depth of the phalanx formation from eight to sixteen men. This enabled the formation to thrust as well as push against an enemy force. Philip also saw the vulnerability of the phalanx's sides and formed mobile light infantry and cavalry to protect the formation's flanks and to exploit breaches. More importantly, Philip paid his soldiers so that he could maintain a standing army, rather than following the tradition of the time: conscripting civilians as warriors when required.

In 346 B.C., the Macedonians conquered the northern Greek province of Phocis and thereby gained a seat on a mostly ineffectual confederation of city-states. Some Greeks opposed acceptance of the Macedonians; Demosthenes of Athens was particularly vocal in speaking against the outsiders. He failed to gain any great support, however, as several of the city-states believed they should unite against the threat from Persia rather than fight among themselves.

By 339 B.C., Philip felt confident enough to march south against other Greek city-states. His timing was fortuitous, as the city-states had weakened themselves further by fighting each other. In addition, they had spent much of their resources on artistic rather than military advances. Athens had even diverted much of its defense fund to finance social projects.

However, when they learned that Philip was on the march, Athens, Thebes, and several small city-states united against the Macedonian invasion. In early 338 B.C., the Greek allies blocked mountain passes that ran along Philip's route southward. Philip broke through in August and pushed the Greek army onto a plain near Chaeronea. The 38,000 Greeks formed a line about a mile long facing west, with the Thebans on the right flank and the Athenians on the left. Both relied primarily on the phalanx formation interspersed with smaller, elite units to respond to trouble areas. The best known of these units was the Sacred Band or Devoted Brothers in Arms—a unit of 300 Thebans said to base their bond on homosexuality.

Philip deployed his army of 40,000 directly across the plain from the Greeks with himself in command of the right flank and his eighteen-year-old son Alexander leading the left. In the initial assault on September 1, the Athenians stopped Philip's advance while the Macedonian left pushed back the Thebans. After several hours of intense combat, Philip briefly withdrew, either as a result of Greek force or as a ruse. When the Athenians advanced, he turned and counterattacked at the same time Alexander committed his cavalry against the exposed flank. The Athenian army broke ranks and fled, leaving 1,000 dead and 2,000 prisoners behind. On the other flank, the Thebans, including the Sacred Band, fought to the death with few survivors.

Philip, displaying that he was as good a politician as soldier, freed the prisoners and sent Alexander to Athens to negotiate a peace. All that Philip asked of the Greeks was for the city-states to unite under his command to fight their common Persian enemies. The grateful Greeks agreed and soon formed the League of Corinth, which ended the autonomy of the city-states and provided a single Greek government led by Philip.

Philip, and later Alexander, continued the traditions of the city-states in advancing trade and the arts. By fighting together rather than against each other, the city-states helped Macedonia defeat the Persians and expand their empire throughout Asia Minor. Along with the military victories came the Greek culture and way of life, which took root in conquered territory and influenced the entire empire—and later, Rome. Alexander continued to develop tactical and strategic innovations as he introduced changes to warfare that would be the model for combat for years to come, earning him the title of "the Great" as well as a place among history's most influential military leaders. Alexander began his career at his father's side at Chaeronea, and that battle significantly influenced the future of Greece and the all the Western World.

52

TET

Vietnam War, 1968

The Tet Offensive of 1968 is history's most prominent example of a battle where the victors lost and the vanquished won. Despite the fact that the United States and South Vietnamese overwhelmingly defeated the Viet Cong and North Vietnamese, the American press propagandized the coordinated surprise attacks into defeat itself and created a dramatic shift in public opinion. Tet eventually led to the withdrawal of U.S. troops and the loss of Vietnam to the communists.

At the end of World War II, the French re-occupied Vietnam to the dismay of Vietnamese who had fought with the Allies against the Japanese. Veteran Marxist Ho Chi Minh and his principal military leader Vo Nguyen Giap resisted the occupation and, with support from the Soviet Union and Communist China, defeated the French at the Battle of Dien Bien Phu (64) in 1954.

After the French withdrew, the Geneva Accords initially split the country into North Vietnam, with Ho and his Communists in charge, and South Vietnam, with a democratic government. The Accords called for elections to be held to select a single leader for Vietnam. However, the United States and other Western countries, fearing that Ho would win, prevented the elections from taking place.

Knowing that the West would never allow him control of all Vietnam at the ballot box, Ho had plans to militarily take over all of Southeast Asia. As early as 1952, Ho's Communist party published documents that stated, "The ultimate aim of the Vietnamese Communist leadership is to install Communist regimes in the whole of Vietnam, in Laos, and in Cambodia."

The United States began sending advisors to South Vietnam in the mid-fifties, shortly after the French defeat. Following the Gulf of Tonkin Incident in August 1964, the U.S. escalated its role, first by bombing the North and then by deploying conventional troop units to Vietnam the next year. By 1967, a half-million Americans, 60,000 Allied troops, and 700,000 South Vietnamese were battling the Viet Cong (South Vietnamese Communists or VC) and North Vietnamese Army regulars (NVA).

Ho and Giap relied on the same strategy against South Vietnam and the Americans that they had employed successfully against the French. Their efforts revolved around a three-phase plan. In Phase One, the insurgents remained on the

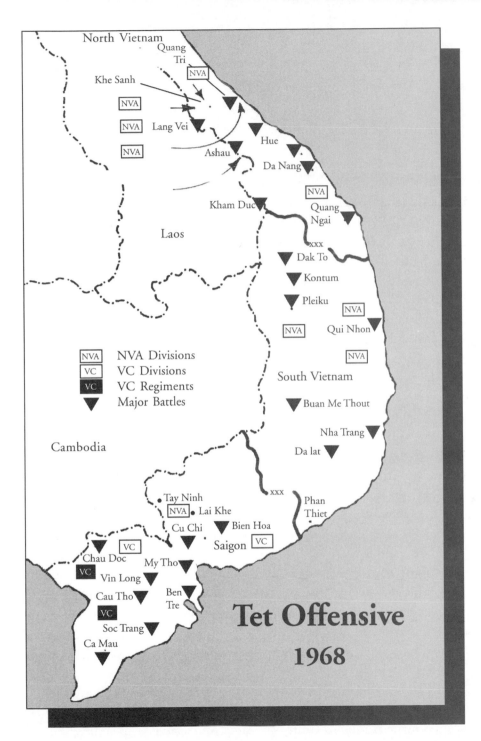

North Vietnam

Quang Tri

Khe Sanh

NVA

NVA   Lang Vei

NVA   Ashau

Hue

Da Nang

Kham Duc

Quang Ngai

NVA

Laos

xxx

Dak To

Kontum

Pleiku

NVA

NVA   Qui Nhon

NVA

South Vietnam

NVA   NVA Divisions
VC   VC Divisions
VC   VC Regiments
▼   Major Battles

Buan Me Thout

Nha Trang

Da lat

Cambodia

Tay Ninh
NVA   Lai Khe
Cu Chi   Bien Hoa
Saigon   VC

xxx   Phan Thiet

Chau Doc
VC   Vin Long
Cau Tho   Ben Tre
VC
Soc Trang
Ca Mau

My Tho

Tet Offensive

1968

defensive while conducting guerrilla and terrorist operations to control as much of the population as possible. In Phase Two, regular military forces formed and attacked isolated government outposts. In Phase Three, large units undertook an offensive to defeat the government force and to establish full control over the civilian population. The concluding step of the final phase was *khoi nghia,* a general uprising of the people to assist in the overthrow of the government.

Throughout the war, the VC and NVA consistently accomplished the first two phases. Communist leaders in Hanoi, while telling their soldiers that victory might take several generations to achieve, nevertheless joined their Viet Cong allies late in 1965 in an attempt to escalate the war into Phase Three with attacks against the newly arrived U.S. First Cavalry Division in the Ia Drang Valley. Although they inflicted heavy casualties on the Americans, the Communists could not sustain a conventional battle. The survivors melted back into the jungle or crossed into Cambodian and Laotian sanctuaries.

For the next two years, the Communists were able to conduct only Phase One and Two operations. Most people in the United States continued to support the war, believing that the democratic South had to be protected from the Communist North and that if Vietnam fell, a domino effect might cause all of Southeast Asia to fall.

After the failure to attain Phase Three in 1965, the Communists replaced many outdated weapons with modern rifles, machine guns, mortars, rockets, and artillery from China and the Soviet Union. By late 1967, Ho and Giap decided that their forces were strong enough once again to escalate to Phase Three. The Communist leaders also thought the people of South Vietnam were ready for *khoi nghia.* Besides, Ho was aware of the swelling American anti-war movement and remarked on several occasions that the war could be won in the newspapers, on the campuses, and in the streets of the United States.

In late 1967, the Communists began infiltrating additional units down the Ho Chi Minh Trail. On January 21, 1968, they attacked the remote firebase at Khe Sanh in the far northwest corner of South Vietnam as a diversion to siphon U.S. and South Vietnamese troops away from more crucial posts. Intelligence leaders remained confident that the rest of the country was secure, believing Khe Sanh to be an isolated incident. South Vietnamese leaders even granted holiday home leave to half their army so they could celebrate the approaching Lunar New Year, or Tet, with their families.

On the night of January 30–31, more than 100,000 Communists attacked Saigon, Hue, Quang Tri, Danang, Kontum, and other major South Vietnamese cities. Of the forty-four provincial capitals, thirty-six came under attack, including ten that the

VC/NVA briefly occupied. A squad of fifteen suicide sappers even breached the outer walls of the U.S. Embassy in Saigon before being killed.

The surprise was complete. The South Vietnamese and Americans, however, rallied quickly to inflict huge numbers of casualties on the enemy. The Communists held out for several weeks in Hue and a few other locations, but by February 24, the attackers were either dead or retreating to their cross-border hideaways. A major failure of the offensive was that there was no *khnoi nghia,* as the people of South Vietnam remained loyal to their government. Some paid a high price for their loyalty. In Hue, the Communists massacred more than 3,000 civilians.

At least 40,000 Communist soldiers died in the Tet Offensive. Most of these were Viet Cong, and their loss so decimated their units that, despite replacements from North Vietnam, they were never again a viable fighting force. The South Vietnamese lost about 2,800, while fewer than a thousand Americans were killed. More than 45,000 civilians died in the crossfire or were murdered by the Communists.

The VC/NVA defeat on the battlefield was complete in the short term, but, in an amazing turn of events, Hanoi moved closer to overall victory. The war-weary Americans watched the battle scenes night after night in their living rooms on their television screens. The psychological impact transformed the Communist defeat on the battlefield into a political victory, especially when Walter Cronkite, America's most trusted newsperson, decided to influence his audience, rather than report the event. On February 27, 1968, from the television studios of CBS News, Cronkite struck the deepest knife-in-the-back to the American military that has ever come from a "friendly" source.

Instead of accurately reporting the facts about the U.S. and South Vietnamese rout of the Communists during Tet, Cronkite delivered an address that Hanoi could not have better scripted when he said, "We have been too often disappointed by the optimism of the American leaders....To say that we are closer to victory today is to believe, in the face of the evidence, the optimists who have been wrong in the past....To say that we are mired in stalemate seems the only realistic, yet unsatisfactory conclusion....it is increasingly clear to this reporter that the only rational way out...will be to negotiate, not as victors, but as an honorable people who lived up to their pledge to defend democracy, and did the best they could."

Following Tet and Cronkite's speech, the American support for the war steadily declined. President Richard Nixon, honoring his campaign promises, began withdrawing U.S. troops in 1969. By 1972, the ground war was in the hands of the South Vietnamese, and Ho once more attempted a Phase Three offensive to take over the country. Again, he failed. This time the South Vietnamese, supported by U.S. air power, destroyed the attacking NVA. Three years later, when South Vietnam no longer had U.S. air support and only a handful of American diplomats and Marine guards remained in Vietnam, Ho's Communists finally achieved victory and united Vietnam under the banner of Communism.

The lasting influence of the Tet Offensive in Vietnam is that, despite a loss on the battlefield, Ho and his followers achieved victory on the TV screens and in the streets of America. U.S. support of the war and of the South Vietnamese steadily eroded after the battle, leaving them unable to resist the continued attacks by the Soviet- and Chinese-supported North Vietnamese.

Tet has arguably been the single greatest influence on U.S. political and military policies. Since Vietnam, the United States has not entered any conflict without a specific mission and without the support of the general population. The overwhelming force buildup and victory in Operation Desert Storm (86) was a direct result of America's "no more Vietnams" policy.

LEPANTO

Holy League-Ottoman War, 1571

The naval battle between the Christians and Ottomans at the mouth of the Gulf of Patras off Lepanto, Greece, ended Turkish domination of the Mediterranean Sea in the sixteenth century and halted more than five centuries of Ottoman expansion. The battle's outcome provided a needed boost to European morale, proving that they could finally stop the spread of the "infidels." The sea battle also was the last major engagement of oar-driven ships.

From the time of Ottoman victories over the Byzantines at Manzikert in 1071 (31), the Crusaders at Hattin in 1187 (81), and the fall of Constantinople in 1453 (41), Muslim Turks had conquered their Christian rivals, expanding their dominance over the Middle East, Asia Minor, and the Mediterranean. Although their land advance was finally blocked at Vienna in 1529 (10), later in the sixteenth century, the Ottoman Turks were looking to expand again into the islands and mainland colonies of the northern Mediterranean.

During this period, the Ottomans benefited from a series of able leaders who united the various Muslim factions into a single force. In Europe, however, Catholics and Protestants spent as much effort fighting each other as opposing the Muslims. France even went so far as to negotiate separate peace treaties with the Ottomans so that it might concentrate its military efforts against its Christian neighbors.

To take advantage of the divided European Christian kingdoms, the Ottoman Turks attacked and occupied the Venetian-held island of Cyprus in 1570. Europe's reaction to the aggression was mixed. Most Christian leaders wanted to retake the island, but they could not agree who should be in charge of the operation. After some debate, Pope Pius V joined with King Philip II of Spain and formed the Holy League to support Venice's efforts to retake Cyprus. The two selected Philip's half-brother, Don John of Austria, as the leader of the expedition.

Don John was a soldier with little naval experience. This, however, was no great determent, as naval warfare of the period closely resembled land combat. Oar-driven galleys usually faced off and rammed each other, and then infantry troops would determine the outcome in hand-to-hand action on the decks.

By the time Spanish, Papal, and Venetian ships assembled in the Italian harbor of Messina in August 1571, the Ottomans had secured all of Cyprus and redeployed their fleet to the Gulf of Patras near Lepanto. Christian and Muslim agents spied on each other's fleets and the opposing leaders had a good idea of the size and composition of their enemy.

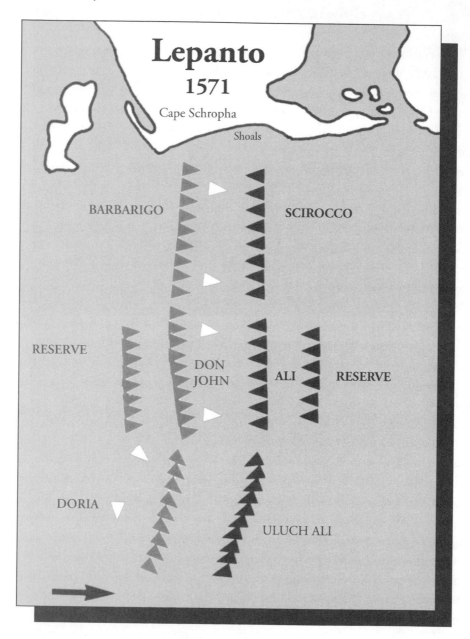

Ali Pasha, the Ottoman commander, had about 250 galleys manned by 88,000 sailors, slaves, and soldiers. Chained slaves, most of whom were Christian captives from previous Ottoman campaigns, provided the galleys' oar-mobility. The real combat power of the Turkish navy was its 16,000 soldiers trained to board and capture enemy vessels.

Don John commanded a slightly larger force of about 300 ships, most of which were also oar-driven galleys that carried soldiers for boarding operations. The Holy League fleet did have an advantage with its six double-sized galleys called galleasses that had crude cannons on their decks capable of firing broadsides. While many of the Christian galleys, as well as the Muslim vessels, had cannons mounted on their bows and sterns, the galleasses possessed far superior firepower. The Christian deck soldiers also had many more muskets than their opponents.

On the morning of October 7, 1571, the two fleets approached each other with their galleys arrayed in lines extending south just off the Lepanto shore. Each commander organized his line into three wings of about an equal number of ships with himself in charge of the middle portion. Both sides displayed huge flags for identification and crew morale. Just prior to the battle, Christian commanders armed their oarsmen and promised freedom to those who were serving criminal sentences. The Muslim commanders did not have that option, as most of their oarsmen were Christian slaves who would turn on their keepers if the opportunity arose.

Don John transferred to a small, swift galley before the battle began and sailed up and down his line, encouraging his force. Their cheers echoed around him as he returned to his flagship and ordered the galleasses to commence firing against the now advancing Turkish line. His cannons stopped the Ottoman center while his flanks sailed forward, effectively breaking the Muslim line. Galleys were soon locked together throughout the Gulf as boarding parties fought with swords, clubs, and pikes. Again the advantage went to the Christians, whose musketeers supported their boarders with shot and shell.

After three assaults, the Christians boarded Ali Pasha's flagship, beheaded the enemy commander, and placed his head on a pike for all to see. Many of the Turkish ships fled.

By afternoon, the Christians had sunk or burned 80 Turkish ships and captured about another 130 along with their crews. Don John lost 17 of his galleys and 7,500 men. By incorporating the captured ships, the Christian fleet was now larger than when the battle began. Crew replacements were also readily available because the victorious Christians freed more than 10,000 slaves.

A single defeat at sea, however, did not end the power and influence of the Ottoman Turks. Their land forces remained in control of their empire and their wealth allowed them quickly to rebuild their fleet. Still, while the Turkish navy was soon back in operation in the Mediterranean, the Turks never regained the power and influence they possessed prior to Lepanto. Europe did not yet rule the sea, but it had gained confidence that it could defeat the Turkish seamen.

In addition to the eventual recovery of the Ottoman navy, other factors decreased the overall influence of Lepanto. Within two years, the Holy League dissolved as its participants negotiated independent treaties with the Muslims and returned to fighting each other. Within a half-century, the former European allies were fighting one another as Catholics and Protestants in what turned into one of history's bloodiest conflicts, the Thirty Years' War.

One lasting influence was the literature written by one of the battle's participants. Miguel de Cervantes, author of *Don Quixote,* served as a young officer aboard a Spanish galley, and his later writings reflect the great battle he witnessed between Christians and Muslims.

The major influence of Lepanto was not in its effect on the Christian-Muslim conflict, but rather how it changed the nature of naval warfare. Sea commanders recognized that large ships armed with multiple cannons had been the deciding factor at Lepanto. Small, oar-driven galleys might be faster for short-range operations, but men alone could not propel heavy cannon-laden warships. Oars gave way to sails. Ships whose cannons could decide a battle's outcome at a distance replaced galleys that delivered boarding parties. Only seventeen years after the Battle of Lepanto, the English navy and Spanish Armada engaged in a battle fought almost entirely with sails and cannons rather than rowers and swords.

54

SARDIS

Persian-Lydian War, 546 B.C.

The Persian victory over the Lydians on the Plain of Thymbra outside Sardis in 546 B.C. opened the way for the formation of the first "world" empire. Through his victory, Cyrus the Great also established himself as one of history's most influential military leaders.

In 612 B.C., Babylon and Media allied with one another to defeat the Assyrians and take control of the region between the Persian Gulf and the Mediterranean Sea. The Babylonians then occupied the southern part of the territory, while the Medians settled in the north along the Caspian Sea, in what is present-day northwestern Iran. Over the next quarter century, the Medians expanded their borders into Asia Minor until they reached lands occupied by the Lydians. In 585 B.C., Media and Lydia peacefully agreed to a border along the Halys River.

Media, however, was at this time experiencing internal struggles that resulted from the excesses of its leaders and religious differences of its people. While most historical "accounts" of this period are more legend than verifiable facts, reliable sources do show that in 558 B.C., a young man named Cyrus, apparently the grandson of the Median king, became the leader of a small Persian district.

In 553 B.C., disgruntled Median military commanders asked Cyrus to lead a rebellion. During a three-year campaign, Cyrus gained control of all of Media and won the support of its citizens because of his fair and just treatment. Media's neighbors, who had been allies with the previous administration, felt threatened by the new ruler. Lydia especially feared Cyrus, and the Lydian leader Croesus began raiding across the Halys River.

Cyrus, aware that he would have to defend what he had taken in battle, assembled an army of about 50,000—estimates range from as low as 20,000 to as high as 200,000—and marched to meet the invaders. The two armies collided late in 547 B.C. near the town of Pteria, where a hard-fought battle ended in a stalemate. Because supplies in the region were exhausted and armies of the period did not fight during the winter months, Croesus withdrew to his capital of Sardis near modern Izmir, Turkey. Along the way, he dismissed many of his Greek mercenary units so he would not have to pay them during the winter months.

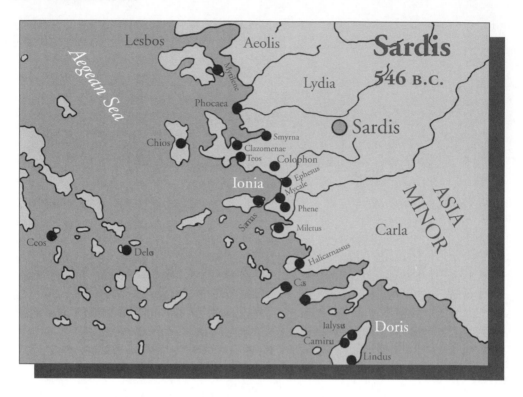

Cyrus, in an innovative move that would lead to his title "the Great," ignored the traditional tactic of not fighting during the winter and, instead of retreating back into Persia, advanced into Lydia. His move was so unorthodox that his army reached the outskirts of Sardis before Croesus was aware of their presence. Despite the surprise, Croesus quickly assembled an army equal to or larger than the Persian force.

In early 546 B.C., the two armies met on the Plain of Thymbra, just outside Sardis. Cyrus formed his army into a huge infantry square with cavalry and chariots slightly to the rear of the flanks. The Lydians approached in long parallel lines of infantry, interspersed with a cavalry that was reputed to be the best in the world. The Lydian horses were not, however, accustomed to the sight and smell of camels, a fact Cyrus knew when he placed his pack camels among his front ranks. As anticipated, the camels spooked the Lydian cavalry, forcing the horsemen to dismount and fight as infantry.

The Persian squares held against the Lydian attack, and then counterattacked with a rain of arrows. Cyrus's cavalry then split the Lydian lines, killed many, and forced the survivors to retreat in disarray back to the walls of Sardis. Cyrus pursued, laid siege to the city, and after two weeks discovered a weak point its defenses where its wall intersected with a cliff. A small Persian force slipped through the gap, stormed Croesus's headquarters, and captured the Lydian leader. The next morning, the city opened its gates and surrendered, its treasures intact. Cyrus again turned enemies into allies through his fair and just treatment of them.

In 539 B.C., Cyrus marched against the rich kingdom of Babylon to his east. Accounts of the campaign vary; some sources say the Babylonians welcomed Cyrus without a fight, while other accounts tell of a two-year resistance. Whatever actually occurred, it is fact that Babylon joined what had by that time become the Persian Empire. As before, in Babylon, Cyrus treated the conquered Babylonians well. His lack of brutality and insistence on religious tolerance again gained allies and support. Of particular note was Cyrus's return of the Jews to their homeland, from where they had been deported by the Babylonians a half century earlier.

Cyrus did not rest after his defeat of the Lydians and Babylonians. What began with his victory at Sardis continued with the expansion of his territory toward India and the inclusion of all of Asia Minor. By the time of his death in about 529 B.C., the Persian Empire had gained the status of the world's first great empire. Not until the passage of two centuries and the arrival of Alexander the Great would there be any substantial threat to the Persian Empire. Even then, parts of the empire that began with Cyrus's victory at Sardis survived for another twelve centuries.

55

POLTAVA

Great Northern War, 1709

For Sweden, the Battle of Poltava ended its reign as the most powerful military force in northern Europe and its claim to having one of the world's strongest armies. For Russia, victory catapulted the backward country to the status of a leading world power for almost three centuries.

During the first quarter of the seventeenth century, Swedish King Gustavus Adolphus had become the most influential military leader of his generation though his innovations in tactics and weapons, as well as his personal leadership. Between 1613 and 1629 he defeated Denmark, Poland, and Russia, thus making Sweden the most powerful country in northern Europe. Despite the death of Gustavus in battle while continuing his expansion into the Rhine Valley in 1632, Sweden remained the principal military power in the region.

After their defeat by Gustavus, Russia languished as a backward nation with little military power. When Peter, soon to be known as the Great, had assumed the Russian throne in 1689, he had begun to modernize all aspects of his country, including its military. A little more than a decade later, Peter had made sufficient progress to join an alliance with Poland and Denmark and declare war against Sweden to reclaim the lands taken by Gustavus three-quarters of century earlier.

Although Gustavus was long dead, the Swedes were more than competently led by Charles XII. The Swedish army stopped the alliance's invasion in April 1700. Charles then counterattacked into Denmark and quickly defeated the Danes. In October, Charles besieged the invading Russians at Narva and in November executed an attack with only 10,000 troops in a driving blizzard to defeat 70,000 of Peter's soldiers. Instead of advancing into Russia, which Charles said "can be beaten at any time," the Swedes marched into Poland and Saxony. By 1705, Charles had defeated all of his enemies in the Baltic except for the remaining Russians.

Over the next two years, Charles built up his depleted forces. Russia sued for a peaceful settlement but Charles decided to launch a land invasion into the Russian heartland from his bases in occupied Poland. Charles invaded Russia early in 1708 and continued his offensive on into the summer, but the Russians refused to engage in a pitched battle, preferring to harass the Swedish army while falling back as they destroyed anything that might be of value or use to the invaders.

Despite one of the most severe winters in history during 1708 and 1709, Charles continued his offensive, refusing to wait out the weather or to delay his advance long enough for reinforcements and supplies to arrive from Riga on the Baltic coast. On October 9, Peter bypassed Charles, attacked the reinforcement column, and captured all of the supplies, including badly needed artillery pieces. Charles ignored the loss and the advice of his generals and ordered his army, now reduced to about 20,000, to advance toward Moscow.

The Russians slowed the Swedish offensive and then stopped it at the town of Poltava located on the bank of the Vorskla River near its juncture with the Dnieper River about eighty-five miles southwest of Kharkov. By May 2, Charles had Poltava in full siege but found it impossible to break through the Russian defenses.

As he continued his assault, Peter assembled the remainder of his army nearby. By the end of July, Peter had 40,000 men and 100 cannons positioned near the Swedish army. Despite the fact that he was low on provisions and gunpowder and had suffered a severe wound in the foot, Charles refused to retreat. As the Russians surrounded his army, Charles, who still had little respect for the fighting abilities of the Russians, ordered an attack. On July 8, the Swedes advanced under withering cannon and musket fire. The Russian lines bent but did not break.

After two hours of close combat, Peter ordered his army forward. They quickly overlapped both of the Swedes' flanks, forcing them to withdraw. Badly outnumbered, Charles continued an orderly resistance until he reached the narrow angle formed by the Vorskla and Dnieper rivers, where the Swedish army began to crumble. Only Charles and a force of about 1,500 escaped. Many of the soldiers he left behind were made prisoners and eventually were used as workers to build St. Petersburg, a tribute to honor the victorious commander, as well as a tribute to the new, modern Russia.

Charles made his way to Turkey, where the traditional Russian enemies provided him sanctuary while he attempted to run his country "in absentia." He eventually made his way back to Sweden and raised another army, and in 1717, he was again on the offensive, this time against Norway, but he was killed in battle the following year. Charles's sister Eleonora succeeded him on the throne and immediately began peace negotiations. In the Treaty of Nystad in 1721, Russia allowed Sweden to maintain its autonomy, but annexed most of the former Swedish Baltic possessions.

Although his final battle took place well over a decade after the Battle of Poltava, the defeat of Charles by Peter signalled the end of Sweden as a military power. In the study of world military history, Poltava is one of the few single battles that ended the control of one long-term power forever and brought a smaller challenger to a superior position that it would maintain for centuries.

Sweden has never regained its military reputation and today is known for its neutrality rather than its military might. Russia replaced Sweden as the dominant power in Northern Europe, and grew in its military influence for nearly three hundred years.

56

PANIPAT

Mogul Afghan Wars, 1526

The invading Mogul army led by Babur defeated the Hindus commanded by Sultan Ibrahim Lodi on the Plains of Panipat on April 21, 1526. Despite facing a much larger army and its supporting herd of elephants, Babur claimed the victory that re-established the Mogul Dynasty, which would rule for the next two centuries the northern two-thirds of what is currently India.

Babur's claim to the region had come from the conquest of his great-grandfather Tamerlane more than a century earlier. Tamerlane, the most influential Central Asian military leader of the Middle Ages, had restored the Mongol Empire of Genghis Khan and extended its borders to the Mediterranean Sea in the west, to India in the south, and to Russia in the north. These conquests, however, had been designed for plunder rather than control of land and people. Once Tamerlane had conquered and looted, he moved on, while the survivors he left behind often rearmed and, with time, became stronger than they had been prior to the Mongol invasion.

Tamerlane's direct descendants had done little to maintain the vast Mongol Empire until the early sixteenth century, when Babur exerted claims over the former empire. Babur, who took the Arabic word Mogul, rather than Mongol, for his people, initially seized control of Kabul in present-day Afghanistan and began operations into Punjab in northwestern India in 1519.

The resident Hindus, ruled by Sultan Ibrahim Lodi, and other natives had opposed the invading Moguls, but they spent as much time fighting each other as the invaders. In 1524, Babur occupied Punjab with little opposition, and over the next two years, he gained support from the local population through peaceful negotiations or by defeating them in battle.

By 1526, Babur expanded southward toward Delhi with an army of about 10,000 Moguls and 5,000 local troops. He learned that Sultan Ibrahim Lodi and his army of 30,000 to 40,000, along with an equal number of camp followers and as many as 1,000 elephants (some accounts say as few as 100–200), were advancing to meet him. Vastly outnumbered, Babur decided to organize a defense rather than risk an attack. On a plain adjacent to the village of Panipat, about 50 miles north of Delhi, he assembled his 700 supply wagons and all others he could gather from the countryside, tying them together to form a barricade with the village of Panipat on their right flank. He left gaps in the wagon-barricade for crude artillery pieces that he had secured from the Turks. These gaps also provided a means for his cavalry to advance or withdraw. Behind the wagons, Babur stationed his archers and musket-armed infantry.

Ibrahim approached the Mogul defenses on April 12, 1526, but did not attack. The two sides faced each other for a week with little or no action. Babur finally became impatient, and on the night of April 19, he attacked with 5,000 men. The Mogul columns became disoriented in the darkness, and by daybreak they were disorganized and exposed in front of the enemy lines. Ibrahim ordered an attack that quickly drove the Moguls back to their wagon defenses.

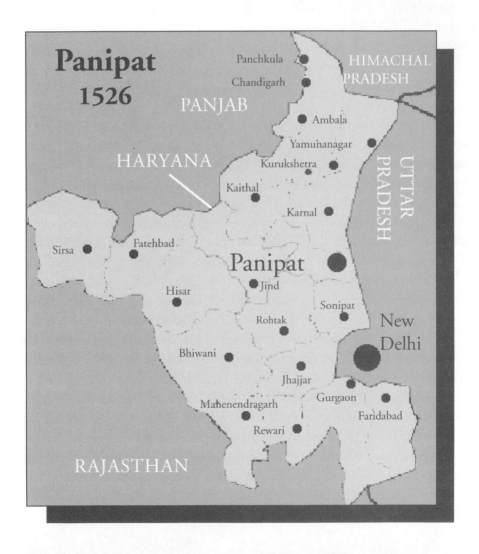

The poor showing by the Moguls convinced Ibrahim that he could successfully attack. On the morning of April 21, he ordered his army forward, directing his main assault against the Mogul right flank where it converged with Panipat. Ibrahim advanced three units abreast with another in front of the center. This movement against the Mogul right flank, however, concentrated the Sultan's army, making it vulnerable to cannon and musket fire, which so unnerved the elephants that they had to be moved to the rear. Although these firearms were crude, they slowed and eventually stopped the attack. Babur then sent his cavalry around both flanks of the attackers until he surrounded Ibrahim and his army. The Sultan and more than 15,000 of his troops soon lay dead on the Plain of Panipat. Many others, including several princes, were captured. They, along with the elephant handlers, swore allegiance to Babur.

The Moguls entered Delhi on April 27, and Babur assumed the throne. Over the next three years, Babur managed to take control of the northern two-thirds of India with only minor opposition. Unlike Tamerlane, the new conqueror treated the residents of the region in a relatively humane manner. But Babur did not hesitate to take whatever he desired. Among the treasures he acquired was the huge Koh-i-Noor diamond, which is believed to have eventually to found its way into the British crown jewels.

After Babur died in 1530, various Indian factions made several attempts to drive the Moguls out of the region. In 1556, Babur's grandson Akbar defeated the Indians at another battle at Panipat and solidified the Mogul Empire. Akbar eventually unified the different factions and the region peacefully prospered for several generations. Jahan, grandson of Akbar, added to India's assets with the construction of the Taj Mahal.

Babur's victory at Panipat in 1526 revitalized the Mogul Empire, which ruled India for more than two centuries. It was not until the 1750s that military and political pressures began to weaken the power of the Moguls. In 1761, in still another battle at Panipat, the Moguls suffered a defeat by an invading Afghan army. Although the Afghans returned home to combat an internal rebellion, all of northwestern India was left in chaos. Mogul King Shah Alam negotiated an agreement with Great Britain, which had become the most powerful nation in Europe after the victory over the Indians and French at Plassey (50) in 1757. The British East India Company soon assumed all but ceremonial powers until the final exit of the Moguls in 1857.

57

SYRACUSE

Peloponnesian War, 413 B.C.

The disastrous two-year siege of Syracuse by the Athenians resulted in the total destruction of the Greek invaders and led to the eventual downfall of Athens. It also produced an environment where Rome and Carthage could rise to dominate the Mediterranean.

As a result of its victories over the Persians in 480 and 479 B.C., Athens had assumed the leadership of the Greek city-states. With the united armies and navies of these city-states, Athens had waged war to expand its empire eastward into Asia Minor while also continuing its long-term rivalry with neighboring Sparta. Athens and Sparta had fought a series of indecisive battles between 460 and 445 B.C. before declaring a truce. In 431 B.C. the two had resumed warfare only to agree to a fifty-year truce in 421 B.C.

The proposed half-century peace agreement lasted only six years before the Athenians decided to attack the city-state of Syracuse on the island of Sicily. Several other city-states on the island were allied with Athens, while the Spartans sided with Syracuse. The Athenian leaders believed that defeating Syracuse would bring the island to their side while also providing a secured base for expansion farther westward.

In the summer of 415 B.C., an Athenian force of about 25,000 soldiers and 15,000 sailors aboard more than 130 warships sailed for Sicily. Three of Athens's most able generals—Alcibiades, Lamachus, and Nicias—commanded the force, but (typical of the period) they were not totally in agreement on who was in charge or how they should proceed with the campaign. Their situation was further complicated by the fact that charges of sacrilege were pending against Alcibiades for destroying statues in Athens during a drunken spree. Also, several Greek colonies on the Italian mainland and in Sicily refused to assist the expedition, preferring to honor the truce with Sparta. Chances for a successful operation eroded further when Alcibiades was recalled to Athens to answer the charges against him. Instead of returning home, he sailed to Sparta, where he revealed Athens's plan of attack.

None of this deterred the Athenian army and navy from their plan. When they landed at Syracuse, they quickly established a beachhead and surrounded the city on land and in the water. Unfortunately, Lamachus fell in an early skirmish, leaving Nicias alone in command. Nicias, who suffered from several medical problems, lacked aggressiveness and decided to besiege the city rather than attack. This allowed the Syracuse army to strengthen their weak defenses, and in the meantime, Spartan reinforcements commanded by Gylippus arrived.

Nicias ordered a double wall be constructed around the city—one to keep the Syracuse army contained, the other to block further reinforcements. Gylippus responded by building counter-walls to intersect the Athenian fortifications. By 414 B.C., he had succeeded in forcing the Athenian invaders onto low ground where malaria and other diseases assisted his efforts to reduce their strength.

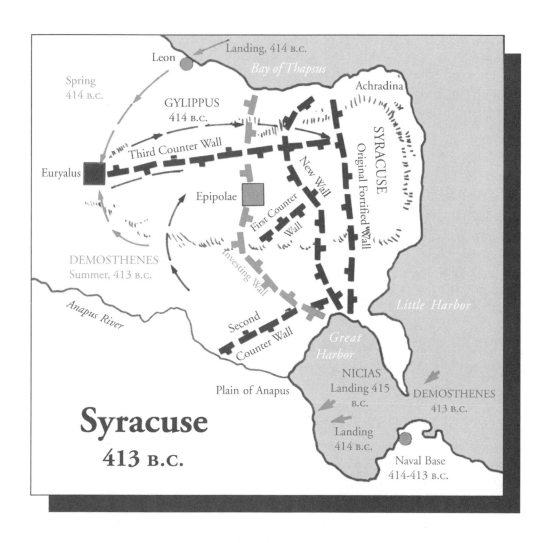

The siege dragged on into 413 B.C., with Nicias unable to gain an advantage. Impatient officials in Athens sent more troops and ships commanded by Demosthenes with orders to attack. Shortly after his arrival, Demosthenes took command of the entire Athenian force and led a night assault to retake the high ground above the city. He was initially successfully, but some of his troops became disoriented in the darkness just as Gylippus counterattacked. Gylippus had taken advantage of the long siege to reinforce the bows of many of his ships so they could act as battering rams against the Athenian fleets. By the time he stopped the final Athenian attack on land, he had also attacked their fleet and gained superiority at sea.

Demosthenes retreated and recommended that the force withdraw back to Athens. Nicias delayed the withdrawal, attempting to come up with a plan for victory. By the time he finally agreed that it was time to go home, Spartan warships had destroyed much of his navy. The only escape route left open was a path through the interior of the island to other Greek colonies.

Gylippus was prepared for the tactic. He attacked the retreating Athenians and divided their column. The Spartans kept the two retreating columns away from water, and by the time they reached the city of Catania, the thirst-crazed Athenians broke ranks to reach a nearby stream. The Spartans attacked with no mercy. In short order, they killed more than 20,000 Athenians and captured 7,000 more, including Nicias and Demosthenes. The captured soldiers were branded and sold into slavery. The two Athenian generals were tortured to death and their naked bodies tossed to the camp dogs.

Unlike many of history's most influential battles, the two-year siege and battle of Syracuse had clear and definable results. Athens's superiority on both land and sea ended with their defeat. Although the city-state survived another ten years before surrendering to Sparta in 404 B.C., it was doomed from the time of its defeat at Syracuse.

The "what ifs" are also more definable from this battle than from most. If the Athenians had assaulted Syracuse immediately upon their arrival rather than laying siege, they likely would have easily defeated the poorly defended city before the arrival of Gylippus and his army. With Syracuse in the hands of Athens, the other city-states of Sicily and mainland Italy would have been forced to join the Athenian alliance. This would have given Athens control of the northern Mediterranean and the bases from which to gain superiority in North Africa. Neither Rome nor Carthage would have had the time nor the means to develop their own empires, which two centuries later competed for control of the region.

Although defeated, the Athenians were not a people to be dominated or ruled by outsiders. The city-states of Greece continued to experience periods of war and peace.

It would take another century before a leader emerged who could bring the Greeks together to reclaim the power they had possessed prior to the battle at Syracuse. Philip of Macedon was able to unite the Greek city-states into one power, which allowed his son Alexander to establish an even greater empire. It is noteworthy, however, that Syracuse still had its influence. After the battle, territory west of Athens never returned to the Greek fold. Alexander the Great built his massive empire in the east rather than the west, for Syracuse had forever stopped Greek expansion in that direction in 413 B.C.

58

BREITENFELD

Thirty Years' War, 1631

The Battle of Breitenfeld and the Protestant victory over the Catholics was the turning point in the Thirty Years' War. In addition to blocking the advance of the Holy Roman Empire, the battle established Sweden as a major European power and introduced a new form of maneuver warfare that dominated future battlefields.

In 1618, a religious revolt in Bohemia had led to a war fought mostly in the German provinces between Europe's Catholic and Protestant countries. The Catholic forces, under the leadership of Johann Tserclaes von Tilly, dominated the first decade of combat. In battle after battle, Tilly proved victorious by deploying his army in an in-depth formation known as a terico, which included pikemen and infantrymen armed with early muskets.

By 1629, Tilly and the Catholics had pushed their borders to the Baltic and appeared ready to take control of all of Europe. Their only remaining obstacle to making the entire continent a Catholic kingdom lay to the north, where King Gustavus Adolphus of Sweden had recently won battles against the Poles, Danes, and Russians. Gustavus, known as the "Lion of the North," favored the Protestant cause, but his real concern was protecting his own borders against the advancing Catholics.

Gustavus built his army around new concepts and technology. He conscripted every young man in Sweden into his army for twenty years but rewarded each with regular pay, land grants, and the first uniforms worn by a large military force. Gustavus also abandoned the in-depth terico and formed his army into smaller, permanent companies that had much greater flexibility in maneuver. These companies were issued modern muskets as well as newly developed paper-wrapped ball-and-powder charges that greatly reduced reloading time. The Swedish army also fielded lighter, more mobile cannons, replacing artillery that was so heavy it could only be moved with great difficulty.

Although Gustavus had the will and the army to meet the Catholics, he found his avenue to them blocked by Saxony. The Saxons, although Protestant, were reluctant to go against Tilly and his Catholic army. It was not until the Catholics looted and killed more than 25,000 inhabitants of Magdeburg on the Elbe River sixty miles northeast of Leipzig in May 1631 that the Saxons finally agreed to ally with Sweden.

The Swedes and Saxons marched toward Leipzig, which fell to Tilly on September 15. A day later, the two armies met just north of Leipzig near the village of Breitenfeld. The 45,000-man Protestant force outnumbered the Catholic army of 36,000 but Gustavus had little faith in the fighting abilities of the 18,000 Saxons.

Tilly deployed his army in a two-mile line with his tericos in the center flanked on each side by his cavalry. Gustavus assembled his army of mobile units in the center on a ridge across a low marsh that separated the two armies. On the right flank he interspersed infantry with cavalry. The Saxons secured his left flank, but Gustavus oriented his center and reserve so they could quickly support the Saxons if they gave way.

Early on the morning of September 17, the battle began with an artillery duel. The Swedish guns did the most damage with their superior accuracy against the tight Catholic infantry formations. Tilly then attacked with his cavalry against both Protestant flanks. On his left, the Swedish infantry, the first in warfare trained to fire in volley rather that individually, stopped the horsemen. The Catholic attack against the Saxons, however, was much more successful. After very little resistance, the Saxons turned and fled; their leader rode fifteen miles before stopping his exhausted horse to check on his army.

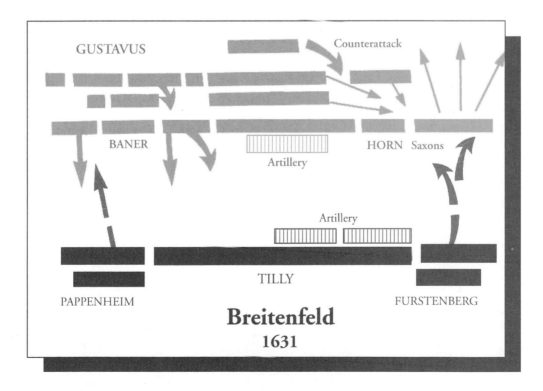

Breitenfeld
1631

Gustavus, anticipating the lack of Saxon resolve, committed his cavalry reserve to fill the breach. Meanwhile, his musketeers and artillery continued to pour shot into the attacking Catholics. Gustavus then personally led his cavalry in a flanking attack that captured Tilly's artillery. Swedish gunners soon were firing into the Catholic rear as their artillery and infantry continued to shred the Catholic front.

By 6:00 P.M., Tilly, wounded three times, withdrew what was left of his army. The Swedes followed, killing or capturing the stragglers. By nightfall, more than 7,000 Catholics lay dead on the battlefield or along the route of withdrawal. All of Tilly's cannons were in the hands of the Swedes, along with their supply trains and 6,000 captives. Many of these prisoners were mercenaries and quickly agreed to join Gustavus against their former employer. These new recruits more than replaced the 2,000 Swedish casualties.

Gustavus's victory at Breitenfeld united Protestant resistance in Europe and led to their victory at Lutzen a year later. The war was far from over as it spread from Germany westward into France, but the Battle of Breitenfeld stopped the Catholic movement northward and elevated Sweden as a European power.

More importantly, Breitenfeld established Gustavus as the "Father of Modern Warfare." Armies all across Europe soon copied his innovations in recruitment, uniforms, weapons, and fighting formations. After Breitenfeld, maneuver rather than mass dominated battlefields.

59

METAURUS RIVER

Second Punic War, 207 B.C.

The Battle of the Metaurus River in 207 B.C. resulted in the first major Roman victory over the Carthaginian invaders. The win then led the Romans to victory in the Second Punic War, control of Spain, and ultimately their destruction of Carthage. This defeat of Carthage gave Rome access to military recruits and other resources that enabled them to dominate the Mediterranean for the next six centuries.

By the mid-third century B.C., Rome and Carthage had advanced to become the two most powerful military forces in the Mediterranean. Each side recognized the other's power, and relations remained fairly amiable as the two conquered more and more territory. It was not until 264 B.C. that the two empires clashed over control of Messina, beginning the First Punic War. After more than a decade of fighting, Rome finally gained the upper hand but not a clear victory. The weary Carthaginians agreed to give up some of their claims, including parts of Spain, and pay reparations to gain an uneasy peace.

Over the next two decades, Rome furthered its power by defeating the Gauls and the Illyrians. Meanwhile, in Spain, a young Carthaginian named Hannibal Barca had assumed command of the army in 221 B.C. Within two years, he had taken control of much of the peninsula. Rome demanded that Carthage turn Hannibal over for trial and cease its military operations. When Carthage refused, Rome declared war, beginning the Second Punic War.

Hannibal had gained his early military experience as he accompanied his father to Spain during the First Punic War. Supposedly at the end of the unsuccessful campaign, Hannibal swore to his father an eternal hatred of Rome and promised to dedicate his life to fighting the Empire.

Hannibal knew that his best chance of success lay not in fighting for Spain but in taking the war directly to Rome. In September 218 B.C., he set out with an army of 50,000 men and about 40 elephants to cross the Alps. Despite heavy loses of men and animals to weather and hostile mountain tribesmen, Hannibal succeeded in his epic fifteen-day trek. He then defeated the Romans in northern Italy, and for the next ten years, he was able to maneuver at will throughout most of the Italian peninsula as he defeated whatever Roman army opposed him.

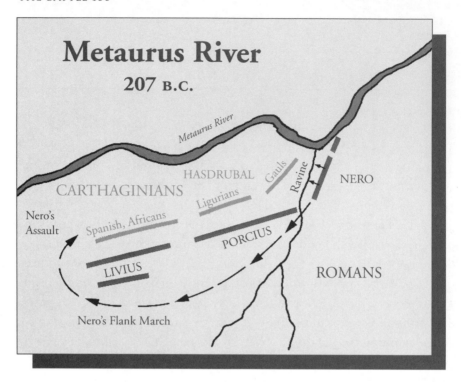

Metaurus River

207 B.C.

Metaurus River

CARTHAGINIANS

HASDRUBAL

Gauls

Ravine

NERO

Ligurians

Nero's
Assault

Spanish, Africans

PORCIUS

ROMANS

LIVIUS

Nero's Flank March

During the decade of fighting, Hannibal recruited some replacements from defeated armies, and others joined him from Spain and Carthage. Despite these reinforcements, Hannibal was never able to muster sufficient forces to attack Rome itself. Finally in 208 B.C., Hannibal sent for his brother Hasdrubal, commander of Carthage's army in Spain, to join him in Italy for a final offensive.

Hasdrubal evaded the Roman army in northern Spain and crossed into Gaul, where he spent the winter adding to and training his army. In the spring of 207 B.C., Hasdrubal crossed the Alps, probably along the same route used by his brother many years before, and marched to the eastern side of the Italian peninsula before turning south down the Adriatic coast. Upon learning of his brother's arrival in Italy, Hannibal started marching north to unite the two armies.

Roman leaders certainly understood the danger of two Carthaginian armies on their soil. For more than a decade, they had been unable to defeat Hannibal and had barely been able to keep him out of Rome. If the armies of the two brothers united, Rome and the Empire would be in grave danger. In response, the Roman senate dispatched two consuls to keep the Carthaginian armies apart. Marcus Livius Salinator rushed northward to intercept Hasdrubal while Gaius Claudius Nero moved south to block Hannibal's march from his base in Lucania.

The two Carthaginian armies were about two hundred miles apart before the Roman armies could maneuver between them. Hasdrubal, attempting to coordinate a meeting with his brother's army, dispatched a courier with his plan. Unfortunately for the Carthaginians, Nero's troops captured the messenger before he could reach Hannibal. Nero exploited the information by rearranging his lines and withdrawing 7,000 of his best infantrymen and cavalrymen to reinforce Salinator.

Hasdrubal recognized that the reinforced northern Roman army had gained the advantage, and he began a withdrawal. However, before he could cross the Metaurus River, the Romans caught up with him, forcing a battle. Both sides arrayed their units in three segments facing each other. The Romans attacked against the center, and although they were outnumbered, the Carthaginians held firm. They were so involved in the fight, however, that they did not notice Nero again withdraw his elite group of 7,000 and swing around to attack Hasdrubal's rear. The invaders were unable to adjust their defenses, allowing the Romans to slash through their flank and kill at least 10,000 with the loss of only 2,000 of their own. Among the dead was Hasdrubal, along with most of his war elephants.

Before the dust of the battle cleared, Nero again led his army on a forced march back to the south and resumed his position opposite Hannibal before the Carthaginian even knew he had been absent. Hannibal first learned of Nero's victory and his brother's defeat when Hasdrubal's head was tossed across the lines into his camp.

The Battle of the Metaurus River was Rome's first significant defeat of Hannibal. Shortly after the destruction of Hasdrubal's army, the Romans defeated the remaining Carthaginian troops in Spain and took control of the entire peninsula. With the loss of his brother's army and Spain, Hannibal had no choice but to remain in Italy for another four years to keep the Roman army occupied so it could not invade Carthage. Hannibal, however, did not win another significant battle and finally withdrew to North Africa, where the Romans successfully concluded the Second Punic War at Zama in 202 B.C. (11)

Despite defeats at the Metaurus River, Spain, and Zama, Carthage managed to survive, and a half-century later once again rose against Rome. This time the Romans gave no quarter as they destroyed the city and killed or enslaved its inhabitants.

If the fight on the Metaurus had gone differently, or if Hasdrubal had been able to join his brother without a battle, it is conceivable that the joint Carthaginian army could have conquered Rome itself. Carthage and North African culture would have then dominated Italy, Spain, and the adjoining regions. Instead, the victory allowed the Romans the complete settlement of Spain and provided manpower from areas previously held by Carthage. The Roman army, with the advantages and confidence gained at the Metaurus River, soon expanded Rome's borders to form the greatest empire of its age.

60

HAMPTON ROADS

American Civil War, 1862

The battle between the USS *Monitor* and the CSS *Virginia* on the waters off Hampton Roads, Virginia, in March 1862 ended in a military draw, giving neither the United States nor the Confederacy a clear victory. The battle was ultimately not so much about rebellion or blockades as it was about the future of naval combat.

From the beginning of naval history, wood had dominated the construction of military and commercial vessels because of its buoyancy and flexibility. Even when small, oar-driven galleys gave way to large, sailing man-of-wars with multiple gun decks, wood remained the material of choice for shipbuilding. However, steel shot and iron shells easily penetrated wooden ships, either sinking them or setting them afire. Shipbuilders and sea captains attempted to make their vessels less vulnerable by using the hardest of woods in multiple layers and placing barriers—cloth, cotton, or iron sheeting—on their most vulnerable areas. While these efforts somewhat "hardened" the sides of their ships, they also restricted their maneuverability and created problems that threatened to capsize the vessels.

Yi Sun-Shin, a Korean admiral, was the first to reinforce his boats with iron. In 1592 Yi covered several of his hundred-foot long vessels with iron studs intended to reinforce their effectiveness as rams. Yi sank several Japanese ships in the Yellow Sea with his "turtle ships" before being fatally wounded. Even though Yi became a Korean national hero, his idea for iron-studded boats was soon forgotten. Other experiments over the years proved that it was impractical to cover ships with iron plating, because the ships then lost buoyancy and maneuverability.

The invention of the steam engine early in the nineteenth century provided both a new means of propulsion for water vessels and, ultimately, a new twist on naval warfare. While these steam-engine vessels with side or stern wheels were effective for commercial use, they were too vulnerable for military operations. One well-aimed shot could completely disable an entire ship. The events that eventually paved the way for the importance of the steam engine in warfare were the invention of internal propellers, which were protected from cannon fire below the water line, and the rebellion by the unindustrialized Confederacy against the United States.

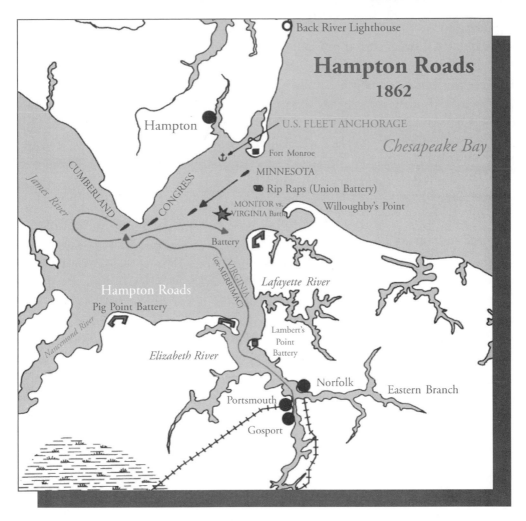

Back River Lighthouse

Hampton Roads
1862

Chesapeake Bay

Hampton

U.S. FLEET ANCHORAGE

Fort Monroe

MINNESOTA

Rip Raps (Union Battery)

MONITOR vs.
VIRGINIA Battle

Willoughby's Point

James River

CUMBERLAND

CONGRESS

Battery

Hampton Roads

Lafayette River

Pig Point Battery

VIRGINIA (ex-MERRIMAC)

Nansemond River

Lambert's
Point
Battery

Elizabeth River

Norfolk

Eastern Branch

Portsmouth

Gosport

At the beginning of the Civil War in the spring of 1861, Confederate successes forced the U.S. Navy to abandon the Norfolk Naval Yard in Virginia. Several ships in the yard for maintenance were set afire rather than be left to fall into rebel hands. These included the USS *Merrimack*, a wooden screw steamer commissioned in 1856. The ship burned to the waterline, but the Confederates raised the wreck, reworked the steam engines, and added four inches of wrought iron bars to its wooden deck and sides. The deck slanted upward from the waterline high enough only for the casement of six nine-inch smoothbore cannons and four six- or seven-inch rifled guns. When launched, the 263-foot ironclad had a draught of 22 feet, complete with a four-foot cast iron ramming prowl. Its two aged six hundred horsepower steam engines could propel the vessel at a top speed of only four knots, and it took the heavy ship, which looked like "a floating barn roof," a full half-hour to turn completely around.

During its reconstruction, the *Merrimack* became known as the *Merrimac*. However, its official name when launched on March 5, 1862 was the CSS *Virginia*.

From the time they first heard about the reconstruction, U.S. Navy leaders feared the damage an ironclad could do to their wooden-ship blockade. Instead of converting wooden ships into ironclads, the Union adopted a design by Swedish inventor John Ericsson for a 172-foot, flat-deck vessel with a 140-ton revolving gun turret containing two 11-inch smoothbore cannons, a design that earned the description of "a cheese box on a raft."

The keel for the USS *Monitor* was laid on October 25, 1861, and she was launched in an amazingly short time of just over a hundred days on January 30, 1862. Despite its strange appearance, the ship, with its eight inches of iron plates on the turret and four and a half inches on its sides and decks, was fast and maneuverable. Although it had only two guns, the independent turret allowed them to reorient quickly without turning the boat itself.

On the morning of March 8, the CSS *Virginia* sailed into the Hampton Roads waterway and attacked the Union blockade. The rebel ironclad rammed and sank the thirty-gun USS *Cumberland* and then forced the fifty-gun USS *Congress* aground. Late in the day, the *Virginia* also ran the USS *Minnesota* aground, but the outgoing tide forced the rebel ironclad to withdraw to deeper waters for the night.

At the dawn of March 9, the *Virginia* moved toward the *Minnesota* with intentions of finishing off the sailing ship. However, between the *Virginia* and the enemy ship, the Confederate sailors found the *Monitor*, which had arrived from New York during the night. At 9:00 A.M., the two ironclads opened fire. During a two-hour battle, the *Monitor* proved more maneuverable, but neither side could damage the other, as their cannonballs bounced harmlessly off the iron plates.

After two hours, the Union boat briefly withdrew to resupply its ammunition but returned to the fight at 11:30 A.M. The *Virginia* now concentrated on the small pilothouse near the bow of the Union ironclad and managed to wound its captain, Lieutenant John L. Worden, with a shot that exploded through his observation hole. The blinded Worden withdrew his ship, and a short time later the *Virginia* returned to its Norfolk port.

While more than 400 Union and 20 Confederate seamen were killed or wounded during the battle on March 8–9, not a single sailor died in the direct clash between the *Monitor* and *Virginia*. While the battle between the ironclads had proven indecisive, the *Virginia* had failed to break the blockade. It remained in port until May 9, when advancing Union ground forces captured Norfolk. The crew of the *Virginia* scuttled the boat rather than allow its capture. The *Monitor* later attempted to sail to a new base but sank in a gale off Cape Hatteras, North Carolina, on December 31, 1862.

Even if the *Virginia* had defeated the *Monitor*, it is doubtful that it would have seriously influenced the outcome of the war. The Confederacy lacked the industry to launch additional ironclads, and the top-heavy, slow-moving *Virginia* would have likely been ineffective outside the inland waterways. With no threat of additional rebel ironclads, the Union placed their resources in other areas to win the war rather than build additional ships.

The real influence of the Battle of Hampton Roads lay not in the fight itself or even in the Civil War overall, but in its effect on the future of ship design. Even though the Union Navy was already successfully placing light armor on the sides of their small steamers on the Mississippi River, and England and France were experimenting with similar armament, it was not until the Battle of Hampton Roads that the world realized the full effect of ironclads. The success of the steam-powered *Virginia* against the sailing ships *Cumberland* and *Congress* on March 8 forever established that wood could not endure against iron. The battle between the *Monitor* and *Virginia* the following day showed that only steel could stand against steel.

Within weeks of the battle, every navy of note in the world began to consider converting to ironclads. Soon sails flew only above pleasure boats and isolated commercial vessels as steel-hulled ships ruled future sea battles. If need had not resulted in the first battle of ironclads at Hampton Roads, some other war would have demonstrated the new technology within a few years or decades. Regardless, the first fight of iron ships occurred at Hampton Roads, elevating that minor battle to one of history's most influential.

61

PYDNA

Third Macedonian War, 168 B.C.

The Roman victory at Pydna in 168 B.C. brought a final end to the empire of Alexander the Great. In addition to establishing Rome as the primary power in the Mediterranean and Near East, the battle proved the superiority of the more maneuverable Roman legions armed with the short sword over the Macedonian phalanx equipped with spears.

In 338 B.C., the Macedonians under King Philip II gained control of the Greek city-states with their victory at Chaeronea (51). Philip's son Alexander participated in the battle, and he assumed command of the Macedonian-Greek army two years later when his father was assassinated. Over the next decade, Alexander earned the title of "the Great" when he defeated Persia and spread his empire eastward.

During this time Alexander had perfected a tactical formation that his father had developed called the phalanx, a tight group of soldiers armed with twelve- to fourteen-foot-long pikes known as sarissas. Supporting the sarissas units were highly mobile light infantry and cavalry troops who exploited the enemy flanks or breaches of their lines.

Alexander's phalanxes achieved victory after victory and provided the avenues for the spread of Greek civilization and culture throughout the Near East. When Alexander died in 323 B.C. at the age of thirty-three, the Macedonian-Greek army remained strong, and their culture continued to greatly influence the region, but the heirless empire began to erode.

While Greece waned, other empires arose. Rome on the Italian peninsula and Carthage in North Africa began to vie for power. A hundred years after the death of Alexander, the Macedonians, led by King Philip V, sided against Rome and provided aid to Hannibal and his Carthaginians in 215–205 B.C. At the end of the war, many of the Greek city-states signed separate peace agreements with Rome, and no significant battle took place between the Macedonians and Romans. Rome finally defeated the Carthaginians at Zama in 202 B.C. (11)

A second conflict between Macedonia and Rome began in 200 B.C., when Philip allied with Syria against Rome. The Roman army marched into Greece and soundly defeated Philip's army at Cynoscephalae in 197 B.C. Following his loss, Philip had to give up his goal of uniting the Greek states, and for a while he supported Rome in their renewed war with Carthage.

Philip died in 179 B.C., leaving the Macedonian throne to his son Perseus. When Perseus forged alliances to again unite the Greek states, the Romans saw the actions as a threat to their own claims in the region. In 171 B.C., the two kingdoms began fighting what became known as the Third Macedonian War.

Shortly after the conflict began, Perseus repulsed a Roman invasion at Larissa on the east coast of Adriatic, but he did not exploit his advantage. Perseus unsuccessfully attempted to gain allies by treaty and cash payment to strengthen his army, but the delay only allowed the Romans to become stronger. In 168 B.C., Rome placed Lucius Aemilius Paulus in command of an expedition against Macedonia. Much debate occurred in Rome regarding the size of Paulus's army and how he should conduct his campaign. Paulus finally announced that anyone wanting to accompany his army could do so; others should stand aside and be quiet.

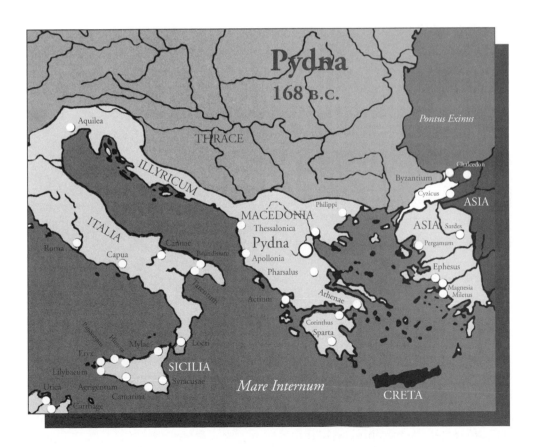

In early summer of 168 B.C., Paulus arrived in Macedonia from the Gulf of Salonika with about 25,000 men. These soldiers were organized into four legions armed with shields and short, double-edged swords. Each legion, thoroughly trained, had the ability to break into smaller groups known as cohorts or maniples. These much more maneuverable legions had proven successful in defeating the Macedonian phalanx at Cynoscephalae thirty years earlier, but Perseus had done nothing since then to modernize his army. The Macedonian leader felt that if the phalanx had been good enough for Alexander the Great, it would be sufficient for him to achieve victory.

Perseus had the advantage of numbers with his army of 40,000 infantry and 4,000 cavalry. Paulus was aware of his enemy's numerical superiority and conducted several flanking maneuvers and a move against the Macedonian supply lines in order to force the Macedonians to move to a location that favored a Roman attack. The Romans finally forced Perseus to move toward Pydna near the Leucus River, where the Macedonians took up a position on a plain facing the Roman legions, who were situated on low hills to their west.

On the afternoon of June 22, 168 B.C., the larger Macedonian phalanxes advanced against the Roman legions. Initially, the Macedonians experienced success as they pushed back the Romans. However, when the plain gave way to hills and gullies, the phalanxes became disorganized. The more maneuverable legions broke into small groups and advanced within sword range, which negated the strength of the Macedonian formation and their long spears.

When the phalanxes came apart, the Roman swordsmen slaughtered the enemy. By the end of the day, more than 20,000 Macedonians lay dead on the field, and another 10,000 were captured as prisoners. Fewer than a hundred Romans were killed in the fight and only 400 were wounded. Perseus briefly escaped with his cavalry, but the Romans captured him and sent him to Italy, where he eventually died in captivity. Paulus took control of Macedonia and the city-states, where he jailed or executed Greek leaders, even those who had previously supported Rome. Except for a brief, unsuccessful revolt in 149–148 B.C., the Greeks never again challenged Rome.

With their victories at Pydna over the Greeks and at Zama over Carthage, Rome was now the only significant military power in the Near East. The Battle of Pydna ended the last vestiges of the empire of Alexander the Great. It did not, however, conclude the influence of the Greeks. While Rome dominated the region for future centuries, the Romans continued to adopt elements of Greek culture, engineering, and philosophy in their daily lives. Pydna elevated Rome to the pinnacle of power, but the Roman victory also allowed the winners to benefit from Greek knowledge and capabilities to make their empire even greater.

62

PEARL HARBOR

World War II, 1941

On December 7, 1941, the Japanese navy launched an air attack against the United States' Pacific Fleet at anchor in Hawaii's Pearl Harbor. In less than two hours, one-half of the major U.S. ships in the harbor lay on the bottom. A day later, the United States declared war on Japan.

Japan had continued to expand its power in the Pacific after defeating the Russians in the Battle of Tsushima (34) in 1905, but a critical lack of raw material in the island nation forced them to import resources, especially oil. In search of more natural resources, the Japanese had occupied Manchuria and much of China by 1937. Then they joined the Axis allegiance with Germany and Italy in 1940 to access even more materials. When France fell to the Germans, the Japanese took over their colony in Indochina with little opposition.

Despite these gains, Japan still lacked sufficient oil resources to reach its goals of expansion and began operations to secure the petroleum fields of the East Indies. The United States had mostly ignored the surge of Japanese expansionism as it dealt with its own economic depression and general post–World War I preference for isolationism. Finally in late 1940, the U.S., a principal exporter of petroleum to Japan, placed an embargo on the shipment of oil and scrap iron and demanded that the Japanese withdraw from China and cease further offensive military operations.

Negotiations continued while both sides prepared for war. The U.S. relocated its Pacific Fleet from West Coast ports to the waters around the Hawaiian islands. A series of naval commanders argued against the move, citing Pearl Harbor as too restrictive and difficult to defend. Officials in Washington, D.C., disagreed, doubting that the Japanese had the will to or the means of attacking that far east. Most Americans believed that if the Japanese mounted an attack at all, it would be against the Mariana Islands or the Philippines.

In Japan, most of the civilian and military leaders were convinced that the United States presented the only viable resistance to their objective of conquering all of Eastern Asia. They believed that if they attacked and destroyed the U.S. Pacific Fleet, the isolationist Americans would sue for peace and leave Japan unopposed to accomplish its objectives.

Admiral Isoroku Yamamoto, commander of the Japanese Combined Fleet, knew that any attack against the Americans would have to be fast and decisive. From his time as naval attaché in Washington in the 1920s, Yamamoto was well aware of the vast resources in the United States. If the Americans were not brought to the peace table within six months, Yamamoto feared that Japan could not win.

Pearl Harbor
1941

OAHU ISLAND,
HAWAII

PEARL HARBOR

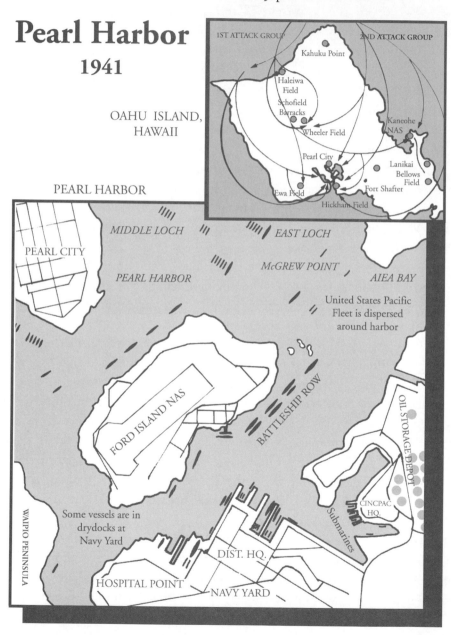

1ST ATTACK GROUP   2ND ATTACK GROUP

Kahuku Point

Haleiwa
Field
Schofield
Barracks
Wheeler Field
Pearl City
Kaneohe
NAS

Lanikai
Bellows
Field
Ewa Field
Fort Shafter
Hickham Field

PEARL CITY

MIDDLE LOCH

EAST LOCH

PEARL HARBOR

McGREW POINT

AIEA BAY

United States Pacific
Fleet is dispersed
around harbor

FORD ISLAND NAS

BATTLESHIP ROW

OIL STORAGE DEPOT

CINCPAC
HQ.

Submarines

WAIPIO PENINSULA

Some vessels are in
drydocks at
Navy Yard

DIST. HQ.

HOSPITAL POINT

NAVY YARD

Yamamoto refined his plans for a carrier-based air attack against the American fleet at Pearl Harbor as negotiations between the U.S. and Japan deteriorated. On November 26, 1941, Yamamoto dispatched a fleet under the command of Admiral Chuichi Nagumo toward the Hawaiian Islands. Six aircraft carriers, along with various support and supply vessels, sailed along the seldom-used northern route.

On November 27, 1941, peace talks were suspended. The U.S. refused to lift its oil and scrap iron boycott; Japan felt its only choice was military action.

By the morning of December 7, 1941, the Japanese fleet had reached a point about 275 miles north of Pearl Harbor, and Nagumo launched his first wave of 183 aircraft. As the flight leader of the first squadron neared Pearl Harbor, he found absolutely no resistance. Surprise was complete. He sent the coded message of "Tora, Tora, Tora" (Tiger, tiger, tiger) to the fleet, letting them know that they were going in unopposed. A second wave of 170 planes followed a little less than an hour later.

Five miniature, two-man submarines joined that attack from beneath the water outside the harbor entrance. While the submarines did little damage, the airplanes spent nearly two hours dropping torpedoes, bombing, and strafing the completely unprepared Americans. By the time the last Japanese planes returned to their carriers, the U.S. battleships *West Virginia* and *California* had sunk, the *Oklahoma* had capsized, and the *Arizona* had been blown to pieces. Four other battleships were damaged, and eleven smaller vessels were on the harbor bottom or badly damaged. In addition, 247 American aircraft had been destroyed or disabled, mostly on the ground before even taking to the air. More than 2,300 Americans lay dead on the island shore, in the harbor, or entombed forever in the wreck of the *Arizona*. Another 1,150 were wounded. Japan's losses totaled 28 airplanes.

The American navy had suffered its worst defeat in history. Yet, beyond drawing America into the war, Japan's victory was neither complete nor even greatly influential. The first two attack waves were so successful that Nagumo decided not to risk a planned third one. As a result, Pearl Harbor's oil storage facilities and much of its repair docks were spared. More importantly, the American aircraft carriers had been away on maneuvers and therefore escaped any damage whatsoever. Within six months, these carriers, along with many repaired ships that had been damaged at Pearl Harbor, would be successfully battling the Japanese in the Coral Sea and at Midway.

The Japanese had been wrong. Defeat at Pearl Harbor did not cause the Americans to withdraw into isolationism; rather the attack united the country toward action. President Franklin D. Roosevelt described the attack as "a day that will live in infamy" when he and the U.S. Congress announced the following day that the U.S. was declaring war against Japan. "Remember Pearl Harbor" joined the historical battle cries of "Remember the Alamo" and "Remember the Maine" in bringing Americans together to prepare for and fight the greatest armed conflict of all time.

Pearl Harbor definitely deserves its place on this list of influential battles, but it is highly unlikely that the U.S. would have been able to remain outside the war for any appreciable time even without the attack. Europe was in danger of falling to Hitler, and those who preferred isolationism were already in the minority. Also, even if the carriers had been present and destroyed in the battle, the U.S. resources and resolve were too enormous. The war might have lasted longer, but Japan was doomed to defeat.

The "sneak" attack by the Japanese on Pearl Harbor so shocked Americans that speculation and rumors were inevitable. Perhaps the most notorious were the rumors that President Roosevelt was forewarned of the attack and failed to alert the Islands. Some stories state that U.S. intelligence sources had intercepted messages about the attack. Actually, the Japanese sent its envoy in Washington a thirteen-part message stating their intention of beginning warfare against the U.S. The envoy was supposed to deliver this message at approximately the same time the attack began, but because of translation and decoding problems, he did not do so until after bombs and torpedoes had already begun to fall. Another story proposes that England's Winston Churchill directly informed Roosevelt that his code breakers knew of the impending attack. Again, there is no sustentative proof that Churchill knew about the attack or shared any information about it.

The background for these and other rumors are quite simple. Americans could not believe or accept that "inferior" Orientals were capable of conducting such a successful operation. There had to be another explanation, but more than sixty years later, only rumors remain, and no facts about any pre-attack knowledge on the part of Roosevelt or others have been uncovered. The real news was that the attack on Pearl Harbor simply hastened American participation in World War II. It provided the spark that fanned into the largest flames of war in history.

63

TANNENBERG

World War I, 1914

The victory by the Germans at the Battle of Tannenberg in 1914 sent the Russians reeling out of World War I and thrust them toward a revolution that would depose the Czar and bring the Communist government to power. Tannenberg's greatest impact, however, was not in Russia but in France. When Germany transferred large numbers of troops to the Eastern Front to defeat the Russians, the French could stop the significantly smaller German force from invading the Western Front at the Battle of the Marne (38).

Peace had prevailed in Europe after the Prussian victory over France in 1871. Both sides, however, had realized that the imbalance of power that resulted would eventually lead to yet another war, and they made alliances and plans in preparation. By the beginning of the twentieth century, France and Russia had allied against Germany and Austria. The uneasy peace continued until a Serb terrorist assassinated Francis Ferdinand, the archduke of Austria, on June 28, 1914. Using the death of one man as an excuse to sacrifice many, Europe went to war a month later.

Germany immediately initiated their Schlieffen Plan, written two decades earlier and periodically updated since then, that called for the quick attack and defeat of France before Russia could adequately mobilize and force a two-front war.

As planned, the Germans massed their armies, attacked west through Belgium, and then hooked south toward Paris. German leaders believed they could capture Paris and secure France's surrender within six weeks. Meanwhile, they left only their Eighth Army in East Prussia along the Polish border as a buffer against the Russians.

The Schlieffen Plan worked as anticipated during its first weeks, but then a Belgian attack slowed the German advance, which would face further resistance from the British Expeditionary Force hurrying across the Channel. French reservists also joined the fight, rushing to the front in Parisian taxicabs. Although delayed, the Germans still had the advantage—until the other part of their plan began to fall apart.

Russia mobilized much more quickly than anticipated and ordered its First Army, commanded by General Pavel Rennenkampf, to attack the Germans from the northeast. Meanwhile, their Second Army commanded by Rennenkampf's archenemy, General Aleksandr Samsonov, attacked the southeast. The Russian First Army defeated the Germans at the Battle of Gumbinnen on August 17 but did not exploit their victory.

The battle did produce significant reactions. The German high command sacked General Max von Prittwitz and replaced him with General Eric von Ludendorff. On the way to the front, Ludendorff and his chief of staff, General Paul von Hindenburg, devised a plan to envelop and destroy the Russian Second Army. When they arrived at the front, they were surprised to discover that an obscure staff officer, Colonel Max Hoffman, had come up with a similar plan and the maneuver had already begun.

The Germans left a single cavalry division to screen against the Russian First Army while maneuvering the rest of their force to surround the enemy Second Army. German planners were correct when they anticipated that the rival Russian army commanders would have little communication with each other and that Rennenkampf would neither attack nor move to assist his fellow general once the envelopment began.

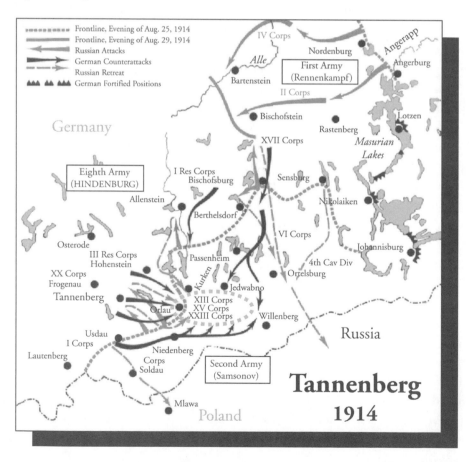

Samsonov, lacking reconnaissance and intelligence, did not recognize that the Germans were concentrating against him and ordered his own attack along the seventy-mile front near the town of Tannenberg in the southeastern region of East Prussia. The Russian's advance in the center actually helped the German assaults on the flanks to surround the Second Army. By August 27, the front had narrowed to forty miles, with about 300,000 men engaged in close combat. The German encirclement was nearly complete.

On August 28, Samsonov left his headquarters and rode on horseback to the front to rally his troops. For the next two days, the Russians attempted to break through the German lines on the east flank across the Masurian Marshes. All their efforts failed. As his army disintegrated, Samsonov committed suicide. In death, he joined 30,000 of his soldiers who had fallen to the German attack. Another 92,000 surrendered and gave up two-thirds of their 600 artillery pieces. The Russian Second Army ceased to exist.

Rennenkampf and his First Army, who had made no effort to come to Samsonov's aid, were soon in retreat from the advancing Germans. A few days later, the overall commander of the Russian army, Grand Duke Nikolai, responded to a question about the losses at Tannenberg. "It's an honor to make such a sacrifice for our allies," he said. While it may have been the honorable thing to do in the Duke's mind, many Russians disagreed, driving them further from the Czar and closer to revolution.

The Battle of Tannenberg ended any major role by Russia in World War I, and they only fought one more significant battle, also a loss, at Kovel-Stanislav two years later (87). The sacrifice of their Second Army, however, did exert its influence on the war's outcome. Germany hailed Ludendorff and Hindenburg as heroes, and they played an influential role in the remainder of the war. More importantly, the rapid mobilization of the Russian army prior to the Battle of Tannenberg created fear in the German high command that they might lose East Prussia. As a result, they pulled troop units from the Battle of the Marne and dispatched them to the Eastern Front. None of these soldiers arrived in time to take part in the Battle of Tannenberg, but their absence did allow the French to stop the German offensive at the Battle of the Marne.

While the Battle of Tannenberg contributed to the rise of Communism in Russia, its major influence was on the Battle of the Marne, where the distribution of forces led to the stagnation of trench warfare on the Western Front and the eventual armistice that ended the war. German victories at both Tannenberg and the Marne would likely have led to their domination of Europe. While this scenario likely would have prevented Adolf Hitler from gaining political and military strength, the imbalance of power certainly would have led to still more warfare.

64

DIEN BIEN PHU

French-Vietnamese War, 1954

The victory of the Viet Minh at Dien Bien Phu in 1954 led to the end of French colonization in Southeast Asia and resulted in the division of Indochina into South and North Vietnam. This defeat of a major colonial power by an unconventional guerrilla force shocked the world and gave hope to rebels everywhere. The confidence-building victory by the Vietnamese Communists at Dien Bien Phu also added to their resolve to reunite the divided Vietnam into a single socialist nation. Their efforts to do so eventually drew the United States into what would become the longest and most unpopular war in American history.

For hundreds of years prior to the nineteenth century, the indigenous peoples who occupied Southeast Asia were constantly at war among themselves or against Chinese invaders from the north. In the latter part of the century, the French had arrived to establish colonies to exploit the region's vast natural resources. By the 1890s, the French had succeeded in conquering most of Southeast Asia.

France maintained rigid control over Indochina until World War II. After the fall of France to the Germans in 1940, the French colonials surrendered all of their territory in Southeast Asia to the Japanese, Germany's ally, without a significant fight. The primary resistance against the Japanese came not from the French but from a Vietnamese nationalist coalition known as Viet Minh. With assistance from the United States, primarily in the form of weapons and advisors, the Viet Minh conducted minor harassment campaigns against their Asian occupiers for the duration of the war.

When World War II ended with Japan's surrender, the Viet Minh attempted to establish their own government, but the French returned and resumed control over what they considered their colony. The Viet Minh, not strong enough to directly resist the French, returned to the jungle under the leadership of Ho Chi Minh to continue the same harassment tactics they had perpetrated against the Japanese. They became even stronger when the Communists took control of China in 1949 and began supplying the Viet Minh with weapons, ammunition, and equipment.

Even so, Ho, along with his military commander Vo Nguyen Giap, quickly discovered they could not match the French in conventional warfare. After several defeats in direct confrontation along the Red River Valley near Hanoi, the Viet Minh withdrew farther into the jungle and restricted their operations to guerrilla tactics. For three years, the French attempted to lure the Viet Minh into a major battle, but Giap engaged only in hit-and-run operations.

In 1953, French general Henri Navarre established a series of interlocking bases nearly two hundred miles west of Hanoi in an isolated valley known as Dien Bien Phu (the rough English translation is "big frontier administrative center"). Navarre thought that by placing his bases in such a remote spot, accessible for resupply only by air, he might provoke a Viet Minh attack. Unfortunately for the French, he was right.

In November 1953, paratroopers of the French Foreign Legion landed in the valley and began preparing landing strips and fortified bases. By early 1954, more than 15,000 French and allied Vietnamese under command of Colonel (later General) Christian de Castries occupied nine fortified positions on the valley floor that extended eleven miles north to south and three miles east to west. Each of the forts was given a feminine name, reputedly after the various lovers of de Castries.

The mountains that surrounded the valley provided excellent observation and firing positions for any potential enemy. However, the French wanted the Viet Minh to see them. They were not concerned about artillery attacks because, according to their intelligence and experience, the Viet Minh had only small arms. Their thinking was that even if the guerillas did possess artillery, it would be impossible for them to maneuver the heavy pieces through the jungle to hillside firing positions.

De Castries and Navarre quickly discovered the errors of their strategy. The Chinese had supplied Giap with more than 200 artillery and anti-air weapons. The Viet Minh broke these into parts and moved them on their backs and on bicycles into the mountains overlooking Dien Bien Phu. There the artillery men reassembled the weapons and armed them with ammunition delivered by the more than 70,000 soldiers who gathered for the great assault the French so wanted.

Giap began his offensive by staging a series of diversionary attacks in Laos and the provinces south of Hanoi. These operations were designed to divert any reinforcements for Dien Bien Phu when he began his main attack. On March 13, 1954, Giap ordered his men into the valley behind a barrage of artillery. They quickly disabled the two airstrips the French needed for resupply and then pushed on against the fortified positions. However, mounting Viet Minh casualties forced Giap to halt the attack.

Over the next few days, paratroopers dropped into the valley to reinforce the French. All supplies and ammunition also had to be delivered by parachute. Monsoon rains soon limited this air resupply and made the already austere camps even less hospitable. French artillery attempted to counter the Viet Minh bombardment, but they were more prepared to face advancing infantry than well-emplaced artillery. The French artillery fire proved so ineffective that their dejected commander, Colonel Charles Piroth, committed suicide.

In mid-March, the Viet Minh began digging a series of parallel trenches that slowly advanced toward the fortified camps. This protected them from French small arms and artillery fire until they could charge across the last few yards. Viet Minh artillery continued to pound the French forts during the digging.

One by one the forts fell. France requested aid from the United States, including, according to some sources, the use of atomic weapons, but received only a few civilian contract pilots in response.

During the night of May 6, the Viet Minh made their final assault on the only remaining French fort. Late in the afternoon of May 7, de Castries radioed his headquarters in Hanoi that he was destroying the last of his ammunition and was preparing to surrender.

More than 2,000 French soldiers and their allies lay dead in the valley. The Viet Minh marched more than 10,000 prisoners, at least half of them wounded, some 500 miles in what many of the French would later compare to the Bataan Death March. By the end of the following summer, only 3,000 were still alive.

The Viet Minh suffered 8,000 dead and twice as many wounded, the majority of these causalities occurring during the human-wave attacks early in the battle. The losses for the Viet Minh were great, but the victory was even greater. A colonial guerrilla army had defeated one of the world's strongest nations. Two months later, a conference partitioned Indochina approximately along the seventeenth parallel into North and South Vietnam. Ho led the government of the North; Giap remained the commander of its armed forces. After that point, colonization of Asia by Europe was as good as over.

Ho continued to receive aid from China and added the Soviet Union to his list of benefactors. It did not take him long to begin operations to reunite the two Vietnams through the military defeat of the democratic South. By 1959, he had agents, known as Viet Cong (or Vietnamese Communist), recruiting soldiers in the South. He also began construction of a series of trails and roads, which became known as the Ho Chi Minh Trail, to resupply the operations against the South. American advisors arrived first to assist the South Vietnamese government, and then regular units were deployed as the war dragged on for more than a decade.

Dien Bien Phu provided the victory that ended French influence in Southeast Asia. The Vietnamese gained confidence that they could defeat a major power if they were patient enough to wait until conditions were favorable before taking large risks. Ho eventually reunited the North and South, but today Vietnam remains one of the world's poorest nations with much of its population desperately seeking refuge outside the country.

65

POLAND

World War II, 1939

The German attack against Poland in 1939 was the opening battle of World War II. In addition to beginning the largest, most costly war in history, the Battle of Poland introduced the "blitzkrieg," or lightning war, where mechanized forces, coordinated with artillery and air support, advanced rapidly through defenses and made an entire nation the battlefield.

The Treaty of Versailles not only brought a formal end to World War I, but it also set the stage for World War II. Its provisions had taken away German territory and levied huge reparations that divided and bankrupted Germany—the perfect environment for the rise of Adolf Hitler, who became the German Chancellor in 1933.

Hitler promised to renew prosperity, so he refused to make further reparation and began rebuilding the German army and navy. When these violations drew little interference from the Western Allies, Hitler proceeded to implement his plans to restore Germany to its former position of power by increasing the country's "living space" and reclaiming regions dominated by German-speaking people for his Third Reich.

Hitler acquired the Rhineland in 1936, Austria and the Sudetenland in 1938, and Czechoslovakia in early 1939. Neither Britain nor France honored treaties to defend the territories taken by the Germans, but in April the British and French reiterated that they would support Poland in the event of a German invasion. Hitler assured them that he had no more territorial demands.

Meanwhile, Germany was supporting the Nationalists in their efforts to take Spain from the Republicans, who were backed by the Soviet Union. Following the Battle of Madrid (71), Germany and Russia signed a non-aggression pact that included provisions for each to acquire additional European territories without opposition from the other.

While these political developments were progressing, several military thinkers in Britain and Germany were developing theories on a new type of warfare. The static, defensive-oriented trench combat of World War I had proven that modern weapons utilized in old-fashioned tactics produced huge numbers of casualties but little acquisition of territory. In 1932, British officer John F.C. Fuller published *Field Regulations III*, which outlined his contention that rapid-moving mechanized operations would be the future of warfare. German General Heinz Guderian studied Fuller's ideas and convinced Hitler to build an armor force and train it to conduct lightning warfare or "blitzkrieg."

In his book *Achtung-Panzer!* Guderian outlined his theory that massed armored units, with artillery and air support, could penetrate enemy front lines and fan out in rear areas to destroy command, control, supply, and reserve units. By moving rapidly and bypassing enemy strongholds and difficult terrain, armies could win battles in days, rather than in months or years as was typical in World War I.

By August 1939, Guderian had five fully operational armor divisions and several others in various stages of preparation. Late in the month, he joined five German armies into a single force composed of 1.2 million men assembled on the Polish frontier. On the evening of August 31, Hitler had an incident staged to make it appear that the Poles had violated the German border. The next day he launched his blitzkrieg into Poland from three directions, with Guderian's armor forces leading the way.

The Polish army of 800,000 was neither trained nor armed to deal with the lightning assault. During the first two days of the battle, 1,400 German aircraft attacked and destroyed the 900-plane Polish air force. The German planes then attacked troop concentrations and provided close air support to the advancing ground columns. By the end of the first week of the battle, the three German columns had penetrated more than 140 miles into Poland, surrounding and annihilating large numbers of Polish units. The Poles fought gallantly, utilizing methods such as futile horse cavalry charges against machine guns, but they were no match for the Germans. By September 8, the German columns had pinched inward around Warsaw, and on the 17th, they completed their encirclement of the city. On this same day, the Soviets joined the war against Poland and their units swept 110 miles into the eastern part of the country in only two days.

Warsaw surrendered on September 27. The next day, the Germans and Russians partitioned the country, and the last significant Polish resistance ceased on October 5. Germany lost about 10,000 killed in the battle while the Poles had at least 65,000 killed and 750,000 taken prisoner. A small number, including General Wladyslaw Sikorski, escaped to London, where they set up a government in exile and provided a few Polish troops to the Allied war effort.

France and Great Britain honored their treaty with Poland and declared war against Germany, but they were unable to provide any assistance before the end of the battle. After the fall of Poland, other countries also aligned with the Allies or the Axis, leading to history's largest and most costly war.

In addition to beginning World War II, the Battle of Poland ended that country's independence for the next half-century. Not long after the battle, the Germans turned against the Soviets and took over the entire country. The Soviet Union later counterattacked and occupied all of Poland, where they remained even after the war concluded. Poland did not break away until its successful labor movement in the 1980s.

By sealing the fate of Poland for the next fifty years, the Battle of Poland showed the world that defensive trench warfare was a thing of the past. Lightning war with rapid-moving mechanized forces supported by artillery and close air support typified the major battles of World War II as well as those since. The Korean War, the series of Arab-Israeli conflicts, and Operation Desert Storm have all included elements of the blitzkrieg that the Germans first employed against the Poles in 1939.

66

LEUCTRA

Greek City-States' Wars, 371 B.C.

The Theban victory at the Battle of Leuctra in 371 B.C. ended Sparta's rule of the Greek city-states and opened the way for the rise of Philip of Macedonia and his son Alexander the Great. Leuctra is also distinctive because of its innovations in the use of cavalry and battlefield tactics.

For several centuries, the Greek city-states had led the world in the advancement of the arts, science, and politics. Despite cultural enlightenments, however, the city-states could not get along and lived in a virtually constant state of war as they vied for overall control of Greece. Athens dominated the other city-states in the latter part of the fifth century B.C., but the Athenians ultimately turned their focus to the arts instead of their military. Sparta, always lagging in the arts but advanced in defense, defeated Athens in 404 B.C. and assumed leadership of the city-states.

After the victory, Sparta raised the taxes of its subordinate city-states and placed puppet governments in charge. Sparta faced few difficulties until it seized the capital of Thebes in 383 B.C. and replaced the Theban government officials with its own.

The usurped Theban leaders immediately began plans to retake their city-state and turned to former enemy Athens for assistance. A joint Theban-Athenian fleet defeated Sparta's navy at Cnidus in 394 B.C., and the allies won several other small naval and land battles over the next decade. In 379 B.C., the Thebans liberated their city-state from Sparta and continued their military operations to bring together several smaller city-states into a Boeotian League.

After more than thirty years of sporadic warfare, Spartan and Theban leaders agreed to peace a conference in 371 B.C. The Theban leader, Epaminondas, did not like the terms offered and walked out of the meeting.

King Cleombrotus I of Sparta realized that the Thebans would resume warfare and that his best course of action was to attack before Epaminondas was prepared. The Spartan army of 10,000 marched into Thebes, where they met Epaminondas's army of 6,000 at Leuctra, ten miles outside the Theban capital.

Most Greek city-states had, by this point in time, adopted the phalanx as their primary battle formation. Phalanxes, squares of soldiers eight to ten men deep protected by breastplates and shields and armed with long spears, could be linked together to break through traditional infantry line defenses and over several decades of use had proven an extremely successful battle formation. When armies that both employed the phalanx met, the formations pushed against each other until one gave way. Training of the soldiers was important, but sheer numbers of phalanxes usually determined the victor.

Although outnumbered, Epaminondas had better knowledge of the terrain, as well as the advantage of several innovations in his organization and tactics. To counter his numerical inferiority, he increased the number of ranks of his phalanx on his left flank to 50. Then to further strengthen this "super phalanx," the Theban leader posted his elite unit of 300 warriors known as the Sacred Band in the center. He next placed his smaller, right flank phalanx further to the rear. An attacker on the weaker right phalanx would now expose its flank to the stronger Theban force on the left.

The Thebans also planned an innovative use of their cavalry. Previously, horsemen had been used more as scouts rather than as warriors. Epaminondas decided to open the battle with his cavalry attacking the Spartan horsemen and driving them from the battlefield to create confusion in the infantry ranks.

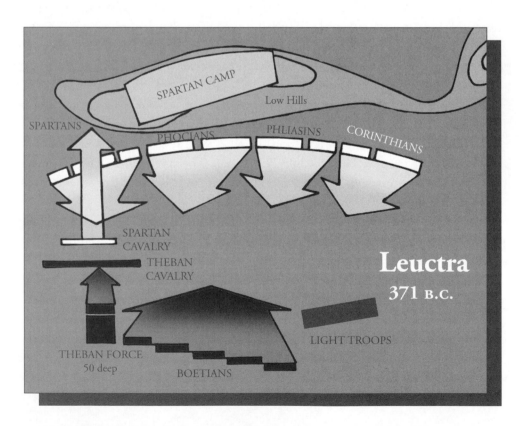

On a morning in July 371 B.C., the two armies faced each other about a mile apart on the plain outside Leuctra. Epaminondas initiated the battle according to his plan with a cavalry charge that easily drove the Athenian horsemen from the field. Some of the horses bolted into the Athenian phalanxes, weakening their formations.

The Theban "super phalanx" advanced and quickly pushed back the smaller Spartan formations on the left flank. Other Spartan phalanxes attempted to take advantage of the Theban penetration and encircled the attackers only to be cut off by the enemy right flank. As the two Theban forces moved forward, the crushed Spartan units disintegrated. Some of the Spartan infantrymen fought their way to the rear, but more than 2,000 were left behind dead on the battlefield.

Theban losses totaled only a few hundred, but the exhausted army was unable to continue the attack. There really was no need to do so; the spirit of the Spartans had been broken to the point where their army would never again achieve prominence. Thebes now was the leader of the Greek city-states, but neither their victory nor their control was complete.

Athens and Thebes, along with various allies, continued to fight for Greece over the next several decades with no result other than weakened regional armies. In 338 B.C., Philip of Macedonia took advantage of the weary city-states and defeated a now-allied Theban and Athenian force at Chaeronea (51). Greece was finally united—but by an outsider rather than a native. Despite his origins, Philip led the united Greece to expand its borders and to spread the country's culture throughout the Mediterranean. Upon his death, his son, Alexander the Great, expanded the Greek territories even farther to make it the largest and most influential empire of its time.

The defeat of Sparta and the ultimate weakening of the city-states by the Battle of Leuctra led to the conquests by Philip and Alexander. It also provided innovations in the structure of the phalanx, battlefield maneuver, and use of cavalry that were adopted by Philip and his son when they led their armies to future victories and per-petuation of Greek culture and politics.

67

CARABOBO

Latin American Wars of Independence, 1821

The South American Patriots defeated the Royalists on the plains of Carabobo in 1821 to secure the independence of Venezuela from Spain. The battle prepared the way for the independence of most of South America and established Simón Bolívar as the "Liberator" of the continent.

Shortly after the voyages of Christopher Columbus, Spanish explorers, settlers, and military leaders had arrived to claim vast areas of the New World. From settlements in the Caribbean Islands, Hernán Cortés conquered Mexico at the Battle of Tenochtitlán in 1521 (12), and Francisco Pizarro defeated the Incas and occupied Peru after his victory at the Battle of Cajamarca in 1532 (6). Just three decades after the "discovery" of the New World, Spain controlled all of Central and South America except Portuguese Brazil and a few small colonies north of Brazil and in the Caribbean.

For the next two centuries, the region's resources, particularly gold and silver, made Spain one of the world's richest kingdoms. Wealth from the New World financed the Spanish army and navy and elevated them to rival those of England and France. As time passed, however, generations born and raised in Latin American felt more kinship with the place of their birth than with their ancestral homeland of Spain. Encouraged by the American and French revolutions at the end of the eighteenth century, many Latin Americans considered independence for themselves.

In 1810, Simón Bolívar led a revolt against the Spaniards in Venezuela and occupied Caracas until the Spanish counterattack drove him and his small army into New Granada (Colombia). Bolívar attempted a second overthrow of the Spanish in Venezuela in 1813, but again he failed.

Bolívar escaped to Jamaica where, in 1815, he approached the newly independent government of Haiti for support. Over the next four years, Bolívar conducted numerous raids back into South America and led two more unsuccessful invasions. However, despite the failure of the expeditions, Bolívar's revolutionary zeal was spreading.

In 1819, Bolívar, with funds provided by Haiti, reinforced his rebel army with English mercenary veterans of the Napoleonic Wars. He then established a base at Angostura, New Granada, and led his 3,200 soldiers across the Andes. On August 7, he defeated the Spanish garrison at Boyaca and three days later "liberated" Bogotá.

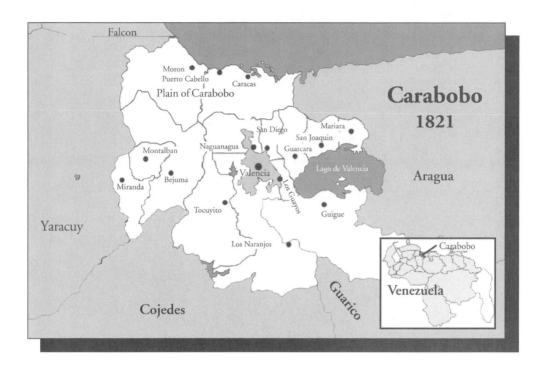

On December 17, 1819, Bolívar proclaimed the independence of the Republic of Colombia and immediately turned his military attention toward the Spanish Royalists from Venezuela. Bolívar's liberation of Colombia attracted more men into his force, and in 1821, he united his army with that of fellow revolutionary José Páez.

Gathered together as the Republican Army, this joint force of 4,000 infantry, 2,500 cavalry, and 350 British mercenaries marched into Venezuela. About a hundred miles west of Caracas, the rebels met an equal-sized Royalist force commanded by Spanish General Miguel de la Torre at the opening to the plain of Carabobo.

The Royalists initially had the advantage because they possessed two light artillery pieces, which Bolívar attempted to neutralize by sending Páez on a flanking movement along the right wing on June 24, 1821. The Royalists caught Páez's force in terrain difficult for maneuvering, and only a bayonet charge by the British mercenaries saved the attack. The Royalists retreated as Bolívar's cavalry lancers assaulted the Spanish center. Despite de la Torre's attempt to rally his defenses at La Guaira, the rebels forced him to surrender.

Five days after his victory at Carabobo, Bolívar entered Caracas and declared Venezuela independent from Spain. With this victory, Bolívar gained the confidence of many other South Americans. Fellow revolutionary José de San Martín, who had defeated the Spanish in Argentina and Chile, turned his army over to Bolívar in 1822, and the united force completed the liberation of Ecuador, Peru, and Bolivia.

South America wanted to be free of European control, and Spain's power had faded to the point where it had neither the resources nor the will to maintain its rule. Had Bolívar not achieved victory at Carabobo, he—or his successor—would have liberated the country elsewhere.

Still, Carabobo was the place of one of history's most influential battles. Bolívar's victory on the Venezuelan plain ensured the success of the revolution that ultimately freed all of South America. Carabobo is not ranked higher on this list, however, because South Americans have yet to take a prominent place in the world community and exert their influence. Bolívar was certainly correct when he wrote, a day after the Battle of Carabobo, "Yesterday a splendid victory confirmed the political birth of the republic." However, the real potential of South America has yet to be realized.

68

CERIGNOLA

Wars for Italy, 1503

The Battle of Cerignola led to Spanish control of Naples and southern Italy, but more importantly, it introduced arquebuses into the infantry arsenal. These early muskets increased the killing ability of the individual soldier and changed methods of warfare.

By the latter part of the fifteenth century, France and Spain had established themselves as the major military powers on the European continent. States on the Italian peninsula, particularly Venice, Milan, Genoa, and Naples, had made great advances in the arts and trade during the Renaissance, but they remained separate and vulnerable to outside attacks.

France invaded Italy in 1494 and quickly moved down the peninsula to occupy Naples. An alliance between Milan, Genoa, and Rome forced the French to withdraw back to their own borders, but France and Spain united in 1499 to take control of the entire peninsula. The French and Spanish differed on the division of the captured territory, and their arguments led to war over Naples in July 1502.

The Spanish dispatched an army to southern Italy, commanded by Gonzalo de Córdoba, a veteran of the wars that expelled the Moors from Spain. Córdoba had fought the French on several occasions in the late 1490s but had been defeated each time. When he returned to Spain, he applied the lessons he had learned to restructure his army. He initiated measures to coordinate his infantry, cavalry, and artillery and divided them into smaller units to facilitate maneuver. Most importantly, Córdoba added firearms to the infantry, which had previously carried only swords, shields, and pikes.

These early matchlock muskets, called arquebuses, fired one-ounce, .75 caliber (three-quarters of an inch) balls that had a killing range of one to two hundred meters. At nearly fifteen pounds each, the muskets had a ground brace on which to rest the heavy muzzle to facilitate aiming. Although the arquebuses took nearly two minutes for the most experienced soldier to reload and would not fire if their powder became damp, these muskets gave the infantryman the capability of firing projectiles that would penetrate shield and armor and kill at a distance.

Córdoba and his army encountered the French at Barletta on Italy's Adriatic coast, and the Spanish leader gained a victory with an assault by his sword-bearing infantrymen. The attack did not favor the use of the arquebuses because of the terrain and weather, and Córdoba held them out of the battle.

On April 28, 1503, Córdoba and his army of 6,000 met a French force of 10,000 in a vineyard about twenty miles inland from Barletta, near the village of Cerignola. Córdoba's infantrymen barely had time dig a defensive trench on a hillside before the French charged their lines. Spread across the Spanish defenses was what later accounts refer to as the "corps" of arquebusmen.

Although the number of infantrymen armed with firearms numbered only several hundred, they quickly made their mark. Rank after rank of the French fell to the musket balls; the few Frenchmen who made it to the trench line were killed by Spanish swords and pikes. The French withdrew to reorganize and then attempted a second assault, but the results were the same. After halting the second French advance, Córdoba ordered a counterattack that cleared the field and captured the French supply wagons and artillery. For the first time in history, individual firearms had won a battle.

Córdoba occupied Naples on May 13, after the French withdrew across the Garigliano River. A stalemate developed as each side waited for replacements and the opportune time to continue the fight. On December 29, under the cover of darkness, the Spanish army moved pontoon bridges into position and conducted a night attack that completely surprised the larger French force. Córdoba's army used musket fire to support the advancing Spanish swordsmen and killed several thousand as they again captured the French supply wagons and artillery.

A month later, the French signed a treaty giving up their claim to Naples and southern Italy. Córdoba returned to retirement in Spain with the title of "the Great Captain."

Struggles over the remainder of the Italian peninsula continued for another fifty years, but battles were never the same after Cerignola. Spanish commanders continued the use of arquebuses and added more muskets to their armies. They also encouraged development of lighter, more reliable weapons. While Spain appreciated the impact of the musket on warfare, other countries did not immediately adopt the new firearms. It took nearly two decades, and the convincing Battle of La Bicocca (92), before the power of arquebuses was widely recognized. Other countries then copied the Spanish maneuver formations and began to acquire muskets of their own, but Spain had the advantage, and its infantry remained the best on the Continent for the next century.

The Battle of Cerignola and the other Italian campaigns had the added impact of spreading the Italian Renaissance to other European countries. While this is important, the fight for the control of Italy in the 1500s did not provide sufficient influence on the world for inclusion on this list except for the introduction of the arquebus. As the smoke from the gunpowder cleared from the hillside vineyard, the defeated French and the victorious Spanish realized the impact of the early muskets. No battle or war would ever again be the same.

69

BOSWORTH FIELD

War of the Roses, 1485

The defeat of Richard III by Henry Tudor at Bosworth Field in 1485 won the crown of England for the House of Tudor. Not only did the battle establish the House of Tudor as the rulers for the next century; it also mirrored the treachery and intrigue that marked the so-called nobles of the period.

After the end of their long, bloody Hundred Years' War with France in 1453, King Henry VI had occupied the English throne. Henry, prone to periods of insanity, had garnered little confidence from his subjects, except members of his own family—the house of Lancaster, represented by a red rose. The house of York, represented by a white rose and led by Richard Plantagenet, opposed Henry's rule. Open civil war had broken out between the houses of red and white roses at the Battle of Saint Albans in 1455.

Six years later, the whites succeeded in deposing Henry VI and placed Richard's son on the throne as Edward IV. However, Henry's wife, Queen Margaret, secured Scottish and French assistance, as well as that of some of the families who had formerly supported Edward IV, to retake the throne in 1470. A year later, the white-rose Yorkists again gained the upper hand at the Battle of Tewkesbury. After more than fifteen years of fighting between the white and red houses, Edward IV finally had a firm hold on the throne and kingdom. Most surviving members of the house of Lancaster fled to exile in France. Some of their supporters went with them, while others swore allegiance to the house of York.

When Edward IV died twelve years later, his son Edward V took his place on the throne. Because Edward V was only twelve years old, his uncle, the Duke of Gloucester, took on the position of Protector. The Duke wasted little time in placing the young king and his brother in the Tower of London for "their comfort." He then proclaimed that Edward IV's marriage to the young king's mother had been invalid, making the two boys illegitimate and ineligible for the crown. A short time later, the boys mysteriously vanished.

On July 6, 1483, the Duke of Gloucester declared himself king of England as Richard III. Richard immediately faced powerful enemies both within and outside his court. The red-rose Lancasterians under Henry Tudor, exiled in France, saw Richard's treachery as an opportunity to regain power. Several of the most influential supporters of the white-rose faction, namely the Stanley Brothers and the Duke of Northumberland, did not approve of Richard or the way he had gained his crown.

On August 1, Henry Tudor sailed to England with family members, allied English nobles, and 2,000 French mercenaries. Six days later, Henry landed near his boyhood home at Milford Haven and began his march toward London. Other anti-Yorkists joined Henry, and his army increased to 5,000.

Richard followed the rebels' advance from his headquarters in Nottingham, where he had assembled his army of about 6,500 infantry, 1,200 archers, and 200 mounted knights. Richard was aware that the Stanleys had met with Henry and that he could no longer depend on their support. However, he assumed they would not join the fight against him because he held one of the Stanley's sons as his hostage.

From this point until the end of the battle between the houses of red and white roses, many of the details, as well as some of the major facts, are unknown or in dispute. Even the exact location of the fight is debatable. While the battle is one of the most influential of its period, it is also one of the most poorly documented. Not a single verifiable eyewitness account of the battle survives. In fact, the most widely known version is the battle's depiction in the fictionalized play *Richard III* by William Shakespeare.

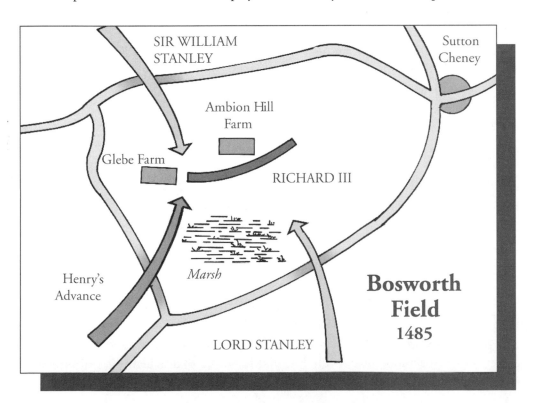

SIR WILLIAM STANLEY

Sutton Cheney

Ambion Hill Farm

Glebe Farm

RICHARD III

Henry's Advance

Marsh

Bosworth Field
1485

LORD STANLEY

It is generally accepted, however, that Richard and his army marched from Nottingham and met Henry's force at Ambion Hill near the village of Market Bosworth. Although Ambion Hill is separate from nearby Bosworth Field, some of the fight may have taken place there, and its name has been generally accepted for the battle.

On the morning of August 21, 1485, Richard went into combat without knowing if he could depend on the Stanleys. Some accounts state that Richard sent them word that he would kill the Stanley's son if they joined the fight, only to receive the reply that the Stanleys had other sons. Whatever actually occurred, Richard did not kill the boy, but neither did the Stanleys participate in the battle initially.

Richard occupied the better terrain on the battlefield but failed to attack when Henry's army became somewhat disarrayed while deploying. When he finally did advance, one of his most experienced subordinates, the Duke of Norfolk, was killed. At about this time, the Stanleys committed their army of 4,000, not to Richard but rather to Henry. The Duke of Northumberland did not support Richard, either because he chose not to or because he was prevented from doing so by the terrain.

King Richard determined that the only way to achieve victory was to kill Henry. Wearing the crown of England on his head and waving a sword, Richard led a party of about eighty knights into the fray toward Henry's position. They fought their way through the infantry and reached Henry's personal bodyguards. Richard managed to strike down Henry's personal standard-bearer before Welsh infantrymen dragged him from his horse and impaled him on their pikes. The leaderless white army quickly surrendered.

Shakespeare later penned the most famous quote of the battle when he wrote that Richard's last words were, "A horse, a horse, my kingdom for a horse." In the heat of battle, Richard had no time for any such speech, and it is more likely he died, like soldiers on battlefields before and after, either cursing his enemies and fate, or calling for his mother.

Richard's naked body was strung across a horse and exhibited in Leicester for two days before burial. Along with Richard, about 1,000 of his soldiers died in the battle at a cost to the rebels of only about 200. As battlefields go, Bosworth Field absorbed little blood given that an entire kingdom changed hands. Henry rewarded the Stanleys for their support but jailed the Duke of Northumberland, adding to the conjecture that he did not betray Richard.

One of Henry's soldiers found Richard's crown near his body and placed it on the head of the new King of England. A few minor battles followed, but the War of the Roses basically concluded at Bosworth Field. Henry VII eventually married the daughter of Edward IV, thus bringing together the houses of white and red roses. The united House of Tudor would rule England for more than a century, during which time its army and navy would grow to make the kingdom a world power.

70

AUSTERLITZ

Napoleonic Empire Wars, 1805

Austerlitz was Napoleon's greatest victory and established the French Emperor as the master tactician of his age. It also strengthened the confidence of the French army, led to the eventual demise of the Third Coalition, temporarily kept Prussia out of the war, and placed Napoleon in power for another decade.

By the spring of 1804, most of Europe was at war against the expansion of Napoleon's French Empire. Great Britain had successfully prevented, or at least postponed, a possible invasion with its victory at Trafalgar (36) on October 21, 1805. With his objective of invading England thwarted, Napoleon had turned eastward into Central Europe. The British had anticipated this move and in April 1805 had formed and financed the Third Coalition with Russia and Austria to stop the French advance.

The Coalition moved much more slowly than the experienced French army. Napoleon occupied Vienna with little opposition in November and continued his march eastward into Moravia. The Austrians, commanded by Emperor Francis II, and the Russians, led by Czar Alexander I, moved to intercept the advancing French. The two opposing armies finally met just west of Austerlitz in what is now the Czech Republic. Unfortunately for the Coalition, Napoleon arrived first and had ample time to study the terrain and devise his plan.

Napoleon deliberately withdrew his army west from the high ground of Pratzen Plateau to a position where he could camouflage most of his troops from observation and lure the enemy into his trap. The advancing Coalition forces occupied the plateau according to plan on December 1. By the end of the day, more than 85,000 Austrian and Russian soldiers supported by 278 cannons faced Napoleon's army of 70,000 men and 140 guns.

While the Russians and Austrians had little confidence in each other, the French were united behind their Emperor. In his order for the battle, Napoleon made clear to his troops the importance of the pending fight: "Soldiers, I shall in person direct all your battalions; I shall keep out of range if, with your accustomed bravery, you carry disorder and confusion into the ranks of the enemy; but if the victory is for a moment uncertain, you shall see your Emperor expose himself in the front rank."

Napoleon also noted the battle would be bloody as he expressed his opinion of the enemy: "Note that no man shall leave the ranks under the pretext of carrying off the wounded. Let every man be filled with the thought that it is vitally necessary to conquer these paid lackeys of England who so hate our nation."

On his right flank in the south, Napoleon had deliberately positioned fewer men in what appeared to be the weak spot in his defenses. In command of the 10,000 French soldiers positioned along Goldbach Brook, however, was Marshal Louis Davout, one of the best generals in Napoleon's army. Early on the morning of December 2, in a misty fog, more than 40,000 Russians commanded by Count Friedrich von Buxhowden advanced against Davout.

Davout's Third Corps held. At 8:00 A.M. Napoleon ordered forward another 20,000 men who had been hidden by the mist and campfire smoke. As they advanced toward the enemy's center, the mist cleared and the sun broke through the clouds. Napoleon and his men accepted this "sun of Austerlitz" as a sign of impending victory.

The Coalition, surprised by the attack on their center, committed their reserve, which slowed but could not stop the advancing French. Napoleon's troops in the north also advanced, and Davout counterattacked across Goldbach Brook. For several hours, the battle roared up and down the line. Fighting was so intense that the French infantry finished off any wounded enemy they passed. This was as much for security of their rear as it was for the battle lust of the warriors. Throughout the line, the French soldiers shouted, "Let no one escape," as they shot and bayoneted their way through the Russian and Austrian lines.

At about 10:00 A.M., the French broke the allied center and poured into their rear. By late afternoon, the Coalition forces were in a hasty, disorganized retreat eastward. They left behind 15,000 dead and wounded as well as 11,000 prisoners. Among the dead were 200 of the Russian Czar's personal escorts. Napoleon observed their bodies, most of which were from the nobility, and remarked, "Many fine ladies in St. Petersburg will lament this day."

The French, exhausted by their long march and the battle, did not pursue. They halted to rest, to bury their 2,000 dead, and to care for their 7,000 wounded. Napoleon later officially adopted many of the orphaned children of his fallen soldiers and gave them his own name. This, along with the stories of the "sun of Austerlitz," added to his growing reputation.

Austerlitz, also known as the Battle of the Three Emperors, gave Napoleon control of Eastern Europe and led to the end of the Third Coalition. On December 26, Francis II of Austria signed the Treaty of Pressburg, ceding great masses of territory to the French. Prussia, which had considered joining the Coalition, instead signed a peace treaty with Napoleon shortly after learning the outcome of Austerlitz.

MURAT

LANNES,
BERNADOTTE

NAPOLEON

KONSTANTIN

Austerlitz

SOULT

Pratzen Plateau

ALEXANDER I,
FRANCIS II

DAVOUT

BUXHOWDEN

Austerlitz
1805

Goldbach Brook

Czar Alexander took the survivors of his army back to Russia. Before he departed he sent a message to the French: "Tell your master that I am going away. Tell him that he has performed miracles...that the battle has increased my admiration for him; that he is a man predestined by Heaven; that it will require a hundred years for my arms to equal his."

Of course, Napoleon's power would last not a hundred years but only ten. Eventually Napoleon's enemies would reunite to defeat his army at Leipzig (4) and send him into exile. Had Napoleon succeeded in his efforts to continue to expand his empire, the Battle of Austerlitz would rank much higher on this list as the great turning point in the future of France. However, Napoleon's later defeats, including the final one at Waterloo (9), decrease its importance. In fact, it might be said that the greatest influence of Austerlitz was to provide another decade of bloody, deadly warfare that filled the cemeteries and emptied the treasuries of all of Europe.

71

MADRID

Spanish Civil War, 1939

The Battle of Madrid ended the Spanish Civil War with a victory for the Nationalists and their leader Francisco Franco who would hold absolute power in Spain for the next thirty-seven years. It also kept Spain out of World War II and led to the short-lived Molotov-Ribbentrop Pact, which established a non-aggression agreement between Germany and the Soviet Union.

By the beginning of the twentieth century, Spain, one of the world's most powerful countries for hundreds of years, was unable to maintain a stable government within its own borders. Its power in Europe had eroded and its colonies around the globe were history.

In World War I, the Spanish had remained neutral, working to stabilize their own government. In 1923, General Miguel de Rivera became the dictator of Spain, only to have his position revoked in 1930 by King Alfonso XIII. Republicans forced Alfonso to leave the country in 1931 and initiated a new Constitution that declared Spain a worker's republic. The Constitution provided measures to break up the large estates, separate church and state, and secularize the schools. In 1936 a popular election increased the Republican power and fueled additional land reforms.

While the Republicans had the support of the general population, it also had strong and powerful enemies in the Church, large landowners, and the military. In June 1936, the army in Spanish Morocco revolted against the Republican government and the rebellion, with General Francisco Franco as its leader, quickly spread to garrisons in Spain. Germany and Italy announced their support of Franco and dispatched men and equipment to support the revolution.

Central and parts of northern Spain remained loyal to the elected government, which requested aid from the world's democracies. Britain and France followed a policy of non-intervention, but they, like the United States, did provide volunteers for the Republican International Brigades. While the major democracies officially remained out of the war, the Soviet Union became the primary source of supplies and equipment for the Republicans.

On July 30, Franco's forces seized Burgos in north-central Spain and then marched south to capture Madrid. Despite poor organization and discipline, the Republicans held the passes and high ground in the Sierra de Guadarrama, thus blocking the Nationalist route to the capital city.

With the attack against Madrid stalled, the Nationalists accelerated their operations in the south, where they captured Toledo in September. In October, the Nationalist offensive, commanded by General Emilio Mola, advanced once more against Madrid, this time in four columns from the south and west. Mola announced that he was confident of victory because, in addition to his four advancing armies, he had a "fifth column" of volunteers within the city who would join the battle.

The fight for Madrid continued into November as the Soviet-backed Republicans and the Nazi-Fascist-supported Nationalists fought each other with the most advanced weapons of the era. Infantry and mechanized forces collided on the ground while aircraft met in the air.

By November 23, the Nationalists had captured about three-quarters of the city, but the Republicans continued to fight. Both sides were so depleted and exhausted that the battle settled into a stalemate along well-fortified trenches. For the next six months, the Nationalists conducted operations to cut roads into the city while the Republicans counterattacked to regain territory.

Franco, now with the title of "generalissimo," recognized that the Battle of Madrid was draining his resources and temporarily halted the attacks while he stabilized his control of the rest of the country. For two years, Franco maintained his siege of Madrid while the Soviet Union, Germany, and Italy tested their modern war tools. By the beginning of 1939, Franco controlled most of the country, and his siege of Madrid was starving the population at the rate of four hundred deaths per day.

On January 26, 1939, Barcelona, the last Republican stronghold in the north, fell to the Nationalists. Great Britain and France recognized the Franco regime as the legitimate government of Spain on February 27, but the Republicans in Madrid continued their defense. On March 6, Communist and anti-Communist factions among the Republicans defenders began their own internal conflict that further weakened the city's defenses.

During the Republican internal revolt, Franco built up his army outside Madrid for a final assault. On March 26, he began his first offensive against the city in two years. The hungry, divided Republican defenses disintegrated as 30,000 surrendered. Thousands more simply laid aside their weapons and uniforms and went home. Franco and his army triumphantly marched into Madrid on March 31.

The Battle of Madrid and the Spanish Civil War cost the Republicans 175,000 soldiers killed and 200,000 civilian battle-related deaths. Another 40,000 Republican soldiers and civilians were executed as war criminals by Franco's army. The Nationalists suffered 110,000 battle deaths. They, too, were the victims of executions, as another 86,000 were killed by Republican firing squads or hangman nooses.

Madrid and the battles that raged around it strongly influenced the development of mechanized vehicles and aircraft that would dominate the early years of the upcoming world war. Much to the displeasure of Germany and Italy, however, strategically located Spain did not join the Axis and remained neutral during World War II, because Franco wanted to consolidate and exploit his power within his own borders rather than risk his already depleted army in a larger conflict. Franco remained in complete control of Spain until his death in 1975.

After the conclusion of the Battle of Madrid, the Soviet Union and Germany discussed how to divide Europe. On August 23, 1939, representatives of the two countries, Vyacheslav Molotov and Joachim von Ribbentrop, agreed on a pact of nonaggression. Neither country would oppose the other when the Soviets occupied the Baltic states of Estonia, Latvia, and Lithuania and Hitler took over Poland

The Battle of Madrid closed the window on the Spanish Civil War and opened the door for the most destructive conflict in history. Many of the weapons and tactics of World War II were field-tested on the Spanish plains and in the streets of Madrid. The outcome directly affected the country for nearly four additional decades under the rule of Franco, whose influence remains in most of the country's activities today.

72

EL ALAMIEN

World War II, 1942

El Alamein was the turning point in North Africa during World War II when the British victory denied the Axis access to Egypt, the Suez Canal, and the Middle East's oil fields. British Prime Minister Winston Churchill later remarked, "Before Alamein we never had a victory. After Alamein we never had a defeat."

When they initiated World War II, the Germans had the best-trained and equipped army in the world. Their blitzkrieg tactics had enabled them to quickly capture France and push the British off the continent at Dunkirk. The greatest limitation had been oil to fuel the mechanized forces.

From the beginning, Hitler had planned to remedy this shortfall by capturing areas rich in petroleum. With his attack on the Soviet southern front, he would occupy the Caucasus, providing access to the Romanian oil fields, while an attack by his Italian allies would secure North Africa and access to the Middle East. In addition to gaining needed oil reserves, the offensives would capture the Suez Canal, giving the Germans easy access to the Indian Ocean, which would allow coordinated efforts with the Japanese.

When Italy declared war on Britain on June 10, 1940, the Italians' first objective was to push the British out of Egypt. However, despite their superior numbers, the Italians fared poorly against the British; their "attack" quickly changed into a retreat across Libya. By February 1941, the British had taken the key port of Tobruk and killed or captured more than 130,000 Italians at the cost of only 500 British soldiers killed and 1,400 wounded.

Hitler, fearing a total Italian collapse, sent an armored corps commanded by Erwin Rommel to regain the initiative in North Africa. Rommel, who had already gained fame for his tactical genius in the battles for Poland and France, arrived in North Africa in February 1941. Within a month, his Africa Corps had the British on the run. They recaptured Tobruk on June 21.

A day later, Hitler promoted Rommel to field marshal. While Hitler could provide a promotion, he could not, because of commitments to the Russian front, provide the number of replacements and amount of supplies Rommel needed to successfully continue his offensive. By 1942, the two armies had settled into defensive positions facing each other along a forty-mile line reaching from El Alamein on the Mediterranean in North Egypt to the Qattara Depression in the south.

On July 1, the Africa Corps attacked the enemy center, but the British responded with a counterattack in the south. General Claude Auchinleck's Eighth Army held during four weeks of thrusts and counterthrusts before the lines settled back along their original positions just sixty miles west of the Nile River.

Despite Auchinleck's fine performance, Churchill replaced him the following month with General Harold Alexander as the overall Middle Eastern commander and placed General Bernard Montgomery in command of the Eighth Army. The arrogant, rude, and vain Montgomery had the ability to motivate his soldiers and rebuild the force.

Rommel tested the new commander with an attack at the end of August at Alam Halfa, but the British lines held. A month later, Montgomery was ready with his own offensive. The British Eighth Army now numbered about 200,000 men and 1,000 tanks—double the number of Rommel's men and machines. Half of Rommel's 500 tanks were inferior Italian models, while the majority of Montgomery's were American-made Grants and Shermans. The British also had the advantage of air superiority over the entire front.

At 9:30 P.M. on October 23, 1942, the Eighth Army began their attack with a diversionary assault on the southern Axis defenses. The real target, however, was in the north at El Alamein. Advancing in the bright moonlight and assisted by engineers, the infantry and armor breached the enemy minefields. The Germans stood fast, but they were leaderless. Rommel was not present to direct counterattacks because he had returned to Germany for a brief visit. His temporary replacement, General Georg von Stumme, died of a heart attack while hurrying to the front. His body was not discovered for twenty-four hours, leaving the Africa Corps without leadership for a full day.

Rommel returned on October 25 to direct counterattacks, and by the next day, the front had stagnated. On the 27th, the British attempted again to break through the German defenses only to be beaten back. Finally, on the 29th, another Allied attack, this time led by an Australian division, penetrated the Africa Corps lines. German anti-tank weapons briefly stopped a follow-on attack on November 1, but the entire Africa Corps was preparing to withdraw on the 3rd. Hitler, despite being unable or unwilling to reinforce the Africa Corps, ordered Rommel to stand and fight to the last man. Rommel refused to squander his army in a pointless battle and began to withdraw westward on November 4.

Axis losses at El Alamein totaled 20,000 casualties and 30,000 prisoners. Nearly all of their tanks and artillery had been destroyed or captured. The British suffered 13,500 casualties and lost half their tanks. Over the next few months, the British pursued the Africa Corps westward toward the Americans who had landed at Casablanca on November 8. The last of the Axis soldiers in North Africa surrendered on May 13, 1943.

The British victory at El Alamein ended the German hopes of occupying Egypt, controlling the Suez Canal, and gaining access to the Middle Eastern oil fields. Besides destroying the Africa Corps, the Allies now occupied all of North Africa from where they could launch an invasion of Sicily that would eliminate Italy from the Axis fold.

El Alamein marked the end of German expansion. With the entry of the United States into the war and the Soviet victories in Russia, El Alamein was a turning point for North Africa as well as World War II. The battle began the march to Italy, onward to Normandy, and finally into the German heartland. As Churchill stated, after El Alamein, the Allies never again knew defeat.

73

SADOWA

Seven Weeks' War, 1866

The Battle of Sadowa in 1866 allowed the Prussians to replace the Austrians as leaders of the German-speaking states. It also demonstrated the military importance of the telegraph and railroads, as well as the effectiveness of breech-loading rifles over muzzle-loaders.

For more than fifty years after the end of Napoleonic Wars, the European nations had struggled to establish their identities and boundaries. Small states and kingdoms had united for their common protection and economic advancement. Generally, these unifications and confederations followed along the lines of ethnic heritage and language.

In an even longer struggle, since the seventeenth century Prussia and Austria had been vying for control of the German states. The two powers united to confront Napoleon, but after his defeat at the Battle of Waterloo in 1815 (9), they had renewed their competition. Prussia wanted the German states under their control. Austria wanted a looser confederation containing the Hungarian, Slavic, and Italian provinces as well as the German states.

By the mid-nineteenth century, Austria had one of the most powerful military organizations on the continent. They possessed more than 700 rifled cannons, which were the most modern and accurate ever fielded. However, in spite of their superior artillery, Austria still armed its infantry with muzzle-loading muskets. Austrian military leaders believed that the newly developed breech-loaders expended too much ammunition for their supply system to support. More importantly, they still believed that the best use of infantry was close fighting with the bayonet rather than with powder and shot.

The Austrians grew complacent in their superiority; the Prussians quietly expanded their army and adopted breech-loading rifles for their infantry. These weapons, known as needle-guns because of their thin, needle-like firing pins, could shoot at five times the rate of muzzle-loaders. Just as important, soldiers could reload them in the prone position rather than having to stand or kneel as muzzle-loaders required.

Prussia also developed superior field commanders, instituted plans to use modern railways to move troops and equipment, and integrated the newly developed telegraph into their communications network. They were ready, but few knew how prepared they were. In 1864, Prussia, under chancellor Otto von Bismarck, invaded and easily subdued the German states of Schleswig and Holstein. Austria, who claimed the states as part of their confederation, negotiated for a peaceful settlement of the crisis before finally declaring war on Prussia on June 14, 1866. Because few European observers had paid attention to the preparations in Prussia, most believed the Austrian army of nearly a million would readily subdue their German-speaking cousins. What they did not know was that Austria could mobilize only 320,000 men, thousands fewer than the Prussians already had in the field.

During the first two weeks of the war, the Prussians, led by General Helmuth von Moltke, captured the German states of Saxe, Hesse, and Hanover. Moltke continued his attack into Saxony and forced 25,000 Saxons to retreat until they joined the 200,000 Austrians, commanded by General Ludwig von Benedek, who were advancing to meet the Prussians.

Benedek chose to move his army to Koniggratz, where the terrain would benefit his defense. However, the Prussians caught up with him at Sadowa near the Elbe River, sixty-five miles northeast of Prague, before he reached his objective. By the morning of July 3, his army occupied hastily prepared defenses along a seven-mile arc. Moltke delayed his attack until his Second Army, containing more than a third of his troops, arrived from the west. However, a broken telegraph line delayed the orders for the Second Army to join the other Prussians.

The Austrians took advantage of their superior numbers and attacked. Despite the withering needle-gun fire, the Austrians closed to bayonet range. On a nearby hillside, Moltke observed the battle alongside Prussian King Wilhelm I and Chancellor Bismarck—one of the last occasions in history where a country's government leaders ventured near enough to a battle to see the fighting. Wilhelm asked Moltke about withdrawal plans. The general replied, "Here there will be no retreat. Here we are fighting for the very existence of Prussia."

Shortly, the Second Army arrived and attacked the Austrian right flank. The fresh troops with their breech-loaders stopped the Austrian advance. When the Austrians attempted several more times to close within bayonet range, the ground was covered with dead and dying Austrians, victims of the Prussian needle-guns. Benedek committed his cavalry, but the needle-gun and the Prussian horsemen dispatched by Moltke stopped them as well.

By 3:00 P.M., the surviving Austrians were in retreat. Even though their artillery covered their crossing of the Elbe to prevent the loss of the entire army, Austria was defeated. On the fields of Sadowa they had lost 40,000 men, half of them prisoners, compared to total Prussian casualties of only 9,000.

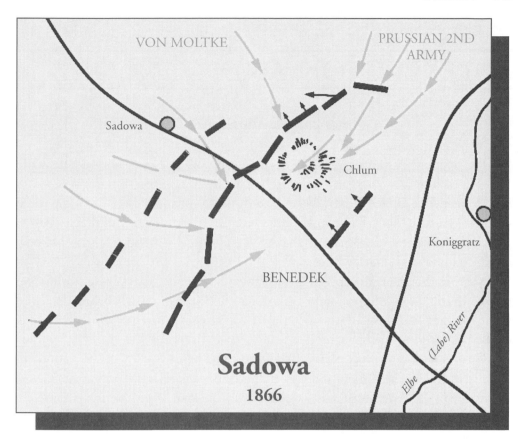

Sadowa

1866

The Prussians briefly pursued the retreating Austrians, but ultimately the Prussian leaders decided that Austria would make a better ally than enemy. Austria agreed to a cease-fire on July 26, 1866, and signed a formal peace treaty on August 23. Although another war would be fought for control of all of Germany, after the Austrian defeat at Sadowa, Bismarck and the Prussians held the upper hand and would ultimately unite the German-speaking peoples into one Empire.

This battle also foreshadowed future technological advances in weaponry. Prussia's infantry demonstrated how deadly the breech-loaders were. Austria displayed the value of accurate, long-range artillery.

The Battle of Sadowa, sometimes referred to as the Battle of Koniggratz, brought the Prussians to the forefront of military prowess. The impact of its outcome rippled across Europe, reinforcing some alliances and changing others. The battle led to a united Germany, yet it also created an imbalance of power that would result in many more conflicts over the next century.

74

LEXINGTON AND CONCORD

American Revolution, 1775

The opening battles of the American Revolution at Lexington and Concord, Massachusetts, led to the independent United States of America less than a decade later. The United States advanced to the status of a world power by the end of the next century. More than two hundred years after its initial revolutionary battles, the United States stands as the world's longest enduring democracy and its most powerful economic and military force.

By the mid-eighteenth century, Great Britain had established colonies throughout the world so that indeed "the sun never set on the British Empire." Britain looked to these colonies as sources of raw materials as well as revenue from duties and taxes. One of its most prosperous sources was its colonies in North America.

Discontented emigrants of the Old World had settled in the North American colonies, bringing with them their rebellious, independent spirit that soon rankled against British rule and regulations. Harsh taxes and trade regulations were imposed on the colonists by the British to pay the bills for the French and Indian Wars, and these measures had fanned the flames of rebellion.

In 1765, the British imposed the Stamp Act on the colonists, which required a tax stamp be purchased and affixed to all legal and commercial papers, newspapers, magazines, pamphlets, and even playing cards and dice. Previous taxation on the colonists had concentrated on various regions or certain products. The Stamp Act, for the first time, taxed all colonists regardless of their location or station. Inadvertently, the British provided the means to unite the colonies in a common cause.

Opponents to the Stamp Act formed secret societies, or adapted previously organized social and political clubs, to oppose the tax. One of the larger organizations, the Sons of Liberty, took direct action by attacking stamp agents and destroying tax stamps and records. When the British repealed the Stamp Act in 1766, the Sons of Liberty did not disband but rather continued to meet to oppose British control. By 1772, they had evolved into the Committees of Correspondence, which initiated interaction between groups in each of the thirteen colonies. In 1774, these committees convened the First Continental Congress.

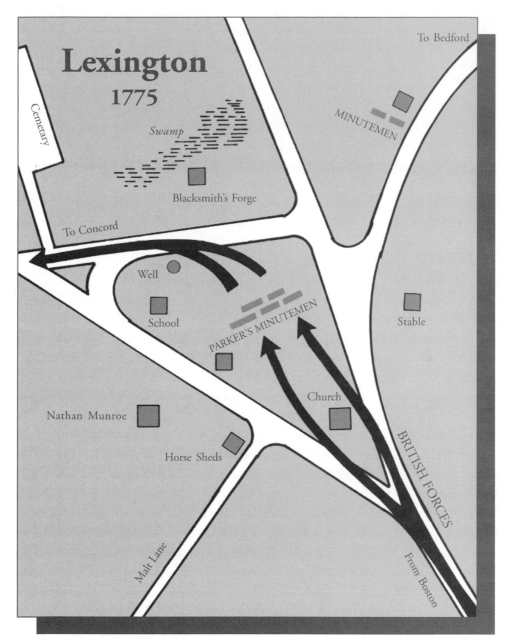

Lexington
1775

Cemetery

Swamp

MINUTEMEN

To Bedford

Blacksmith's Forge

To Concord

Well

School

PARKER'S MINUTEMEN

Stable

Nathan Munroe

Church

Horse Sheds

BRITISH FORCES

Malt Lane

From Boston

While they were organizing politically, the colonists were also hoarding arms and ammunition in the event of future military operations. On September 1, 1774, British troops, on the orders of General Thomas Gage, destroyed an arms depot in Cambridge, Massachusetts, where they met no resistance.

Despite this setback, the colonists continued to stockpile military supplies and munitions as more and more Americans favored independence from Great Britain. On April 18, 1775, General Gage learned of a new stockpile and issued the following order in Boston to the Tenth Regiment Foot: "Having received intelligence that a quantity of Ammunition, Provisions, Artillery, Tents and small Arms have been collected at Concord, for the Avowed Purpose of raising and supporting a Rebellion against His Majesty, you will march with the Corps of Grenadiers and Light Infantry, put under your command, with the utmost expedition and Secrecy to Concord, where you will seize and destroy…all Military Stores whatever."

Rebel patriots in Boston learned of the order, and Williams Dawes and Paul Revere rode toward Concord warning the villagers en route that "the British are coming." By the time the column of 700 British soldiers reached Lexington, sixteen miles from Boston, early on the morning of April 19, militia Captain John Parker had seventy "Minutemen" assembled on the town's common.

British Major John Pitcairn rode forward on his horse and demanded, "Disperse, ye rebels, disperse!"

For a while both sides stood their ground. Parker reportedly exclaimed to his men, "Stand your ground! Don't fire unless fired upon! But if they want to have a war, let it begin here."

The Americans, keenly aware they were vastly outnumbered, began to walk away, but they did not lay down their muskets. Suddenly a single shot rang out, and then several, followed by a general volley by the British infantry. Who fired first remains undetermined, but this brief fire fight, which left eight dead, including Parker, and ten militiamen and one British soldier wounded, was the first battle of the American Revolution.

The confident British continued their march to Concord, where they were only partially successful in destroying the rebel stores and provisions before Minutemen from surrounding villages arrived. Rebels soon outnumbered the British. After a brief skirmish at Concord's North Bridge that felled fourteen Redcoats, the British hastily retreated back to Boston.

Unhampered by any rules of warfare and angered by their losses at Lexington and Concord, the Americans began sniping at the retreating British from behind fences, trees, and buildings. By the time the British reached their garrison in Boston, they had suffered 73 killed, 174 wounded, and another 26 missing. American casualties totaled 49 dead, 41 wounded, and five missing.

Lexington and Concord were not decisive by any means. They were, however, "the shots heard around the world," the opening battles of the American Revolution. The brief skirmishes also proved to the rebel colonists that, despite their small numbers and lack of military training, they could use unconventional warfare to survive in fights against superior numbers.

If not at Lexington and Concord, the Revolution's first fights would have been elsewhere in a short time. The Americans were ready for independence and prepared to fight for it. Many battles lay ahead, including the pivotal fight at Saratoga (15) and the final victory at Yorktown (1), but the United States of today can trace back its military lineage to those first shots fired at Lexington Green and Concord's North Bridge.

75

GOLAN HEIGHTS

Israeli-Arab Six-Day War, 1967

The Battle of Golan Heights in 1967 secured Israel's northern border and helped bring an end to the Six-Day War. Since that time, occupation of the Heights has reduced attacks from Syria and Lebanon and protected Israeli settlements and water sources in the region. Although the Israelis successfully defended the territory in the Yom Kippur War of 1973, the Golan Heights remain today a point of military and political crisis.

According to the Bible, Abraham led nomadic, Hebrew-speaking tribes into Canaan in about 1800 B.C., where they would later be enslaved by the Egyptians. In 1200 B.C., Moses gained the Hebrews' freedom from Egypt and returned them to Canaan. Over the next thousand years, the Jews settled and defended much of what is today modern Israel. In the first century A.D., Rome dominated the region and put down several Jewish revolts. The Jews began their final revolt against the Romans in A.D. 130 but were totally defeated over the next five years. In 135, the surviving Jews were exiled, and the area became known as Palestine.

While the Jews formed communities around the world, various nations fought over Palestine for the next two centuries. The Crusaders briefly held part of the region after their occupation of Jerusalem in 1099, but Palestine remained mostly controlled by the Muslims.

In the latter part of the nineteenth century, European Jews had formed the Zionist movement that encouraged Jewish nationalism and the establishment of a homeland. By 1914, more than 60,000 Jews had immigrated to Palestine. Britain had gained control of the region as a spoil of World War I but made promises to both the Jews and the Arabs about the occupation of Palestine. During the 1930s, many Jews had immigrated—legally and illegally—to Palestine to escape Nazi persecution. More had followed after the liberation of the German concentration camps at the end of World War II.

For the next few years, the British attempted to stop illegal immigration into Palestine while the Jews and Arabs fought over the land. In 1947, the United Nations proposed dividing the region into Arab and Jewish states, but neither side agreed. Both believed that the region was theirs and theirs alone.

The British attempted to maintain some semblance of order, but when their mandate granting them control of Palestine expired on May 14, 1948, they withdrew and left the Jews and Arabs to decide their own fate. A few hours before the last British officials departed, David Ben-Gurion, commander of the Jewish military, declared Israel's independence. The United States quickly recognized the new nation.

Neighboring Arab countries joined local Palestinians in the fight for the country, but the Jews now numbered 650,000 with an army of 60,000. The disorganized Arab force fared poorly against the Israelis and on January 7, 1949, agreed to a cease-fire, but still refused to recognize Israel's right to exist.

Open warfare broke out again in 1956 when Egypt nationalized the Suez Canal and barred Israeli shipping. Israel attacked Egypt and drove all the way to the Suez Canal before another truce was negotiated.

The truce did not lead to peace, as the Arabs and Jews continued to conduct raids and terrorist attacks against each other over the next decade. Both sides also rearmed, as Israel received aircraft, weapons, and equipment from the United States, Britain, and France, while the Arab states relied on the Soviet Union for arms and equipment.

In 1967, Egypt, Syria, and Jordan began amassing their forces on the Israeli borders to avenge their previous defeats. Israel did not wait to be attacked but instead initiated the war themselves on the morning of June 5 with a surprise assault on enemy airfields. In a matter of hours, the Israeli air force had destroyed, mostly on the ground, more than three-quarters of the Egyptian air fleet; the following day they did the same to Syria.

A ground offensive followed the air campaign, and by June 8, Egyptian and Jordanian forces were in retreat on all fronts. The United Nations proposed a cease-fire, but the Israelis had one more objective to secure before agreeing to stop their offensive. On June 9, they moved against Syrian defenses on the Golan Heights along their northern border.

The Golan Heights, more than 480 square miles of rocky, basalt earth, rise from four to seventeen hundred feet to overlook Israel to the west and Syria to the north and east. The area dominates routes to and from Lebanon and controls access to fresh water reservoirs that serve much of Israel. Whoever controls the Golan Heights controls the entire region.

The Israelis began their attack with raids by helicopter-delivered infantrymen against key points. Bulldozers then breached the outer defenses and filled anti-tank ditches so their armor could advance. Over the next thirty-six hours, small and large fights broke out on the Heights with one common result—the Israelis dominated every engagement. By the end of the battle, the surviving Syrians were retreating

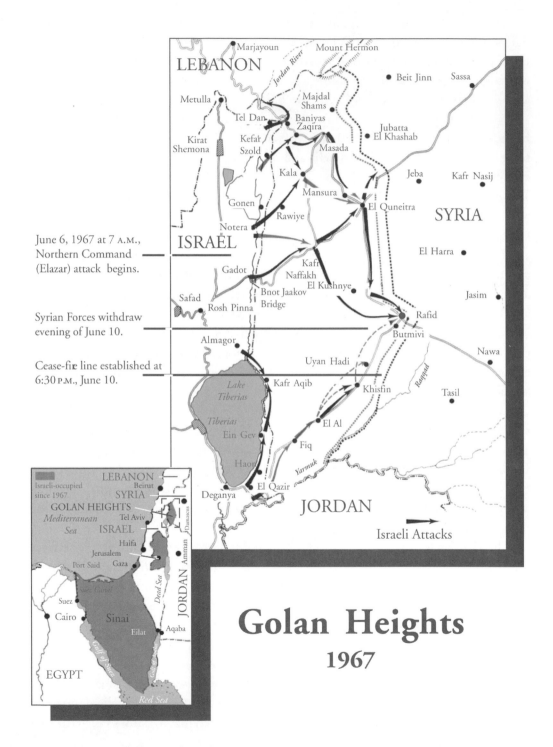

Marjayoun
Mount Hermon
LEBANON
Jordan River
Beit Jinn
Sassa
Metulla
Majdal Shams
Tel Dan
Baniyas Zaqira
Jubatta El Khashab
Kirat Shemona
Kefar Szold
Masada
Jeba
Kafr Nasij
Kala
Mansura
Gonen
El Quneitra
SYRIA
Rawiye
Notera
El Harra
June 6, 1967 at 7 A.M., Northern Command (Elazar) attack begins.
ISRAËL
Gadot
Kafr Naffakh
Jasim
Safad
Bnot Jaakov Bridge
El Kushnye
Rosh Pinna
Rafid
Syrian Forces withdraw evening of June 10.
Butmivi
Nawa
Almagor
Cease-fire line established at 6:30 P.M., June 10.
Uyan Hadi
Lake Tiberias
Kafr Aqib
Khisfin
Raggad
Tasil
Tiberias
Ein Gev
El Al
Fiq
Haon
Yarmuk
Deganya
El Qazir
JORDAN
Israeli Attacks

Israeli-occupied since 1967
LEBANON
Beirut
SYRIA
GOLAN HEIGHTS
Mediterranean Sea
ISRAEL
Tel Aviv
Damascus
Haifa
Jerusalem
Gaza
JORDAN
Amman
Port Said
Dead Sea
Suez
Cairo
Sinai
Aqaba
Eilat
Gulf of Suez
EGYPT
Red Sea

Golan Heights
1967

toward Damascus, leaving behind more than 2,500 dead, 100 tanks, and 200 artillery pieces. Israel's losses totaled only 115 killed and 306 wounded.

Both sides agreed to a cease-fire on June 10, but skirmishes continued for several weeks. The Arabs still refused to recognize the right of Israel to exist, and with more assistance from the Soviets, they again began to rearm. Israel also replaced destroyed equipment and rebuilt its army.

Egypt and Syria, humiliated by their defeat in the Six-Day War, once again attacked Israel on October 6, 1973. The Arab alliance caught the Israelis off guard and gained the advantage in the Sinai and the Golan Heights. Over the next two weeks, however, the Israelis regrouped to seize the initiative, drove the Egyptians and Syrians back, and doubled the pre-war size of occupied territory before the cease-fire on October 22.

Both the Six-Day and Yom Kippur Wars exerted influence far beyond the borders of Israel. The world watched the battles between war machines provided by the West and the Soviet Union as a prelude to possible warfare between NATO and the Warsaw Pact. The Soviets were embarrassed by the poor performance of their tanks and other weapons, while the United States and allies were extremely proud of the dominance of their weapons and equipment. Both wars forced the Soviets to spend more to modernize and update their equipment—expenditures that would help eventually bankrupt the country and bring down the Communist government.

The Yom Kippur War of 1973, like the Six-Day War, did not bring peace but merely another cease-fire. Small raids and terrorism continue in the region today while the constant state of crisis threatens to escalate into full-blown combat at any time. Israel continues to occupy the Golan Heights, and the Syrians continue to claim it is rightfully theirs. Today Israel, Palestine, and their neighboring countries remain one of the most volatile threats to world peace. Proposals have been made and rejected, agreements established and broken. There is no peace in the Middle East, only lulls between wars.

While the Battle of the Golan Heights is influential in that the occupation provides Israel a degree of security from its strategic heights, only time will determine the future of Israel. Its enemies are many, its friends few. The Golan Heights will play an important role in the destiny of the entire region.

76

INCHON

Korean War, 1950

The landing of United Nations' forces more than one hundred miles behind the North Korean lines in 1950 ranks as the most successful amphibious assault in history. The resulting battle stopped the attempt by the Communist North to take over the Democratic South. More importantly, it provided the first opportunity to display that the United Nations would stand together to oppose Communist expansion.

Decisions made at the Potsdam and Yalta Conferences at the close of World War II had outlined the procedures for the surrender of the Japanese who occupied the Korean Peninsula. The Soviet Union accepted the surrender north of the thirty-eighth parallel in 1945, while the Americans assumed that responsibility south of the latitude. In 1947, the Soviet Union announced that the North Koreans wanted to establish their own Communist government. The newly formed United Nations countered with a proposal that general elections be held to determine the government, but the Soviets refused. In August 1947, the Democratic People's Republic of Korea began governing the North, while the Republic of Korea took charge in the South.

Skirmishes began almost immediately along the thirty-eighth parallel border. The Soviets provided weapons, ammunition, and advisors to form a strong army in the North, while the United States less enthusiastically provided aid to the South. North Korea continued their military buildup through the late 1940s as their leader, Premier Kim Il-sung, prepared to forcibly reunify the country under his Communist flag.

Kim, however, remained reluctant as long as it appeared that the United States supported the government in the South. In January 1950, U.S. Secretary of State Dean Acheson unwittingly stated in a speech at the National Press Club in Washington that American interest in the Pacific included Japan, but he made no mention of Korea. Kim took this declaration, along with the fact the U.S. was in the process of withdrawing troops from Korea, as a clear message that the Americans would not defend the South.

After traveling to Moscow to confirm that he would have the backing of Joseph Stalin, Kim strengthened his army and assembled it near the border. On June 25, 1950, more than 100,000 North Koreans, led by 125 Soviet-made tanks, crushed the South's border defenses. Within forty-eight hours, the Communists were at the outskirts of the capital city of Seoul, and the South Korean army was in total retreat.

American President Harry Truman, at the request of South Korean President Syngman Rhee, appealed to the United Nations for assistance. The UN Security Council passed a resolution, with no veto from the boycotting Soviet Union, that the attack cease. When the North Koreans ignored the demand and continued their assault, the Security Council passed another resolution that authorized military assistance to repel the invasion.

On June 28, Truman ordered General Douglas MacArthur, commander of the Far Eastern Command in Japan, to provide immediate air support and to deploy additional ground troops to the peninsula as soon as possible. American troops from Japan began landing at the southern port of Pusan and pushed inland to join the retreating South Koreans. Small units from other United Nations armies followed, and on July 8, MacArthur assumed the leadership of the United Nations Command.

The UN force attempted to stop the Communist advance 150 miles south of the thirty-eighth parallel at Taejon but failed. By the end of July, the North Koreans had pushed the poorly prepared and under-trained UN force into a defensive perimeter around Pusan about seventy miles wide and sixty miles long. However, despite a hard-fought Communist attack, the Pusan Perimeter held strong as more UN forces joined the lines. Commanders on both sides assumed that MacArthur would assemble a large army around the port and then counterattack, but the American general had a better plan.

MacArthur proposed a bold amphibious counterattack at the port of Inchon just twenty-four miles southwest of Seoul. Critics expressed concerns about the plan not only because of the distance behind the lines, but also because the tides at Inchon varied more than thirty feet, allowing only a narrow time frame for success. MacArthur ignored the criticism, stating, "We shall land at Inchon, and I shall crush them."

In early September, MacArthur assembled Task Force Seven, composed of 320 warships, including four aircraft carriers and 70,000 men from nine UN countries. The principal units, the U.S. First Marine and the U.S. Army Seventh Infantry Divisions, became the X (Tenth) Corps.

After five days of aerial bombardment and two days of naval gunfire, MacArthur launched Operation Chromite early in the morning on September 15, 1950. Beacons, set by forward reconnaissance units who had secretly gone ashore several days previously, guided the lead elements ashore. Marines of the Fifth Regiment, with only seventeen men wounded, quickly overran the critical island of Wolmi-do, which guarded the approach to the mainland. A few hours later, more Marines from the First Division went ashore and fought their way inland through light resistance.

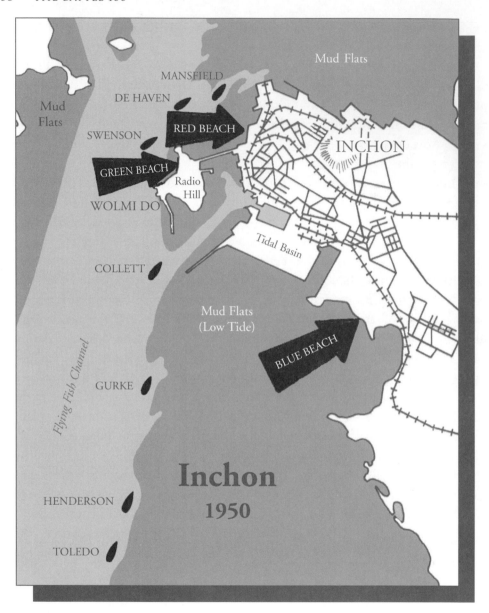

By the end of the day, Inchon was secured. Its thousand defenders were dead, captured, or retreating wildly toward Seoul. Marine casualties totaled 20 dead and fewer than 200 wounded. On September 16, the Seventh Infantry Division came ashore to push toward Seoul and its important airfield at Kimpo.

Within days, the X Corps secured the airfield and the capital while suffering fewer than 300 total casualties. At the same time, the UN forces in the Pusan Perimeter broke out and drove the North Koreans back. On September 26, the UN forces from Pusan and Inchon linked up near Osan, cutting off and ultimately destroying more than eight divisions of North Koreans. The Communist soldiers who had escaped retreated back across the thirty-eighth parallel, and by October 1 all of South Korea was in UN control.

The UN forces crossed the thirty-eighth parallel, continued their pursuit, and by Christmas occupied most of North Korea. Only a large-scale intervention by Communist China prevented a UN victory. Eventually, the battle lines stabilized back near the thirty-eighth parallel, and a cease-fire was finally declared on July 17, 1953. Technically, and at times in actuality, the two countries have remained at war ever since.

This continuing stalemate in Korea, instead of a decisive victory, lessens the impact of the landing at Inchon, but the battle is still extremely important. While the breakout of the Pusan Perimeter would have likely been a success without Inchon, the landing made it easier and reduced the number of potential friendly casualties. More importantly, Inchon proved to the world that the United Nations could and would unite to stop international aggression.

77

AYACUCHO

Peruvian War of Independence, 1824

The Battle of Ayacucho marked the end of Spanish control of South America, which had lasted for more than three hundred years. With an army of less than 6,000, rebel leader Antonio José de Sucre freed most of the continent from European control, allowing the formation of independent nations that still exist.

From the time of the exploratory voyages of Christopher Columbus and the conquests of Hernán Cortés and Francisco Pizarro, Spain had claimed and ruled most of Central and South America. The extensive natural resources of the region, especially silver and gold, financed Spain's ascension to the role of the world's most powerful military and trade force. Not until the destruction of the Spanish Armada in 1588 (16) did anyone defeat Spain. The rise of Britain and France diminished the status of Spain in Europe, but it easily maintained its holdings in the New World for an additional two hundred years.

Each succeeding generation born and reared in the New World increasingly resented Spanish officials sent to govern and tax. The successful rebellion by the United States against Great Britain fueled the growing independence movement. The French Revolution inspired even greater desire for independence in South America.

When Napoleon occupied Spain in 1808, the Latin American colonies swore continued allegiance to Spain's deposed King Ferdinand VII, but they enjoyed this period when Spain had little control over their activities. Some, including Simón Bolívar and José de San Martín, took advantage of the situation to begin direct military action to gain independence.

When Ferdinand regained his throne in 1814, he sought to regain control of the New World colonies, but the South American-born Spanish population resisted. Spain relied on small military units sent to organize and lead locals who remained loyal to the crown. The rebels recruited their members from Spanish citizens who wanted independence from local natives and from mixed races. By 1821, Bolívar had liberated much of the northern part of the continent at the Battle of Carabobo (67) while Martín had defeated the Spanish in Argentina and other areas in the south. In 1822, the two liberators met in Ecuador, where Martín, after some disagreement, turned over his command to Bolívar for the final operations to gain independence for all of Spanish South America.

Spain continued to fight the rebellion with loyal South Americans led by officers from Spain. Spanish wealth and assets were already dwindling, but their decline was also influenced by the recently declared Monroe Doctrine of the United States. In December 1823, President James Monroe declared that the United States would consider any effort by a European country to establish or re-establish colonies in the Western Hemisphere "as dangerous to our peace and safety" and would resist any such incursion. Spain, like other European nations, viewed this declaration with amusement or contempt, but none, including the Spanish, sent any more troops to South America.

Bolívar, with General Antonio José de Sucre as his second-in-command, began a major offensive against the Spanish early in 1824. After several small skirmishes, the cavalry forces of the two armies met at Junín, about ninety-five miles northeast of Lima, on August 6. In a forty-five-minute battle fought with saber and pike, the revolutionaries drove the Spanish force from the field.

Skirmishes continued for several months, but the victory at Junín had given the rebels a huge boost in morale and they gained support, both in recruits and supplies, from the local population. Bolívar was so confident of a final victory that he left Sucre in charge of the army and returned to Lima to organize the new government.

Sucre's rebels and the Royalists, commanded by José de la Serna, maneuvered against each other for the next several months with no decisive action. Finally, on December 8, the two forces met on the plain of Ayacucho. In the local native language, Ayacucho means "dead corner," both for the previous fights there during the early Spanish conquest and for its general geography. The plain measures only 1,300 yards from east to west and about half that from north to south. To the north and west are mountains, and the plain falls off into gorges in the east.

Serna led an army of about 9,000 supported by fourteen cannons. However, only about 500 of his men, mostly officers and sergeants, were regular Spanish soldiers. The rest were volunteers or draftees from the local villages who had varying degrees of training and motivation. Across the field, Sucre had only one artillery piece and about 6,000 men, but they were enthusiastic and confident from their victory at Junín.

On the morning of December 9, Serna ordered his infantry forward against the rebel left and center. Both held firm. On the right flank, the commander of the rebel Second Colombian Division, General Cordova, drew his sword and deliberately killed his own horse. He then shouted to his men, "There lies my horse; I have now no means of escape, and we must fight it out together!" He then waved his hat about his head and declared, "Onward with the step of conquerors."

Sucre committed his cavalry reserve when Cordova's troops gained the advantage. By early afternoon Serna and his troops were in full retreat. Sucre pursued and by nightfall had captured all of the Spanish artillery as well as Serna, most of his officers, and 1,000 soldiers. Another 1,800 lay dead at Ayacucho or along the line of withdrawal. Sucre's casualties totaled about 300 killed and twice that number wounded.

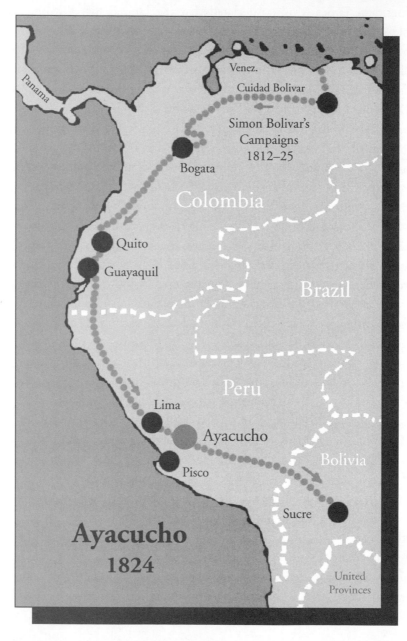

Several minor skirmishes followed Ayacucho, but for all practical purposes, the rebels had succeeded. Spanish officials quickly left the country or joined the new independent government. Spain's holdings in the New World were reduced to a few Caribbean islands. With its status as a world power greatly reduced, Spain was well on its way to its later defeat in the Spanish-American War of 1898.

Unfortunately, the revolution in South America did not mirror that of North America, where the states were united into a single country. The many opposing factions within South America, combined with its vast geography and lack of established communications, led to many countries instead of one. Although most of these countries still exist, South America has never been able to unite sufficiently to influence world affairs or to project power beyond their own shores.

Even if the Spanish had won at Ayacucho, they were on the decline, and victory would have ultimately gone to the rebels. Spain had neither the power nor the will to maintain its control; independence was inevitable. Spain might have maintained some role in South America if it had been willing to share power, such as Great Britain did to maintain its Commonwealth. But Spain wanted all or nothing, and they achieved the latter.

Although Ayacucho is deserving of its comparison to the American victory at Yorktown (1) in that it successfully concluded the revolution, the long-term results and influence of the battle were not nearly so significant. South America remains today a rich region that has yet to achieve its potential. While its countries are mostly democratic, many of its governments remain in an almost constant state of turmoil.

78

PORT ARTHUR

Russo-Japanese War, 1904

The surprise attack by the Japanese against the Russian Pacific Fleet anchored off Port Arthur, and the subsequent land siege and attack against the city, set the stage for Japan's victory over Russia in the early years of the twentieth century. Port Arthur led to additional successes, including the decisive victory in the Battle of Tsushima Strait (34) that drew Korea and parts of China into Japanese control. More importantly, the combined victories elevated Japan to the status of world power and displayed for the first time in modern history that an Asian country could defeat the Europeans.

From the time it opened its shores to visitors in 1854, Japan had studied the industrial and military developments of other countries. Within a short period of a half-century, the Japanese had advanced from a primitive state to become one of the world's technological leaders. The ambitious Japanese, however, lacked the natural resources for their continued modernization and had to look outside their home islands for raw materials.

In 1894, Japan went to war with China over control of Korea and the Liaodong Peninsula with its strategic harbor of Port Arthur. Although the Japanese were successful in their war, they lost in peace when European nations diplomatically forced them to return their gains. The disappointed Japanese became even angrier when China agreed to lease Port Arthur to the Russians and allow them to build a railway connecting the seaport with the Russian interior.

On February 8, 1904, the first great war of the twentieth century began when the Japanese launched a surprise attack against the Russian Pacific fleet anchored off Port Arthur. The Japanese, commanded by Admiral Heihachiro Togo, damaged two Russian battleships and a cruiser and blockaded the remaining ships in the Port Arthur harbor. When the Russian commander, Admiral Stepan Makarov, attempted to break the siege on April 13, his flagship *Petropavlvosk* struck a mine and sank with the loss of 600 Russian sailors, including the admiral. The remainder of the fleet returned to Port Arthur and the Japanese navy again blockaded the harbor entrance.

With the Russian navy neutralized, the Japanese landed five infantry divisions above Port Arthur on May 5. For the next three weeks, the Japanese army under

General Yasukata Oku attacked the Russian defenses at Nanhan commanded by General Anatoly Stesel. Finally, on May 27, the Japanese overran Nanhan and forced the Russians to withdraw to a defensive position outside Port Arthur.

By June 1, more than 80,000 Japanese surrounded the 42,000 Russians defending the city. Over the next several months, the battle settled into trench-like warfare that provided a preview of later combat in World War I. Machine guns, artillery, and naval gunfire raked the Russian lines, but despite casualties, illness, and declining supplies, the Russians held on.

On December 5, the Japanese infantry overran key high ground known as 203 Meter Hill. They quickly moved some of their heavy guns to the heights and shelled the remaining Russian ships in the harbor below. The last four Russian battleships soon were at the bottom of the harbor. Finally, on January 2, 1905, Stesel surrendered. Although victorious, the battle had been costly for the Japanese. More than 58,000 of their soldiers had been killed or wounded in the seven-month siege.

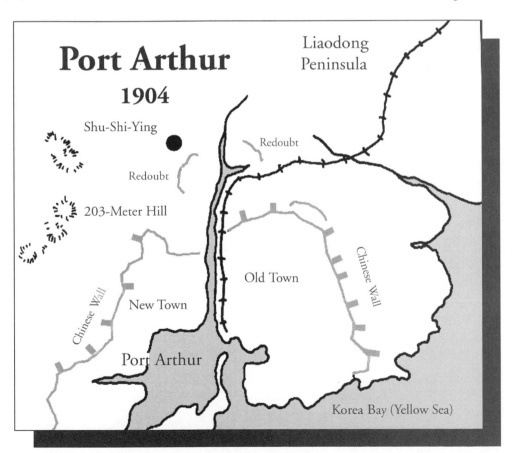

During the Battle of Port Arthur, other Japanese units landed in Manchuria and Korea, where they experienced similar success against the Russians. Their victory at the Battle of Mukden on March 10, 1905, further weakened Russian resolve, which then went to the bottom of the sea when its Western fleet finally arrived only to be soundly defeated in the Battle of Tsushima Strait on May 27.

The Japanese victory at Port Arthur over the Russian sea and land forces set the stage for the future battles that brought Russia to the peace table. While it is not as influential as the Battle of Tsushima Strait, it played a significant role in winning the war and establishing Japan as a world power. Both battles proved to an astonished Western world that an Asian country could fight and win against a modern European power.

The Japanese welcomed their new power and status. The nationalism and political strength that resulted from their military victories at Port Arthur and Tsushima Strait would make them the aggressor in another war less than forty years later, when they would be crushed by the United States and the Allies.

The defeat at Port Arthur pushed the Russians closer to revolution against the Czar, which ultimately led to the establishment of the Communist Soviet Union. While they did not declare war against Japan in World War II until after the Americans dropped their atomic bombs (7), the Soviets applied many of the lessons learned in the trenches outside of Port Arthur to their later successful defense of major cities against the Nazis.

Even though Port Arthur had significant impact, it was not as influential as it should have been. The Americans ignored the example of Japanese sneak naval attacks, leaving themselves unprepared at Pearl Harbor (62) in 1941. Except for the use of aircraft, there were many similarities between Port Arthur and the attack against the Hawaiian islands.

The long siege of Port Arthur brought observers from most of the world's major military powers. Despite the obvious effectiveness of machine guns and mass-produced heavy artillery, only the Germans understood their possible impact on future conflicts. Much of the Germany's early success in World War I came from what they learned at Port Arthur. France and Great Britain would pay in blood for the lessons they did not learn from that battle.

79

AGINCOURT

Hundred Years' War, 1415

The victory by the much smaller English army over the French at Agincourt on October 25, 1415, revealed the power of the common soldier armed with the longbow over armor-covered, horse-mounted knights. Immortalized nearly two hundred years later by William Shakespeare's *Henry V,* Agincourt has become one of history's most famous battles.

In the mid-fourteenth century, England and France had differed over who should sit on the French throne as well as over territorial claims throughout the region. For more than a century, the two had fought with various degrees of intensity in what became known as the Hundred Years' War.

Despite the English victory early in the war at Crécy (33) in 1346, neither side had been able to sustain an advantage. For the next half-century they continued intermittent warfare on land and at sea. In August 1415, newly crowned King Henry V of England decided to invade France and end the hostilities. After only a few weeks of campaigning in Normandy, however, Henry's army suffered from combat casualties, hunger, and disease. Henry determined that his best course of action was to march northeast to the port of Calais and return home to regroup. After all, in a war that had already been going on for more than fifty years, there was no need to be hasty.

Heavy rains slowed Henry's army of about 5,000 archers and 1,000 cavalry, requiring them to detour around the flooded Somme River. This delay allowed Charles d'Albret, the constable of France, to assemble an army of more than 20,000 men, mostly titled knights, and move toward Calais.

On October 24, at the village of Agincourt, about 35 miles northwest of Arras, d'Albret blocked Henry's route. The English king, realizing the French outnumbered his army three or four to one, sought a truce, but d'Albret refused his terms. Henry quickly deployed his force on the far side of a freshly plowed, rain-soaked field, positioned between two patches of forest that were about 1,200 yards apart. He dismounted his cavalry into three divisions abreast and placed his archers on each flank.

Across the field, d'Albret deployed his force three ranks in depth with the cavalry forward. For the rest of the day and the night the two sides faced each other with neither taking the offense.

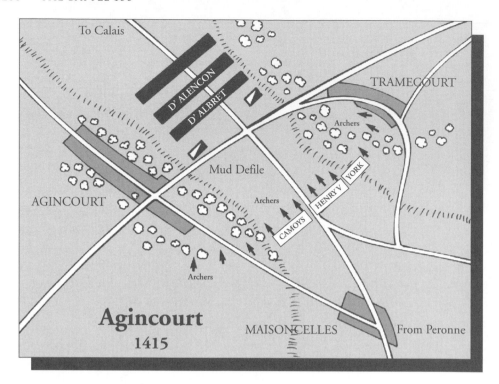

To Calais

D' ALENÇON

D' ALBRET

TRAMECOURT

Mud Defile

Archers

AGINCOURT

Archers

YORK

HENRY V

CAMOYS

Archers

Agincourt
1415

MAISONCELLES

From Peronne

On the morning of October 25, Saint Crispin's Day, Henry maneuvered his archers with their longbows forward until they were within range of the French lines. Their hail of arrows killed or wounded many of the Frenchmen, but more importantly, the action enraged the defenders into advancing against the archers, for the French still fancied the mounted knight with his sword over modern weapons, such as the longbow. According to plan, the English bowmen withdrew to their infantry lines and continued to fire their missiles at the advancing French cavalry and infantrymen. The narrow opening between the forests so restricted the number who could join the attack that their total only equaled the number of defending Englishmen. The muddy field further slowed the French advance, allowing the longbow men to continue their slaughter. When the French finally reached the English lines, the archers dropped their bows and joined the defense with swords and axes.

The first two French ranks fell in front of the English defenses. Those not killed were taken prisoner and quickly withdrawn to the rear. As the third rank prepared to attack, a small number of French camp followers infiltrated Henry's rear area to plunder his supplies. Henry, thinking his rear was threatened, ordered the execution of all prisoners. It was a needless massacre. By the time the French third rank neared the English defenses, the heaps of their dead so discouraged them that they withdrew.

Among the dead were d'Albret, more than 500 French noblemen, and more than 5,000 French soldiers. English casualties, nearly all common soldiers with the exception of the Duke of York, were only about a thousand, although accounts vary from as few as 200 to as many as 1,600.

Despite the decisive victory, Henry was neither willing nor strong enough to exploit his advantage. He resumed his march to Calais and sailed to England, but he did return two years later to conquer most of Normandy. The English were not, however, able to sustain their success in France, and the Hundred Years' War continued for another four decades after Agincourt. The depleted and exhausted two countries finally concluded the war in 1453 without the benefit of a formal peace treaty.

Agincourt was indeed a decisive victory achieved by a badly outnumbered army. It did not, however, end the war or even greatly influence its outcome. Much is made of the success of the English longbow men in the battle, but the effectiveness of the weapon was no surprise, as it had already been proven a half-century earlier at Crécy. The day of the heroic armor-clad knight of nobility was already in decline, and Agincourt merely proved that their time of dominance on the battlefield was past.

Agincourt certainly deserves its honored place in history, particularly among the English. But its place on this list is not only for what occurred on Saint Crispin's Day, 1415. Rather its greatest and most lasting influence began nearly two centuries after the battle when William Shakespeare penned *Henry V.* Shakespeare's memorable lines about a "small band of brothers" achieving victory over vast numbers of foes continues to awe readers and audiences and inspire military leaders to this day. Henry may have won the battle at Agincourt, but it was the Bard who provided the lasting influence of the fight. In addition to the play's pure entertainment and dramatic appeal, it has left a lasting influence on soldiers of all countries who have felt for one reason or another that their efforts were not supported properly or were underappreciated.

In *Henry V,* Act 4, scene 3, Henry's men are tired and fearful of fighting such a numerically superior force. They remark to their king that things might be different if more of their countrymen had joined the campaign. King Henry responds, in words often quoted in military circles today:

This story shall the good man teach his son
And Crispin Crispian shall ne'er go by,
From this day to the ending of the world,
But we in it shall be remembered,
We few, we happy few, we band of brothers.
For he to-day that sheds his blood with me
Shall be my brother; be he ne'er so vile,

This day shall gentle his condition;
And gentlemen in England now a-bed
Shall think themselves accurs'd they were not here,
And hold their manhoods cheap whiles any speaks
That fought with us upon Saint Crispin's Day.

(4.3.61–72)

80

YENAN

Chinese Civil War, 1934–1935

The six-thousand-mile retreat by Mao Zedong and his followers from Jiangxi (Kiangsi) Province in southern China to Yenan in the northern province of Shaanxi (Shensi) saved the Chinese Communist movement from extinction. Veterans of this "Long March" formed the core of the Communist Party that took control of China thirteen years later, after their victory over the Nationalists at the Battle of Huai-Hai (8) in 1948.

As late as the start of the twentieth century, warlords were still fighting with each other over various regions of China as they had for hundreds of years. During World War I, Japanese invaders had occupied part of the country and the newly formed Soviet Union threatened the northern provinces. Two major factions of Chinese had tried to unite to oust foreign occupation. Chiang Kaishek led the KMT, or Nationalists, while several leaders, including Mao Zedong, headed the CCP, or Communists.

Because of opposing philosophies and goals, the Nationalists and Communists ended the partnership in 1927. The Nationalists generally focused on control of the urban and industrial areas while the Communists concentrated on the rural populations. The Nationalists had the larger army as well as access to more weapons and supplies. However, the Communists controlled Jiangxi Province and its fifty million people in southeastern China.

The stronger Nationalists surrounded the Communist-held province, blockaded it from receiving food or other supplies, and began military operations against the Communists. During the seven-year campaign, the Communist sector steadily shrank as a million soldiers and civilians died of wounds, disease, and starvation.

In 1934, the surviving Communists realized that they had to escape the encirclement or they would be totally destroyed. On the night of October 16, about 90,000 men and women broke through the Nationalist lines and began the Long March north to Shaanxi Province, where the terrain and local Communist partisans would provide them safety.

Over the next year, the Communists trekked across twenty-four rivers and eighteen mountain ranges in all types of weather. Along the way, they fought pursuing Nationalists as well as various feudal and provincial armies who resented the Communist intrusion into their territory.

The Communists, however, did more than fight on their Long March. Mao, who rose to the primary leadership position during the march, used the journey to recruit additional followers and to promote his ideas of Communism. As he passed through villages, he instituted land reforms that redistributed ownership from the rich to the peasants. He also ensured that his soldiers took no food or other supplies from the peasants without payment. Unlike the Nationalists, who took whatever they wanted, the Communists left behind friends and converts rather than enemies. Mao also left behind cells of loyal followers who continued to promote the advantages of Communism. Many of the regions through which Mao and his Long March passed had never heard of the Communists before their arrival. While few openly welcomed him or picked up arms to join his cause, the kind treatment and ideas of reform of the Communists made such an impression on the citizens that they were easily recruited in later years as Mao became more powerful.

After marching 6,000 miles, fighting Nationalists and local militias, and enduring harsh weather and climate, the Communists finally made their way to Yenan in Shaanxi Province, where they joined a local army of 10,000 Communists on October 20, 1935. Only 20,000 of the original 90,000 survived the Long March, but the bond and trust between the survivors influenced all future Communist actions.

In 1937, the Nationalists and Communists once again put aside their differences to join to fight another invasion from Japan. Both sides accepted aid from the United States and the Soviet Union but hoarded many of these arms and supplies rather than use them against the Japanese. When World War II concluded, the Nationalists and Communists, each now well-armed, continued their fight for the control of China. This time, the Communists gained the upper hand, and after defeating the Nationalists at Huai-Hai in 1948, founded the People's Republic of China the following year with Mao as its chairman.

Yenan was more a destination than a battle, but it is worthy of inclusion on this list of influential conflicts. The Communists had to win every engagement along the route of the Long March. A single defeat would have meant their extinction, but they could not declare victory until they reached the Yenan sanctuary.

If the Communists had not reached Yenan, the Long March would have failed. If the Long March had failed, the Communists would have had no role in China's participation against Japan in World War II, nor would they have emerged from the war to renew their takeover of the country that concluded with their victory at Huai-Hai. While Huai-Hai is more influential because it gave the Communists the total control of China that they still possess today, it might not have happened at all if not for the success of the Long March.

Without Yenan and Huai-Hai one can only speculate on the influence of a Nationalist rather than a Communist China. The Korean and Vietnam wars would have been different or perhaps not have taken place at all. Also, Communist Chinese arms and advisors would not have supported Marxist groups around the world. But the Communists did successfully complete their Long March and eventually assumed the leadership of all of China, a country that is today one of the last centers of socialism and the source of the primary threat to regional and world peace.

81

HATTIN

Christian Crusade/Muslim War, 1187

The victory of the Muslim army led by Saladin over the Crusaders at Hattin ended dominance of the Holy Land that the Christians had gained a century earlier. It also established Saladin as the most influential military leader of the period and further united the Muslims in their efforts to expel European invaders from their territory.

By the eleventh century, the Western world had basically settled into two religious camps: Christian and Muslim. While factions within these two groups differed greatly and often fought among themselves, nothing could unite Christian or Muslim factions faster than the prospect of fighting each other—particularly when it came to control of the regions of Palestine and Syria that they both considered their Holy Land.

Catholic and Byzantine Orthodox Christians disagreed on numerous tenets of the faith, but they came together when confronted by Islam. For centuries, however, Catholic Western Europeans fought among themselves while the Byzantine Empire spread Christianity eastward toward Islam's westward advances.

The Muslim world, while not without internal turbulence of its own, managed to unite in 1071 to defeat the Byzantines at Manzikert (31). This allowed the Muslims, mostly Turks, to threaten Constantinople and tighten their control over the Holy Land.

In 1095, Pope Urban II called for a crusade to free the Holy Land from the "infidels." An army of knights and common soldiers sailed to Palestine and occupied the major holy sites and cities in 1099. The Christian crusaders soon spread throughout the coastal region and into Syria. Their presence did not bring peace. The Crusaders often did not get along themselves, and their feudal control angered Christian settlers as well as Jewish and Muslim natives.

Subsequent Crusades occupied additional parts of the region over the next century while the Muslims frantically sought a leader who could retake what they considered their own holy sites. That person did not emerge until the mid-twelfth century. As a youth, Saladin learned and served as a small unit leader in the Turkish-Syrian army that opposed the various Crusades. In 1164, he participated in the successful campaign to drive the Christians from Egypt. Following that battle, Saladin took charge of the Egyptian government, and over the next two decades, he united the various Muslim factions from Egypt to Baghdad.

In 1187, Saladin, now in control of all of the Middle East except for the Crusader states in Palestine, called for a jihad, or holy war, to expel the Christians. The Muslim leader was aware that the Christian settlements were well-defended and that they could quickly reinforce each other in the event of an invasion. He therefore decided that, rather than attack them directly, he would lure the Christians out of their fortifications into more open territory.

Saladin began by occupying the lightly defended town of Tiberias on the Sea of Galilee with his army of 20,000 men. The Christian king, Guy of Lusignan, immediately assembled his army. Despite the advice of several of his subordinates that Saladin might be forming a trap, Guy ordered a march to rescue Tiberias. Although he realized the dangers, Guy feared appearing weak and losing control of his own kingdom if he failed to do so. Also, Guy had a piece of the "True Cross" under which his army would march, and therefore he believed that God would be on his side.

Guy gathered the largest Christian army ever formed in the Holy Land. More than 1,200 knights and 14,000 soldiers, armed with swords, bows, and crossbows, stood ready to march from their assembly area at Saffuriya. The route to Tiberias was not long, but the fifteen-mile journey led across a barren desert with no access to shade or water. Along the route Saladin positioned archers to harass and rain arrows on the advancing column.

By mid-morning of the first day, the Christians were out of water and suffering under the heat and showers of arrows. Guy turned his advance from Tiberias to the Springs of Hattin in the northeast—the only nearby source of water. Again, Saladin dispatched his archers to harass the march. On a plateau just short of the springs, the main Muslim army blocked the Christian advance. Guy pitched a tent to house the fragment of the True Cross and camped his army around the relic.

During the night of July 3, Saladin's men burned what little vegetation was available on the camp's upwind side. The smoke and heat added to the misery of the thirsty Christians. At daylight on the morning of July 4, 1187, the Christians resumed their march to the springs. Once again, Saladin's archers attacked the columns. When the thirst-crazed men began to break ranks, the Muslim cavalry swept in, dividing the force. Guy attempted to rally his army around the bit of the True Cross, but the Muslim horsemen slashed their way through his ranks and captured the holy relic. Christian resolve melted. Only a small group of knights, probably fewer than 200, fought their way through the Muslim encirclement and escaped. The remainder of Guy's army either died or was captured.

Among the prisoners was Guy himself, whom Saladin provided with water and humane treatment. One of Guy's subordinates, Reynald of Chatillon, did not fare so well. Saladin had promised to personally kill the knight in revenge for the death of a relative. Shortly after the battle, he did so. He then offered the other Christian leaders the option of converting to Islam or execution. Most chose the latter. The common Christian soldiers were not provided an option but rather were sold into slavery.

Within months of their victory at Hattin, the Muslims captured most of the major Christian cities in Palestine. Although the Europeans launched another half-dozen crusades over the next century, none was successful in regaining control of the Holy Land. Some of these Crusaders were more interested in looting than in establishing control, while others were too weak to make an impact on the strong Muslim forces that Saladin left behind.

There is also evidence that Guy's defeat while fighting under the protection of the fragment of the True Cross eroded the beliefs of many Christians that their God would provide victory regardless of the obstacle or cause. Whatever the reason, Islam remained in control of the region for more than seven hundred years and broadened their area of dominance with the victory at Constantinople in 1453 (41).

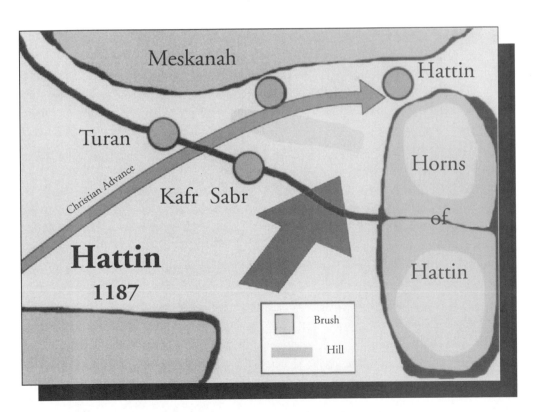

Hattin, therefore, was a turning point in the struggle for control of the Holy Land. Guy's poor plan led to the destruction of his army and the end of Christian dominance in the region. Even without his victory at Hattin, however, Saladin likely would have achieved the same result if the Christians had remained in their fortified cities. Saladin was the better general with access to a far greater number of soldiers and supplies. The Christians were a great distance from home, few in number, and representative of too many kingdoms and peoples to unite strongly enough to resist the Muslim army. The Crusaders were doomed from the start; Hattin simply expedited their demise.

82

GUADALCANAL

World War II, 1942–1943

The Battle of Guadalcanal was the first time during World War II that Americans defeated the Japanese army. The long and bloody battle served as a training ground for American men, weapons, and tactics that secured the Solomon Islands and began the long, island-hopping campaign toward the Japanese homeland.

Within months of the carrier attack against Pearl Harbor (62), the Japanese naval and land forces had defeated the major Allied strongholds in the Western Pacific. On February 15, 1942, the British had surrendered Singapore in what Prime Minister Winston Churchill declared "the worst disaster and largest capitulation in British history." The Americans in the Philippines had put up a better fight, but they too had surrendered on May 6–18.

In early May, the Japanese had landed unopposed on Guadalcanal and Tulagi on the far eastern end of the Solomon Islands. Soon after landing, they began building an airfield on the north central shore of Guadalcanal while their infantry fortified the island. The Japanese planned to use these islands to enable them to cut off, and possibly invade, Australia.

About the time the Japanese were landing at Guadalcanal, the Americans were seizing the initiative at sea. On May 7, U.S. carriers drove the Japanese fleet out of the Coral Sea and then soundly defeated them at Midway (44) in early June. Now that they were gaining the advantage at sea, the Americans turned to block the Japanese land advance.

Two months after Midway and only eight months after Pearl Harbor, the U.S. initiated operations to reclaim the Solomon Islands. On August 7, 1942, the U.S. First Marine Division, commanded by General Alexander Vandegrift, landed on the north side of Guadalcanal and on Tulagi. The 16,000 marines quickly secured all their objectives from the Japanese, including the airfield at Lunga Point that was near completion.

The Japanese, caught off guard by the invasion, immediately responded with air attacks, bombardments from ships, and infantry reinforcements to retake the airfield. The marines, mostly raw recruits just out of boot camp but led by seasoned sergeants who were veterans of intervention operations from the Caribbean to China, dug in around the airfield in a four-by-seven-mile perimeter. On August 20, the first planes began operations from the airstrip now called Henderson Field in honor of a marine major killed at Midway. That same day, the Japanese infantry made their first assault on the marine defenders. By the end of the month, they were threatening Henderson Field while American and Japanese aviators and sailors were fighting for superiority of the air and control of sea lanes that would allow the delivery of reinforcements and supplies.

From September 12–14, the Japanese infantry attacked the marines from the east and south along the Lunga River and Bloody Ridge. The marines repulsed each attack, sometimes resorting to hand-to-hand fighting.

On September 18, the Second Marine Division and the U.S. Army American Division came ashore to reinforce the defenses. On the eastern end of the island, so many additional Japanese units were landing that by the end of September, they outnumbered the Americans. On September 27, the marines attempted to expand their positions to the west along the Matanikau River only to be beaten back by superior enemy numbers.

For the next two months, the Japanese repeatedly tried to pierce the perimeter around Henderson Field. Both sides fought against each other as well as the harsh jungle, tropical diseases, and a shortage of supplies. The American marines and soldiers, however, stopped each attack, as they frequently killed ten or more Japanese for each friendly casualty.

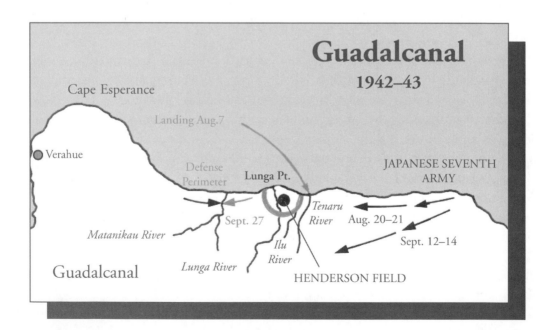

While the armies battled on land, the American and Japanese navies were also fighting over control of the sea-lanes to Guadalcanal. The Japanese gained the upper hand in the Battle of Savo Island on August 9, but subsequent battles in September and October brought equal losses to either side. Finally, during a battle lasting from November 13–15, the U.S. Navy gained superiority in the waters off the island. The Japanese made one more attempt to reinforce the island by sea on November 30, only to lose many of their troop transports to American naval gunfire.

The Japanese army on Guadalcanal was now cut off except for an occasional resupply ship that slipped through the American fleet at night. At the end of November, the Marines and soldiers began counterattacks that slowly expanded their lines out from Henderson Field. By December, the Americans had gained the advantage, and the Japanese were retreating inland.

On December 9, the command of the island passed from the marines to the army as the First Marine Division withdrew to be replaced by the Army's 25th Infantry Division. By New Year's Day, there were more than 50,000 Americans on the island.

The Japanese continued to resist, but other than a few fanatical charges, they were unable to inflict much damage on the growing American force that now ruled on the sea and in the air. From February 7–9, the Japanese slipped several high-speed destroyers to the northwest tip of the island at Cape Esperance and extracted 12,000 troops. They left behind more than 14,000 killed during the six months of battle, and another thousand were taken prisoner.

American deaths in the Battle of Guadalcanal totaled 1,600, with another 4,200 wounded in action. Thousands more were evacuated from the lines due to malaria and other diseases.

Guadalcanal secured the way for the capture of other islands in the Solomons and then other chains as the Americans moved closer to the Japanese homeland. Sea routes to Australia were also now secured so the Allies could use that country for the buildup of men and equipment to recapture the entire Pacific.

Guadalcanal marked the first land victory by the Americans over the Japanese. The win boosted the morale of the Americans, but more importantly, it provided lessons on how to fight, survive, and win against the Japanese. Guadalcanal was the initial step in a long journey that would lead to Tokyo and victory a little more than two and a half years later.

83

NASEBY

English Civil War, 1645

The victory by the Parliamentary forces over those of King Charles I at Naseby in 1645 led to the end of the absolute English monarchy and the establishment of the Commonwealth. Refugees from both sides who fled to North America took with them prejudices and passions that provided much of the basis for the American Revolutionary War a little more than a century later.

For nearly two centuries following the War of the Roses (69), the leadership of England remained fairly stable. The king ruled while a relatively impotent Parliament tended to minor administrative matters. Over the years, however, internal struggles within the royal family widened the distance between the king and the people represented by Parliament. Tensions between Anglican and Presbyterian factions were increasing at the same time the king was raising taxes to finance his armies fighting on the continent.

In 1642, many leaders of Parliament, representing mostly the middle-class and merchants, revolted against the king. Although some nobles joined the revolt as members of Parliament, generally the gentry and the peasants remained loyal to the crown. Geographically, the northern and west-central parts of England stood with the king while London and the south joined the Parliamentarians.

Early in the revolt, the Royalists, also known as Cavaliers, maintained an advantage over the Parliamentary forces (called "Roundheads" because of their distinctive haircuts). Prince Rupert, Charles's nephew, led the small Royalist army composed mostly of aristocrats. While they had the advantage of combat experience, they were often undisciplined because most considered themselves leaders rather than followers.

Conversely, the Roundhead army quickly gained strength and discipline. A former member of Parliament named Oliver Cromwell organized a cavalry troop despite his lack of previous military experience and his advanced age of forty-three. Cromwell expected both officers and men to meet the highest standards of moral character and honesty, and he demanded instant responsiveness to commands and forbade looting, swearing, or any other "ungodly" conduct. The aged leader armed his men with the most modern weapons and mounted them on the best available horses. He also provided sufficient pay for their services and delivered it in a timely manner, and he later introduced the uniform red coats that would be the symbol of the English army for generations to come.

The key to Cromwell's success in his first command and in the larger forces he later led was discipline. Repetitive drills and strong leaders enabled Cromwell to recall his attacking units to reorganize for subsequent charges or to completely change their direction in the middle of battle. By the end of the first two years of revolt, Cromwell's cavalry had earned the name "Ironsides," as they consistently defeated the Royalists.

While Cromwell remained subordinate to Lord Thomas Fairfax, the overall Roundhead leader, his system of organization and discipline spread to the entire Parliamentary force, resulting in what became known as the New Model Army. In 1644, the New Model Army soundly defeated Prince Rupert at the Battle of Marston Moor, reducing the size of the Royalist army and the territory it controlled.

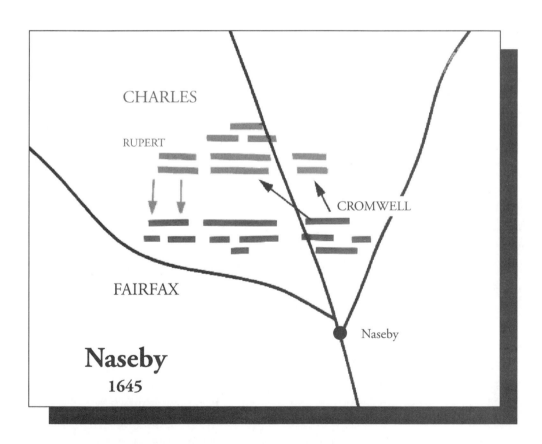

CHARLES

RUPERT

CROMWELL

FAIRFAX

Naseby

Naseby
1645

Despite the loss, King Charles and Prince Rupert renewed their efforts to crush the rebellion the following spring. They began by marching north from their head-quarters in Oxford to regain lands lost in the previous year's campaign. Rupert initially had some success in capturing several towns, but when he learned the Roundheads were to his rear and preparing to besiege Oxford, he turned back south. Near the town of Naseby, about fifty miles north of Oxford, the Royalists and Roundheads finally met.

Neither side was prepared for the encounter, but by chance, the Royalists, whose 4,000 cavalry and 3,500 infantry were outnumbered by the 6,500 cavalry and 7,000 infantry of the Roundheads, occupied a very defendable hillside. However, when Rupert saw the Roundheads withdrawing, he thought they were retreating instead of only moving to high ground of their own. He ordered his army to advance.

The two forces deployed with infantry in the center flanked by cavalry. Rupert personally led the Royalist horsemen on the west flank while Cromwell commanded the best Roundhead cavalrymen on the east and opposite wing. As a result, when the battle finally began at about 10:00 A.M. on June 14, 1645, both Rupert and Cromwell were able to push back their opposition. King Charles, located behind the infantry center, could have committed his reserve to shore up the flank now giving way to Cromwell, but he hesitated, likely fearing for his own life. Cromwell began to turn the flank and surround the Royalist infantry.

On the western flank, the less disciplined Royalist cavalry under Rupert pursued the retreating Roundhead horsemen and even stopped to loot the supply trains. By the time Rupert turned them back to the main battle, the Royalist infantry were mostly dead or captured by Cromwell's sword-and-pistol-wielding cavalry. By noon, more than a thousand Royalists lay dead on the hills outside Naseby, and another 4,000 were taken prisoner. Total Roundhead casualties numbered only about a thousand. Rupert finally returned to the battle but was too late to influence its outcome other than to lead King Charles to safety.

Charles and Rupert continued their fight for two more years. Although they achieved several minor victories, they were never again able to stand against the New Model Army after their defeat at Naseby. In March 1647, Charles finally surrendered to the Parliamentary forces and remained in place as a puppet king. Charles, however, continued plots to regain his power, and Parliament executed him two years later.

Parliament eventually restored the throne for Charles II in 1660 but retained most of the powers that led to the English governmental system. England would still have a king, but the real power now lay in its Parliament.

While the Battle of Naseby certainly influenced the future of England, its major impact was on the future of the British colonies in North America. During and after the British civil war, residents of the north, who were threatened by the Roundheads, sailed for the American colonies. Many in the south who felt threatened by the Royalists did likewise. Each group took with them loyalties and beliefs that they passed on to their children. While other English colonists who supported neither side and simply sought new opportunities joined both of these groups, definite opinions and passions about powers of royalty and parliaments influenced the thinking in the American colonies, resulting a century later in the Revolutionary War.

84

KADESH

Egyptian-Hittite Wars, c.1294 B.C.

Neither the Egyptians nor the Hittites won a decisive victory at Kadesh, but the battle ranks as one of history's most influential because it is the earliest conflict for which sufficient details were recorded so that succeeding generations could know the numbers, formations, and tactics. The battle also provides one of the earliest examples of a military commander using propaganda and public relations to turn a poor performance on the battlefield into a great victory.

During the fourteenth century B.C., the Egyptians were the most advanced and powerful empire in the world. About this time a people known as Hittites surfaced as a kingdom in Asia Minor in what is presently Syria. Little is known about the Hittites except that they were able to fashion iron weapons when the Egyptians and other nations still primarily used bronze.

Between Egypt and the Hittites were smaller kingdoms and loosely organized tribes who swore allegiance to whomever had the most power. In the early 1200s B.C., the small kingdom of Amurru defected from Egypt to join the Hittites. Egyptian King Ramses II decided to regain Amurru while also stopping the Hittite advance into what is present-day Israel and Lebanon.

In the mid-1290s B.C.—estimates of the exact date vary from as early as 1299 B.C. to 1250 B.C.—Ramses assembled an army of 20,000 infantrymen and charioteers into four corps and marched northwest. Commoners filled the ranks of the infantry while noblemen manned the chariots. Ramses was so confident of success that he did not deploy scouts to his front or flanks; his corps were often separated on the march by as much as ten miles.

The Hittite army of about 16,000, commanded by Muwatallis, did use scouts to follow the Egyptian advance as they awaited their opportunity. The chance came when Ramses crossed the Orontes River near the town of Kadesh in the area known in present-day as western Syria. Ramses had only one of his corps across the river when Muwatallish attacked with 2,500 chariots, each of which was manned by three warriors. The chariots quickly surrounded the Egyptian corps, and only the personal leadership of Ramses, at least according to his version of the fight, prevented their annihilation.

The Hittites might have taken a clear victory had not so many stopped to loot the enemy camp rather than finish off the Egyptians. Reinforcements from the three other corps arrived to drive off the Hittites and rescue Ramses. The Egyptians then counterattacked toward Kadesh but could not defeat the town's defenses.

Phase I

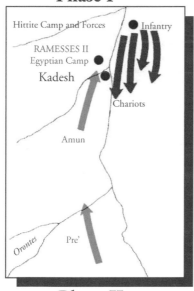

Phase III

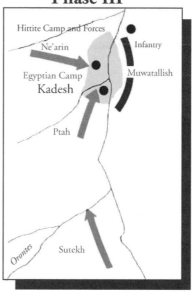

Phase II

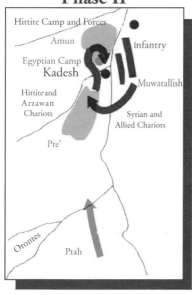

Kadesh
1294 B.C.

Kadesh provided neither side a great advantage. Less than half the available forces, either Egyptian or Hittite, actually engaged in combat. In essence, the battle was more a skirmish that prevented a larger fight from taking place.

Ramses and his army returned home. For seventeen additional years, the Egyptians and Hittites warred over the coastal territory that divided their two kingdoms, with neither gaining the advantage. Eventually, Ramses married the daughter of a Hittite leader and the two kingdoms ceased their fighting. Egypt and the Hittite kingdom signed a peace treaty that became another first—history's first verifiable example of diplomacy between two nations. The country between the two nations remained semi-independent, but internal and external wars for control have continued up to the present. It is doubtful that a decisive victory by either the Egyptians or the Hittites at Kadesh would have done anything to promote a long-term peace in the region.

The actual battle of Kadesh had little influence on the status of the warring kingdoms or on the future of warfare itself. Although the Hittites had the advantage of iron weapons over the bronze of the Egyptians, the battle was indecisive. In fact, if Ramses had not made a great effort to record the details of the fight, history's first recorded battle account, Kadesh would have not been included in this list of influential battles.

Although historians are grateful to Ramses for his writings and for the monuments he dedicated to the fight, the Egyptian was much more interested in promoting himself than in recording facts. Ramses would not be the last soldier to understand that history is kinder to the leader who writes his own accounts of his battles.

On his return to Egypt, the king began to erect monuments and temples to record his "great victory" at Kadesh. Every inscription on the monuments referred to the Hittite commander as the "vanquished chief." According to Ramses, he alone was responsible for the great victory, declaring, "None of you was there…None rose to lend me his hand in the fight."

Ramses also admitted that he alone had to promote his accomplishments, saying that his fellow Egyptians did not later "tell the story of his great deeds."

Despite the records left by Ramses, the Battle of Kadesh was not a great victory. Although Ramses was apparently brave in battle, he ignored several important basic rules of warfare by separating his forces and not properly employing reconnaissance. Perhaps the most significant outcome of the battle was the personal aggrandizement practiced and accomplished by Ramses. He was the first, but certainly not the last, military commander to declare victory when there was none; to blame his failures on his subordinates; and to declare himself the smartest, bravest, and most courageous leader in history. One has only to look at the huge public relations sections that follow and record each action of today's generals and admirals to understand Ramses's true legacy.

85

CHARLESTON HARBOR

American Civil War, 1864

The assault by the CSS *H.L. Hunley* against the United States naval fleet off Charleston Harbor in 1864 marked history's first successful submarine attack. While the sinking of the USS *Housatonic* did not significantly influence the Civil War, the event proved the value of submarines and modified the future of naval warfare.

Experimentation with submersible watercraft predates the American Civil War by more than two millennia. Aristotle wrote about an underwater craft used in 332 B.C. by Alexander the Great to place obstacles on the seabed. There is also evidence that the Chinese experimented with primitive submarines as early as 200 B.C. In 1578, Englishman William Borne designed the first submarine complete with ballast tanks, but Borne's idea never got beyond the drafting table. It was not until 1620 that Cornelis Drebbel successfully launched and recovered an underwater vessel in the Thames River.

In 1776, American David Bushnell launched an egg-shaped submersible that carried a crew of one. The *Turtle*, piloted by Sergeant Ezra Lee, became the first combat submarine when it unsuccessfully attempted to place a mine on the side of the HMS *Eagle* in New York harbor on September 6, 1776.

Robert Fulton, another American inventor, experimented with a submarine he called the *Nautilus* in 1798, but he dropped the project when he failed to receive government support. Engineers from other countries during this period also attempted to build submarines; Germany launched the *Sea Devil,* which made several successful voyages in 1850.

When the Confederacy broke away from the United States in 1861, the North blockaded the South, preventing the export of agricultural products and the import of military supplies. The Confederacy attempted to break the blockade with an ironclad warship at Hampton Roads (60) in 1862, but neither these nor other efforts were successful.

In 1863, several Southern inventors decided that the most economical method of breaking the Union blockade was with submersibles. Construction began at Mobile, Alabama, in 1863, on the *H.L. Hunley,* named in honor of its principal financial backer. The *Hunley,* fashioned from an iron steam boiler, was slightly less than forty feet long. Its design included a hand-cranked propeller driven by a crew of eight with only enough additional space for the captain, who steered the boat and controlled its depth. Ballast tanks on each end of the *Hunley* were flooded or emptied with hand pumps. Additional iron weights on the bottom of the boat could be released from inside if an emergency called for added buoyancy.

The submarine's only armaments were explosives attached to the end of a long bow spar. To attack, the boat had to maneuver underwater close enough to attach the explosive charge to the side of an enemy vessel and then detonate it with a rope as the submarine backed away.

In the fall of 1863, the builders shipped the *Hunley* by rail to Charleston, South Carolina. Shortly after the submarine's arrival and launch, it attempted to attack the Union blockade outside the harbor, but it was swamped by a wave that drowned the entire crew save the captain, Lieutenant John Payne. The boat was recovered only to sink twice more during sea trials in October. Two seamen survived the first sinking; all hands, including H.L. Hunley, died in the second.

Once again the *Hunley* was recovered. On February 17, 1864, the *Hunley*, captained by Lieutenant George Dixon, one of the submarine's builders in Alabama, pushed away from its Charleston dock, slipped below the surface, and made its way toward the Union fleet. Silently it approached the 23-gun, 1,800-ton Union sloop *Housatonic*.

The next day, Lieutenant F. G. Higginson, U.S. Navy, wrote the following report: "Sir: I…make the following report of the sinking of the USS *Housatonic*, by a rebel torpedo off Charleston, S.C., on the evening of the 17th instant. At about 8:45 P.M., the officer of the deck, Acting Master J.K. Crosby, discovered something in the water about 100 yards from and moving toward the ship. It had the appearance of a plank moving in the water. It came directly toward the ship, the time from when it was first seen till it was close alongside being about two minutes. During this time the chain was slipped, engine backed, and all hands called to quarters. The torpedo struck the ship forward of the mizzenmast, on the starboard side, in a line with the magazine. Having the after pivot gun pivoted to port we were unable to bring a gun to bear upon her. About one minute after she was close alongside the explosion took place, the ship sinking stern first and heeling to port as she sank."

Higginson included a list of the five men killed in the attack. He concluded with an explanation that he was making the report because his captain had been wounded by the explosion.

The *Hunley* did not return from the attack. On March 10, 1864, the assistant adjutant of the Confederate command in Charleston wrote in an official report, "…I regret to say that nothing since has been heard either of Lieutenant Dixon or the torpedo boat. It is therefore feared that that gallant officer and his brave companions have perished."

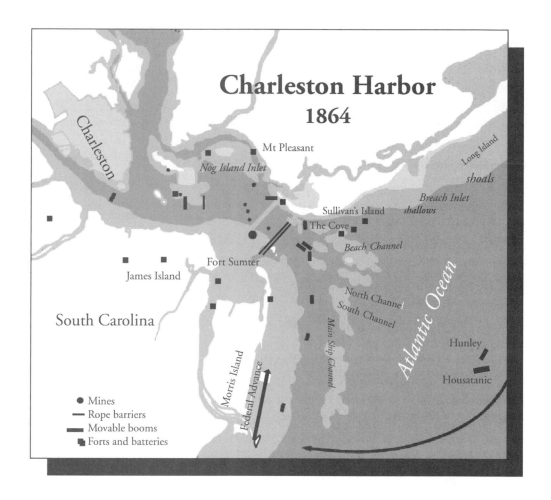

The *Hunley's* fate remained unknown for the next 131 years, until underwater archeologists discovered it on the ocean floor in 1995. Divers raised the submarine in 2000 and transported it to a special preservation tank at the Charleston Navy Yard. Since that time, the hull has been opened and artifacts and human remains recovered. The exact cause of sinking remains undetermined.

Despite its loss and the inability of the Confederacy to launch subsequent underwater attacks, the *Hunley* earned the distinction of being the first submarine to sink an enemy warship. Both the United States and other countries took note of the battle and increased their submersible research. The U.S. Navy launched its first successful submarine, the USS *Holland,* in 1898. It was not until 1914 that a German submarine matched the *Hunley's* success in sinking an opposing country's ship. From that time forward, submarines have played an important role in every major war. Today, U.S. Navy nuclear-powered and armed submarines are constantly at sea, serving as deterrents to future threats.

Although the *Hunley* sank but one ship and was lost itself, the Confederate submarine earned the honor of conducting the first successful combat mission by a submarine. It changed the future of naval warfare. No longer would navies fight only on the surface; after the Battle of Charleston Harbor, every sea captain had to also defend against an attack from under the waves.

OPERATION DESERT STORM

Liberation of Kuwait, 1991

The defeat of Iraq in Operation Desert Storm in 1991 liberated Kuwait and its oil fields. While the brief war did not remove Iraqi leader Saddam Hussein from power, it did demonstrate the ability of the United Nations to form a multinational coalition to defend one of its members.

During the war between Iraq and Iran in the 1980s, other Arab nations, as well as the United States and the Soviet Union, had provided military aid to Hussein in order to prevent expanded Iranian control of the Middle Eastern oil fields. Even though the war ended in a draw, Iraq had come out of the conflict with a well-equipped and well-supplied military force that had grown to become the fourth largest in the world. Hussein had also used poison gas against Kurdish rebels within his own borders, and he was nearing development of nuclear weapons.

However, Iraq had incurred huge debts for financial support from its neighboring Arab countries. Hussein saw a solution in Kuwait. By annexing his neighbor, Hussein could cancel his debt to that country at the same time he acquired its rich oil fields and ports on the Persian Gulf. In early 1990, Hussein declared Kuwait an Iraqi province and began massing his army along the border. After several weeks of ignored threats, Hussein's armor forces swept into Kuwait and quickly occupied the country on August 2–3.

The reaction to the invasion was immediate. Great Britain, the United States, and other members of the United Nations, including fellow Arab states who might be next, condemned the takeover. Saudi Arabia agreed to allow the United Nations Coalition use of its territory on the borders of Kuwait and Iraq to assemble a force. Ground and air units from around the world began to arrive while warships filled the Persian Gulf. The bulk of the forces, however, came from the United States, and General H. Norman Schwarzkopf assumed command of the Coalition buildup operations, dubbed Operation Desert Shield.

Schwarzkopf and the American Chairman of the Joint Chiefs of Staff, General Colin Powell, as veterans of the Vietnam War, believed that the fight against Iraq must be run by the military and that maximum force should be applied. President George Bush agreed and allowed his generals to plan the operation.

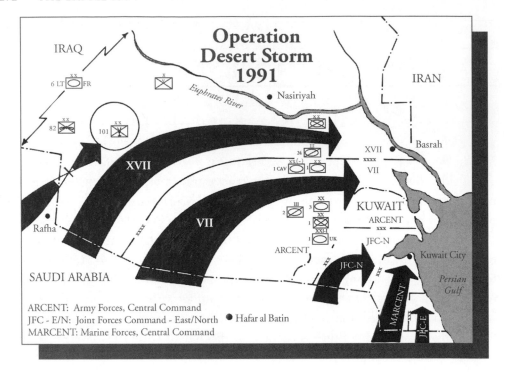

Operation Desert Storm 1991

After a huge buildup that brought the total number of Coalition force troops up to more than 650,000, the UN issued an ultimatum for Iraq to withdraw from Kuwait. Hussein, confident that his veteran proclaimed "million-man army" could win and convinced that neither the U.S. nor the UN would fight a prolonged war, ignored the demand.

Actually, Hussein's army had only about a third of the men he claimed, and many of his best troops had fallen in the war against Iran. Hussein also had over the years relieved or killed a number of his most proficient officers because he feared they might attempt to take control of the country.

Early in the morning of January 17, 1991, Coalition bombers and fighter aircraft swept across Iraq, destroying Hussein's anti-aircraft defenses and communications networks. Most of his air force was destroyed on the ground. For two weeks, the coalition aircraft flew across Iraq at will as they destroyed military facilities and ground forces.

Despite his losses and the ineffectual defenses of his military, Hussein refused further demands to withdraw from Kuwait. On January 29, he dispatched a mechanized division to attack Saudi Arabia south of Kuwait. The attack advanced eight miles before Coalition forces destroyed more than 80 percent of the Iraqi vehicles and men and sent the remainder hurrying back across the border.

Hussein next attempted to divide the Coalition by deploying intermediate-range ballistic missiles against Israel. If the Israelis entered the conflict, many of their long-time Arab enemies might drop from the Coalition. When the missile attacks against Israel failed to get the expected reaction, Hussein turned his missiles against allied staging areas in Saudi Arabia. Other than inflicting a few casualties, this attack also proved ineffective.

Hussein continued to ignore demands for his withdrawal. After it became apparent that air-attacks alone would not succeed, the land force prepared to cross into Kuwait and Iraq. On February 24, 1991, Schwarzkopf executed Operation Desert Storm with diversionary attacks along the Kuwaiti border while the bulk of the Coalition force swung in a wide hook on the west flank. The "Hail Mary" advance across the desert met practically no resistance. Iraqis surrendered to anyone who approached, including rear support troops and even news reporters. Hussein's great army gave up almost without a fight. Within a hundred hours of the beginning of the Coalition attack, Kuwait was free. Later claims put the Iraqi dead at 60,000 to 100,000 but these numbers were vastly inflated. Actual Iraqi casualties totaled somewhere between 8,000 and 15,000, with another 25,000 wounded. More than 85,000 were prisoners of war. Coalition casualties numbered fewer than 500.

Although significant, the Coalition victory was not total. Incorrect intelligence had inflated the Iraqi numbers, causing commanders on the west flank to move slowly with extreme caution as they executed their "Hail Mary" hook. As a result, when Hussein asked for a cease-fire on February 28, many of his best armor units had withdrawn to safety. His retreating troops also set fire to hundreds of oil wells, leaving Kuwait ablaze and the air black with smoke.

Across the world, people rejoiced that Hussein had been defeated with so few Coalition casualties. The rapid extinguishing of the oil fires added to the post-war euphoria. In the United States, many, including President Bush, claimed that the support of the American public for the successful military operation had finally removed the Vietnam War stigma from the United States people and military. Schwarzkopf and his army were welcomed home with the largest parades and greatest enthusiasm since World War II.

The passage of time, however, has dimmed the brightness of the victory in Kuwait. While the country was freed and Hussein's nuclear efforts slowed, if not stopped, more than a decade after the war, the Iraqi leader remains in power. The allied generals who led the offensive have retired, and the Coalition political leaders are out of office, but Hussein is still in absolute control of Iraq and continues to provide a threat to peace and a base for terrorism.

Despite its failure to eliminate Hussein, Desert Storm ranks as one of history's most influential battles for its demonstration that the world's nations could and would unite in a coalition to combat aggression. This first major post-Cold War effort by the United Nations serves as a reminder to others who might consider acts of war against their neighbors. Had this Coalition managed to expel Hussein from power and eliminate Iraq as a threat to regional peace, Desert Storm would have earned an even higher ranking on this list.

87

KOVEL-STANISLAV

World War I, 1916

The Battle of Kovel-Stanislav, also known as the Brusilov Offensive, was the last significant battle on the Eastern Front in World War I. In addition to inflicting almost a million casualties on each side, the battle led to the downfall of the Russian and the Austrian monarchies.

Following the Battle of the Marne in 1914 (38), the Western Front had settled into trench warfare where the French and British faced the Germans. During the next two years, each side launched an occasional offensive, but massive casualties were the only results as the two sides fought back and forth for the same few kilometers of territory.

By defeating the Russians at the Battle of Tannenberg the same year (63), the Germans had been able to continue their offensive, but by the end of 1915, the Eastern Front had also stagnated along a line reaching from Riga on the Baltic Sea for nearly a thousand miles south to the Carpathian Mountains on the Russian-Romanian border.

In February 1916, the Germans had launched a major offensive at Verdun on the Western Front. The French, barely able to hold the line, had requested that Russia attack on the Eastern Front to relieve some of the pressure on their lines in a manner similar to their actions two years earlier at Tannenberg. Once again, the Russians had agreed to the French request; but once again, the results had been the same. The Russian attack against the Germans at Lake Naroch produced little except a hundred thousand casualties.

In May, Russia received another plea for help, this time from Italy. When Austria attacked Italy at Trentino, the Italian's begged the Russians to attack to help relieve the pressure on their front. Czar Nicholas saw the request as an opportunity for his army to regain its prestige and for his government to improve the morale at home. However, all but one of his generals responded that they were unprepared and too short of ammunition and supplies to undertake an offensive.

Alexei Brusilov, Commander of the Southwest Army Group, was the only general to claim he was ready to attack. In truth, General Brusilov, a new commander wanting to impress his Czar with his willingness to fight, suffered the same supply shortages as the other units. His aggressiveness also alienated the other generals, who resented his ambition. As a result, they did little or nothing to help him prepare for the offensive.

Nevertheless, Brusilov assembled his army along the 300 miles reaching from the Romanian border north to the Pripet Marshes. The Russians had several advantages in the battle's early states. The Austrian army, unaware of the Russians amassing on the other side of the lines, did not anticipate an attack. Brusilov also had the advantage of being forced to use innovative tactics because of his limited supply of artillery ammunition.

World War I battles almost always began with massive artillery barrages to soften the enemy lines. While the shells did inflict damage, they also warned the enemy of a pending attack and turned ground and forest into mud and entanglements that slowed the advancing infantrymen.

Unable to begin his offensive with a sustained artillery barrage, Brusilov concentrated his infantry against strong points and positions that dominated the lines. In this way, his superior numbers were able to break through the Austrian lines and force the entire front to withdraw.

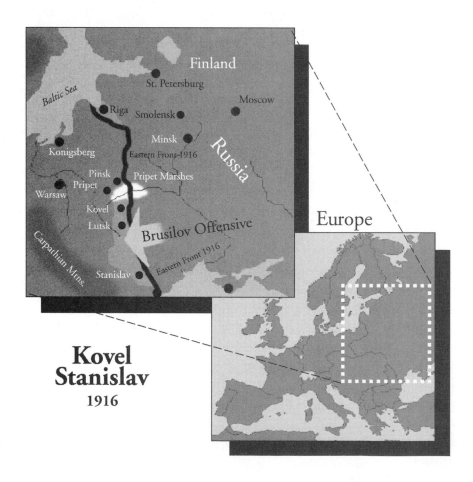

Kovel Stanislav
1916

The Russians began their attack on June 4 and quickly pushed the surprised Austrians back. In the northern sector, Brusilov captured Lutsk on June 6 and during the next four days advanced fifty miles to the outskirts of the important rail center of Kovel. The southern part of the offensive experienced similar success and reached the town of Stanislav a short time later.

Brusilov's offensive reaching from Kovel to Stanislav began to slow in late June. Germany, using the superior railways within their lines, rushed reinforcements forward to assist the Austrians. Both the Czar and Brusilov wanted the other Russian armies to attack in their sectors, but the generals—tired of losing so many men, low on supplies, and jealous of Brusilov—remained in place. The Czar did provide additional artillery ammunition to the offensive, but this actually did more harm than good; Brusilov used the additional ammunition to revert to massive artillery attacks followed by infantry advances on a broad front. The results were piles of bodies and a stalemated front.

By September, the Russians were short of men, ammunition, and supplies. The exhausted Germans and Austrians were satisfied to let the front settle into static trench lines.

About a million men on each side were killed, wounded, captured, or deserted during the three months of the Battle of Kovel-Stanislav. Its influence, however, reached far beyond the hospitals, graveyards, and prison camps. The battle finished Russia as an active participant in the war, having used up the last of its available men and military supplies. Food shortages soon caused more casualties due to starvation. Soldiers and civilians lost confidence in their Czar. A year after the battle, the Russian Revolution was well underway.

Austria's losses on the front and its reliance on Germany to come to their rescue ended most of its decision-making influence. Austria never recovered from the Battle of Kovel-Stanislav and ceased being a major military power from that time forward. Austrians, too, lost confidence in their leader, and within a year the Hapsburg Empire collapsed, leaving Austria and Hungary to form separate republics.

The battle also had drastic effects on Romania, which had previously remained neutral. With Brusilov's initial success, that country had allied with the Russians, expecting victory. A year later, Romania was invaded and overrun by Germany's ally Bulgaria.

Brusilov's Offensive did accomplish part of its original mission. It took the pressure off the French at Verdun that helped prevent a German breakout. While it is better known than Kovel-Stanislav, Verdun ended with few results other than the typical World War I extensive casualty list. The Battle of Kovel-Stanislav, on the other hand, toppled two monarchies and removed one of the war's major players from the conflict.

88

SANTA CLARA

Cuban Revolution, 1958

The Battle of Santa Clara concluded the politico-military revolution in Cuba that brought Fidel Castro and the first viable Communist state into the Western Hemisphere. In 1962, less than four years later, Castro took delivery of Soviet missiles which put the batteries only ninety miles off the coast of the United States, an action that brought the Americans and Russians to the brink of nuclear war.

Within a decade after the discovery voyages of Christopher Columbus in the final years of the fifteenth century, Spanish settlers began to develop Cuba as an agricultural center and as an assembly point for further exploration of Central and South America. Over the next three centuries, the native inhabitants, imported black slaves, and immigrant colonials became unhappy with the exploitation and harsh laws of the Spanish rulers. They began a series of independence movements in the 1860s that in 1895 erupted into a revolution led by Jose Marti.

The United States intervened in 1898, leading to the Spanish-American War and the expulsion of Spain from Cuba. A treaty in 1899 made Cuba an independent republic under U.S. protection. Internal revolts, however, continued for the next thirty years, causing the U.S. to send troops to restore order in 1912 and again in 1917. In 1934, Fulgencio Batista, an army sergeant, led a coup to overthrow the government and established the island nation's first stable leadership since the expulsion of the Spanish.

Batista maintained his power by being friendly with the United States while ruthlessly jailing or executing his opposition at home. His police state tactics allowed American investors to establish resorts, casinos, and industry on the island for the enrichment of both those investors and Batista himself, who demanded payoffs and bribes.

The wealth enjoyed by the Batista regime did not extend to the general Cuban population, and the seeds of revolution again sprouted across the island. On July 26, 1953, Fidel Castro, a twenty-five-year-old University of Havana law graduate, led 160 fellow revolutionaries in an attack against the Moncada army barracks in Santiago de Cuba. Castro's objective was to capture weapons and supplies for his revolt and to encourage local civilians to rally to his cause. All of his objectives failed. Government troops killed or captured most of the rebels, and Castro and his brother Raul were caught and imprisoned.

A year later Castro was freed in a general amnesty of political prisoners. His revolutionary zeal still ablaze, Castro went to Mexico to organize another rebellion that he called "26th of July" in honor of his failed attack against Moncada. Castro, in command of an "army" of 81 rebels, including his brother and Argentinian doctor Che Guevara, landed on the southern coast of Cuba on December 2, 1956. Again Castro faced disaster as Batista's army captured all but a dozen of the rebels within a few days of their landing.

Fidel, Raul, Che, and a few others fled into the Sierra Maestra Mountains where they began guerrilla operations and conducted a propaganda campaign to win support from the peasants and middle class. In the following months, the 26th of July movement gained followers and momentum as much from the excesses and cruelty of Batista as from Castro's activities. Castro gained power by merely maintaining a presence as he recruited citizens who were unhappy with the current government.

In the summer of 1958, Batista conducted a campaign to find and destroy Castro in his mountain camps. When the campaign failed, Castro assumed the offensive with his army that had grown to 2,000. Fidel took half the rebels and marched toward Santa Clara, the capital of Las Villas Province, 150 miles from Havana, while his brother led the remaining men to Santiago on the island's southern coast. The plan was to cut the island in half.

On December 28, 1958, Castro's rebels, after a brief fight, defeated the 3,000 government troops guarding Santa Clara. Santiago fell to Raul a short time later. Batista ordered troops in Havana to travel by rail to Santa Clara to retake the city, but the soldiers refused. Batista, already cut off from aid by the United States because of his corruption and harsh rule, fled to exile in the Dominican Republic on New Year's Day, 1959.

Castro marched into Havana on January 8 and assumed the Cuban leadership. The United States initially welcomed Castro and the democratic government they thought he would bring. They soon discovered just how wrong they were. Although Castro had promised freedom of the press and individual and private property rights, he quickly executed more than a thousand of Batista's supporters and began to socialize the island's economy. He confiscated more than a billion dollars of American assets and spoke out against "Yankee imperialism." On January 31, 1961, the U.S. broke off diplomatic relations with Cuba. Later that year, Castro, admitting he had always been a Marxist, began accepting assistance, including military aid, from the Soviet Union and Communist China.

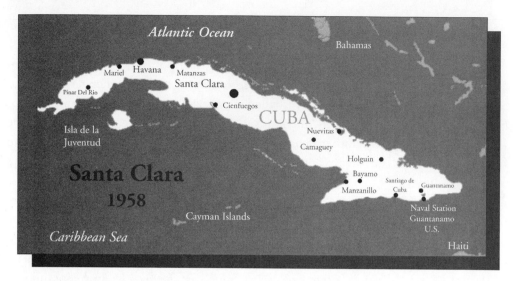

Castro solidified his control over Cuba with his defeat of the U.S.-supported, poorly planned Bay of Pigs invasion on April 17, 1961, which attempted to depose him. The following October, Americans discovered that Castro and the Soviet Union had installed on the island medium-range, nuclear-armed missiles capable of reaching the United States. The resulting Cuban Missile Crisis almost triggered a nuclear World War III before the Soviet Union agreed on October 28 to dismantle the weapons and ship them out of Cuba.

While the Battle of Santa Clara shed little blood and deserves only the briefest of mention as a "battle," the fight made up in impact what it lacked in action. Santa Clara rallied Cuban civilians to Castro's side and even convinced Batista's army that they were backing the wrong leader. Santa Clara led Castro to Havana from where he brought the world as close as it has come to nuclear war. Although Castro's efforts to export his Communist revolt to other Latin American countries and to support Marxist movements in Africa have failed over the years, Cuba remains one of the world's few surviving Communist countries and the only one in the Western Hemisphere. Castro's power and influence has faded with each folding of other Communist regimes, yet he remains in power and still represents the primary, if not only, threat to peace in the region.

89

JIDDA

Hejaz War, 1925

The capture of Jidda after a year-long siege in 1925 gave control of the entire Arabian Peninsula to Abdul Aziz Ibn Saud and led to the establishment of Saudi Arabia. Descendants of Ibn Saud continue today to rule the country, which has become one of the richest in the world with the discovery of its vast oil fields.

The early history of the Arabian Peninsula is a mystery because its oppressive heat and expansive desert kept all but the staunchest nomads from its interior. Only its western ports along the trade route to the East had contact with the outside world. The prophet Muhammad united the region's tribes in the seventh century under the Islamic faith. When the center of Islam moved to Damascus and then to Baghdad, only the peninsula's holy cities of Mecca and Medina retained any importance on the peninsula.

In the sixteenth century, the Ottoman Turks had occupied the peninsula only to lose most of it to the Wahabis, a strict Muhammadan sect, in the mid-eighteenth century. Throughout this period, tribes and families fought for control of various parts of the region. By the turn of the twentieth century, the Ottoman Turks had regained much of coastal Arabia now known as Hejaz, while the Wahabi and Rashid tribes controlled the desert interior, known as the Nejd.

Between 1901 and 1906, the two tribes had fought over the Nejd, and the Wahabis emerged victorious. Ibn Saud, the grandson of Faisal—who had ruled central Arabia before the arrival of the Ottoman Turks and the rise of the Rashid—led the victors. He added the former Turkish province of Al-Hasa to his budding empire in 1913 and captured the Asir region in 1920.

During World War I, the Ottoman Turks lost their hold on the Hejaz section of the peninsula to the British and an Arab army advised by English officer T.E. Lawrence, the famous "Lawrence of Arabia." In 1916, Sherif Hussein ibn-Ali, the leader of the Arab forces, proclaimed Arabian independence and himself as the King of the Hejaz.

In 1924, Ibn Saud attacked Hejaz with the objective of uniting the peninsula. His Wahabis army captured the town of Taif and massacred the survivors. When Ibn Saud's army approached Mecca, the holy city's defenders, mindful of Taif, gave up without a fight on October 24, 1924. A year later, Islam's other holy site of Medina fell to Ibn Saud.

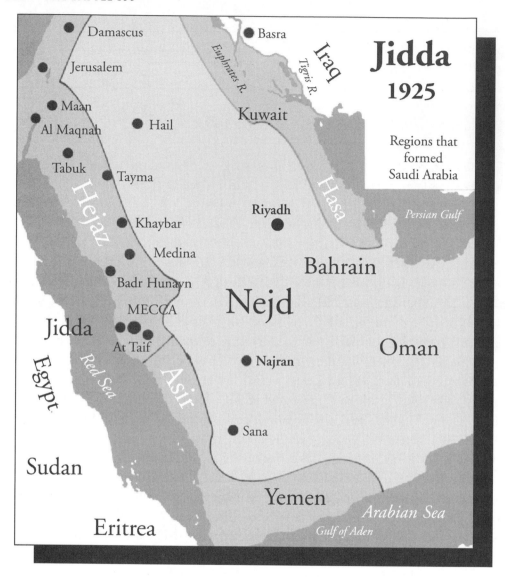

In January 1925, the Wahabis besieged the Red Sea port of Jidda, forty-six miles west of Mecca. Jidda, the last Hejaz stronghold, had ample defenses and a resupply route by sea. Little combat took place over the next months as Ibn Saud maintained his siege and negotiated with Hussein and his followers. On December 19, 1925, Hussein agreed to abdicate in favor of his son. Four days later, the new leader of Jidda surrendered the city to Ibn Saud.

On January 8, 1926, Ibn Saud declared himself the King of Hejaz and Nejd. Three years later, some of his followers rebelled because they believed that the king was not fanatical enough in his Muslim beliefs. The Royal army defeated the rebels at the Battle of Sibilla on March 30, 1929, killing more than a thousand with a loss of only 200.

In 1932, Ibn Saud renamed his kingdom Saudi Arabia and ruled the country as an absolute monarchy until his death in 1953. Although there have been fights within the family, direct descendants of Ibn Saud have continued to rule the kingdom until the present time.

For many years, the world paid little attention to the internal fights on the Arabian Peninsula. Other sea and land routes had taken away its minimal importance as a way to the East, and few outside the region saw any value in the vast, hot desert. Jidda would be a minor footnote in history, and certainly not a candidate for this list of most influential battles, if petroleum deposits had not been discovered by the United States' Standard Oil Company in 1936. Further exploration proved that the world's largest oil deposits lay beneath the sands of Saudi Arabia.

Oil from Saudi Arabia brought unparalleled wealth to King Saud and his family, who are today among the richest people in the world. Saudi Arabia's wealth, combined with King Saud's leadership, resulted in formation of the Arab League in 1945 and later, to the formation of the Organization of the Petroleum Exporting Countries (OPEC) which continues today to influence the entire world with its management of oil production and prices. Saudi Arabia has been a stabilizing force in the Middle East, and generally, the oil-dependent nations have maintained a favorable relationship with the Ibn Saud family.

If not for Ibn Saud and the Battle of Jidda, there would be no Saudi Arabia today. The vast country and its riches would have likely been divided into many small kingdoms similar to the neighboring Gulf States. As long as the oil reserves hold out, the influence of Ibn Saud, Jidda, and Saudi Arabia will continue.

90

MALPLAQUET

War of the Spanish Succession, 1709

The Battle of Malplaquet was a meeting of superlatives: it was the bloodiest fight of the eighteenth century between the two largest armies ever assembled in the Western world to date led by two of the greatest military leaders of all time. Yet, the battle produced no clear victor; its real influence was in the revelations, which went mostly unheeded, of the lethality of modern combat.

By 1709, the War of the Spanish Succession was in its eighth year as Europeans fought over who should assume the throne of Spain. French King Louis XIV had claimed the crown for his grandson when Spanish King Charles II died in 1700 without an heir. Spain, England, the Netherlands, and the Holy Roman Empire formed an alliance in 1702 and declared war against France to prevent that country from seizing the crown and increasing its power.

More countries joined the fight as the war progressed, escalating the size of the armies and the magnitude of the battles. Leaders emerged who proved to be among the most influential of all time. Eugene of Savoy, born to French parents who had been exiled because of their plots against King Louis XIV, had joined the Austrian army when his native country turned down his services. By the time of the War of the Spanish Secession, Eugene was a master of mobility, the strategic use of terrain, and motivation of his subordinates.

John Churchill, the Duke of Marlborough, joined Eugene in leading the Allies. Marlborough brought with him superior tactical and strategic talents to coordinate vast armies from divergent areas and a record of never having lost a battle or a siege.

Marlborough and Eugene worked together to win the Battle of Bleheim (48) in 1704 and reunited again in September 1709 to besiege the French army at Mons. The French commander, Marshal Duc Claude de Villars, assisted by Marshal Duc Louis de Boufflers, concentrated their primary defenses ten miles south of Mons near the village of Malplaquet.

The Allied commanders realized that they had to neutralize Malplaquet before capturing Mons, and so they maneuvered their army of 100,000 against the 90,000 French defenders who had built a mesh of entrenchments, abates, and obstacles. On the morning of September 11, 1709, Marlborough and Eugene attacked the French using the same basic plan that had proven successful at Blenheim. The Allied infantry assaulted both flanks while their 30,000-man cavalry force, led by Marlborough, prepared to attack the center once the wings were pushed back.

French artillery battered the infantry advance and their cavalry counterattacked any breach in their lines. The French stopped the Allies on the left wing, but Eugene, leading the assault on the right, broke through the enemy lines. After seven hours of infantry fighting, Marlborough led the allied horsemen against the center as planned and forced the French to retreat. Boufflers, now in command after Villars had been wounded, maintained discipline and led an orderly withdrawal. The Allies proceeded to Mons, which fell to their siege on October 26.

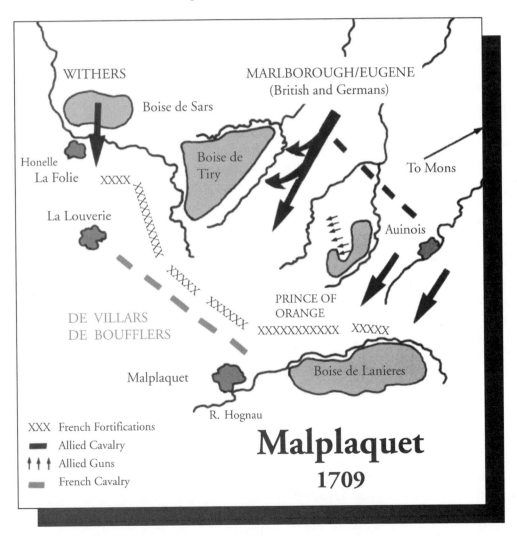

The Allies claimed victory because of the French withdrawal from Malplaquet and the ultimate surrender of Mons, but it had been a costly win. Nearly one-fourth of the Allied army were killed or wounded in the battle. Eugene, although wounded in the assault against the French flank, recovered and fought Austria's wars for the next twenty-five years, earning a well-deserved place on the list of history's most influential commanders.

Marlborough returned to England where the House of Commons passed a motion that declared, "The astounding progress of Her Majesty's arms under the Earl of Marlborough has brilliantly restored the honor of the English nation."

Marlborough had indeed been the primary force in establishing Britain as a world military power, but Malplaquet would be his last battle. Undefeated on the battlefield, Marlborough did not fare so well in the political arena. The opposition party in England used the huge number of casualties at Malplaquet to declare him a "butcher" and to force his relief from command. By the time the War of Spanish Succession ended with a series of treaties in 1713 and 1714, the Duke was living in comfortable retirement at Blenheim Palace, a mansion built for him by a grateful country.

The total combined 190,000 combatants at Malplaquet were the most heretofore ever assembled for any one battle in the Western world. The 12,000 French and the 24,000 Allied casualties made Malplaquet the bloodiest fight of not only the war but also the entire century. Not until the wars of Napoleon a hundred years later would more soldiers be killed and wounded in a single battle.

Despite these massive casualties, Malplaquet had no far-reaching influence. Future commanders did learn from the battle that frontal attacks by large armies against prepared defenses were deadly, but this was a lesson that had been presented countless times in previous conflicts. Battles after Malplaquet were smaller for the next century but this was as much because of the lack of resources as from any lessons learned on the bloody battlefield outside Mons. Malplaquet's real influence lies only in its size, its number of casualties, and its effects on the great leaders involved in the battle. Unfortunately, despite the great loss of lives, the battle provided insufficient influence for it to be included anywhere other than near the end of this list.

91

SAN PASQUAL

U.S.-Mexican War, 1846

The Battle of San Pasqual was the only significant military action in California during the war between the United States and Mexico. Although they suffered a greater number of casualties and had to retreat, the members of the U.S. "Army of the West" regrouped and pacified the area from San Diego to Los Angeles to claim the territory that eventually became the state of California.

From the time of its independence from Great Britain, the United States had steadily added to its territory by occupying unclaimed regions and by taking lands from the Native Americans. The U.S. greatly expanded its borders with the Louisiana Purchase from France in 1803 and the purchase of Florida from Spain in 1819. By the mid-nineteenth century, many Americans supported the policy that said the United States should reach from the Atlantic to the Pacific.

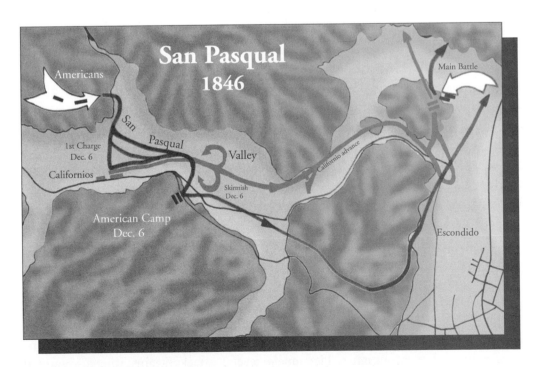

In 1845, Texas, which had won its independence from Mexico in 1836, applied for statehood, but Mexico, refusing to recognize that the region was no longer its territory, broke off diplomatic relations with Washington when the United States admitted Texas into the Union. In the end, however, the dispute between Mexico and the U.S. was the location of the Texas border. Mexico claimed the Nueces River, while the United States put the border much farther to the southwest along the Rio Grande. Border skirmishes led to the U.S. declaration of war on Mexico on May 13, 1846.

Most of the battles between the two countries took place in Mexico, but the Americans were interested in far more than just the confirmation of the Texas border; they were after the spoils of war. While many Americans looked at Texas as a vast wasteland, they coveted California with its fertile lands and magnificent harbors that could open the Pacific to the U.S. Despite its riches, California had a population of only 7,000 Mexicans, 70,000 Native Americans, and a thousand foreigners, mostly Americans, by the early 1840s.

Prior to the outbreak of the Mexican War, President James Polk had attempted to buy California, but Mexico refused. After the declaration of war in 1846, President Polk took action to acquire militarily what he had failed to gain diplomatically or financially. Six weeks after the war began, Polk ordered Colonel Stephen Watts Kearny to proceed westward.

Kearny and his 1,700-man Army of the West departed Fort Leavenworth, Kansas, on June 29. They arrived at Santa Fe on August 18 and occupied the town with no opposition from the Mexican officials. On September 25, Kearny left the majority of his force behind to secure New Mexico and marched toward California with only about 120 soldiers.

It took more than six weeks for Kearny's army to cross the harsh Southwestern desert. His small army was exhausted and nearing starvation when they finally neared San Diego, where the U.S. fleet commanded by Commodore Robert F. Stockton could resupply them. However, between Kearny and the coast stood about a hundred Mexican-Californians led by Captain Andres Pico.

The Mexicans were fewer in numbers, but they rode fresh horses and carried eight- to ten-foot-long lances. The Americans were riding tired mules after their horses had died on the long journey, and they carried sabers. Both sides possessed pistols and muskets, but a cold rain dampened their powder and made the early firearms inoperative.

On December 6, in the San Pasqual Valley, about forty miles northeast of San Diego, the Mexicans made a frontal charge against the Americans. Their long lances proved superior over Kearny's sabers and the Americans retreated to a hilltop in the nearby Escondido Mountains. Pico made several attacks against the dismounted

Americans but could not break through their defenses. During the night, Kearny sent a messenger to San Diego, and four days later, a detachment of marines and sailors from the American ships arrived and guided them to safety.

Kearny lost eighteen men killed and another thirteen wounded at the Battle of San Pasqual, nearly a third of his force. Mexican casualties were likely fewer.

Pico's attack against the Army of the West was the only significant resistance by the Mexican-Californians. Kearny and Stockton occupied Los Angeles the following January where John C. Fremont, who had led the Bear Flag Revolt of American settlers in Northern California in December 1845, joined them. Mexican officials formally surrendered California on January 13 to Fremont rather than Kearny or Stockton. This created quarrels among the American leaders but did nothing to endanger the U.S. claim to California established when Mexico ceded it to the United States in the Treaty of Guadalupe Hidalgo signed on February 2, 1848.

The Battle of San Pasqual was small by any standard; even its exact location remains unknown. At best, the Americans could only claim the battle was indecisive, as neither side surrendered. In the actual fighting, there is little doubt that Pico's lancers had the advantage over the saber-wielding Americans, but the fight's real influence was not in its casualties, but in the fact that it actually took place. Kearny's presence at San Pasqual showed America's resolve to include California in its Manifest Destiny. His survival of the battle, occupation of San Diego and Los Angeles, and his presence gave the U.S. a fair claim to California when it came time to negotiate the end of the Mexican War.

At the cost of fewer than thirty-five casualties, the Americans acquired one of its largest states and reinforced its claims to lands that spanned from the Atlantic to the Pacific. The California ports opened the way for trade with the Far East, and the discovery of gold in 1849 enriched the entire nation.

92

LA BICOCCA

French Wars in Italy, 1522

The Battle of La Bicocca was a contest between Spanish arquebusiers and Swiss pikemen hired to fight for the French. The arquebusiers won, verifying that earlier victories achieved with firearms were not aberrations but rather the future of warfare. In addition, the battle ended the Swiss reputation as Europe's finest offensive troops.

From 1450 to 1550, the Renaissance flourished in Italy as Italians made great strides in the arts and intellectual pursuits. Politically, however, the Italian peninsula was divided into five major states whose internal quarrels had made all of them vulnerable to outside attack.

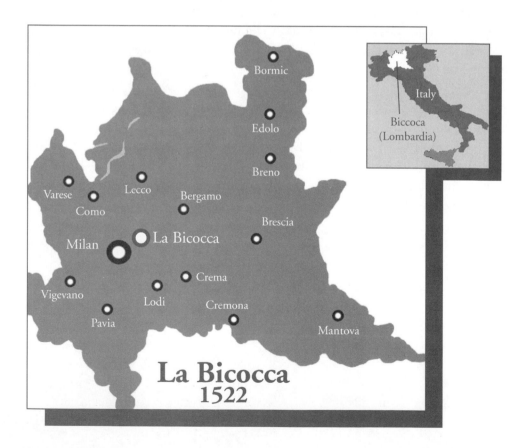

France invaded the peninsula in 1494, and five years later, Spain joined it in occupying most of Italy. The two countries collided over control of Naples in 1502. Most of the battles between the French and Spanish, like those among the Italian states, accomplished little other than adding to the numbers of widows and orphans. Possession of territory went back and forth as allegiances were made, broken, and then renegotiated.

The real significance of the wars in Italy came not from territory seized or lost but from the use of arms and tactics. On April 28, 1503, Spanish commander Gonzalo de Córdoba positioned his army of 10,000 in hillside defensive positions in a vineyard twenty miles inland from Barletta near the village of Cerignola. Among his swordsmen and pike carriers, Córdoba had several ranks of infantrymen armed with early matchlocks known as arquebuses. When they charged the Spanish, hundreds of French soldiers fell to the one-ounce balls fired from the arquebuses, thus ending the attack and driving the survivors into retreat.

The Battle of Cerignola (68) had introduced the potential of firearms on the battlefield, but it was not until the Battle of La Bicocca that the arquebuses completely delivered on their promise. In the meantime, the various factions had signed a peace agreement in 1516. It did not last long. The rivalry between King Francis I of France and Charles V, who wore the crowns of both Spain and the Holy Roman Empire, again led to war on the Italian peninsula.

After several skirmishes, Charles's army, composed mostly of Spanish soldiers and German mercenaries, encountered the French near the village of La Bicocca a few miles north of Milan. Despite their experience at Cerignola, the French had not yet included muskets in their arsenal, relying still on sword, pike, and Swiss mercenaries, reputed to be the best assault troops in Europe, as their hired reinforcements.

The Spanish prepared their defenses along a sunken road just outside La Bicocca. Four ranks of Spanish arquebusiers made up the center, while German pikemen took up their rear and flanks. A small section of the musketmen also covered a bridge that led to the Spanish rear.

The battle opened on April 27, 1522, with an assault by the Swiss pikemen against the Spanish center. As each rank of the arquebusiers fired, the soldiers in the row knelt to reload while the rank behind shot their muskets into the advancing Swiss. Despite the lengthy reloading time, the Spanish gunners maintained a steady rate of fire into the Swiss soldiers. The Swiss pikemen had heretofore prided themselves on their ability to break through any formation, but the Spanish stood firm. After losing nearly half their numbers to musket fire, the Swiss soldiers agreed to attack again only if their officers left the relative security of the rear and led from the front. The officers did so, most of them joining the 3,000 dead Swiss soldiers stacked in front of the Spanish arquebusiers.

After the Swiss frontal attack failed, the French cavalry tried to flank the defenders by traversing the bridge guarded by the detachment armed with muskets. The French horsemen either died or fled.

The Swiss continued to provide mercenaries to various armies after the Battle of La Bicocca, but they never again regained the reputation they possessed prior to the battle. Switzerland was later able to preserve its sovereignty as a neutral nation largely based on its naturally defensive, mountainous location. Their willingness to serve as an arbitrator, banker, or refuge to people with influence and money, no matter what their cause, has also helped them maintain their independence.

What had begun at Cerignola in 1503 came to fruition at La Bicocca in 1522. Spanish arquebusiers proved that they could decisively defeat the best infantry in Europe. Musket fire had won a battle and destroyed the fighting spirit of an entire country. Armies that ignored the lessons of Cerignola and La Bicocca faced only ruin and defeat as successful forces decreased loading time, improved reliability, and increased the accuracy of shoulder-held firearms. No battlefield would ever be the same after gunpowder and lead took the place of swords and pikes.

Although the Battle of La Bicocca merely confirmed what the Spanish had shown the French and the world at Cerignola two decades earlier, it is well deserving of inclusion on this list, because even though it was not the first successful use of firearms on the battlefield, it was the fight that finally convinced the nonbelievers.

93

MEGIDDO

Egyptian-Kadesh War, c. 1479 B.C.

The Egyptian victory over the Kadesh alliance in the Battle of Megiddo re-established Egypt's control of Palestine and provided much of the riches to build its temples and monuments. Megiddo also takes its place as an influential battle because it is the earliest military conflict for which partial accounts by eye-witnesses survive.

From the time of the unification of Upper and Lower Egypt in about 2900 B.C., the Egyptian Empire flourished. In less than five hundred years, its kings erected the Great Pyramids, and for another thousand years, Egypt ruled the region with little opposition. However, by the eighteenth century B.C., the kingdom was losing power to its own residents as well as to neighboring tribes.

When Ahmose became king in about 1575 B.C., he initiated plans to regain power and to expand the Empire into the northeastern frontier. For more than a century, Ahmose, and later his grandsons, successfully pushed the Egyptian border to include current-day Palestine and Syria. In about 1520 B.C., King Thutmose II died, leaving the throne to his young son. Because of the age of Thutmose III, his mother, Hatshepsut, initially ran the empire as her son's regent, but ultimately she openly assumed the role of pharaoh.

Hatshepsut did well in taking care of her people and in building new temples and monuments. However, she did little to maintain a strong military or to control her far-flung territories. By the time of her death in about 1480 B.C., the King of Kadesh, supported by the powerful Mitanni tribes along the Euphrates River, had declared the regions of modern Palestine and Syria free of Egyptian rule.

Thutmose III, now of age, enthusiastically assumed Egypt's leadership. While it is unknown if he was responsible for his mother's death, he did remove her name from all public buildings and monuments. Meanwhile, he rebuilt and trained the Egyptian army that had been mostly ignored for more than two decades.

In 1479 B.C. (varying accounts estimate ten to twenty years earlier or later), Thutmose III led his army into Gaza and on into Palestine. Historians generally assume that his force numbered between 20,000 and 30,000 men. A few aristocrats accompanied the army in horse-drawn chariots armed with archers, but the bulk of the force were infantrymen armed with shields, bronze swords, and axes. The Kadesh alliance army was probably about the same size and armed with similar weapons.

In the late spring, the Egyptian army reached the mountains leading to the town of Megiddo. The King of Kadesh placed a heavy ambush along one of three passes that he thought the Egyptians would use and arrayed the remainder of his army between the passes and Megiddo. Thutmose III correctly anticipated the enemy's plan and selected a more restricted route that his opponent had discounted as too dangerous.

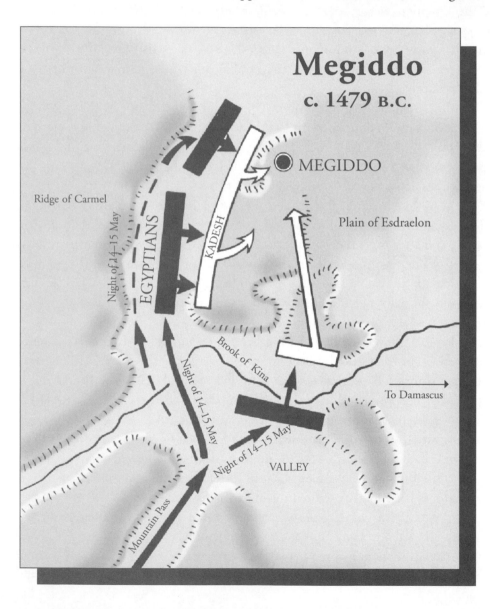

The Egyptian army negotiated the unguarded pass and attacked the unsuspecting Kadesh force, driving it back within the walls of Megiddo. No detailed accounts of the formations employed or other aspects of the fight have survived. Thutmose ordered the construction of his own wall around the city to protect his army and to prevent any escape. After a siege of several months, the town surrendered. The King of Kadesh escaped, but the Egyptians captured his army, nearly a thousand chariots, more than two thousand horses, and about four hundred pounds of gold and silver.

Thutmose continued his offensive after the fall of Megiddo and neutralized all of his opposition as he expanded Egypt's border beyond the Euphrates. Generally, he treated conquered tribes humanely, but he always took the sons of leaders back with him to Egypt to hold as hostages and to teach an appreciation for the empire. He also demanded large payments of gold and other resources that he used to further strengthen his army and to begin an era of construction of temples and memorials rivaled only by the Pyramids.

Thutmose and his heirs fought on numerous occasions to maintain the empire, including the Battle of Kadesh in 1290 B.C. (84). Shortly after this period, however, Egypt's power started to erode as other empires began to rise.

While the Battle of Megiddo added several hundred years to Egypt's rule in Palestine, its real influence lay in the records left by the chroniclers who accompanied the Egyptian army. Although these early correspondents did not record an account of the actual battle, their writings on the march and general campaign are the first of their kind in recorded history.

Even this record is vague at best. Information on the campaign and siege were recorded on a roll of leather and later stored in the Temple of Amon. Unfortunately, the scroll itself did not survive, but sufficient references to it in later writings confirm its existence.

Undoubtedly, battles and wars took place long before Megiddo, and it is likely that many had far more influence than the Egyptian victory over the Kadesh alliance. It remains important in history and worthy of this list not for its direct influence, but simply because it is the first that was recorded by eyewitnesses.

While it does not impact on its original influence, it is also noteworthy that according to the Bible's Book of Revelations, history's last battle will be fought between good and evil at Armageddon. In Hebrew, the word for Megiddo is Armageddon.

94

ROCROI

Thirty Years' War, 1643

The Battle of Rocroi resulted in the beginning of the end of Spanish military land power in the seventeenth century. It also introduced France as the rising influence and Louis II de Bourbon, Prince de Conde, as one of history's most influential military commanders.

In 1618, a revolt in Bohemia began as a struggle between Catholics and Protestants. Over the next decade, the conflict expanded from a religious contest to a political fight between the major monarchs of Europe. Although most of the combat took place in Germany, where half the local population died as a result of the fighting, most of Europe became involved in one of history's bloodiest conflicts to date.

By the time the Thirty Years' War had been raging for more than a quarter-century, most of the original monarchs and military leaders were dead or retired. Their young replacements brought renewed vigor to add to the body count and property destruction.

The death and ruin brought on by the war were the result not only of religious zeal and crown loyalty but also the advances in tactics and weaponry. Improvements in the range, accuracy, and reloading time of muskets and cannons made gunpowder dominant over sabers and pikes. The Spanish in particular had incorporated musket-bearing infantrymen into formations known as tericos.

By 1643, the prolonged war had weakened Spain's military despite the defeat of their French rivals and occupation of much of Germany and the Netherlands. In the spring of 1643, the commander of the Spanish army in the Netherlands, Don Francisco Melo, decided to take the war into France. Heading an army of 18,000 infantry and 8,000 cavalry, he crossed what is now the border of Belgium and France and besieged the small fortress of Rocroi, located fifty-five miles northeast of Reims. Eight thousand Spanish infantrymen armed with muskets made up the core of Melo's army. The remaining 10,000 infantrymen were Germans, Italians, and other allies who were not as well-trained or motivated as the Spaniards.

As soon as the French commander, Prince de Conde, learned of the invasion, he marched his army of 15,000 infantry and 7,000 cavalry to relieve the besieged city. Conde, only twenty-two years old and in command for less than a year, wanted a decisive engagement with the Spanish. He would soon get his wish.

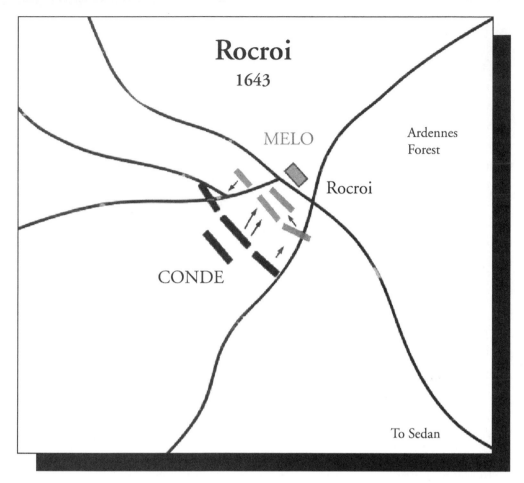

Rocroi stood in a small clearing surrounded by flat marshes in the Ardennes Forest. The only high ground was a slight ridge two miles southwest of the town, which the fast-moving French occupied before Melo could react, leaving the Spanish to position themselves between the ridge and Rocroi.

By May 18, each side had its infantry in the center and its cavalry on the flanks. While the entire Spanish army was on their front line, Conde held back about a third of his infantry and cavalry behind his formation as a reserve. Before the French army was completely in position, however, one of Conde's cavalry subordinates charged without orders. The French horsemen were quickly repulsed by the Spanish, which ended the day's only fighting.

The next morning, Conde opened the battle with an artillery barrage against the Spanish infantry. The French cavalry, with Conde personally leading the horsemen on his right flank, advanced. Conde's column pierced the Spanish cavalry and drove them backward. On the left flank, however, the Spanish repulsed the French cavalry and forced them to withdraw. The Spanish cavalry then turned into the French center and briefly captured their artillery before being repulsed by the reserve that came forward to support the front line.

When Conde saw that his left flank had given way, he turned toward the center, slashed his way through Melo's infantry, and separated the Spanish tericos from the Germans and Italians. The Spanish infantry, up to that time considered the most superior foot soldiers, fought valiantly but ultimately fell, surrounded and outnumbered. Late in the battle, the surviving Spanish officers attempted to surrender. However, when the French came forward to accept, a group of Spanish soldiers who either did not get the word to cease shooting or refused to do so, fired at the approaching soldiers. The French resumed their assault until they killed nearly all of the elite Spanish infantrymen.

At the end of the day more than 8,000 of Melo's soldiers, mostly infantrymen, were dead. Another 7,000 were taken prisoner. French losses totaled 2,000 dead. Despite the casualties and the complete French victory, the Battle of Rocroi did not end the Thirty Years' War, which would last another five years.

Rocroi did, however, greatly influence the war's end and the future European balance of power. Spain never could replace its elite infantry, and its power declined through the remainder of the conflict. Before Rocroi, Spain had the dominant army in Europe. After the battle, the French took that position and over the next half-century rose to become the most powerful nation in the world.

Rocroi also introduced Conde, soon to be known as the Great Conde. Over the next thirty years he added to his masterful victory at Rocroi and became one of France's most popular and influential military commanders.

While Rocroi catapulted France and Conde to positions of influence and served as the war's turning point, its long-term influence is not very significant. The Thirty Years' War was yet another example of nations and peoples being disseminated because of differing religious beliefs and competing "royal" families. All of the countries involved would rise and fall again and again as they continued to fight through the centuries for various gods and kings. The influence of these wars, like the battle of Rocroi, lay more in rotting corpses and burning villages than in any long-term changes in borders and governments.

95

CARTHAGE

Third Punic War, 146 B.C.

After their victory over Carthage in 146 B.C., the Romans destroyed the city and sold its inhabitants into slavery. Although Rome had defeated Carthage in a series of previous battles and wars, making the outcome of this final fight inevitable, the Battle of Carthage is nonetheless significant because it symbolizes the necessity for nations to maintain a strong military or face annihilation.

In the third century B.C., Rome in central Italy and Carthage in North Africa had emerged as the leading military and trade powers in the Mediterranean. The political and economic rivalry between the two empires had led to war in 264 B.C. over control of the city of Messina on the island of Sicily. Over the next fifteen years, Rome and Carthage fought on both land and sea. Rome's navy defeated the Carthaginians in the Battle of the Aegates Islands off Sicily in 241 B.C. to end the First Punic War. In the negotiations that ended the conflict, Carthage gave up its claims to Sicily and agreed to pay an indemnity to the victors.

Despite its loss, Carthage had remained economically and militarily powerful. Over the next two decades, Carthage further strengthened its military under the leadership of Hannibal and his brother Hasdrubal. In 218 B.C., Carthage resumed its war with Rome, and two years later, Hannibal led an attack over the Alps into Italy while his brother occupied Spain.

Hannibal succeeded in a series of battles in Italy over the next decade, but he was unable to attack and defeat Rome itself. In 207 B.C., Hasdrubal marched from Spain to join his brother for an assault against the Roman capital, but Gaius Claudius Nero and his Roman legions intercepted and defeated the Carthaginians in northern Italy at the Metaurus River (59).

After Hasdrubal's departure from Spain, Roman general Scipio defeated the remaining Carthaginians on the Spanish peninsula and three years later sailed to North Africa, a move that forced Hannibal to withdraw from Italy to defend his homeland. Scipio defeated Hannibal at the Battle of Zama in 202 B.C. (11), and the Carthaginians once again had to negotiate peace with the Romans to end the Second Punic War. This time they gave up most of their territory outside of North Africa and paid an even larger indemnity.

For the next half-century, Carthage languished militarily but regained its commercial prowess, a turn of events that many Romans resented. After all, the Romans had defeated the Carthaginians in two wars, and the defeated were once again enjoying the riches of trade. One Roman leader, Marcus Cato, lobbied for the elimination of their North African economic rival and ended each of his speeches with the declaration, "Carthage must be destroyed."

In 150 B.C., Rome dispatched an army to North Africa on the pretext of protecting its ally Numidia from neighboring Carthage, who had done virtually nothing to rebuild its military after its defeat at Zama. Knowing they had little chance in an armed conflict with Rome, the Carthaginians proposed that they surrender their arms and pay additional reparations. They even offered three hundred children from their leading families as hostages to prove their nonaggression.

Rejecting the offer, Rome demanded that the Carthaginians give up their trade routes, abandon their city, and move to the interior. When the Carthaginians refused, the Romans besieged the city. A poorly trained Roman army led by inept commanders facing triple walls of defense allowed Carthage to hold out for three years.

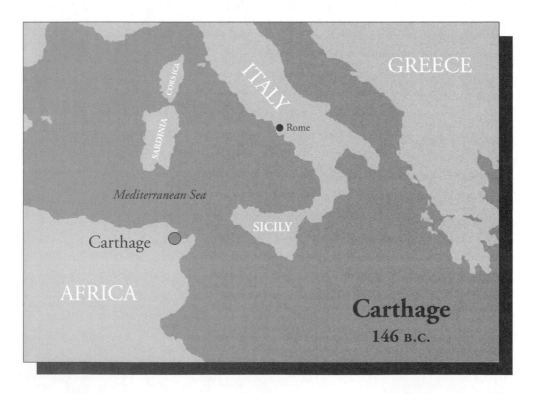

Finally, in 146 B.C., Scipio Aemilianus, the adopted grandson of the victorious Roman commander at Zama, took charge of the army. He led an attack that breached the walls and then captured the city after six days of fighting. Much of the city and many of its inhabitants were destroyed in the battle, but 50,000 Carthaginians survived to surrender.

Scipio Aemilianus and his fellow Romans intended for this Third Punic War to be the last. Some accounts state that the Romans leveled the city, poisoned its water wells, and salted the fields so nothing would again grow on Carthaginian soil. There are also reports that the surviving adult males were executed, the females ravished, and the children enslaved. While these stories are exaggerated, the Romans did sell the Carthaginians into slavery and raze the remaining walls and buildings. During the years following the battle, most of the city's stone and other building materials were hauled away to other towns and villages for reuse. What at one time had been the most powerful trade and military power on the Mediterranean simply ceased to exist.

The lasting influence of Carthage has been its example as a nation that failed to maintain a viable military force. Even though Carthage regained its commercial viability after the Second Punic War, it did not rebuild its military to defend itself. There was no Fourth Punic War, and Carthage never rose from the ashes of its defeat.

96

THAMES RIVER

War of 1812, 1813

The Battle of Thames River in 1813 secured the Northwest Territories for the United States and encouraged the British to agree to a peace treaty the following year that ended the War of 1812. In addition to losing the battle, the British lost Tecumseh, their most important Native American ally, who was mortally wounded. Tecumseh's death also influenced the future of native tribes all across North America, as he had proven to be the only leader capable of uniting Native Americans against the westward expansion by the whites.

Even though the British had signed a treaty following their defeat at Yorktown in 1783 (1) that acknowledged the independence of the United States, many Englishmen did not accept the American colonies' departure from the empire. Continuing requirements for men and material to battle Napoleon on the Continent gave Britain an excuse to impress American sailors into their navy and interfere with American trading vessels. In addition, British soldiers in Canada were arming Native Americans to fight against U.S. expansion into the Great Lakes and the Northwest Territories.

Since shortly after the arrival of the first white colonists on the Atlantic coast early in the seventeenth century, various native tribes had attempted to halt the settlement of their lands and hunting grounds. Many of these natives were brave, proficient individual warriors, but none of the tribes approached fighting in terms of military organization or tactics. Except on the rare occasions where they possessed overwhelming numbers or had the element of complete surprise on their side, the Native Americans met defeat.

By the early part of the nineteenth century, white settlers had exterminated the native tribes or pushed them inland from New England and the Atlantic Coast. It was not until 1801 that Tecumseh, chief of the Shawnees in Ohio, united many of the surviving tribes from Canada to the Gulf of Mexico into a single confederation so that the Native Americans could significantly threaten white expansion.

Tecumseh, whose father had been killed by whites, believed that all of North America belonged to the Native Americans and refused to sign any treaty that stated otherwise. As a boy, Tecumseh had learned sufficient English to negotiate several disputes between whites and his people. He continued his education, learning to read and write, and eventually he became a convincing orator in English and several native languages.

Between 1801 and 1811, Tecumseh traveled from the Great Lakes to Alabama and Mississippi, convincing tribes to join his Red Stick Confederacy. Most of the independent-minded tribesmen refused to join, but a sufficient number did so to get the attention of the whites. Tecumseh placed his brother, The Prophet, known for his visions of native superiority, in charge of a refuge and training center called Prophetstown at the juncture of the Tippecanoe and Wabash Rivers in Indiana.

On November 7, 1811, U.S. militiamen commanded by William Henry Harrison attacked Prophetstown, drove The Prophet into flight, and destroyed the town. Harrison's discovery of British-supplied arms in the camp further outraged the Americans, who by that time were tired of British interference.

Neither the U.S. nor the British were prepared for the War of 1812. The United States had few soldiers, sailors, weapons, or ships; the British were better armed and organized, but they faced a greater enemy on the Continent who threatened their own shores. As a result, the battles of the War of 1812 were generally small and focused on the control of the Canadian border, the Great Lakes, and the Northwest Territories.

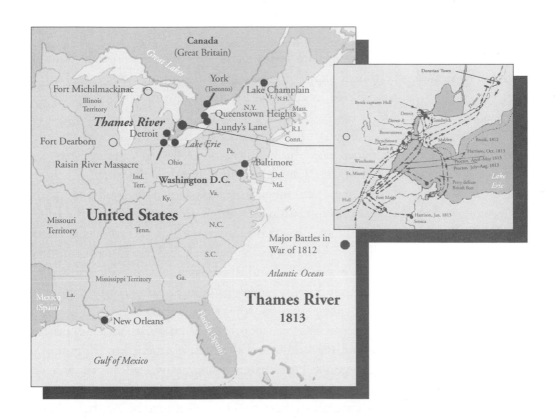

Early in the war, Tecumseh and his native allies sided with the British in hopes that they would return lands occupied by white Americans. The British discovered that the Native Americans were impossible to train into regular infantry units and used them primarily for reconnaissance and screening operations. They also found them useful as a propaganda tool with which to terrorize white Americans, who were well aware of the atrocities committed by various native tribes. In January 1813, this threat became even more real when a group of Native Americans tortured and killed fifty wounded white men left behind at the Battle of Raisin River in southeastern Michigan.

Campaigns early in the war did not go well for the United States until, finally, on April 27, Americans commanded by Zebulon Pike overran the British garrison at York, Canada. The following September, Oliver Perry defeated the British flotilla on Lake Erie to gain control of the Great Lakes.

Following Perry's victory, an army of 4,500, again led by Harrison, crossed Lake Erie into Ontario on September 27. The British army of 800 regular infantrymen commanded by General Henry Proctor and reinforced by 1,200 Native Americans led by Tecumseh, evacuated Detroit and Fort Malden. Proctor not only fled, he did so in a state of near-panic, leaving behind supplies for the Americans and failing to destroy bridges or to block roads to impede their pursuit.

On October 5, Harrison caught up with Proctor's army on the north back of the Thames River in southeastern Ontario. A reconnaissance patrol reported to Harrison that the enemy were not arrayed in a massed formation but rather were spread out with spaces between the soldiers. Despite the dense forest and flanking swamp, Harrison began his attack with a charge by a regiment of Kentucky cavalrymen armed with muskets. These horsemen easily broke through the British defensive gaps and turned to fire into their rear as the American infantry assaulted the front.

Proctor, along with a small detachment of Dragoons and mounted Native Americans, fled the field early in the battle. Tecumseh attempted to rally the tribes-men but fell to multiple gunshots. The native leader was one of forty-eight British and Native Americans killed or wounded in the battle; another 475 were captured. American losses amounted to fifteen killed and thirty wounded.

These relatively few losses produced great returns. In addition to the capture of Proctor's supply train and official papers, the Americans now controlled the Northwest Territories as well as the Great Lakes. The death of Tecumseh ended the British-Indian alliance between the British and the Native Americans. More impor-tantly, it finished what had begun at Prophetstown—no native leader again ever had any success in uniting the tribes against white expansion. Except for a brief coalition of tribesmen that defeated Custer at Little Big Horn (100) in 1876, after Thames

River, the Native Americans suffered defeat after defeat until their tribes were decimated and the survivors moved to permanent reservations.

Because of the superiority of the white's weapons and military organization, they would have successfully defeated the Native Americans regardless of a confederation established by Tecumseh or any other leader. However, if he had lived to make his vision a reality, the white victory over the Native Americans would have been much more costly and not nearly as swift.

97

PAARDEBERG

Second South African War, 1900

The Battle of Paardeberg was the largest and bloodiest fight of the Second South African War, and the British victory opened the way for the annexation of the Boer republics. While South Africa produced great wealth for Britain, especially in the forms of diamonds and gold, the strict post-war policy of racial separation called Apartheid created a state of inequality and unrest that remains in the region today.

Settlers for the Dutch East India Company first came to the Cape of Good Hope in 1652 to protect the profitable trade route to Indonesia. During the Napoleonic Wars, the British realized the strategic value of South Africa and seized the territory from the Dutch. The British and the Dutch "Boers" did not agree on much except their perceived superiority over the black natives of the region. In 1835, the Dutch became so tired of British control that they loaded their possessions on ox carts and made the "Great Trek" inland to establish their own colonies of Transvaal and the Orange Free State.

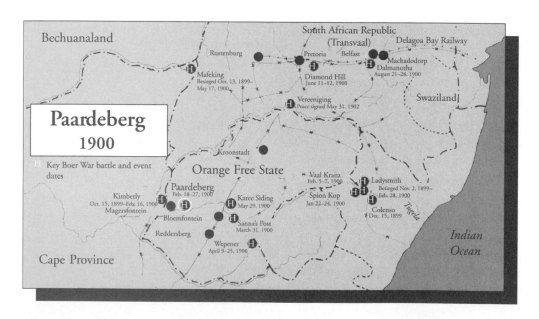

The British, glad to be rid of the troublesome Boers, recognized the independence of the Boers' new countries. Tensions, however, continued between the British and the Boers, eventually leading to the First South African War after Britain annexed Transvaal in 1877. When the Boers won two battles in 1881, the British decided the area was not worth a fight and once again recognized the independence of Transvaal.

A few years later, the British again changed their minds with the confirmation of diamond deposits and the discovery of huge gold deposits in the Boer states. Even though Boer officials attempted to limit the numbers, British miners and settlers moved into Boer territory and by the early 1890s outnumbered the Dutch. British settlers in Transvaal resented paying taxes to the Dutch government while being denied the right to vote. The British in the Cape Colony supported several attempts to overthrow the Boer government, pushing both sides closer to war. Finally in October 1899, Transvaal, allied with the Orange Free State, went to war against the British.

Initially, the Boers had the advantage because there were so few British troops in the region. The Boers were superb horsemen and excellent shots; most carried the most up-to-date German rifles. While their military organization was far from rigid, the Boers worked well together and knew the countryside intimately. Early in the war, they took the initiative and besieged the predominantly British towns of Ladysmith and Mafeking, as well as the Kimberly diamond-mining center.

The British responded by dispatching soldiers from throughout the empire, including Australia and Canada, to South Africa. By February 1900, the British had assembled 37,000 soldiers, 113 pieces of artillery, 12,000 horses, and 22,000 transport animals under the command of two of Britain's most able and influential officers, Frederick Roberts and Horatio Kitchener.

British operations around Kimberly lifted the siege on February 15. The Boer commander, Piet Cronje, then consolidated his force about twenty-three miles southeast of the diamond center at Paardeberg on the Modder River. Cronje's force totaled about 5,000, but many of these were women and children who accompanied the soldiers.

On February 18, four British brigades assaulted the Boer defenses across the flat, treeless plain. The Boers allowed the advancing soldiers to close within one hundred yards before opening up with concentrated rifle fire. In a few hours, more than a thousand British soldiers lay dead before the Boer defenses.

The British withdrew the attack force, surrounded the defenses, brought their artillery forward, and bombarded the Boer positions. On February 27, the Boers surrendered after more than a thousand had fallen to the British artillery.

After Paardeberg, the Boers were forced to adopt guerrilla warfare to continue the conflict. The British responded by herding more than 120,000 Boers and their families into concentration camps. On May 31, 1902, the Boers finally surrendered, leaving Transvaal and the Orange Free State to become part of British South Africa.

The united British and Boers still differed on many things, but they were in complete agreement in their belief of their superiority over the native Africans. Louis Botha, a Boer, became the first Prime Minister, and South Africans began to identify themselves more by color than national origin.

South Africa sent soldiers to support the Allies in World War I and again in World War II. The country continued to provide security for trade lanes around the African cape, as well as riches of gold, diamonds, and other resources until South Africa finally cut its links with Britain and became a republic in 1961.

During this period when few nations, including the United States and Great Britain, recognized any significant degree of equality of the races, South Africa stood out for its intense repression and separation of its black population. South Africa's official Apartheid policy kept blacks from holding skilled jobs, restricted where they could live and travel, and in all aspects of society kept them separate from the white population. Despite pressure from other countries and world organizations, South Africa maintained strict Apartheid until they finally began some reforms when Frederick de Clerk assumed the leadership of the country in 1989. Not until 1996 did South Africa adopt a constitution that guaranteed equal rights for blacks and whites.

The Battle of Paardeberg assured the continued British and white dominance of South Africa and its exploitation as a source of wealth and resources for the empire. Unfortunately for the native population, the British victory meant nearly another hundred years of second-class citizenship. It also established the concept of Apartheid as one of history's most unfair and unjust social decrees, and adds that word to the long list marking man's inhumanity to his fellow men.

98

TEL-EL-KEBIR

Egyptian Revolt, 1882

The victory by Sir Garnet Wolseley's regulars over the Egyptian rebels at the Battle of Tel-el-Kebir in 1882 led to British control of the region for the next three-quarters of a century. It also secured the Suez Canal for Britain, and the British occupation of Egypt provided resources for campaigns against Islamic fundamentalists in Sudan and for operations against Turkey.

From time immemorial, internal and external factions have fought to control the area that Egypt occupies today. The geographical location and natural resources make it a strategic center for North Africa, the Middle East, and the Mediterranean Sea. For centuries, the Ottoman Empire, after its victory at Constantinople in 1453 (41), exerted the most influence over Egypt and the region.

By the nineteenth century, the Ottoman Empire was waning and Russia was threatening it. During the 1850s, only the intervention of European countries prevented the Russians from gaining control of the Bosporus and Black Seas. For this assistance, Great Britain and France received the rights to develop businesses and to protect their citizens in the region.

In 1869, the Suez Canal opened between the Mediterranean and the Red Sea, drastically shortening the sailing distance from Europe to India and the East. Egypt retained a large financial interest in the canal, but poor management and overspending forced the Egyptians to sell their remaining shares to the British in 1875. When the entire Egyptian government declared bankruptcy the following year, Britain took an even greater role in running the country, including selecting Egyptian leaders.

In September 1881, Colonel Arabi Pasha led a revolt of the Egyptian army that ousted the British-backed government. Arabi rallied the country behind the banner of "Egypt for Egyptians" and promises that included control of the profitable Suez Canal. Britain and France agreed that they had to protect the canal as well as the stability of the region, and they planned to oust Arabi and his rebels.

Within weeks, the French Parliament voted to withdraw its support of the operation. The British, however, did not waver, dispatching a navy flotilla and an army commanded by Sir Garnet Wolseley to reestablish hegemony. On July 11, 1882, the Royal Navy attacked the rebel defenses at the port of Alexandria, which guarded the entrance to the Nile. Two days of bombardment demolished the Egyptian defenses, and the British army landed unopposed.

On August 20, Wolseley and his army of 40,000 captured the town of Ismailia at the mouth of the Suez Canal. Arabi now had about 60,000 men in his rebel army, but he had to spread his force to cover several possible routes of attack. He established his primary defenses with 24,000 men at Tel-el-Kebir, sixty-five miles north of Cairo. There he had his army dig a trench line about three miles long on a sloping ridge that faced several miles of open ground. Interspersed with his infantry were seventy pieces of artillery.

Wolseley also had to spread out his troops to secure other areas, and as a result, he approached the Egyptian defenses with only about 17,000 men. Five miles from the Egyptian trenches, he halted and sent out reconnaissance. When the scouts returned with a description of the enemy defenses and numbers, Wolseley realized that a traditional daylight attack would be murderous.

Instead he ordered preparations for a night assault. This was not a tactic for which his army was trained, but Wolseley took measures to ensure its success. He allowed five hours for the advance and assigned guides with compasses to lead the march. He also brought in naval navigators to use celestial navigation to keep the marchers on course.

Despite the extremely dark night, the advance progressed flawlessly. Before dawn on September 13, the British army had closed to within two hundred meters of the trenches and positioned their artillery between infantry divisions on each side. Cavalry stood ready on the flanks of the infantry, and the Royal Marines waited behind the formation in reserve.

When the Egyptians spotted the army assembled to their front at first light, they barely had time to fire but a few volleys before the British infantry swept through their lines. The rebel withdrawal turned into a wild retreat when the British cavalry joined the attack. Resolve further eroded when British bugles blew and the order of "fix bayonets" rang out across the lines of infantrymen. Within approximately one hour, 2,500 of Arabi's troops were dead, wounded, or captured. All of his artillery was in British hands. Wolseley's troops had suffered only 58 dead and 400 wounded. Two days later, Wolseley marched into Cairo, where Arabi surrendered without further resistance.

The British restructured the government and taxed the wealthy rather than the peasants. Much of this revenue went to repay Egyptian debts to the British, but improvements were also made to educational, transportation, and medical facilities. Additionally, the British reorganized the Egyptian army with their own officers in charge and soon found themselves defending the southern border with Sedan against Islamic fundamentalists.

During this time, Egypt remained officially a possession of the Ottoman Empire, but the Turks had little influence over the country. Although they called Egypt a "protectorate," it was for all practical purposes a British colony. When World War I broke out in 1914, the British and Turks were on opposite sides. Egypt did not support the Ottomans but rather served as a base of operation for the allies. Conferences and treaties that ended World War I rewarded Britain with Egypt and the entire Persian Gulf region, including oil-rich Iraq.

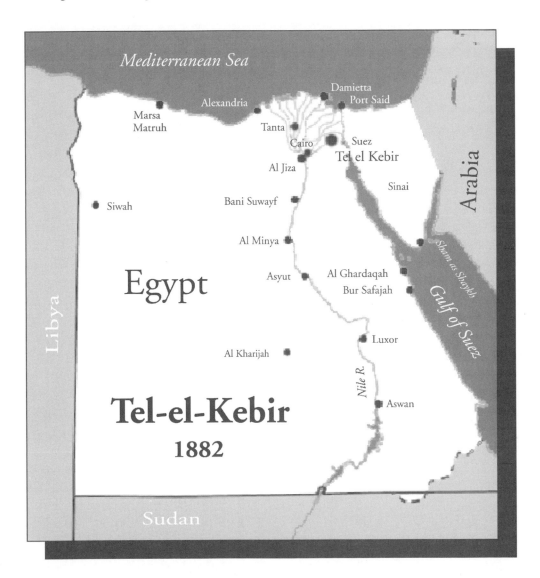

At the cost of fewer than sixty dead, the British gained control of Egypt for more than seventy-five years, providing them with control of the Suez Canal and a profitable trade with their colony of India. In fact, it was not until the British Empire, like the Ottoman Empire before it, began to fade that another Egyptian revolt, this time led by Gamal Abdel-Nasser, finally ended Britain's control of the country in 1956. By that time India had already gained its independence and the British had little left to protect.

99

VYBORG

Finnish-Russian War, 1918

The existence of Finland as a free and independent country is a direct result of the anti-Communist White Army's defeat of the Soviet-backed Red Army at Vyborg in 1918. Vyborg also introduced Finnish General Carl Gustav von Mannerheim as one of history's most influential military leaders.

The narrow space of land between Russia and Sweden that was to become Finland was first settled in the seventh century by tribes from the Volga and Urals who forced the native Lapps to move farther north. Sweden conquered the region in 1157 and ruled it until it lost the area to Russia in 1809. Following their occupation, the Russians set up Finland as a Grand Duchy, but over the years replaced the Finnish language and military system with their own.

Early in the twentieth century, the unrest in Russia over the Czar's rule spread to Finland. When this unrest in Russia manifested itself in the March Revolution in 1917, the Finns proclaimed their own freedom on July 20. While most Finns supported their country's independence, they were deeply divided with regard to what form of government they should adopt.

The government that declared Finland's independence was mostly from the middle and upper classes who favored some type of democratic republic. Their strongest support came from shooting and social clubs known as White Guards who practiced military organization and training procedures. On the other side were the working class, called Reds, who favored the Soviet model of Communism and wanted Finland to become a socialist state either separate from or part of the Soviet Union. Further complicating the division was the presence of 50,000 Russian troops still garrisoned within Finland's borders.

When the presiding government recognized the Whites as the official army of Finland on January 25, 1918, a civil war broke out across the country. The separation into Whites and Reds along social lines was far from absolute, and Finns from all walks of life joined one side or the other. Soon villages divided against each other and in some instances even family members picked up arms against one another.

The Finnish government placed General Carl von Mannerheim in command of its White Army. Mannerheim, a native Finn, had served as an officer in the Russian army and had participated in the honor guard of Czar Alexander's coronation in 1895. He had also gained combat experience in the Russo-Japanese War of 1904–5 and in World War I before returning home during the Russian Revolution.

Mannerheim, with an army of 80,000, first moved against the Russian garrisons in northern Finland and easily defeated them while capturing much-needed arms and ammunition. Mannerheim then marched southward to expel other Russian troops and to secure the city of Helsinki. During this period, Finns referred to the fighting as Civil War, Class War, Red Revolt, and Liberation War, but by whatever name, death and destruction were its results. Along the way, skirmishes between the Whites and Reds escalated into battles where little quarter was given as brother fought against brother and friend against friend.

By late March, the Whites had pushed the majority of the Red Army into defensive positions at the town of Tampere, about a hundred miles north of Helsinki. Mannerheim encircled the town and began the largest battle of the war. On April 6, more than 11,000 Reds surrendered, opening the way to Helsinki. Mannerheim, now supported by a German force commanded by General Colmar von der Goltz who joined the Whites to fight the Communists, occupied Helsinki on April 13.

The surviving Reds and their Russian supporters realized that the war was lost and hurriedly retreated eastward toward Russia. Mannerheim pursued and caught up with the retreating army at Vyborg on the narrow strip of land between the Gulf of Finland and Lake Ladoga. On April 29, Mannerheim attacked Vyborg, killed many of the Reds, and drove the remainder into Russia.

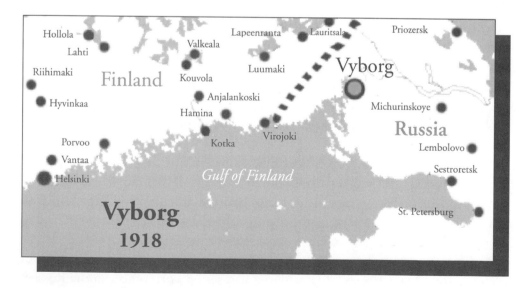

A week later, the last pockets of Red resistance in Finland surrendered. Total battle deaths during the three-month war were about 3,230 Whites and 3,360 Reds. Non-battle deaths, including executions and starvation in prison camps, numbered about 1,650 Whites and 8,380 Reds.

Following the war, the people of Finland remained deeply divided between former White and Red allegiances until 1939 when the Finns, still ably led by Mannerheim, united and turned back a Soviet invasion. A subsequent Soviet attack in 1940 defeated the Finns, but in 1941 they again allied with the Germans against the Russians—until changing sides one more time in 1944. Mannerheim remained in command during all of these changes, and his military and diplomatic leadership are directly responsible for Finland's maintenance of its independence. Shortly after World War II, his grateful country rewarded him with the republic's presidency.

The Battle of Vyborg completed the Whites' victory over the Reds and eliminated future internal socialist threats to an independent Finland. Had the Reds proven victorious, Finland would probably have become just another province of the USSR without its freedom for another seventy years until the final breakup of the Soviet Union.

Although Finland has not had a great influence in world affairs, it deserves recognition as one of the few countries that has successfully fought both Nazi Germany and the Soviet Union to maintain its independence. This autonomy, and the fact that Finland is still a republic, began at Vyborg, thus earning that battle a place on this list.

LITTLE BIG HORN

U.S.-Indian Wars, 1876

The defeat of a portion of the Seventh Cavalry by the Sioux Indians and their allies along the Little Big Horn River in 1876 marked the greatest victory Native Americans ever experienced over the United States Army. While it has become one of the most famous and studied fights in history—resulting in hundreds of books, films, and even songs—the battle appears on this list not because of its military influence, but because of its continued popularity as a fascinating story.

From the time they arrived in North America, white European settlers negotiated for, bought, or simply took land from the native inhabitants. Despite the vast territory and seemingly unlimited resources, the Native Americans had warred among each other for centuries over hunting areas, for slaves, or just for sport. Without steel or wheels, they had relied on bows and arrows, spears, and clubs for weapons. While the typical Native American was a capable individual warrior, bands and tribes had no concept of massing forces, maneuver, or tactics.

Other than raids against isolated farms or individual travelers, the Native Americans experienced little success against the white settlers armed with muskets and organized into militias. During the late eighteenth and early nineteenth centuries, the U.S. Army easily defeated the tribes in the eastern United States and placed the survivors on reservations. Other than the few occasions that the Europeans, particularly the French, had armed and trained them, the Native Americans never had resembled a military force.

By the mid-nineteenth century, the U.S. had eliminated or neutralized the Native Americans along both the East and West Coasts. Only the tribes of the Great Plains hindered the United States from reaching from "sea to shining sea."

During the American Civil War, most of the military forces that protected settlements in the Midwest had withdrawn to fight in the East. Local militias had filled in for the absent regular army, and these frontiersmen frequently displayed a degree of savagery that rivaled or exceeded that of the Native Americans. At Sand Creek, Colorado, on November 29, 1864, militia units had attacked a village of Cheyenne and Arapahoe, killing more than four hundred Native Americans, including women and children.

The massacre at Sand Creek led to a general uprising of the Plains Indians. This included the Sioux, the largest tribe, who resisted the construction of a military trail across their lands in Wyoming and Montana. In 1868, the United States agreed to abandon the trail when the Sioux accepted a treaty that provided them a reservation in Dakota Territory.

An uneasy peace lasted for a few years before the Sioux left their reservation in protest of the white gold rush into the Black Hills and the construction of a railroad through their lands. Other tribes soon joined the Sioux in renewing their raids against the whites. On January 31, 1876, the U.S. ordered all Native Americans back to their reservations, threatening that those who failed to obey would be considered hostile and hunted down by the army.

The Native Americans ignored the ultimatum. Most had no desire to return to reservation life and were prepared to fight. The few who wanted to return were unable to because of the extremely harsh winter.

In the spring, the U.S. Army began a three-pronged attack against the native camps involving more than 2,500 soldiers. General George Crook advanced north from Fort Fetterman, Wyoming; General John Gibbon moved east from Fort Ellis, Montana; and General Alfred Terry moved west from Fort Lincoln, Dakota Territory. Their intelligence estimate was that the hostile tribes could field only five to eight hundred warriors armed with bows and arrows and a few ancient muskets.

On June 17, Crook's column of 1,200 troops encountered 1,500 Sioux warriors on the Rosebud River in southeastern Montana. While the tribesmen still lacked a formal military organization, they were following the leadership of Chief Crazy Horse and several other tribal leaders. In a six-hour battle, they killed 10 cavalrymen and wounded another 32. While it was indecisive, the battle revealed far larger numbers of Native Americans armed with repeating rifles than the army had anticipated. These weapons were either captured from settlers or bought from traders. For the first time in the Indian Wars, U.S. soldiers were not only outnumbered, but with their single shot rifles, they were also outgunned.

Crook, delayed by the fight, had no means to communicate this information with the other two columns. When Gibbon and Terry met at the mouth of the Rosebud a few days later, they continued their march despite the absence of Crook. Based on the discovery of a mile-wide network of trails, the generals concluded the Native Americans must be at a major encampment at what the Sioux called Greasy Grass along the Little Big Horn River in southern Montana.

The commanders planned to continue their advance in two columns to envelop the camp. On June 22, Terry dispatched Lieutenant Colonel George Armstrong Custer and his Seventh Cavalry Regiment as an advance reconnaissance. Custer, having had poor intelligence on the number of natives and their arms, left his Gatling guns behind because the unnecessary weapons would slow his march If he discovered any tribesmen, he was to drive them toward the larger columns. Custer, who had achieved general's stars in the Civil War while in his early twenties by making quick decisions and reacting aggressively, had experienced success in previous battles with the Native Americans. He knew they preferred to hit fast and then disappear, and getting them to stand and fight would be extremely difficult.

Custer pushed his column more than fifty miles in a single day and reached high ground near the Little Big Horn late on June 24. Despite a report from his native scouts about the size of the camp and his own visual reconnaissance, Custer planned an attack for the next morning. While much speculation then and since suggests Custer foolishly attacked so he would not have to share the glory with the other commanders, it is more likely that previous experiences of chasing bands of tribesmen for weeks only to have them run away without a fight made Custer want to engage them as soon as possible.

On the morning of the 25th, Custer divided his command into three columns, a tactic that reinforces the notion that he had no idea of the size and arms of his opponents. Custer sent Major Marcus Reno to the south side of the river while he advanced to the north bank. A smaller unit, including his supply train, commanded by Captain Frederick Benteen, followed Reno.

Reno had advanced to within a few miles of the camp when he encountered a superior force of Native Americans that drove him back across the river. The cavalrymen went into a hasty defensive position on a ridge, where Benteen, who had received a courier message to join Custer, arrived and joined the fight. The attacking Sioux prevented either column from reinforcing Custer. During the fight that lasted the remainder of the day and into the 26th, 53 of Reno's and Benteen's men were killed and about that many more wounded.

Shortly after Reno and Benteen joined forces, they heard sounds of a battle nearer the native camp along Custer's route of advance. Heavily engaged themselves, they could not move to support their commander. On the morning of June 27, Terry's and Gibbon's columns arrived to relieve Reno. When they looked for Custer, they discovered more than 200 corpses.

There were no white survivors of what became known as Custer's Last Stand. Only conflicting Native American accounts of what happened at the Battle of Little Big Horn are available. Apparently Custer initially charged the village until he saw he was up against as many as 3,000 warriors, many armed with repeating rifles. He withdrew up the hillside east of the river and hastily formed a defense behind dead horses. The tribesmen, under the leadership of Sitting Bull, Gall, and Crazy Horse, closed their circle until a final rush overran the few survivors.

Shortly after the battle, the *Bismarck Tribune* published a brief account stating, "General Custer attacked the Indians on June 25, and he, with every officer and man in five companies were killed."

Despite the fact that the Little Big Horn was the greatest victory by the Native Americans over the whites in American history, it had little direct immediate or long-range impact. After the battle, the Native Americans broke into small groups and fled. Disease and hunger reduced their numbers as the cavalry relentlessly pursued. Within a year, the surviving Sioux and their allies were back on the reservation. Except for some minor uprisings, the Sioux never again exhibited any military power whatsoever.

The news of the battle in Washington did increase the U.S. military budget, which provided additional men and improved arms for the army. However, the battle had no significant influence on the U.S. or its military, except to motivate the army to avenge its losses. In fact, the only lasting impact was the formation of an insurance cooperative by the small officer corps who saw how little care was provided to the widows and orphans of Custer's command.

Since Custer's Last Stand, thousands of books and articles have been written about the battle. When motion pictures became popular in the twentieth century, a new Custer film appeared nearly every decade—their plots and prejudices about the heroes and villains generally reflecting the political climate of the time. Little Big Horn has become one of the most discussed and documented battles in history. While it decided little or nothing, the questions of what happened and why remain popular items of conjecture. It joins this list not because of its influence, but because of its popularity and notoriety.

INDEX

BIBLIOGRAPHY

Adcock, R.E. *The Greek and Macedonian Art of War.* Berkeley, CA: University of California Press, 1957.

Allen, Peter. *The Yom Kippur War.* New York: Scribner, 1982.

Alpert, Michael. *A New International Study of the Spanish Civil War.* New York: St. Martin's, 1994.

Anderson, Fred. *Crucible of War: The Seven Years' War and the Fate of the Empire In British North America, 1754–1766.* New York: Alfred A. Knopf, 2000.

Anderson, M.S. *Peter the Great.* New York: Longman, 1995.

Antal, Sandy. *Proctor's War of 1812.* East Lansing, MI: Michigan State University Press, 1997.

Aronson, Theo. *The Fall of the Third Napoleon.* London: Cassell, 1970.

Ashley, Maurice. *The Battle of Naseby and the Fall of King Charles I.* New York: St. Martin's, 1992.

Atkinson, Rick. *Crusade.* Boston: Houghton Mifflin, 1993.

Babur. *The Baburnama: Memories of Babur, Prince and Emperor of Hindustan.* Washington, D.C.: Smithsonian Institution, 1996.

Bahn, Paul G. *Lost Cities.* New York: Welcome Rain, 1997.

Bak, Richard. *The CSS Hunley: The Greatest Undersea Adventure of the Civil War.* Dallas: Taylor, 1999.

Baker, G.P. *Hannibal.* New York: Cooper Square, 1999.

Baldwin, Hanson W. *World War I.* New York: Grove, 1963.

Balyuzi, H. M. *Mohammad and the Course of Islam.* Oxford: Ronald, 1976.

Baudot, Marcel, editor. *The Historical Encyclopedia of World War II.* New York: Facts on File, 1980.

Bauer K. Jack. *The Mexican War, 1846–1848.* New York: Macmillan, 1974.

Beeching, Jack. *The Galleys at Lepanto.* New York: Scribner's, 1983.

Bengtsson, Frans G. *The Sword Does Not Jest: The Heroic Life of King Charles XII of Sweden.* New York: St. Martin's, 1960.

Bennett, Michael. *The Battle of Bosworth.* New York: St. Martin's, 1985.

Blair, Clay Jr. *Forgotten War: America in Korea.* New York: Times Books, 1987.

Blond, Georges. *Admiral Togo.* New York: Macmillan, 1960.

Boatner, Mark M. III. *The Civil War Dictionary.* New York: David McKay, 1959.

———. *Encyclopedia of the American Revolution.* New York: David McKay, 1966.

Borza, Eugene. *In the Shadow of Olympus: The Emergence of Macedon.* Princeton, NJ: Princeton University Press, 1990.

Bourne, Peter G. *Fidel: A Biography of Fidel Castro.* New York: Dodd, Mead, 1986.

Bresler, Fenton. *Napoleon III: A Life.* New York: Carroll & Graff, 1999.

Brusilov, Alexei A. *A Soldier's Notebook: 1914–1918.* Westport, CN: Greenwood Press, 1971.

Bunson, Matthew. *Encyclopedia of the Roman Empire.* New York: Facts on File, 1994.

Busch, Noel F. *The Emperor's Sword: Japan Versus Russia in the Battle of Tsushima.* New York: Funk and Wagnalls, 1969.

Caidin, Martin. *The Tigers Are Burning.* New York: Hawthorn, 1974.

Carrell, Paul. *Hitler Moves East.* New York: Little, Brown, 1965.

Carruthers, Bob. *The English Civil Wars, 1642–1660.* London: Cassell, 2000.

Carter, John M. *The Battle of Actium: The Rise & Triumph of Augustus Caesar.* London: Hamilton, 1970.

Cassius, Dio. *Dio's Roman History.* New York: Macmillan, 1924.

Catton, Bruce. *The Army of the Potomac.* 3 Vols. Garden City, NY: Doubleday, 1952.

Chandler, David G. *The Campaigns of Napoleon: The Mind and Method of History's Greatest Soldier.* New York: Macmillan, 1966.

———, editor. *A Guide to the Battlefields of Europe.* London: Hugh Evelyn, 1965.

————. *Marlborough as Military Commander.* New York: Scribner, 1973.

Chidsey, Donald B. *The Spanish-American War: A Behind-the-Scenes Account of the War in Cuba.* New York: Crown, 1971.

Chubarov, Alexander. *The Fragile Empire: A History of Imperial Russia.* New York: Continuum, 1999.

Churchill, Winston. *The Second World War.* 6 Vols. Boston: Houghton Mifflin, 1948–1953.

Clark, Alan. *Barbarossa: The Russian-German Conflict 1941–45.* New York: Quill, 1965.

Clarke, Dwight L. *Stephen Watts Kearny: Soldier of the West.* Norman, OK: University of Oklahoma Press, 1961.

Clayton, Tim and Phil Craig. *The Finest Hour: The Battle of Britain.* New York: Simon and Schuster, 2000.

Cobb, Richard. *The French and Their Revolution: Selected Writings.* New York: New Press, 1998.

Cole, Juan R. *Colonialism and Revolution in the Middle East: Social and Cultural Origins of Egypt's Urabi Movement.* Princeton, NJ: Princeton University Press, 1993.

Coles, Henry. *The War of 1812.* Chicago: University of Chicago Press, 1965.

Collier, Richard. *The War in the Desert.* Alexandria, VA: Time-Life, 1977.

Connaughton, R.M. *The War of the Rising Sun and Tumbling Bear: A Military History of the Russo-Japanese War 1904–5.* New York: Routledge, 1988.

Corbett, Julian S. *Maritime Operations in the Russo-Japanese War, 1904–1905.* Annapolis, MD: Naval Institute Press, 1994.

Costello, John. *The Pacific War: 1941–1945.* London: Collins, 1981.

Cragg, Dan. *Generals in Muddy Boots: A Concise Encyclopedia of Combat Commanders.* New York: Berkley, 1996.

Craven, Brian. *The Punic Wars.* London: Weidenfeld and Nicolson, 1992.

Creasy, Edward Shepherd. *Fifteen Decisive Battles of the World: From Marathon to Waterloo.* New York: Harpers, 1851.

Davis, Paul K. *100 Decisive Battles: From Ancient Times to the Present.* Santa Barbara, CA: ABC-CLIO, 1999.

Davis, William C. *Duel Between the First Ironclads.* Mechanicsburg, PA: Stackpole, 1994.

Davis, William Stearns, editor. *Readings in Ancient History: Greece and the East.* 2 Vols. Boston: Allyn and Bacon, 1912–1913.

Dear, I.C.B. and M.R.D. Foot, editors. *The Oxford Companion to World War II.* New York: Oxford, 1995.

De Gaury, Gerald. *The Great Captain.* London: Longmans 1955.

de Selíncourt, Aubrey, trans. *Herodotus: The Histories.* Baltimore: Penguin, 1954,

Dodge, Theodore Ayrault. *Caesar: A History of the Art of War Among the Romans Down to the End of the Roman Empire.* New York: Da Capo Press, 1997.

Dower, John W. *War Without Mercy: Race & Power in the Pacific War.* New York: Pantheon, 1986.

Duffy, Christopher. *Austerlitz 1805.* London: Seeley Service, 1977.

Dupuy, R. Ernest. *World War II: A Compact History.* New York: Hawthorne, 1969.

———— and Trevor N. Dupuy. *The Encyclopedia of Military History, From 3500 B.C. to the Present.* New York: Harper and Row, 1970.

Dupuy, Trevor N. *The Evolution of Weapons and Warfare.* New York: Bobbs-Merrill Company, 1980.

Eastman, Lloyd E. *Seeds of Destruction: Nationalist China in the War and Revolution, 1937–1949.* Stanford, CA: Stanford University Press, 1984.

Editors, Time-Life Books. *Ramses II: Magnificence on the Nile.* Alexandria, VA: Time-Life Books, 1993.

Eggenberger, David. *An Encyclopedia of Battles: Accounts of over 1560 Battles from 1479 B.C. to the Present.* New York: Dover, 1985.

Eisenhower, John S.D. *So Far From God: The U.S. War With Mexico, 1846–1848.* New York: Random House, 1989.

Esposito, Vincent J. *A Concise History of World War I.* New York: Praeger, 1964.

———— and John R. Elting, editors. *A Military History and Atlas of the Napoleonic Wars.* New York: Praeger, 1964.

Evans, Geoffrey. *Tannenberg: 1410–1914.* London: Hamish Hamilton, 1970.

Fall, Bernard. *Hell In a Very Small Place: The Siege of Dien Bien Phu.* Philadelphia: Lippincott, 1967.

Farwell, Byron. *The Great Anglo-Boer War.* New York: Harper and Row, 1976.

———. *Queen Victoria's Little Wars.* New York: Harper and Row, 1985.

Fehrenbach, T. E. *Lone Star: A History of Texas and the Texans.* New York: American Legacy, 1968.

Fernandez-Artmesto, Felipe. *The Spanish Armada: The Experience of War in 1588.* New York: Oxford, 1988.

Ferrill, Arther. *The Origins of War: From the Stone Age to Alexander the Great.* New York: Thames and Hudson, 1985.

Foote, Shelby. *The Civil War: A Narrative.* New York: Random House, 1958–1974.

Freeman, Edward. *The History of the Norman Conquest of England: Its Causes and Results.* Chicago: University of Chicago, 1974.

Freidin, Seymour and William Richardson, editors. *The Fatal Decisions.* New York: Sloane, 1956.

Friedrich, Otto. *Blood and Iron: From Bismarck to Hitler, the Von Moltke Family's Impact on German History.* New York: Harper Collins, 1995.

Friendly, Alfred. *The Dreadful Day: The Battle of Manzikert, 1071.* London: Hutchinson, 1981.

Frye, Richard N. *The Heritage of Central Asia: From Antiquity to the Turkish Expansion.* Princeton, NJ: Markus Wiener, 1996.

Fuller, J.F.C. *The Generalship of Alexander the Great.* New Brunswick, NJ: Rutgers University Press, 1960.

———. *A Military History of the Western World: From the Earliest Times to the Battle of Lepanto.* 3 vols. New York: Funk and Wagnalls, 1954–1956.

Gailey, Harry A. *The War in the Pacific: From Pearl Harbor to Tokyo Bay.* Novato, CA: Presidio Press, 1994.

Galvin, John R. *The Minutemen: The First Fight: Myths and Realities of the American Revolution.* Washington, D.C.: Brassey's, 1989.

Gardiner, Alan H. *Egypt of the Pharaohs: An Introduction.* New York: Oxford University Press, 1961.

Gardner, Brian. *The East India Company.* London: Hart-Davis, 1971.

Gascoigne, Bamber and Christina Gascoigne. *The Great Moghuls.* New York: Harper & Row, 1971.

Gaunt, Peter. *Oliver Cromwell.* Cambridge: Blackwell, 1996.

Glantz, David and Jonathan House. *The Battle of Kursk.* Lawrence, KS: University Press of Kansas, 1999.

Goldsworthy, Adrian K. *The Punic Wars.* London: Cassell, 2000.

Graham, W.A. *The Story of the Little Big Horn: Custer's Last Fight.* Lincoln, NE: University of Nebraska Press, 1952.

Grant, Michael. *Constantine the Great: The Man and His Times.* New York: Scribner's, 1993.

———. *Julius Caesar.* New York: M. Evans, 1969.

Green, Peter. *The Greco-Persian Wars.* Berkeley, CA: University of California Press, 1996.

Haley, James L. *Sam Houston.* Norman: University of Oklahoma Press, 2001.

Hallam, Elizabeth, editor. *The War of the Roses.* New York: Weidenfeld & Nicolson, 1988.

Hamilton, Edward P. *The French and Indian Wars: The Story of Battles and Forts in the Wilderness.* New York: Doubleday, 1962.

Hammond, N.G.L. *The Genius of Alexander the Great.* Chapel Hill, NC: University of North Carolina, 1997.

———. *A History of Greece to 322 B.C.* Oxford: Clarendon Press, 1967.

Hanson, Victor D. *The Wars of the Ancient Greeks and Their Invention of Western Military Culture.* London: Cassell, 1999.

Hardin, Stephen L. *Texian Iliad: A Military History of the Texas Revolution, 1835–1836.* Austin, TX: University of Texas Press, 1994.

Harvey, L.P. *Islamic Spain: 1250–1500.* Chicago: University of Chicago Press, 1990.

Harvey, Robert. *Clive: The Life and Times of a British Emperor.* New York: St. Martin's, 2000.

Hassig, Ross. *Mexico and the Spanish Conquest.* New York: Longman, 1994.

Held, Robert. *The Age of Firearms.* New York: Harper Brothers, 1957.

Hemming, John and K.C. Jordan, illustrator. *The Conquest of the Incas.* New York: Harcourt Brace, 1973.

Herodotus. *The Histories.* Baltimore: Penguin, 1954.

———. *History of the Persian Wars* (Vol. 6 of *Great Books of the World*). Chicago: Encyclopedia Britannica, 1952.

Herzog, Chaim. *The War of Atonement.* Boston: Little, Brown, 1975.

Hibbert, Christopher. *Agincourt.* London: Pan Books, 1968.

Hibbert, Christopher. *Cavaliers and Roundheads: The English Civil War, 1642–1649.* New York: Scribner, 1993.

Hicks, Brian. *Raising the Hunley: The Remarkable History and Recovery of the Lost Confederate Submarine.* New York: Ballantine, 2002.

Hindley, Geoffrey. *Saladin.* New York: Barnes and Noble Books, 1976.

Hixon, Carl K. *Guadalcanal: An American Story.* Annapolis, MD: Naval Institute Press, 1999.

Hoehling, A.A. *Thunder at Hampton Roads.* Englewood Cliffs, NJ: Prentice-Hall, 1976.

Hogarth, D.G. *Philip and Alexander of Macedon: Two Essays in Biography.* Freeport, NY: Books for Libraries Press, 1971.

Honan, William H., editor. *'Fire When Ready Gridley!': Great Naval Stories from Manila Bay to Vietnam.* New York: St. Martin's, 1993.

Hooton, E.R. *The Greatest Tumult: The Chinese Civil War 1936–49.* Washington, D.C.: Brassey's, 1991.

Howarth, David. *1066: The Year of Conquest.* New York: Penguin, 1977.

Hughes, Lindsey. *Russia in the Age of Peter the Great.* New Haven, CT: Yale University Press, 1998.

Innes, Hammond. *The Conquistadors.* New York: Knopf, 1969.

Jarman, Rosemary H. *Crispin's Day: The Glory of Agincourt.* Boston: Little, Brown, 1979.

Johns, Sally Cavell. *The Battle of San Pasqual.* San Diego, CA: University of San Diego Libraries, 1973.

Johnson, J.E. and P.B. Lucas. *Glorious Summer: The Story of the Battle of Britain.* London: Stanley Paul, 1990.

Johnson, John J. *Simon Bolivar and Spanish American Independence, 1783–1830.* Princeton, NJ: Van Nortrand, 1968.

Jones, David E. *Women Warriors: A History.* Washington, D.C.: Brassey's, 1997.

Jutikkala, Eino an Kauko Pirinen. *A History of Finland.* New York: Dorset Press, 1988.

Kagan, Donald. *The Outbreak of the Peloponnesian War.* Ithaca, NY: Cornell University Press, 1969.

Karnow, Stanley. *Vietnam: A History.* New York: Viking, 1983.

Karol, K.S. *Guerrillas in Power: The Course of the Cuban Revolution.* New York: Hill & Wang, 1970.

Keegan, John. *The Face of Battle.* New York: Viking, 1976.

Keen, Maurice, editor. *Medieval Warfare: A History.* New York: Oxford University, 1999.

Kemp, Anthony. *D-Day and the Invasion of Normandy.* New York: Harry N. Abrams, 1994.

Ketchum, Richard M. *Saratoga: Turning Point of America's Revolution.* New York: Henry Holt, 1997.

Knaplund, Paul. *The British Empire: 1815–1939.* New York: Fertig, 1970.

Kostiner, Joseph. *The Making of Saudi Arabia 1916–1936: From Chieftancy to Monarchical State.* New York: Oxford University Press, 1993.

Kousoulas, D. George. *The Life and Times of Constantine the Great, the First Christian Emperor.* Danbury, CT: Rutledge Books, 1997.

Lacey, Robert. *The Kingdom.* New York: Harcourt Brace Javanovich, 1982.

Lamb, Harold. *Babur the Tiger: First of the Great Moghuls.* Garden City, NY: Doubleday, 1961.

———. *The Crusades: Iron Men and Saints.* Garden City, NY: Doubleday, 1930.

———. *Cyrus the Great.* Garden City, NY: Doubleday, 1960.

———. *Suleiman the Magnificent, Sultan of the East.* Garden City, NY: Doubleday, 1951.

Lancel, Serge. *Carthage.* Cambridge: Blackwell, 1995.

Langer, Herbert. *The Thirty Years' War.* New York: Dorset Pres, 1990.

Langley, Michael. *Inchon Landing: MacArthur's Last Triumph.* New York: Times Books, 1979.

Leckie, Robert. *From Sea to Shining Sea: From the War of 1812 to the Mexican War, the Saga of America's Expansion.* New York: Harper Collins, 1993.

Liddell Hart, Basil H. *Great Captains Unveiled.* Navato, CA: Presidio Press, 1990.

———. *History of the Second World War.* New York: Putnam, 1971.

———. *The Real War: 1914–1918.* Boston: Little, Brown, 1930.

———. *Scipio Africanus: Greater than Napoleon.* New York: Da Capo Press, 1994.

Lister, R.P. *Genghis Khan.* New York: Stein and Day, 1969.

Lockhart, James. *The Men of Cajamarca: A Social and Biographical Study of the First Conquerors of Peru.* Austin, TX: University of Texas, 1972.

Lloyd, Alan. *Marathon: The Story of Civilizations on a Collision Course.* New York: Random House, 1973.

Longstreet, Stephen. *War Cries on Horseback: The Story of the Indian Wars in the Great Plains.* Garden City, NY: Doubleday, 1970.

Lucas, James S. *War in the Desert: The Eighth Army at El Alamein.* New York: Beaufort Books, 1983.

Lynch, John, editor. *Latin American Revolutions, 1808–1826.* New York: Knopf, 1965.

MacDonald, Peter G. *Giap: A Biography of General Vo Ngyen Giap.* New York: W.W. Norton, 1992.

Macksey, Kenneth and William Woodhouse. *The Penguin Encyclopedia of Modern Warfare, 1850 to the Present Day.* New York: Viking, 1991.

Maclear, Michael. *The Ten Thousand Day War: Vietnam, 1945–1975.* New York: St. Martin's, 1981.

Madej, Victor, and Steven Zaloga. *The Polish Campaign.* New York: Hippocrene Books, 1985.

Maenchen. O.J. *The World of the Huns: Studies in Their History and Culture.* Berkeley, CA: University of California Press, 1973.

Mahan, Alfred Thayer. *The Life of Nelson: The Embodiment of the Sea Power of Great Britain.* Annapolis, MD: Naval Institute Press, 2001.

Mallett, Michael E. *Mercenaries and Their Masters: Warfare in Renaissance Italy.* Totowa, NJ: Rowman and Littlefield, 1974.

Manceron, Claude. *Austerlitz: The Story of a Battle.* New York: Norton, 1966.

Mandel, Paul. *Great Battles of the Civil War.* New York: Time, 1961.

Mannerheim, Carl. *The Memoirs of Marshall Mannerheim.* New York: E.P. Dutton, 1954.

Mansel, Philip. *Constantinople: City of the World's Desire.* New York: St. Martin's, 1996.

Margiotta, Franklin D. Editor. *Brassey's Encyclopedia of Military History and Biography.* Washington, D.C.: Brassey's, 1994.

Marshall, Robert. *Storm From the East: From Genghis Khan to Khubilai Khan.* Berkeley, CA: University of California Press, 1993.

Mattingly, Garrett. *The Armada.* Boston: Houghton Mifflin, 1959.

McPherson, James M. *Battle Cry of Freedom.* New York: Oxford, 1988.

Meier, Christian. *Caesar.* New York: Basic Books, 1995.

Meyer, Michael C. *The Course of Mexican History.* New York: Oxford, 1995.

Millar, Fergus. *The Roman Near East: 31 B.C.–A.D. 337.* Cambridge, MA: Harvard University Press, 1993.

Mitchell, Joseph B. *Decisive Battles of the American Revolution.* New York: Putnam, 1962.

Morelock, J.D. *The Army Times Book of Great Land Battles: From the Civil War to the Gulf War.* New York: Berkley, 1994.

Morison, Samuel E. *The Two Ocean War: A Short History of the United States Navy in the Second World War.* Boston: Little, Brown, 1963.

Motzki, Harald. *The Biography of Muhammad: The Issue of the Sources.* Boston: Brill, 2000.

Murray, Oswyn. *Early Greece.* Cambridge, MA: Harvard University Press, 1993.

Nelson, H.H. *The Battle of Megiddo.* Chicago: University of Chicago Press, 1913.

Norwich, John Julius. *Byzantium: The Decline and Fall.* New York: Knopf, 1995.

———. *A Short History of Byzantium.* New York: Alfred A. Knopf, 1997.

Oberdorfer, Don. *Tet! The Turning Point in the Vietnam War.* Baltimore: Johns Hopkins University Press, 2001.

Official Records of the Union and Confederate Navies in the War of the Rebellion. Washington, D.C.: Government Printing Office, 1921.

Olmstead, A.T. *History of the Persian Empire.* Chicago: University of Chicago Press, 1959.

Oman, C.W.C. *A History of the Art of War in the Middle Ages.* 2 Vols. New York: Franklin, 1959.

O'Toole, G.J.A. *The Spanish War: An American Epic—1898.* New York: W.W.Norton, 1984.

Overy, Richard. *Why the Allies Won.* New York: W.W. Norton, 1996.

Pages, Georges. *The Thirty Years' War, 1618–1648.* London: A. and C. Black, 1970.

Pakenham, Thomas. *The Boer War.* New York: Random House, 1979.

Palmer, David R. *Summons of the Trumpet: U.S.-Vietnam in Perspective.* Novato, CA: Presidio Press, 1978.

Parker, Robert. *Military Memoirs of Marlborough's Campaigns, 1701–1712.* Mechanicsburg, PA: Stackpole Books, 1998.

Perez-Stable, Marifeli. *The Cuban Revolution: Origins, Course, and Legacy.* New York: Oxford University Press, 1999.

Perroy, E.M.J. *Hundred Years' War.* New York: Oxford, 1952.

Peters, F.E., editor. *A Reader on Classical Islam.* Princeton, NJ: Princeton University Press, 1994.

Pflanze, Otto. *Bismarck and the Development of Germany.* 3 Vols. Princeton, NJ: Princeton University Press, 1990.

Pohl, James W. *The Battle of San Jacinto.* Austin, TX: Texas State Historical Association, 1989.

Pollard, A.J. *Richard III and the Princes in the Tower.* New York: St. Martin's, 1991.

Powell, Anton. *Athens and Sparta: Constructing Greek Political and Social History from 478 B.C.* Portland, OR: Aeropagitica Press, 1988.

Prange, Gordon. *At Dawn We Slept: The Untold Story of Pearl Harbor.* New York: McGraw-Hill, 1981.

Pratt, Fletcher. *The Battles That Changed History.* Garden City, NY: Doubleday, 1956.

Prawdin, Michael. *The Mongol Empire: Its Rise and Legacy.* London: G. Allen and Unwin, 1961.

Prescott, William H. *Conquest of Mexico.* Garden City, NY: Blue Ribbon, 1943.

———. *History of the Conquest of Peru.* New York: Modern Library, 1998.

———. *History of the Reign of Ferdinand and Isabella the Catholic.* New York: Limited Editions Club, 1967.

Preston, Paul. *The Spanish Civil War: 1936–39.* New York: Grove Press, 1986.

Radosh, Ronald, Mary R. Habek, and Grigory Sevostianov, editors. *Spain Betrayed: The Soviet Union in the Spanish Civil War.* New Haven, CT: Yale University Press, 2001.

Ragan, Mark K. *Union and Confederate Submarines in the Civil War.* Mason City, IA: Savas, 1999.

Regan, Geoffrey. *The Guinness Book of Decisive Battles.* New York: Canopy Books, 1992.

Richards, J.F. *The Mughal Empire.* New York: Cambridge University Press, 1993.

Rihani, Ameen F. *Maker of Modern Arabia.* Boston: Houghton Mifflin, 1928.

Roberts, Michael. *Gustavus Adolphus and the Rise of Sweden.* London: English University Press, 1973.

Roberts, Russell. *The Rulers of Ancient Egypt.* San Diego, CA: Lucent Books, 1999.

Ross, Charles. *Richard III.* Berkeley, CA: University of California Press, 1981.

Roth, Stephen J., editor. *The Impact of the Six Day War: A Twenty-Year Assessment.* New York: St. Martin's, 1988.

Roy, Jules. *The Battle of Dien Bien Phu.* New York: Harper & Row, 1965.

Runciman, Steven. *The Fall of Constantinople, 1453.* Cambridge: Cambridge University Press, 1965.

Russell, Don. *Custer's Last Stand; or, The Battle of the Little Big Horn.* Fort Worth, TX: Amon Carter Museum, 1968.

Sachar, Howard M. *A History of Israel: From the Rise of Zionism to Our Time.* New York: Knopf, 1996.

Salisbury, Harrison Evans. *The Long March: The Untold Story.* New York: Harper & Row, 1985.

Scales, Robert H. Jr. *Certain Victory: The U.S. Army in the Gulf War.* Washington, D.C.: Brassey's, 1993.

Schoolfield, George C. *Helsinki of the Czars: A Cultural History.* Columbia, SC: Camden House, 1996.

Schwarzkopf, H. Norman. *It Doesn't Take a Hero: The Autobiography of General H. Norman Schwarzkopf.* New York: Bantam, 1992.

Selby, John. *The Road to Yorktown.* New York: St. Martin's, 1976.

Seward, Desmond. *The Hundred Years War: Trial by Battle: The English in France, 1337–1453.* New York: Atheneum, 1978.

Showalter, Dennis E. *Tannenberg: Clash of Empires.* Hamden, CT: Archon Books, 1991.

Singletary, Otis A. *The Mexican War.* Chicago: University of Chicago, 1960.

Smith, Digby G. *1813, Leipzig: Napoleon and the Battle of the Nations.* London: Greenhill, 2001.

Smith, Justin H. *The War With Mexico.* 2 Vols. Gloucester, MA: Peter Smith, 1963.

Stacy, C.P. *Quebec.* Toronto: Macmillan, 1959.

Starn, Orin, Carlos I. Degregori, and Robin Kirk, editors. *The Peru Reader: History Culture, Politics.* Durham, NC: Duke University Press, 1995.

Stokesbury, James L. *A Short History of World War II.* New York: William Morrow, 1980.

Sugden, John. *Tecumseh: A Life.* New York: Henry Holt, 1998.

Sumption, Jonathan. *The Hundred Years' War: Trial by Battle.* Philadelphia: University of Philadelphia Press, 1988.

Sweetman, Jack, editor. *Great American Naval Battles.* Annapolis, MD: Naval Institute Press, 1998.

Taylor, F.L. *The Art of War in Italy, 1494–1529.* London: Greenhill, 1993,

Thompson, Leonard M. *A History of South Africa.* New Haven, CT: Yale University Press, 1995.

Thomson, George M. *The First Churchill: The Life of John, 1st Duke of Marlborough.* London: Secker and Warburg, 1979.

Thucydides. *The Landmark Thucydides: A Comprehensive Guide to the Peloponnesian War.* New York: Free Press, 1996.

Toland, John. *In Mortal Combat: Korea, 1950–1953.* New York: Morrow, 1991.

———. *Infamy: Pearl Harbor and its Aftermath.* New York: Berkley, 1982.

Tolbert, Frank X. *The Day of San Jacinto.* Austin, TX: Pemberton Press, 1959.

Trask, David F. *The War With Spain in 1898.* New York: Macmillan, 1981.

Trench, Charles C. *A History of Marksmanship.* Chicago: Follet, 1972.

Tuchman, Barbara. *The Guns of August.* New York: Macmillan, 1962.

Turner, Henry Smith. *The Original Journals of Henry Smith Turner with Stephen Watts Kearny to New Mexico and California, 1846–1847.* Norman, OK: University of Oklahoma Press, 1966.

Van der Vat, Dan. *The Pacific Campaign: World War II: The U.S.-Japanese Naval War, 1941–1945.* New York: Simon and Schuster, 1992.

Vassiliev, Alexei. *The History of Saudi Arabia.* New York: New York University Press, 2000.

Viola, Herman J. *Little Bighorn Remembered: The Untold Indian Story of Custer's Last Stand.* New York: Times Books, 1999.

Warner, Oliver. *Great Sea Battles.* New York: Macmillan, 1963.

Warner, Rex, translator. *Julius Caesar: War Commentaries of Caesar.* New York: New American Library, 1960.

Warraq, Ibn, editor and translator. *The Quest for the Historical Mohammad.* Amherst, NY: Prometheus Books, 2000.

Warry, John Gibson. *Warfare in the Classical World: An Illustrated Encyclopedia of Weapons, Warriors and Warfare in the Ancient Civilizations of Greece.* Norman, OK: University of Oklahoma Press, 1995.

Wedgwood, C.V. *The Thirty Years War.* New York: Methuen, 1981.

Weigall, Authur. *The Life and Times of Marc Antony.* New York: Putnam's, 1931.

Werth, Alexander. *Russia at War 1941–1945.* New York: Dutton, 1964,

Westmoreland, William C. *A Soldier Reports.* New York: Doubleday, 1976.

Wetzel, David. *A Duel of Giants: Bismarck, Napoleon III, and the Origins of the Franco-Prussian War.* Madison, WI: University of Wisconsin Press, 2001.

White, Theodore H. and Annalee Jacoby. *Thunder Out of China.* New York: Da Capo Press, 1980.

Wilson, Dick. *The Long March, 1935: The Epic of Chinese Communism's Survival.* New York: Viking, 1971.

Windrow, Martin and Francis K. Mason. *A Concise Dictionary of Military Biography: Two Hundred f the Most Significant Names in Land Warfare, 10th to 20th Century.* New York: John Wiley, 1991.

Wood, Derek. *The Narrow Margin: The Battle of Britain and the Rise of Air Power.* Washington, D.C: Smithsonian Institute Press, 1990.

Worcester, Donald Emmet. *Bolivar.* Boston: Little, Brown, 1977.

Yang, Benjamin. *From Revolution to Politics: Chinese Communists on the Long March.* Boulder, CO: Westview Press, 1990.

Zhukov, Goergi. *From Moscow to Berlin: Marshal Zhukov's Greatest Battles.* New York: Harper & Row, 1969.

ABOUT THE AUTHOR

Michael Lee Lanning retired from the U.S. Army after more than twenty years of service. He is a decorated veteran of the Vietnam War, where he served as an infantry platoon leader and company commander. Lanning has written fourteen books on military history, including *The Military 100: A Ranking of the Most Influential Military Leaders of All Time*. He lives in Phoenix, Arizona.